REMAPPING BLACK GERMANY

REMAPPING BLACK GERMANY

NEW PERSPECTIVES ON AFRO-GERMAN HISTORY, POLITICS, AND CULTURE

EDITED BY
SARA LENNOX

UNIVERSITY OF MASSACHUSETTS PRESS
Amherst and Boston

Printed in the United States of America

ISBN 978–1-62534–231–7 (paper); 230–0 (hardcover)

Designed by Sally Nichols
Set in Arno Pro
Printed and bound by Sheridan Books, Inc.

Cover design by Sally Nichols

Library of Congress Cataloging-in-Publication Data
A catalog record for this book is available from the Library of Congress.

British Library Cataloguing-in-Publication Data
A catalog record for this book is available from the British Library.

CONTENTS

PREFACE

This book has been a long time in the making, and I have incurred many debts along the way. This volume could not even have been conceived without the efforts of Peggy Piesche and Fatima El-Tayeb, whose brilliant grant-writing skills won us an Alexander von Humboldt Foundation TransCoop grant for a project on Black German studies and a Volkswagen Foundation grant for a project on Black European studies. I am indebted to those foundations for providing us with the funding that enabled us to develop a scholarly focus on Black Germany in the context of Black Europe, and I thank the Provost's Office at the University of Massachusetts for providing the matching funds that enabled us to accept the TransCoop grant. I am also grateful to Randolph Ochsmann, who was willing to become our senior German partner for both projects, and to Tobias Nagl, who moved to Western Massachusetts to become a research associate for the Black German project, engaged vigorously in its activities, and helped to conceptualize this book. Their efforts, along with Beverly Weber's organizational support, made it possible to host the conference "Remapping Black Germany: New Perspectives on Afro-German History, Politics, and Culture" at the University of Massachusetts in April 2006, the event from which this volume sprang.

Other friends and colleagues helped me think more deeply about Black Germans and race in Germany. Dagmar Schultz and Ika Hügel-Marshall first told me about Black Germans and generously introduced me to members of the Black German community. I am likewise grateful to Rosemarie Peña, whom I first met when she attended "Remapping Black Germany," and who was energized by the conference to take over the leadership of what became the Black German Heritage and Research Association (BGHRA). This book and my understanding of the Black German experience have benefited from the BGHRA's three conferences that Rosemarie, Tina Campt, Leroy Hopkins, and I co-organized. Panels on race and Blackness in Germany over the past decade and a half at the conferences of the German Studies Association, along with two recent seminars on Black Germans chaired by Tiffany Florvil and Vanessa Plumly, have also shaped my thinking and left their imprint on this book. I have learned and continue to learn from my graduate students in German and Scandinavian studies at UMass, especially Jamele Watkins and Kevina King, whose work focuses on Black Germans.

Friends have also helped me continue to challenge my own whiteness, with special thanks owed to Arlene Avakian and John Bracey. Anna Schrade, Peggy Piesche, and two anonymous reviewers for the University of Massachusetts Press kindly made detailed suggestions for improving the multiple drafts of my introduction. Julia Demmin and Stephanie Keep know very well the gratitude I owe them. I am also grateful to the contributors to this volume for their patience as they waited for the book to appear.

Finally, my son, Jonathan Lennox, and my partner, Arthur Cohen, have borne with me over the years that I have worked on this book, and I thank them now and always for their love, support, and understanding.

REMAPPING BLACK GERMANY

Introduction

SARA LENNOX

The Black German historian Fatima El-Tayeb observed in 2001 that prior to the publication of her own monograph, *Schwarze Deutsche: Der Diskurs um "Rasse" und nationale Identität 1890–1933* (Black Germans: The discourse on "race" and national identity, 1890–1933), only three historical studies had even acknowledged the existence of a Black population group in Germany.[1] Now, only a decade and a half later, Black German studies is a recognized and growing field, as increasing numbers of scholars, including the contributors to this collection, turn their attention to the history and culture of Black people in the German-speaking territories. The essays in this volume, which originated in a 2006 conference at the University of Massachusetts, "Remapping Black Germany," build on and advance this research. The cartographic metaphor in the title of the conference and this book recognizes scholars' efforts to fill in the blank spots on the map of what is known about peoples of African descent in Germany while also emphasizing that the new knowledge they are producing does not simply add details to an otherwise unchanged map of Germany. Rather, the attention recent scholars have directed to the situation of Black people in Germany has universalizing rather than minoritizing implications (to employ terminology that Eve Kosofsky Sedgwick advanced for another purpose),[2] demanding that many other aspects of Germany—its history, its politics, its philosophy, its literature, its music—also be reconceived once the contributions of Black Germans are acknowledged.

To that end, my aims for this volume are threefold. First, it contests the presumption that Germany is a country of white people alone by documenting the presence of Black Germans over many centuries of German history. It also demonstrates the major role that attention to race, and to Black Germans more specifically, has played at different points in the German past. Were white scholars of German studies to embrace these positions, they might find it necessary to reconceive German history and culture in ways that extend far beyond merely understanding Black Germans as a small niche population.[3] Attention to Black Germans within a transnational context might also contribute to the larger project of "deprovincializing Germany"[4] by helping Germans to look beyond their own boundaries, situating Germany's treatment of race and peoples of color within the larger framework of a comparative examination of such practices within countries like and unlike itself.

As well, I want this collection to serve as an introduction to Black German studies for people who know little about the field or about Black Germans themselves. In her introduction to *Showing Our Colors,* Audre Lorde wrote that she hoped that the book's translation would fulfill her dream "of making the stories of our Black German sisters—and Afro-German history as a whole—available to the English-speaking Diaspora."[5] I hope that *Remapping Black Germany* also can contribute to a greater understanding of the variety of Black experiences and the particular history of Black Germans within the African diaspora. Finally, over the past decades US scholars' elaboration of new perspectives on the German experience—in the form of exile studies, GDR studies, feminist studies, migrant and migration studies, and colonial and postcolonial studies—has not only fundamentally transformed US German studies but also legitimated those academic fields within Germany and encouraged German scholars to address them too. If US attention to Black German studies could similarly exert pressure on the German academy to acknowledge the field's importance and to employ Black German scholars to research and teach about it,[6] I would be proud that this book had played a small role. This book may, I hope, make it ever more difficult for other scholars to write German history without taking Black German history into account as it enables scholars of Africana studies also to take Black Germany into consideration.

Of course I want *Remapping Black Germany* also to benefit scholars of Black German studies, as well as Black Germans themselves. I hope that Black Germans will accept the book as a gesture of solidarity and a contribution to the production of critical knowledge that will at least indirectly benefit their community as it confronts present and future challenges. Optimally this book will also contribute to transforming the academy and Western thought more generally, a project to which many scholars of Black German studies are committed. Though "mapping" historically has often been an activity undertaken to serve colonialist ends,[7] the "remapping" intended by this volume endeavors instead to contribute to challenges to what has been termed "the coloniality of power"—the social classification of the world's population around the idea of race to justify white Europeans' domination over the globe.[8] This volume is intended to contest the sway of the coloniality of power over Germany, thereby changing circumstances for Black Germans and for everyone else there too. In such ways it will, I hope, contribute to drawing new maps both of Black Germany and of territories that lie beyond it.

As demonstrated by the quite varied "new perspectives" advanced by this volume's essays, whose authors include Black Germans and a Black American as well as white scholars from Germany, the United States, and the United Kingdom, *Remapping Black Germany* makes no effort to advance a cohesive account of "Black German history, politics, and culture," and I hope its chapters will be understood to diversify and revise established critical paradigms of Black German scholarship. This introduction provides a context for those essays. I first offer an overview of the Black German movement and Black German achievements and then briefly present current research on the history of Black people in Germany before summarizing the individual essays. However, the introduction intentionally neither adjudicates other scholars' contributions to Black German studies nor articulates a vision for the field. As a white American woman who necessarily perceives the world from a different vantage point than that of Black Germans, I am keenly aware of the perils of what Linda Alcoff some decades ago called "the problem of speaking for others."[9] Black Germans inaugurated and have sustained this field, and an assessment of its accomplishments and future directions should, I think, properly be left to them.

I

Until recently, the publication of *Farbe bekennen: Afro-deutsche Frauen auf den Spuren ihrer Geschichte* in 1986 has been regarded as the moment at which the Black German movement was born. But Black German poet Philipp Khabo Koepsell argues for a new narrative of Black German activism that situates the current movement within the larger and longer history of transnational Black social engagement on German soil. As Koepsell emphasizes, before the First World War migrants from the German colonies in Africa demanded justice for their country people as their fellows in the colonies rebelled against German rule. After the war, migrants in Germany organized to provide mutual support, and in the late 1920s, joined by comrades from elsewhere in the African diaspora, they associated themselves with the international antiracist efforts of the Communist Party. In the 1960s militant African American GIs published underground newspapers, protested racist treatment within and outside the military, and opposed the Vietnam War. In the seventies and eighties a range of African, African American, and Black German writers, often students, published texts in both German and English, though these works are what Koepsell terms "the invisible archive," since the white German mainstream is mostly unaware of them. However, Koepsell argues, "it was the activism, solidarity work and the leadership of the African students that created the structures and the fertile ground for a modern Black German movement to evolve."[10]

The 1984 encounter of African American lesbian feminist poet Audre Lorde with Black German women in Berlin marked what Asoka Esuruoso and Koepsell call a "transition point" in Germany's Black activist movement,[11] encouraging organization by German-born Black people and moving Black women into the movement's leadership. In the summer semester of 1984 Lorde offered a poetry workshop and a course on Black American women poets at the Free University of Berlin. "During this period," Lorde recalled, "I wanted to get to know particular German women about whose existence I knew, but about whom I couldn't find out anything in New York: Black German women."[12] The women in her course let her know that there was no common word to designate them—as one told her, "The nicest thing they ever called us was 'warbaby.'"[13] Out of their discussions emerged the new term "*afro-deutsch*" (Afro-German) that would begin to transform the lives of Black people in Germany. (The terms "Afro-German" and "Black German" are generally treated as synonymous, though "Black German" is now thought to be more inclusive and is more widely used.) Lorde remembered how another Black German woman responded to that new name: "'I've never thought of Afro-German as a positive concept before,' she said, speaking out of the pain of having to live a difference that has no name; speaking out of the growing power self-scrutiny has forged from that difference."[14]

In 1983 a feminist press in Berlin had published *Macht und Sinnlichkeit* (Power and sensuality), a collection of poetry and essays by Lorde and white feminist poet Adrienne Rich, and planned to issue another volume by Lorde. But, as May Ayim recalled, Lorde laid down her pen and declared, "I won't write anything more until I hear and read something by Black women in Germany."[15] Thus *Farbe bekennen* came into being, edited by Black Germans Katharina Oguntoye and May Opitz (who would later claim her father's name, Ayim) and white German feminist publisher Dagmar Schultz. The volume juxtaposed multigenerational autobiographical accounts, interviews, photographs, poems, and conversations among Black German women, framed by three sections written by Opitz, based on her master's thesis, that compiled the first account of Black German history. (In 1992 the University of Massachusetts Press published the book in English translation as *Showing Our Colors: Afro-German Women Speak Out.*) As Fatima El-Tayeb puts it, *Farbe bekennen* "contextualised experiences that had been perceived as aberrant and individual, pointing them out as collective traits in the life of a population that up until that point was neither perceived nor had defined itself as a community—black Germans."[16] The book's emphases would shape the new Black German movement from its outset, as El-Tayeb stresses: "The focus on a female perspective in *Showing Our Colors* as well as its explicitly feminist context made sure that here, black identity was not presented as male; instead it was women's voices that first articulated experiences that laid the groundwork in constituting a larger sense of community."[17] As Peggy Piesche has remarked, *Farbe bekennen* was pathbreaking because it was a book by, about, and for Black German women.[18]

Until the movement's emergence, particularly Afro-Germans in northern areas of Germany had lived in isolation from other Black people, and, from potentially quite different backgrounds—the children of African American GIs, of African students, of African American, Caribbean, or African travelers, of Black people who had lived in Germany for generations—they did not necessarily recognize their commonalities or their connections to other people from the diaspora in Germany.[19] Neither was it clear (nor is it even today) how many Black people lived in Germany, since Germany has no racial category in its census due to ongoing concern about the Nazis' misuse of such categories. As well, until the year 2000 German citizenship law, based on *jus sanguinis* or the "law of blood," granted citizenship only to those possessing German "blood," which for Black Germans meant only those with at least one, almost always white, German parent. Since 2000, children born in Germany of immigrant parents who meet certain other conditions can claim German citizenship (and, since 2014, also retain the citizenship of their parents). Naturalization is possible after eight years of legal residence in Germany. These provisions mean that refugees, asylum seekers, migrants, and other Black people choosing to live in Germany temporarily or permanently may well not hold German citizenship and hence legally do not count as Germans. The Black German population today is estimated at about 500,000, but it is not entirely clear who belongs to that category.

Responding to these circumstances, the two major organizations of Black German advocacy formed shortly after the appearance of *Farbe bekennen* have opted to address the issues of all Black people in Germany, not just of those with German passports. ADEFRA, short for Afro-DEutsche FRAuen, or "Afro-German women" (though its founders were also happy to discover that it also meant "woman who displays courage" in Amharic)[20] was founded by Black German women (all of them lesbians—and lesbians have continued to function as the motor of the organized Black German women's movement). Now ADEFRA identifies itself as concerned with both "Black German women and Black women in Germany." The other organization's acronym, ISD, originally stood for Initiative Schwarze Deutsche (Initiative of Black Germans). Though the acronym has not changed, the organization has since expressed its recognition of the limitations of national identification by changing its name to Initiative Schwarze Menschen in Deutschland (Initiative of Black people in Germany), indicating that it too regards all Black people in Germany as its constituency.[21]

ADEFRA and the ISD set themselves the task of overcoming Black isolation and bringing Black people together, and activists from those organizations term Black people in Germany collectively the "community," using the English word. Together they have created autonomous spaces for Black encounters. As one of ADEFRA's founding members put it, from the outset the movement committed itself to deep emotional investments in people.[22] Such connections are taken to be a vehicle for "empowerment" (the English word is used here too), which ADEFRA conceives as the effort to support and strengthen Black consciousness, self-determination, and self-organization.[23] As another ADEFRA founder recalled: "More and more people joined who could recognize themselves in others' stories and suddenly drew their whole previous lives into question. . . . We started calling that the 'Afro-flash.' "[24]

One of the ISD's most important networking events is the annual Bundestreffen (nationwide meeting), a weekend gathering open only to Black people and held every year since 1985 that is devoted to workshops, lectures, children's and youth activities, films, performances, readings, and parties. The Bundestreffen is an important site for education about Black history and culture, as have been the Black History Month events held in Berlin from 1990 to 2001 as well as periodically in other cities.[25] The ISD also initiated *Homestory Deutschland,* a photo exhibition featuring twenty-seven historical and contemporary Black figures that since 2006 has toured Germany and many countries in Africa, accompanied at some sites by a changing program of readings, lectures, workshops, and artistic presentations.

In their effort to combat racism, Black activists have insisted on their right to determine the names by which they are known, choosing to be called Afro-Germans or Black Germans rather than other terms they regard as insulting and demeaning. Vigorous struggles have taken place against the use of terms they regard as derogatory, including a Berlin theater's use on its marquee of a term activists designate as the N-word.[26] Recent initiatives that have provoked heated discussion among mainstream German groups have addressed racist language in older German children's books, including *Pippi Longstocking* and *Die kleine Hexe* (The little witch). Currently the ISD is engaged in a campaign that calls for the recognition of racial profiling as discrimination,[27] for instituting antiracism training for police, and for establishing structures for reporting police misconduct.

On its website, the ISD indicates that it especially supports groups organized by refugees, engaging itself on behalf of refugees' rights and regularly mobilizing campaigns against deportations and other state measures, against residency requirements, and against the extreme Right. This work enables the ISD to forge links with and advocate for Black people who are otherwise without the connections and resources that could enable them to survive in Germany. The organizations also pursue transnational contacts, with one activist asserting that ADEFRA "conceives of itself as part of the larger international community of Black women / people,"[28] including African Americans, Africans, Black people from the former East Germany after the fall of the Berlin Wall, and other Black Europeans.

Though ADEFRA and the ISD are the largest and most visible organizations advocating for Black people in Germany, many other groups and individuals also focus on Black issues. In 2005 a Black German coalition spearheaded by the ISD garnered national and international support for a campaign against an "African village" exhibited in the Augsburg Zoo that recalled the *Völkerschauen* (ethnographic exhibitions) of Imperial Germany; in 2014–2015 another coalition protested racist structures in the German university. Broad coalitions have repeatedly demonstrated against racist murders of Black people and against racism more generally. Black Germans have joined with white allies to organize walking tours of German cities that draw attention to visible reminders of German colonialism. In 2010 the Black community successfully lobbied for the name of a street in Berlin-Kreuzberg commemorating a man who had erected a seventeenth-century West African slave fortress to be changed to that of May Ayim.[29] In 2013 the first two Black Germans were elected to the German Bundestag: Charles Huber for the Christian Democrats and Karamba Diaby for the Social Democrats.

The texts of Black German writers that began to emerge in the mid-eighties also contributed to Black German pride and efforts at self-definition. May Ayim and Katharina Oguntoye had included their own poems in *Farbe bekennen* as well as those of GDR poet Raya Lubinetzki. Ayim, poet, educator, activist, and source of inspiration to many other Black Germans, is regarded as Black Germany's premier author. In 1996 she suffered a mental and physical collapse and took her own life at the age of thirty-six. One volume of her poetry was published during her lifetime, and a second volume and a collection of essays appeared posthumously. In 1991 the ISD published a volume of Black German poetry, *Macht der Nacht* (Power of night); *Talking Home: Heimat aus unserer eigenen Feder: Frauen of Color in Deutschland* (Home from our own pen: Women of color in Germany), a collection edited by Black German poet Olumide Popoola and Turkish-German poet Beldan Sezen that includes poetry by many Black women, appeared in 1999; and *Arriving in the Future: Stories of Home and Exile,* edited by Asoka Esuruoso and Philipp Khabo Koepsell and published in 2014, is the newest anthology of poetry and other creative writing by people of the African diaspora living in Germany. Beginning with Ika Hügel-Marshall's *Daheim unterwegs: Ein deutsches Leben* (1998, translated as *Invisible Woman: Growing Up Black in Germany*) and Hans J. Massaquoi's *Destined to Witness: Growing Up Black in Nazi Germany* (1999), the autobiographical impulse that *Farbe bekennen* initiated has subsequently been taken up by many Black Germans, who document a Black presence at different times and places, revealing the variety of the Black German experience and providing a language to address the Black

German condition.[30] Quite recently several all-Black theater ensembles, including abok and Label Noir, have been established, and the plays *Real Life: Deutschland, Heimat, bittersüße Heimat* (Homeland, bittersweet homeland), and *Kosmos BRD* have featured all-Black casts; the performance space Ballhaus Naunynstraße serves as a center for Black German theater and performance in Berlin, while the organization Bühnenwatch vigorously opposes blackfacing and other racist practices in German theaters. In 2012 editors Sandrine Micossé-Aikins and Sharon Dodua Otoo launched the Black book series Witnessed with the publishing house Edition Assemblage, publishing English-language texts by Black people in Germany. In July 2016, Otoo, also a talented author, won that year's Bachmann Prize, one of German-speaking Europe's most prestigious awards for contemporary literature. As Koepsell urges, the literary production of African migrants in Germany should also be recognized as belonging to the Black German literary tradition.[31] From the 1980s onward, African immigrants and travelers have written in German about their temporary or permanent lives in Germany, their autobiographies, fiction, and poems juxtaposing violence in Africa with the xenophobia and economic hardships of post-unification Germany while envisioning future harmonious relations in their new homeland or back in Africa.[32]

Since the eighties, a range of other media have also promoted networking among Black people and education about Black issues and have undertaken political advocacy on their behalf. Numerous periodicals have been published, including the newspaper *afro look;*[33] ADEFRA's journal *Afrekete; blite,* a magazine for young people; and *X, Das Magazin für AfroKultur.* AFROTAK TV cyberNomads is a social media network that has produced videos, compiled a databank, and preserved an archive about the African diaspora in Germany. Filmmakers/screenwriters like Fatima El-Tayeb, Oliver Hardt, John A. Kantara, Branwen Okpako, and Pierre Sanoussi-Bliss now increasingly garner attention within the German mainstream and internationally. Schwarze Filmschaffende in Deutschland (Black filmmakers in Germany), founded in 2006, advocates both for Black people in the film industry and for more accurate portrayals of Black people in film; in 2007 SFD presented a program of films at the Berlin International Film Festival, the first time Black filmmakers in Germany were represented there. In 2001 der braune Mob was founded as Germany's first Black media watch organization and continues to campaign vigorously against all forms of racism in the media and public life.

Responsible for what El-Tayeb terms a shift in "gender visibility" in the Black German movement,[34] Black German hip-hop has allowed mostly male Black German hip-hop artists to emerge as spokespeople for antiracist causes. Two members of the group Advanced Chemistry, founded in 1987 and one of the first groups to rap in German, were Black Germans, and in 1992 the group became a voice for minority issues in Germany with the album *Fremd im eigenen Land* (Foreign in my own country). In 2000 a group of German rap, reggae, and soul musicians led by Black Germans established the transnational antiracism project Brothers Keepers. After skinheads in Dessau murdered Alberto Adriano, a German of Mozambiquan origin, in June 2000, Brothers Keepers released the militant rap single "Adriano: Letzte Warnung" (Final warning),[35] which gained national media attention and reached the German top ten in 2001. Numerous other Black Germans are active as hip-hop artists or in other musical genres. Black Germans are also increasingly represented in the visual arts, with Marc Brandenburg, Yvonne Buntrock, Christina Grotke, Manou Holzner, Ika Hügel-Marshall, Stephen Lawson, Guy St. Louis, Raja Lubinetzki, Ingrid Mwangi, Sabina Odumosu, Ricky Reiser, Daniel Kojo Schrade, and others working in a range of mediums, including painting, sculpture, photography, performance, and video.

To recognize the richness and variety of Black cultural production in Germany and celebrate its connections to the transnational Black diaspora, the May Ayim Award, the first international Black German literary award, was established in 2004. Over one hundred submissions in both German and English were received from around the world, and the best contributions were presented at a gala event hosted by the House of World Cultures in Berlin on October 29, 2004. They were subsequently collected in a volume displaying images of sculptor Stephen Lawson's *Black Germania* on its cover and with an accompanying DVD featuring the event's multimedia performances. In her introduction, Peggy Piesche asserts that it might be claimed of the three first-prize winners—Mario Curvello, an Afro-Brazilian prose writer living in Berlin; Olumide Popoola, a Nigerian-German poet living in London; and MC Santana, a Black German English-language rapper from Darmstadt—what was maintained of Ayim herself: that they are "as committed as [they are] passionate." No longer merely reactive vis-à-vis dominant discourses, Piesche declares, the authors in the collection inscribe themselves within their own traditions, referring backward and pointing forward toward a Black European art adequate to Black European identity.[36] The volume's editors situate the anthology within the tradition established by the 1991 collection *Macht der Nacht* and emphasize that it too should be considered a "survival reflex" that makes connections transcending national and linguistic boundaries. "May this book open paths for our children," they urge. "Keep jammin.'"[37]

II

Though *Afro-German Women Speak Out* was the subtitle of the English translation of *Farbe bekennen,* the original German subtitle stressed another aspect of the Afro-German project: *Afro-deutsche Frauen auf den Spuren ihrer Geschichte,* "Afro-German women [in search of] the traces of their history." That subtitle placed the endeavor to recover the history of African-descendant people in Germany at the forefront of Black German women's efforts to define their own identities and situate themselves both as Germans and as people of the African diaspora within the continuum of German and global history. The account of Black German history that Ayim offers in *Farbe bekennen* has not been challenged in the intervening years, though since then Black German and other scholars have filled in many details. This section of the introduction provides an overview of what is now known about the history of Black people in Germany, particularly emphasizing studies written by Black people themselves.

As Ayim's account suggests, Black German history can be understood as the attempts of successive generations of people of African background in the German-speaking territories to claim the right, individually and sometimes collectively, to name and speak for themselves as political subjects and subjects of discourse as they confronted various obstacles to that undertaking. In contrast to the history of the Americas and of some European countries, the presence of people of African descent in Germany is not a consequence of the violent mass dispersal of slavery and only to a lesser degree the result of the European colonization of Africa. Instead, for centuries Black people, more often male than female, came to Germany mostly individually, brought, likely as slaves, to adorn princely courts, to serve as soldiers in armies from the eighteenth century to the twentieth, to entertain Europeans as participants in colonial expositions, to study at German universities, or, as economic migrants, to seek a better life. In legal or extralegal alliances with white German women, those Black men often fathered children who grew up in a majority-white society frequently in isolation from other people of color and whose descendants were to various degrees absorbed into the general German population.[38] Records of these lives are difficult to retrieve, as the subtitle of *Farbe bekennen* acknowledged by alluding only to historical "traces." No inclusive and continuous Black German history can as yet be written, and accounts must presently be limited to what the 2007 volume *re/visionen: Postkoloniale Perspektiven von People of Color auf Rassismus, Kulturpolitik und Widerstand in Deutschland* (Re/visions: Postcolonial perspectives of people of color on racism, cultural politics, and resistance in Germany) terms "*Geschichtssplitter*,"[39] historical shards or fragments, of which this volume hopefully provides a number more.

As Ayim observes, it is impossible to know "when the first Africans came to Germany and when the first Afro-Germans were born."[40] Possibly African soldiers accompanied Roman armies to the German lands;[41] chronicles report that, when Holy Roman Emperor Frederick II traveled to Germany in 1235, he was accompanied by "dark-skinned Ethiopians" who guarded his imperial treasury;[42] and various works of medieval art attest to artists' familiarity with African physiognomy.[43] Wolfram von Eschenbach's *Parzival,* dating from the first decade of the thirteenth century, is the first German literary text to feature a Black figure, Belacâne, the first wife of Parzival's father, Gahmuret; their son Feirefiz, with skin described as piebald, both black and white, is the first Black child represented in a German literary text. In the period of political decentralization following the death of Frederick II in 1250, rulers over smaller German principalities increasingly regarded the inclusion of Africans in their retinues as evidence of their access to the riches of far-flung lands, and greater and lesser German nobles and wealthy merchants gradually followed suit.[44] These Africans are often portrayed in paintings of the period, their presence highlighting the status, and the white skin, of their masters and mistresses. Blacks attached to German courts, aristocrats, and merchants could be reduced to passive roles, exchanged, for instance, as gifts between rulers, but they also frequently exercised significant agency in positions of varying status, working as musicians, valets and ladies' maids, barbers, waiters, carpenters, gardeners, stableboys, midwives, and washerwomen.[45] Scholars are only slowly beginning to recover and chronicle these lives.

Two Africans brought to German-speaking countries in the eighteenth century achieved significant recognition in their own time. Anton Wilhelm Amo, born around 1700 in what is now Ghana, was taken to Amsterdam by the Dutch West India Company, which in 1707 presented the boy as a gift to Duke Anton Ulrich of Braunschweig-Wolfenbüttel; the duke baptized the boy with his own and his son's names and raised him as a member of the ducal family. Amo attended the University of Halle, ending his studies there with a "disputation" in Latin, likely the first defense of Black people written on German soil, titled *De iure Maurorum in Europa* (On the rights of Moors in Europe); he then continued on to the University of Wittenberg, where he was permitted to deliver lectures as he wrote his dissertation (also in Latin), *On the Absence of Sensation in the Human Mind and Its Presence in Our Organic and Living Body,* publicly defending it in 1734. In 1738 Amo completed his major study *Treatise on the Art of Philosophizing Soberly and Accurately,* a work aligning him with Enlightenment thinkers Leibniz and Christian Wolff. He taught university courses in philosophy in Halle and then in Jena before returning to Ghana in 1747, where he died sometime after 1753. Cameroonian-German philosopher Jacob Emmanuel Mabe considers it Amo's accomplishment as an Enlightenment thinker to have advocated for the extension of human rights to non-Europeans, to have advanced a notion of the "thing in itself" years before Kant, to have argued for a conception of hermeneutics long before Schleiermacher, and, in theorizing the spirit-body dualism, to have situated this metaphysical problem vis-à-vis his African antecedents.[46]

Angelo Soliman was born around 1721 and taken to Sicily as a child slave, where he was given to its imperial governor. From 1754 onwards he lived in Vienna, becoming the *Cammerherr* (head of a staff of servants) of a Viennese prince. Member of a reform-minded lodge of Freemasons that included aristocrats, high government servants, and elite members of the bourgeoisie, Soliman is known to have met Mozart several times in Masonic contexts.[47] Yet, the recognition Soliman had garnered during his life notwithstanding, upon his death in 1796, possibly at the command of Emperor Franz II himself,[48] Soliman's body was skinned, stuffed, and—adorned with a belt and headdress of red, white, and blue ostrich feathers—exhibited in the emperor's newly founded natural history cabinet, despite the vigorous efforts of Soliman's daughter to secure the release of her father's remains for burial.[49] In 2006 a Black Austrian research team associated with the project "*Verborgene Geschichte/n* (Hidden history/ies): Remapping Mozart" undertook the project of reclaiming and rewriting the history of Soliman and other Black people whose presence could be documented in Austria around the time of Mozart.[50]

The first larger group of Africans to live for longer periods of time in Germany arrived in the second half of the nineteenth century, with some two-thirds coming from Cameroon and Togo, African colonies that, along with German East Africa and German Southwest Africa, Imperial Germany had acquired in the Berlin West Africa Conference of 1884–1885 (and would lose in the First World War). In her groundbreaking 1997 study *Eine afro-deutsche Geschichte: Zur Lebenssituation von Afrikanern und Afro-Deutschen in Deutschland von 1884 bis 1950* (An Afro-German history: On the life situation of Africans and Afro-Germans in Germany from 1884 to 1950), Katharina Oguntoye (a coeditor of *Farbe bekennen*) compiled information about colonial migrants in Germany from the archives of the Reichskolonialamt (Imperial colonial office) to dispute the claim, as she puts it, "that there certainly weren't any, and if Africans had lived here, they couldn't have survived in the 'hostile' German environment."[51] More recently, Robbie Aitken and Eve Rosenhaft have built on Oguntoye's research to show the ways in which "young men with dark faces who hailed from Germany's new African colonies became the founding generation for a substantial black presence in Germany."[52] Deriving from different territories and ethnic groups, the colonial migrants nonetheless recognized their commonalities from the outset, terming each other *"Landsleute,"* compatriots. Though their reasons for traveling to Germany varied, many came or were brought to participate in one of the popular ethnographic exhibitions then widespread across Europe and the United States that featured "primitive" or "savage" peoples dressed in exotic garb; they lived, often for months at a time, in replicated villages and pursued what were alleged to be traditional activities. Africans, frequently members of colonial elites, often agreed to take part in the exhibitions for financial reasons and to secure free passage to Europe and after hours pursued more cosmopolitan activities. Andrew Zimmerman has noted, for example, that at the 1896 Colonial Exhibition, "after the visitors had gone home and they no longer had to perform, the East Africans amused themselves with German folksongs and even sang 'Deutschland über Alles,' accompanied by a violin played by a member of the group."[53] Pascal Grosse observes that, though quantitatively colonial migration was an insignificant phenomenon within the history of migration to Germany, qualitatively the presence of colonial migrants required Germany to develop political, legal, and intellectual criteria to organize ethnocultural difference as racial politics,[54] with ominous consequences for Germany's future. Mpundu Akwa, a colonial migrant and member of a Duala royal family, published the first periodical by Black people in Germany, *Elolombé ya Kamerun* (Sun of Cameroon), a fifty-two-page magazine advocating for more African sovereignty in Cameroon that appeared in German and Duala in 1908.[55]

Conditions worsened for the colonial migrants in the period between their first arrival and the 1920s. Racial attitudes hardened after 1900, partly in response to the Herero-Nama War of 1904–1906 in German Southwest Africa (during which the commanding German general issued the genocidal command to exterminate the Herero) and the Maji-Maji War of 1905–1907 in German East Africa. In the context of those hostilities, which many colonists interpreted as "race wars," racial purity took on a new importance, and race mixing was construed as treason. In several African colonies, mixed marriages, which would have produced mixed-race children entitled to German citizenship, were administratively forbidden (though they were never outlawed in Germany itself), and any such existing marriages were annulled.[56] Such attitudes would have an impact on Germany extending far beyond the colonial period; as El-Tayeb has maintained, "German colonialism was both fed by and produced racialized notions of national identity, notions whose traces have been visible in German citizenship policies throughout the twentieth century."[57]

White German opposition notwithstanding, many colonial migrants (about half of the eighty-two men of the first generation, overwhelmingly from Cameroon, who lived longer than four years in Germany)[58] chose to marry or enter into partnerships with white German women,[59] establish families, and raise mixed-race children. Despite their efforts, very few migrants were ever able to acquire German citizenship; recognized as subjects but not citizens of Germany before World War I, they were classified as stateless after the colonies were lost, and from 1932 to the end of the Nazi period migrants and other Black Germans were issued only a *Fremdenpass* (alien's passport) with the explicit specification that "the bearer does not possess German nationality."[60] Though Germany sought to repatriate some migrants, returning home was frequently not an option: both before and after World War I, German officials refused to grant migrants permission to take their white wives back to Africa,[61] and without passports Black Germans were often unable to leave Germany. In 1918 colonial migrants organized the Afrikanischer Hilfsverein (African aid association) to provide assistance in dealing with authorities, employers, and landlords; possibly the first such

Black organization in Germany, it was open to "every member of our Black race and every person of color."[62]

World War I and its immediate aftermath intensified racial hostilities. Around 485,000 soldiers of color from French colonies and 160,000 from British colonies, along with two divisions of African American troops, fought on European battlefields.[63] Germans regarded the Allies' decision to use colonial troops as evidence that their enemies had declared race war against them, and they stylized themselves as sole protectors of the honor of the white race.[64] The intensive wartime propaganda effort set the stage for a massive postwar campaign against what was termed the "Black Shame" or "Black Horror on the Rhine," the stationing of some twenty thousand French colonial troops in the occupied Rhineland beginning in 1919.[65] As Tina Campt, Pascal Grosse, and Yara-Colette Lemke-Muniz de Faria put it, "Black soldiers intensified the trauma of defeat because they inverted the established colonial relationship of domination between 'whites and blacks' on German soil."[66] Though relationships between the French soldiers and the German communities in which they were stationed were generally unproblematic, newspaper articles, cartoons and caricatures, posters, pamphlets, novels, plays, films, songs, poems, leaflets, postcards, and postage stamps drew on vicious stereotypes to portray sexually menacing, degenerate, and probably syphilitic Black soldiers, often represented as apes, who were prepared to despoil white German womanhood and engender "mongrel" children. From what were probably in the main consensual relationships between the colonial soldiers and white German women, about six to eight hundred children were born; termed "*Rheinlandbastarde*" (the German word *Bastard* means both "illegitimate" and "mongrel"), they were unquestionably of German nationality, since citizenship of "illegitimate" children passed through the mother. As Tina Campt has observed, "the Rhineland Bastard is the first representation of a domestic, German-born Black native."[67]

Yet in great contrast to racist representations of Black people during World War I and the Rhineland occupation, the enthusiastic reception of African American expressive culture during the Weimar Republic attested to a quite different conception of Blackness, connected instead to new notions of Americanization and modernity and thought to represent sexual liberalization and a vitality absent from a Germany crushed by war. (To some great degree, of course, this "Negrophilia" rested on positive inversions of the racist assumptions about Black primitivism that had fueled the Black Horror.) Once the hyperinflation of the early twenties had been brought under control, a number of enormously popular Black American entertainers toured Germany.[68] In May 1925 the "Chocolate Kiddies" revue, featuring music by a young Duke Ellington, brought forty-five African American musicians, actors, and dancers to the Berlin stage, including Sam Wooding's eleven-man orchestra, who performed the first "authentic" Black jazz to be heard in Germany. Later that year African American dancer, choreographer, and actor Louis Douglas brought his "Revue Nègre" to Berlin; the show's breakout star was not Douglas or his wife, the dancer Marion Cook, or the saxophonist Sidney Bechet but the glamorous erotic dance sensation Josephine Baker.[69] We know little about contacts between traveling Black entertainers and the approximately 2,500 to 3,000 Black people from various areas of the African diaspora living in Germany during the Weimar Republic.[70] But it is not improbable that they encountered each other in Berlin's "*Biguine*," which advertised itself as Germany's first *Negerbar* (Negro bar), opening on February 26, 1932, and closing shortly before the Nazis took power. The staff of the Biguine was entirely Black, and Black American, Black British, and Caribbean entertainers are known to have performed there.[71] Tobias Nagl regards such establishments as "important crystallization points of Black German everyday life in the Weimar Republic,"[72] and the presence of, and German enthusiasm about, Black performers from elsewhere in the world in this and other venues must also have encouraged Black people in Germany to conceive of themselves as members of a much larger and more far-flung African diaspora.

Moreover, during the Weimar Republic not just the entertainment industry enabled encounters between Black people in Germany and those from elsewhere. By the late 1920s especially Black people in Hamburg and Berlin were drawn into the international orbit of the Communist Party by its efforts on behalf of Black workers, including publication of the English-language journal *Negro Worker* by the Hamburg office of the International Trade Union Committee of Negro Workers; organization of the first International Congress of Negro Workers in Hamburg by Trinidadian George Padmore, with delegates from the United States and the Caribbean as well as Europe; and a 1932 tour through Germany by the mother of one of the "Scottsboro Boys" (nine young African American men accused of raping two white women) as part of an international solidarity campaign mounted by the party.[73] In Communist efforts coordinated by Padmore, Brent Hayes Edwards observes, "we encounter . . . a nascent discourse of black internationalism, that is at once inside communism, fiercely engaged with its ideological debates and funneled through its institutions, and at the same time aimed at a race-specific formation that rejects the Comintern's universalism, adamantly insisting that racial oppression involves factors and forces that cannot be summed up or submerged in a critique of class exploitation."[74] A number of colonial migrants in Germany joined the German Communist Party or involved themselves in activities associated with it, including the German section of the League for the Defense of the Negro Race, organized under the aegis of the Comintern. By March 1930 the French police had received a report that the League had two hundred German members, with branches in Hamburg and Frankfurt as well as Berlin.[75]

The Nazis of course put an end to such activities on the part of Black people and others. But except for the sterilization of 385 Rhineland children in 1937,[76] National Socialists formulated no specific policies directed at Black people, nor were Blacks targeted for extermination, since, in contrast to Jews, they were regarded as both too powerless and too small in number to warrant policy directives. As well, the Nazis hoped that Africans in Germany could serve as useful mediators once the lost colonies had been regained and did not wish to jeopardize African goodwill. In practice, the Nazi treatment of Black people was contradictory and inconsistent, dependent on the arbitrary decisions of local Nazi officials. Blacks were prohibited from participating in any activities closed to "non-Aryans," which meant that they were dismissed from schools, denied employment in positions that required membership in the Deutsche Arbeitsfront (German labor front), and forbidden to marry or have sexual relations with Germans. Some Black people found jobs, refuge, and connections to other people from the African diaspora in the Nazi film industry, where they were needed to portray "natives" in Nazi colonial films and exotic characters in other movies. From 1936 to 1940 some also found employment with the state-sponsored Deutsche Afrika-Schau (German Africa show), a touring ethnographic exhibition. Black people could also be the recipients of ordinary Germans' acts of kindness, protection, and solidarity, especially when those Germans knew them in local and personal contexts. Autobiographies by Black Germans Hans Massaquoi, Marie Nejar, Gert Schramm, and Theodor Michael, as well Tina Campt's interviews with Hans Hauck and Fasia Jansen in *Other Germans: Black Germans and the Politics of Race, Gender, and Memory in the Third Reich,* provide insight into the conditions of everyday life for Black Germans under the Nazis.[77]

In the wake of the Allied defeat of the Nazis, Black German children born of postwar relationships between white German women and Black Allied occupation soldiers, in the main African American GIs, became the largest group yet of Black people born on German soil. Because, for racist reasons, US authorities rarely allowed African American GIs to marry their German sweethearts, most children born of these unions were "illegitimate," frequently raised by their white mothers alone or together with a white stepfather or relinquished to orphanages or foster care. (Due to the single-handed efforts of Mrs. Mabel Grammer, the wife of a Black US officer stationed in Germany, up to 700 Black German children were adopted by African Americans.) Though they constituted only a small minority (4,776) of the 67,770 children fathered by occupation troops between 1945 and 1955,[78] the Black German children received disproportionate attention. Rita Chin and Heide Fehrenbach maintain that in West Germany "the question of race remained at the very center of social policy and collective imagination during the occupation years," though differently configured than during the Nazi period: now West Germans increasingly adopted "an American model of race, based upon skin color and a black-white binary"[79]—within which Black Germans featured prominently.

In 1952, the year the first cohort of Black German children entered school, West German Bundestag members debated how best to integrate their new Black population into German society because they recognized that the Federal Republic's treatment of the children would be regarded internationally as a measure of how thoroughly Germans had repudiated National Socialism. (As US schools were still segregated at this point, the children's successful integration into German schools would also reveal West Germany's moral superiority to Americans, who had undertaken to teach them democratic values.) However, by the late 1950s, as the children entered adolescence, West Germans conceived new purposes for them. It was now assumed they would choose to emigrate, likely to the tropical regions for which their racial constitution allegedly suited them, where they could live "among their own kind" while serving Germany's economic, commercial, and diplomatic interests by functioning as a bridge between Africa and their birth country. In the view of Campt, Grosse, and Lemke-Muniz de Faria, the promotion of emigration for Germany's Black population (at a point in their lives at which they could be expected to become sexually active) suggests that, by the late fifties, "integration was no longer the ultimate goal, but rather the segregation of white from black Germans."[80]

The plot of the 1952 West German feature film *Toxi* aptly represented German fantasies about the convenient disposal of this new generation of mixed-race children in Germany: after all members of an extended German family demonstrate their post-Nazi racial rehabilitation by welcoming a small Afro-German girl into their home, they are spared the long-term consequences of acquiescing to a Black presence in Germany when Toxi's African American father arrives like a deus ex machina to whisk her back to the United States.[81] As Lemke-Muniz de Faria puts it, "The exportation, both planned and realized, of these Afro-German children was deeply political in that it was often an external attempt to arbitrarily simplify the complex situation of a German-born, non-white population."[82]

No history of Black Germans in either West or East Germany has as yet been written, though many autobiographies by quite differently situated Black Germans reveal commonalities in their often harrowing experiences, and Marion Kraft's *Kinder der Befreiung: Transatlantische Erfahrungen und Perspektiven Schwarzer Deutscher der Nachkriegsgeneration* (Children of liberation: Transatlantic experiences and perspectives of Black Germans of the postwar generation) collects moving autobiographical and analytical accounts from children of African American GIs.[83] El-Tayeb writes: "Since the existence of a population that was not white and still German was as unthinkable after 1945 as it was before, history was both ignored and repeated. The persecution of black Germans under fascism, the hysteria around the 'Rhinelandbastards' and the anti-miscegenation laws miraculously vanished from public consciousness. At the same time, the old positions continued to guide discussions about non-white Germans, this time under the heading 'occupation children.'"[84] Michelle Wright terms Black Germans "Others-from-Within from Without": like the Black populations of countries like the United States, the United Kingdom, or France, Black Germans are treated as "Others-from-Within," "physically part of the nation, but in all other ways utterly foreign and thus utterly incapable of being integrated into that nation." But, Wright argues, they are simultaneously also regarded as "Others-from-Without": though "born and raised in Germany they are consistently misrecognized as *Africans,* even after extensive conversation has established a German birthplace, parents, and education."[85]

Perceived as not belonging in Germany, even regarded as testimony to their mothers' or their country's shame (since their fathers were assumed to have been members of a military force that defeated Germany), Black German children in West Germany were often taunted and harassed by white playmates and classmates, with teachers refusing to intervene or discriminating themselves in the form of more severe punishments and lower grades. The children were not represented or acknowledged in school curricula and were frequently tracked into vocational training instead of being encouraged to prepare for university study. They also were attributed with characteristics and behaviors stereotypically associated with Black people: heightened physical skills, musical and rhythmic abilities, laziness and lack of discipline, impetuousness, low intelligence, hypersexuality. As children and adults they were reproved or penalized for misdemeanors that would have been overlooked if committed by whites. Jobs and apartments they applied for were suddenly no longer available. They were desired as exotic sexual objects but rejected as more permanent romantic partners. White Germans felt free to stare at them, to fondle their hair, to comment publicly on their skin color, appearance, and behavior. Much less has been published about and by Black East Germans, usually children of Africans studying or working in the German Democratic Republic, but existing evidence suggests that their treatment was no better.

German unification and the upsurge in nationalism and racism that accompanied it only worsened conditions for Black Germans and other people of color: as May Ayim put it in her poem "blues in black and white," "a reunited germany / celebrates itself in 1990 / without its immigrants, refugees, jewish and black people / it celebrates in its intimate circle / it celebrates in white."[86] Despite political struggles on the part of Black Germans since the emergence of their movement in 1986, two books by Black German authors published in the past decade—*Plantation Memories: Episodes of Everyday Racism* by Grada Kilomba[87] and *Deutschland Schwarz Weiß: Der alltägliche Rassismus* (Germany Black and white: Everyday racism) by Noah Sow[88]—indicate that in united Germany, very much has still not changed.

III

This volume's essays acknowledge and celebrate the Black German agency recognized in the first section of this introduction but attest as well to the obstacles with which Black Germans have had to contend that the second section addresses. The essays also demonstrate the ways in which the Black German experience can be illuminated using multiple approaches and from a range of perspectives and positionalities.

The first three essays explore the enormous energy loosed by the emergence of the Black German movement. A major figure in Black German studies and the only Black German to hold a tenured professorship in the humanities or social sciences at a German university, Maureen Maisha Eggers underlines the important links between social movement work and the production of knowledge within the Black German women's movement. She emphasizes the ways that Black women's engaged scholarship has informed how Blackness has been conceptualized in Germany, promoted epistemic change, and contributed to decolonizing knowledge itself. Eggers's essay provides an account of the movement from the perspective of someone participating in it and situates the movement transnationally by drawing on anglophone postcolonial, diasporic, and African feminist theories to understand it.

Also a Black German scholar-activist, Nicola Lauré al-Samarai turns to African American literary scholar Houston Baker's notion of "spirit work" to explore the creative impulses that shape Black German cultural production. Literary texts, films, visual arts, and music, this lyrical essay shows, constitute a communal resource enabling Black Germans to resist racist violence, exclusion, and their erasure from German history, define themselves, and connect to wider Black cultural traditions globally. The essay provides an invaluable overview of cultural products and scholarship produced by Black Germans.

Dirk Göttsche examines more recent Black German literary texts in greater detail, showing how they connect to diasporic traditions and transnational cultural referents while continuing to focus on struggles against German racism but also, particularly in the case of celebrities, emphasizing individual achievement. Göttsche determines that postmillennial publications manifest increased self-confidence, engagement with mainstream culture, interventions into debates about national identity, and a growing presence in contemporary German literature. Göttsche's essay helps to embed Black German literary production within a larger framework of diasporic/transnational writing.

The next sequence of essays adds more historical detail to this introduction's account of Black German history. Robert Bernasconi addresses the history of German antipathy to race mixing, with special emphasis on physical anthropologist Eugen Fischer, whose work connects colonial and Nazi racial ideology. In his 1913 investigation of the mixed-race Rehoboth "mongrels" in German Southwest Africa, Fischer argued that the absorption of the blood of inferior peoples would doom Europeans to decline, and he later appropriated Mendelian genetics to maintain that, once despoiled, racial purity could never be restored. Appointed director of Berlin's university by the Nazis, Fischer provided "scientific" support for Hitler's policies and authorization for the sterilization of the Rhineland children. This essay makes an important contribution to critical race studies through its international, comparative discussion of racial mixing, anthropological science, and antimiscegenation laws, the last being particularly relevant because many Black Germans have one white German parent.

Tobias Nagl focuses on two Cameroonians in 1920s Germany to raise theoretical questions about how to read the colonial archive against the grain. Nagl is able to discern moments of resistance and subversion in archival accounts of the pathology and criminality of Wilhelm Munumé and Peter Makembe, perpetrators of an elaborate scam involving counterfeit bills and other documents. Munumé and Makembe's deft performative manipulation of racial stereotypes, along with their appeals for Black German citizenship and protest against colonial atrocities, highlights the complex strategies Black Germans employed to protest racist violence, contest the racial underpinnings of Germanness, and claim belonging. This essay elaborates new strategies for writing Black German history beyond the oral histories and autobiographies on which it has mostly been based hitherto and also establishes a new origin for Black German literature by terming a poem by Munumé in defense of his Germanness "the inaugurating moment of Black German postcolonial writing."

Christian Rogowski examines the Rhineland occupation by contrasting French and German sources and by focusing on Black voices rather than white propaganda. Using a letter from the Afrikanischer Hilfsverein as a springboard, Rogowski explores the reactions of Black people across the diaspora to the campaign against the French troops to show how it provided an occasion for Blacks in Germany to distinguish themselves as African *Germans* but situates their efforts within those of the larger African diaspora, including the francophone elite. Rogowski's essay raises important methodological issues about subaltern speech and contributes to comparative scholarship on racist and colonial ideologies.

Maria Diedrich shows us that the travel reports, letters, and diaries of the substantial number of members of the African American elite who traveled to Germany in the 1930s mostly fail to mention Black people there, instead consistently representing Germany as white. Diedrich particularly faults W. E. B. Du Bois, a Germanophile who in 1937 maintained that Blacks in Germany faced no traces of racial hatred. Diedrich suggests that such refusal to engage more centrally with issues touching on Black people in Nazi Germany was a self-protective move by members of the African American elite, an attempt to preserve Germany as a privileged site where they were not touched by racism like that of the United States.

Tina Campt focuses on the ways that Black Germans were part of German society during the Nazi period, not on how they were excluded from it. She analyzes traces of Black German lives under the Nazis that can be retrieved through the examination of casual snapshots of everyday life. Her sensitive readings of these photos reveal them to be illustrative of defiance and refusal: in contradistinction to what National Socialism asserted, these Black people insisted on being Germans. But the comfortable relationships revealed in the photos also tell us that some white Germans were willing to include Black Germans "in the tightly woven fabric of community." This essay makes a major methodological contribution to Black German studies by identifying and showing us how to interpret sources beyond the written archive.

As the first account of Black German life under the Nazis to see print, Martha Stark's "My 13 Years under the Nazi Terror," originally reported in 1949 in the *Pittsburgh Courier* and only recently rediscovered, is a seminal document of Black German history. Stark enjoyed a happy and unremarkable childhood in an elite German family until the Nazis took power, after which she was targeted for discrimination, though she also was protected by other Germans' acts of friendship, kindness, and support. Felicitas Jaima's introduction situates Stark's story in the context of remembrances of National Socialism by other Black Germans, shaped by what Jaima terms the "peripheral inconsistencies" of their sometimes more, sometimes less antagonistic treatment by the Nazis.

Heide Fehrenbach shows that, though regarded as taboo after the defeat of Nazism, the category of race, now reduced to the Black-white binary, nonetheless remained formative for the new West German state after 1945. Anti-Black racism, she argues, motivated the disproportionate attention West Germans paid to the mixed-race children born of romantic relationships between Black occupation troops and white German women. West German authorities encouraged their international adoption, social scientists determined that they manifested traits stereotypically associated with Black people, and popular magazines continued to exoticize them into the

1970s. This essay documents attitudes that continue to impact the lives of today's Black Germans.

Peggy Piesche, a highly regarded Black German scholar-activist who grew up in East Germany, focuses on Black German children who, beginning in the 1960s, were born of relationships between foreign students or workers in the German Democratic Republic and white East German women and were forced to contend with East Germany's unwillingness to engage with difference in schooling, youth publications, and elsewhere. However, though Piesche shows that racism coexisted easily with GDR socialism, she also argues that the racism of united Germany derives from legacies of colonialism and nationalism that both Germanies share. Written from an insider's perspective, this essay remains one of few to address the situation of Black East Germans.

The volume's final three contributions envision futures for Black German studies and the Black German movement. Black German historian and literary and film scholar Fatima El-Tayeb encourages Black Germans to think beyond national and Black paradigms and build alliances with other Black Europeans and European minority groups, especially second- and third-generation migrants. Drawing on queer theory, she urges Black Germans / Europeans to understand diaspora as a "permanent productive dislocation" of the future rather than a relationship to a lost home in the past and to forge "queer" counter-memories and counter-histories. She thereby situates Black German / European politics within the tradition of women of color (lesbian-) feminism that shaped the Black German movement from its outset.

The final chapter is a 2012 discussion among four Black German women activists who, centrally involved in bringing the Black German women's movement into being, recollect their experiences, assess the current moment, and look forward to what is to come. Their exchange shows how the movement changed the lives of Black people in Germany and, by producing critical knowledge about Black Germans and their history and conceptualizing a Black German (female) subject who understood herself as part of that history, enabled Black German studies. Bringing together different generations of Black German women, East and West Germans, and activists with academics, this moving and inspiring interchange celebrates almost thirty years of movement history.

The volume concludes with an epilogue consisting of a conversation between Peggy Piesche and me about the role of white scholars in Black

German studies. Like Eggers in the first essay of this book, Piesche asserts that the epistemic turn for which Black German studies is responsible derives from the specific positionality of Black Germans. Initially she contends that white scholars can have no legitimate role to play within Black German studies, since it is impossible for them to abandon a positionality implicating them in hegemony and whiteness. But when I explain that I am pursuing Black German studies in my own interest, because I too want to live in a better world no longer founded on white hegemonic principles, Piesche agrees that such a critical white perspective, directed also at engaging other white people in efforts to promote social change, could indeed contest hegemony. That is my hope for this volume: that in various ways it elaborates positions critical of hegemonic perspectives, including those of whiteness, and in those regards can also contribute to changing them.

NOTES

1. Fatima El-Tayeb, *Schwarze Deutsche: Der Diskurs um "Rasse" und nationale Identität 1890–1933* (Frankfurt/M: Campus, 2001), 8.
2. In terms that are, *mutatis mutandis,* relevant for Black Germans too, Sedgwick distinguishes between a minoritizing view of "homo/heterosexual definition" as an issue of primary importance to a relatively small number of homosexuals, and a universalizing view of it as "an issue of continuing, determinative importance in the lives of people across the spectrum of sexualities." See Eve Kosofsky Sedgwick, *Epistemology of the Closet* (Berkeley: University of California Press, 1990), 1.
3. For such a rewriting of German history informed by the Black German experience, see Rita Chin, Heide Fehrenbach, Geoff Eley, and Atina Grossmann, *After the Nazi Racial State: Difference and Democracy in Germany and Europe* (Ann Arbor: University of Michigan Press, 2009).
4. "Deprovincializing Germany" was a conference hosted by the University of Massachusetts Amherst in April 2001 from which, after learning of the conference's title, the German consulate in Boston withdrew its support.
5. Audre Lorde, foreword to *Showing Our Colors: Afro-German Women Speak Out,* ed. May Opitz, Katharina Oguntoye, and Dagmar Schultz, trans. Anne V. Adams in cooperation with Tina Campt, May Opitz, and Dagmar Schultz (Amherst: University of Massachusetts Press, 1992), viii–ix.
6. For a passionate statement about Black German scholars' exclusion from the German academy, see Noah Sow, "The Beast in the Belly: Schwarze Wissensproduktion als angeeignete Profilierungsressource und der systematische Ausschluss

von Erfahrungswissen aus Schwarzen Kulturstudien," Heimatkunde—migrationspolitisches Portal, Heinrich-Böll-Stiftung, December 8, 2014, http://heimatkunde.boell.de/2014/12/08/beast-belly.

7. See Noah Sow's critique of white scholars' "tradition of cartography and its fatal consequences" in Sow, "Beast."
8. See Aníbal Quijano, "Coloniality of Power, Eurocentrism, and Latin America," *Nepantla: Views from South* 1, no. 3 (2000): 533–80, and Quijano, "Coloniality and Modernity/Rationality," *Cultural Studies* 21, nos. 2–3 (March/May 2007): 168–78.
9. Linda Alcoff, "The Problem of Speaking for Others," *Cultural Critique* 20 (Winter 1991–92): 5–32.
10. Philipp Khabo Koepsell, "Literature and Activism," in *Arriving in the Future: Stories of Home and Exile,* ed. Asoka Esuruoso and Philipp Khabo Koepsell (Berlin: epubli, 2014), 42. See also Esuruoso and Koepsell, "Introduction Alpha," 12–13, and Esuruoso, "A Historical Overview," 14–35, in the same volume.
11. Esuruoso and Koepsell, 12.
12. Audre Lorde, "Gefährtinnen, ich grüße euch," in *Farbe bekennen: Afro-deutsche Frauen auf den Spuren ihrer Geschichte,* ed. Katharina Oguntoye, May Opitz, and Dagmar Schultz (Berlin: Orlanda, 1986), 13.
13. Lorde, foreword to *Showing Our Colors,* vii.
14. Ibid., vii–viii.
15. Nicola Lauré al-Samarai in discussion with the activists Katja Kinder, Ria Cheatom, and Ekpenyong Ani, "'Es ist noch immer ein Aufbruch, aber mit neuer Startposition': Zwanzig Jahre ADEFRA und Schwarze Frauen/Bewegung in Deutschland," in *re/visionen: Postkoloniale Perspektiven von People of Color auf Rassismus, Kulturpolitik und Widerstand in Deutschland,* ed. Kien Nghi Ha, Nicola Lauré al-Samarai, and Sheila Mysorekar (Münster: Unrast, 2007), 352.
16. Fatima El-Tayeb, "'If You Cannot Pronounce My Name, You Can Just Call Me Pride': Afro-German Activism, Gender, and Hip Hop," *Gender & History* 15, no. 3 (November 2003): 471.
17. Fatima El-Tayeb, *European Others: Queering Ethnicity in Postnational Europe* (Minneapolis: University of Minnesota Press, 2011), 67.
18. Peggy Piesche, personal communication with author, October 21, 2014.
19. In southern West Germany's US zone of occupation, where African American GIs were stationed, Black German children grew up to a greater degree in the company of other Black people, thus possessed a securer sense of their own Black identity and a wider awareness of Black culture and politics transnationally (Michael K. Fisher, telephone conversation with the author, July 3, 2016).
20. Lauré al-Samarai, 348.
21. The volume *Spiegelblicke: Perspektiven Schwarzer Bewegung in Deutschland,* ed. Denise Bergold-Caldwell, Laura Digoh, Hadija Haruna-Oelker, Christelle Nkwendja-Ngnoubamdjum, Camilla Ridha, and Eleonore Wiedenroth-Colibaly (Berlin: Orlanda, 2015), contains moving testimonials to the important role the ISD has played for many Black Germans.

22. Ekpenyong Ani, Jasmin Eding, Maisha M. Eggers, Katja Kinder, and Peggy Piesche, "Transformationspotentiale, kreative Macht und Auseinandersetzungen mit einer kritischen Differenzperspektive—Schwarze Lesben in Deutschland," in *In Bewegung bleiben: 100 Jahre Politik, Kultur und Geschichte von Lesben,* ed. Gabriele Dennert, Christiane Leidinger, and Franziska Rauchut (Berlin: Querverlag, 2007), 165.
23. Ekpenyong Ani, "Die Frau, die Mut zeigt—der Verein ADEFRA: Schwarze Deutsche Frauen/Schwarze Frauen in Deutschland e.V.," in *TheBlackBook: Deutschlands Häutungen,* ed. AntiDiskriminierungsBüro Köln von Öffentlichkeit gegen Gewalt e.V. and cyberNomads (Frankfurt/M: Interkulturelle Kommunikation, 2004), 145–49.
24. Lauré al-Samarai, 349–50.
25. See Nigel Asher, "Die Geschichte des Black History Month in Deutschland," in *Spiegelblicke,* 44–50.
26. In contrast to "Negro," which English speakers view as outmoded but only somewhat offensive, the term's German translation "*Neger*" is regarded as demeaning and defamatory. On that issue, see Grada Kilomba Ferreira, "'Don't You Call Me *Neger!*'—Das 'N-Wort,' Trauma und Rassismus," in *TheBlackBook,* 173–82; Grada Kilomba, "The N-word and Trauma," in *Plantation Memories: Episodes of Everyday Racism,* 3rd ed. (Münster: Unrast, 2013), 100–106; and Susan Arndt, "Neger/Negerin," in *Afrika und die deutsche Sprache: Ein kritisches Nachschlagwerk,* ed. Susan Arndt and Antje Hornscheidt (Münster: Unrast, 2004), 184–89. The term *"Mohr"* (moor) is likewise regarded as racist.
27. In Bergold-Caldwell, Digoh, Haruna-Oelker, Nkwendja-Ngnoubamdjum, Ridha, and Wiedenroth-Coulibaly, see Jamila Adler, Laura Digoh, and Jadija Haruna-Oelker, "Racial Profiling—eine menschenrechtswidrige Praxis," 250–54, and Abyel, "Racial Profiling—Bedeutung eines Präzedenzfalls," 259–61.
28. Ani, "Die Frau, die Mut zeigt," 147.
29. For further discussion of Black German activism, see Eleonore Wiedenroth-Coulibaly, "Zwanzig Jahre Schwarzer Widerstand in bewegten Räumen: Was sich im Kleinen abspielt und aus dem Verborgenen erwächst," in *re/visionen,*, 401–22.
30. See note 17 in chapter 2 for a complete list of Black German autobiographies published to date.
31. See Koepsell.
32. For more information on writing by African authors in Germany, see Sara Lennox, "Postcolonial Writing in Germany," in *The Cambridge History of Postcolonial Literature,* ed. Ato Quayson (Cambridge: Cambridge University Press, 2012), 1:639–44.
33. See Francine Jobatey, "*afro look:* Die Geschichte einer Zeitschrift von schwarzen Deutschen," PhD diss., University of Massachusetts Amherst, 2000; and Jeannine Kantara, "Die Geschichte der Zeitschrift *afro look* und die Anfänge der ISD," in *Black Berlin: Die deutsche Metropole und ihre afrikanische Diaspora in Geschichte und Gegenwart,* ed. Oumar Diallo and Joachim Zeller (Berlin: Metropol, 2013), 165–76.
34. El-Tayeb, "If You Cannot," 474.
35. Adé Odukoya, a Black German hip-hop artist with whom the idea for Brothers Keepers originated, reports on the origins of the group and its tour of East German

schools in 2002 in "Die Brothers Keepers Story," *TheBlackBook,* 345–49. The same volume contains an interview with Tyron Ricketts, another Brothers Keepers member (Angela Kamara, "'... man selber sollte die Stimme erheben!': Interview mit Tyron Ricketts," 313–26). As El-Tayeb notes, the members of Brothers Keepers consistently referred to themselves as Afro-German, thus situating themselves in the context of the movement that coined that name (El-Tayeb, "If You Cannot," 461).

36. Peggy Piesche, "'der käfig hat eine tür': Eine Einleitung," in *May Ayim Award: Erster internationaler schwarzer deutscher Literaturpreis 2004,* ed. Peggy Piesche, Michael Küppers, Ekpenyong Ani, and Angela Alagiyawanna-Kadalie (Berlin: Orlanda, 2004), 13.
37. Michael Küppers and Angela Alagiyawanna-Kadalie, "Macht der Nacht II," in *May Ayim Award,* 10.
38. For one story about such a family, see Gorch Pieken and Cornelia Kruse, *Preußisches Liebesglück* (Berlin: Propyläen, 2007).
39. Ha, Lauré al-Samarai, and Mysorekar, 111, 171, 207, 281, 399.
40. Opitz, Oguntoye, and Schultz, *Showing Our Colors,* 3.
41. Peter Martin, *Schwarze Teufel, edle Mohren* (Hamburg: Junius, 1993), 15, 367.
42. Ibid., 18.
43. Paul H. D. Kaplan, "The Calenberg Altarpiece: Black African Christians in Renaissance Germany," in *Germany and the Black Diaspora: Points of Contact, 1250–1914,* ed. Mischa Honeck, Martin Klimke, and Anne Kuhlmann-Smirnov (New York: Berghahn, 2013), 21–37.
44. Martin, 41–52.
45. Anne Kuhlmann-Smirnov, "Ambiguous Duty: Black Servants at German Ancien Régime Courts," in *Germany and the Black Diaspora,* 57–73. See also Kuhlmann-Smirnov, *Schwarze Europäer im Alten Reich: Handel, Migration, Hof* (Göttingen: V&R unipress, 2013).
46. Jacob Emmanuel Mabe, *Anton Wilhelm Amo interkulturell gelesen* (Nordhausen: Traugott Bautz, 2007).
47. Rüdiger Wolf, "Fürsten und Freimaurer: Angelo Soliman als Diener dreier Herren," in *Angelo Soliman: Ein Afrikaner in Wien,* ed. Philipp Blom and Wolfgang Kos (Vienna: Wien Museum/Christian Brandstätter, 2011), 97–105.
48. Philipp Blom, "Straußenfedern, Muscheln und Glasperlen: Soliman und andere Präparate in Museen, zwischen Wissenschaft und Ideologie," in *Angelo Soliman,* 117.
49. Walter Sauer, "Angelo Soliman: Mythos und Wirklichkeit," in *Von Soliman zu Omofuma: Afrikanische Diaspora in Österreich 17. bis 20. Jahrhundert,* ed. Walter Sauer (Innsbruck: Studienverlag, 2007), 79–86.
50. See Simon Inou, "Remapping Mozart—Geschichte Schwarzer Menschen in Österreich," *afrikanet,* March 12, 2006, http://www.afrikanet.info/archiv1/index.php?option=com_content&task=view&id=345&Itemid=2.
51. Katharina Oguntoye, *Eine afro-deutsche Geschichte: Zur Lebenssituation von Afrikanern und Afro-Deutschen in Deutschland von 1884 bis 1950* (Berlin: Hoho Verlag Christine Hoffmann, 1997), viii.

52. Robbie Aitken and Eve Rosenhaft, *Black Germany: The Making and Unmaking of a Diaspora Community* (Cambridge: Cambridge University Press, 2013), 2.
53. Andrew Zimmerman, *Anthropology and Antihumanism in Imperial Germany* (Chicago: University of Chicago Press, 2001), 26. For an account of a colonial migrant who became an impresario in Germany and Europe, see Rea Brändle, *Nayo Bruce: Geschichte einer afrikanischen Familie in Europa* (Zurich: Chronos, 2007).
54. Pascal Grosse, "Koloniale Lebenswelten in Berlin 1885–1945," in *Kolonialmetropole Berlin: Eine Spurensuche,* ed. Ulrich van der Heyden and Joachim Zeller (Berlin: Edition, 2002), 200. See also Grosse, *Kolonialismus, Eugenik und bürgerliche Gesellschaft in Deutschland 1850–1918* (Frankfurt/M: Campus, 2000).
55. Koepsell, 36–37.
56. See Lora Wildenthal, *German Women for Empire, 1884–1945* (Durham, NC: Duke University Press, 2001).
57. Fatima El-Tayeb, " 'Colored Germans There Will Never Be': Colonialism and Citizenship in Modern Germany," in *Extending the Diaspora: New Histories of Black People,* ed. Dawne Curry, Eric Duke, and Marshanda Smith (Urbana: University of Illinois Press, 2009), 226.
58. Aitken and Rosenhaft, 88.
59. Oguntoye, 68.
60. Aitken and Rosenhaft, 67–87.
61. Oguntoye, 150–51; Aitken and Rosenhaft, 107–10.
62. Peter Martin, "Der Afrikanische Hilfsverein von 1918," in *Zwischen Charleston und Stechschritt: Schwarze im Nationalsozialismus,* ed. Peter Martin and Christine Alonzo (Munich: Dölling und Galitz, 2004), 73–80.
63. Christian Koller, "Der 'dunkle Verrat an Europa': Afrikanische Soldaten im Krieg 1914–1918 in der deutschen Wahrnehmung," in *Zwischen Charleston,* 111–12.
64. Grosse, *Kolonialismus,* 205.
65. Koller, "Verrat." See also Christian Koller, *"Von Wilden aller Rassen niedergemetzelt": Die Diskussion um die Verwendung von Kolonialtruppen in Europa zwischen Rassismus, Kolonial- und Militärpolitik (1914–1930)* (Stuttgart: Franz Steiner, 2001).
66. Tina Campt, Pascal Grosse, and Yara-Colette Lemke-Muniz de Faria, "Blacks, Germans, and the Politics of Imperial Imagination, 1920–60," in *The Imperialist Imagination: German Colonialism and Its Legacy,* ed. Sara Friedrichsmeyer, Sara Lennox, and Susanne Zantop (Ann Arbor: University of Michigan Press, 1998), 207.
67. Tina M. Campt, *Other Germans: Black Germans and the Politics of Race, Gender, and Memory in the Third Reich* (Ann Arbor: University of Michigan Press, 2004), 28.
68. For an account of earlier Black American entertainers in Germany, see Rainer Lotz, *Black People: Entertainers of African Descent in Europe and Germany* (Bonn: Birgit Lotz, 1997).
69. Annette Dorgerloh, "Josephine Baker: Zwischen Bananenröckchen und 'neuer Frau' der zwanziger Jahre," in *Zwischen Charleston,* 290.

70. Christine Alonzo, Gerd Fleischmann, Peter Martin, Horst Matzerath, and Achille Mutombo-Mwana, "'Besondere Kennzeichen: Neger': Schwarze im NS-Staat," NS-Dokumentationszentrum, Cologne, Germany, November 8, 2002–February 23, 2003, http://www.museenkoeln.de/ausstellungen/nsd_0211_schwarze/aus_01.asp.
71. Jonathan Wipplinger, "'Biguine': The African Diasporic Presence at Weimar's End" (paper presented at the Black German Heritage and Research Association Convention, Amherst College, Amherst, MA, August 9, 2013).
72. Tobias Nagl, *Die unheimliche Maschine: Rasse und Repräsentation im Weimarer Kino* (Munich: text + kritik, 2009), 733.
73. Ibid., 620–35; Peter Martin, "George Padmore," in *Unbekannte Biographien: Afrikaner im deutschsprachigen Raum vom 18. Jahrhundert bis zum Ende des Zweiten Weltkrieges*, ed. Ulrich van der Heyden (Werder an der Havel: Kai Homilius, 2008), 266–73.
74. Brent Hayes Edwards, *The Practice of Diaspora: Literature, Translation, and the Rise of Black Internationalism* (Cambridge, MA: Harvard University Press, 2003), 245.
75. Aitken and Rosenhaft, 205–9.
76. Gisela Bock, *Zwangssterilisation im Nationalsozialismus: Studien zur Rassenpolitik und Frauenpolitik* (Opladen: Westdeutscher Verlag, 1986), 354.
77. Hans J. Massaquoi, *Destined to Witness: Growing Up Black in Nazi Germany* (New York: Morrow, 1999); Marie Nejar, *Mach nicht so traurige Augen, weil du ein Negerlein bist: Meine Jugend im Dritten Reich* (Reinbek bei Hamburg: Rowohlt, 2007); Gert Schramm, *Wer hat Angst vorm Schwarzen Mann: Mein Leben in Deutschland* (Berlin: Aufbau, 2011); Theodor Michael, *Deutsch sein und Schwarz dazu: Erinnerungen eines Afro-Deutschen* (Munich: Deutscher Taschenbuch Verlag, 2013); Campt, *Other Germans*.
78. Yara-Colette Lemke-Muniz de Faria, "'Germany's "Brown Babies" Must Be Helped! Will You?' U.S. Adoption Plans for Afro-German Children, 1950–1955," *Callaloo* 26, no. 2 (2003): 344.
79. Rita Chin and Heide Fehrenbach, "Introduction: What's Race Got to Do with It? Postwar German History in Context," in *After the Nazi Racial State*, 6, 18.
80. Campt, Grosse, and Lemke-Muniz de Faria, 227.
81. Angelica Fenner, *Race under Reconstruction in German Cinema: Robert Stemmle's* Toxi (Toronto: University of Toronto Press, 2011).
82. Lemke-Muniz de Faria, "Germany's 'Brown Babies,'" 358.
83. Marion Kraft in collaboration with Ika Hügel-Marshall, ed., *Kinder der Befreiung: Transatlantische Erfahrungen und Perspektiven Schwarzer Deutscher der Nachkriegsgeneration* (Münster: Unrast, 2015).
84. Fatima El-Tayeb, "'Blood Is a Very Special Juice': Racialized Bodies and Citizenship in Twentieth-Century Germany," *International Review of Social History* 44, supplement 7 (1999): 166–67.
85. Michelle M. Wright, "Others-from-Within from Without: Afro-German Subject Formation and the Challenge of a Counter-Discourse," *Callaloo* 26, no. 2 (Spring 2003): 297.

86. May Ayim, "blues in black and white," in *Blues in Black and White: A Collection of Essays, Poetry, and Conversations*, trans. Anne V. Adams (Trenton, NJ: Africa World Press, 2003), 4.
87. Grada Kilomba, *Plantation Memories: Episodes of Everyday Racism* (Münster: Unrast, 2008).
88. Noah Sow, *Deutschland Schwarz Weiß: Der alltägliche Rassismus* (Munich: Goldmann, 2008).

1

Knowledges of (Un-)Belonging

Epistemic Change as a Defining Mode for Black Women's Activism in Germany

MAUREEN MAISHA EGGERS

Black women's activism has been fundamental to the formation and existence of the Black movement in Germany and at defining moments has been a motor for the constitution of the organized Black community.[1] The struggle for public, political, and academic recognition is largely fueled by contestations led and organized within the Black women's movement. Scholarship by Black women and the communication of their analyses and findings at Black community events and meetings have intimately informed how Blackness is conceptualized in Germany. This essay's main focus is to explore this engagement with critical thought and to determine how dominant patterns of belonging are contested and transformed not just by social movement work but by focusing on the production of knowledge. Scholarship is then of strategic importance, because the focus shifts from social mobilization alone toward epistemic production and consequently toward epistemic change, from merely contesting racist representations toward dismantling legitimized and historicized racialized knowledges. I draw on the work of postcolonial, diasporic, and African feminist scholars to explore the relationships between intellectual work and social movement work,[2] between social mobilization and epistemic production, between the state and social movement contexts, and between alternative education, narration, and knowledge sharing.

To outline changing understandings and objectives associated with belonging, this essay highlights three periods that represent paradigmatic shifts in the (self-)perception of the Black movement in Germany, especially with respect to knowledge production about Blackness in Germany. These are an outward movement, an inward movement, and a movement toward transformative action. Each period is determined by different perceptions of social movement work and also by a specific definition of the relationship of this organizational work to the (hegemonic) mainstream.

My focus on the context of the Black women's movement is based on its significance as a driving force during key moments in the constitution of the organized Black community in Germany. The Black women's movement is the site within which issues of scholarship on Black Germany, belonging, and the relationship to the state are mainly situated. Black women activists acted as catalysts in the naming of the movement ("*afro-deutsch*" [Afro-German], later "*Schwarze Deutsche*" [Black German]). Black women activists were pivotal in defining the movement's content (knowledge production about Black German history, developing concepts of alternative education). They were also at the forefront of politicizing the Black movement in Germany (linking it to wider critical social movements).

This essay is divided into three parts. The first section focuses on the moments at which the Black (women's) movement in Germany was constituted. It informs about a period of exploration and experimentation. Critical scholarship is theorized here as an initial orientation. Epistemic production is directed outward. The scholarly work of Black women activists at this time is mainly addressed to the (white) German public. The second section focuses on the effects of scholarship for the movement itself. The creation of *autonomous spaces*[3] for epistemic production on Blackness becomes a pressing concern. Attention shifts from educating the public to transformational (inner) social movement education. The third section is concerned with the 1990s and beyond. The focus is not on the content of knowledge production itself, or on the relationship to the state in itself, but much more on actively using epistemic production to change the position of the movement within German society and thus transform society as a whole. The role of epistemic change as a form of *symbolic revolution*[4] becomes increasingly evident. The movement's most recent orientation is characterized by a venture not only to increase epistemic production but to actually effect epistemic change as a long-term solution.

Emerging into Existence: The Role of Narration

MOVING OUTWARD: THE (FIRST HALF OF THE) 1980S

The organized Black (women's) movement in Germany began in the 1980s. Black women activists were at the core of actions that led to the creation of initiatives and discussion groups on Blackness in Germany and eventually to the definition of Black Germanness. This initiatory movement can be more precisely described as a move toward claiming symbolic space. With the emergence of Black women activists, first individually and then collectively, *belonging* became a particular interest that required addressing. As activists entered spaces of political articulation, the discussion of understandings of Blackness, as well as contradictions and intentions in organizing, became increasingly significant. The spaces in question were mainly within the broader context of the (dominantly white) women's movement. The scenes were national feminist conferences, the annual lesbian spring meetings, and the women's cultural and club scenes in Berlin, Hamburg, Bremen, and Munich. Black women activists who were interested in feminist theories and politics met and opened discussions on Blackness and feminism.[5]

The term "*afro-deutsch*" was coined in 1984 by Audre Lorde together with a group of Black women activists in Berlin. This is considered the moment at which the Black movement in Germany was born.[6] The naming project set out to embrace and acknowledge the position of subjects of African ancestry/heritage and German lineage/situatedness/identity. At the same time, it symbolized a conscious endeavor to discard derogatory (German) terms connoting Blackness. Political self-definition as Afro-Germans, later Black Germans, initiated a new sense of collective identity and self-appreciation.

This movement can be characterized as an advance toward shattering the complacency of symbolic nonexistence. A series of actions began whose goal it was to contest dominant myths such as the claim that "there are no Black people in Germany, and if there are any, they have nothing important to say." Black women activists now actively sought contact with each other. This was followed by efforts to create spaces for exchange and experimentation (weekend workshops, exchange programs with other Black activists from the Netherlands, etc.). Finally, racism was collectively placed on the agenda of emancipatory movements in Germany. Addressing feminist and leftist emancipatory discourses, Black women activists pushed for the recognition of the struggles of Black people in daily interactions and spaces. Crucial to this was the challenge of making the realities of Black female subjects visible and thus open to contestation and transformation.

Translation as an Act of Resistance

The movement outward was linked to the project of weaving Black presence (critically) into the daily realities of Germany. Blackness was identified as already intimately intertwined with daily consumer cultures, cultures of representation, cultures of (white) charity, etc. The goal was to subvert those oppressive and paternalistic connotations of Blackness and to open up a field for creative *critical positionings.* Three levels of action can be determined as significant to this project. The first level concerns the role of political self-definition, which is to say, the role of naming Blackness in the German language (see above). The second level is the role of autobiographical texts in asserting *belonging.* The third level is the role of counter-discursivity and transformative impulses (appropriating key themes and local/regional/national discourses) and their reinterpretation from the vantage point of critical Black perspectives.

The Role of Autobiographical Texts and Literary Production

This move was characterized by the emergence of texts and poetry that inscribed Black and female realities and perspectives into the German language. May Ayim (formerly May Opitz)—renowned for the force and grace with which she appropriated the German standard/imperial language—initiated a push toward opening the German language to improvisation, contestation, and subversion. In a sense, she made a meaningful contribution to transforming the German language itself, pushing it to accommodate and adapt itself to subverted meanings, hybrid definitions, and articulations. Guy Nzingha St. Louis published *Gedichte einer schönen Frau* (Poems of a beautiful woman),[7] opening up a substantial field in which intense discussions ensued about the challenges and possibilities of anti-heteronormative self-definitions, self-concepts, and self-designs. The book *Farbe bekennen: Afro-deutsche Frauen auf den Spuren ihrer Geschichte* (later translated as *Showing Our Colors: Afro-German Women Speak Out*), published by the women's publishing house Orlanda in 1986, is acknowledged as a tangible manifestation of the critical presence of Black (female activist) Germans in Germany. This publication gave the Black community in Germany a huge boost. The book earned international acclaim and contributed to changing the face of German literary and cultural studies in the United States. Theorizing Black Germanness and teaching Black German history led to the creation of interdisciplinary and transnational links to German studies, cultural studies, Black studies, and diaspora studies.

The Role of Counter-Discursivity and Transformative Impulses

Understanding Germanness now in many contexts also entails acknowledging the presence of people of color in general and of Black Germans in particular. Furthermore, it requires an understanding of how colonialism, naturalization policies, post–World War II occupation policies, and migration have contributed to cultural, national, and racialized hybridity in Germany. Theorizing the causes, forms, and effects of this hybridity is closely bound up with the transdisciplinary project of documenting Black German histories, a key part of which is the quasi-archaeological process of sifting through footnotes and records in search of evidence for the Black presence in Germany.[8] Black women activist-historians like Katharina Oguntoye, Fatima El-Tayeb, and Paulette Reed-Anderson are at the center of this movement. A major emphasis of their scholarship involves German colonial history as well as the history of battles for citizenship fought by mixed-parentage Afro-Germans in the colonies and by African colonial citizens who migrated to Germany. Another focus concerns the occupation of the Rhineland by (Black) French soldiers after the First World War and the Afro-German children who resulted from unions between these soldiers and white German women. Historians have also studied Black (German) experiences in the Third Reich and Hitler's campaigns for new German colonies in Africa. Significant areas of post–World War II Black German history include the role of Afro-Germans in East Germany, such as the Black children of contract workers, as well as Black students from the young postcolonial Communist states (Cuba, Angola, Mozambique) or from freedom movements like SWAPO (Namibia). Post–World War II Black West German history again includes the consequences of military occupation, this time by American, British, and French troops, and the generation of Afro-German children (the so-called occupation children) born to Black soldiers and white German women. Later topics include the migration of African students to (West) Germany from the 1960s onward, the migration of African refugees to Germany, and the children born to African migrants and their white German partners.

Cultural studies as an analytical framework gained importance in situating the autobiographical accounts and life-stories of Black German subjects (or Black subjects in Germany) within different and specific periods. Black cultural studies activist-scholars like Peggy Piesche—whose biography is Black East German—contributed complex perspectives on the intersections between population policies, national political alliances, personal negotiations of contact prohibitions, and Black East-Germanness.[9]

Communicating these findings became a project leading to proposals for alternative education that brought Black (female activist) educationists to the fore. Belonging became a concern that was discussed and debated at virtually every meeting. The annual meetings of ADEFRA (formerly Afro-German Women, now Black Women in Germany) and the ISD (Initiative of Black People in Germany) became forums at which workshops were presented on Black German histories, on Black feminism, etc. All three levels—acts of self-naming, acts of translation through autobiographical writing, and acts of initiating counter-discourse—spurred a move toward transforming the consciousness of Black activists / collectives in Germany, which was now literally being written into the German language.

Emerging Scholarship on Black Germany

The extensive work of Black women activists from this period consists of cultural commentaries and critiques that have profoundly impacted German society. Epistemic production (verbal, visual, and social texts) in this phase is intimately linked to narration. Narrating is understood by Linda Tuhiwai Smith—quite literally—as emerging into visibility and therefore as "opposition being made visible."[10] The effects and implications of narrating have been discussed widely. In the context of social movement work, the impact of political, cultural, and literary interventions, cultural analysis, and critical (re-)interpretations of culture, and how these aspects determine belonging, is extremely relevant. Narration is considered central to changing perceptions of normalcy.[11] Since narration creates and preserves normalcy, dismantling legitimized and historicized dominant knowledges requires counter-narration. The power of normalcy in upholding the symbolic order has been thoroughly analyzed in the critical work of Pierre Bourdieu. His term "gentle violence" (soft violence, soft power) signals compliance with knowledge systems.[12] At the same time, it equally signals oppositional possibilities of disrupting and dismantling dominant and repressive systems and symbolic orders through critical scholarship—which is not surprising, as Bourdieu strongly links intellectual work to social movement work.

With regard to the transformation of language as a cultural symbol, German has become a vessel within which articulations of subordinated "hyphenated Germans"—such as *Afro-Deutsche* (Afro-Germans / Black Germans), *Asiatisch-Deutsche* (Asian Germans), *Türkisch-Deutsche* (Turkish Germans), or *Sinti/Roma-Deutsche* (German Sinti/Roma)—have found, or more precisely made, spaces. In this vein, a variety of the German language created as a brand name associated with people of color from migrant backgrounds (*Kanaksprak*) has become popular with young Germans from all kinds of backgrounds. The various levels of translation constitute acts of appropriation, subversion, and resistance—as exemplified in the work of Ayim, St. Louis, Raya Lubinetzki, and other activists.

Epistemic Production and Social Movement Work

MOVING "INWARD": THE SECOND HALF OF THE 1980S

Through intense engagement with the specific history of Blackness in Germany, the focus had gradually shifted from communicating outward to the (white) German public to a communication inward within the Black movement itself. The symbolic manifestation of the movement and the project of claiming visibility continued—but lost urgency in comparison to determining the actual content and thus the envisioned orientation of the Black movement in Germany. The founding of the nationwide organizations ADEFRA and ISD in 1985/1986 facilitated the changing focus toward a more intense discussion among Black activists themselves.

Defining and clarifying collective positions on issues affecting the quality of the daily lives of Black subjects in Germany took center stage. Motivated by the desire to create definitions outside the hegemony of white and (symbolically) male-dominated German society, debates on the necessity of positioning ensued. This led to an orientation toward a *critical difference positioning*. The impetus behind that move was a conscious decision not to be compared to, or merely compounded into, a structure already diagnosed as highly oppressive and intensely myopic. A temporary answer was found to the age-old dispute about "difference versus sameness" or "separation and/or equality" that periodically reappears in any social movement taking a critical stance toward existing power structures.

This effort was fueled by an intense investment in a perspective that would allow and nurture spaces for closeness and intimate interchange, promote affirmations of Black female creative expression, and affirm the struggles and survival knowledge of Black female activists. The need for intense exchange to enable experimentation with reconstructing the meaning of Blackness from self-perspectives and to facilitate the reevaluation of experiences of Blackness by nurturing Black consciousness led to the creation of separate spaces. Black women activists began to organize their own meeting spaces within the broader women's movement and within the wider Black movement that also involved Black men. This period also intensified the search for and creation of spaces where Black women activists from Germany could meet and network with other Black women activists from other parts of Europe and the United States. This period was characterized by regular weekend seminars on topics such as health, sexuality, relationships, meaningful employment, political strategies, and alternative knowledge production.

This phase of "inward" movement was a period in which links between the experiences of activism, scholarship, and teaching became focal points. Conceptual meetings saw debates on the role of social movements in epistemic production and alternative education. ADEFRA's programs were now geared toward understanding the implications of being socialized within a society whose dominant code made whiteness the standard. This resulted in a period of intense self-exploration. The aim was to analyze the ways in which Black activists themselves contribute to upholding the dominant logic and the symbolic order through their perceptions and actions. The objective was to explore how (self-)knowledges could create new spaces for action. Gayatri Spivak observes that social mobilization without epistemic change leads mostly to mere short-term solutions.[13] It became increasingly clear that the experiences of the activists involved would be fundamental to the movement. Action could lead to short-term results while in the long run leaving much of the overall structure of dominance unchanged. The connections between oppositional action, scholarship, and education (teaching) eventually led to the realization that the movement needed to gain access to feasible methods of influencing and changing the symbolic order. It was also necessary to assess what kind of content(s) would have the impact needed to disrupt racialized dominance. This in turn led to critical debates about the envisioned relationship of the movement to the German state and the range of possibilities for influencing it.

Decolonization: Striking at the Foundations of Dominant Projections

TRANSFORMING MOVEMENT INTO CREATIVE POWER: FROM THE 1990S ONWARD

Black women activists—including the founders and other long-term activists of ADEFRA—were by now in public service, working in (educational) institutions and (national) projects. In the 1990s the movement's orientation indicated a shift toward influencing mainstream contexts through critical thought and positioning. The epistemic work done by Black historians in Germany had laid the groundwork for the collective project of contextualizing Black presence in Germany. The movement of Black activists had become a site for critical knowledge production, not only for cultural critique but, more significantly, for academic critique. Black women activists had begun to nurture topics identified as being of key relevance to Germany's Black community. Afro-diasporic perspectives and realities of migration were at the center of scholarship on Black Germany at this stage. Interventions into discourses of nationhood and Europeanness had followed. Pushing forward the engagement with postcolonial perspectives in theorizing German history and contemporary debates had become a fundamental concern.[14]

The emergence of a new collective sense of self was reflected in the twentieth-anniversary celebrations of ADEFRA and the ISD (2005/2006), both of which were marked by exhibitions, namely *Generation ADEFRA: 20 Jahre Schwarze Frauenbewegung in Deutschland* (Generation ADEFRA: 20 years of the Black women's movement in Germany) and *Homestory Deutschland: Schwarze Biografien in Geschichte und Gegenwart* (Homestory Germany: Black biographies in past and present).[15] Innumerable literary and media productions have emerged from the context of the Black communities in Germany. Even the 2009 winner of the TV casting show *Deutschland sucht den Superstar* (Germany is looking for the superstar—the German equivalent of the American program *American Idol*), is a Black German—who, in addition to being a brilliant artist, also made substantial waves via his openly gay self-positioning. Again, a cultural statement sparked a wide-ranging discussion of anti-heteronormativity, this time not only in the Black community but—thanks to the mass media—nationwide.[16]

Charmaine Pereira's text "Between Knowing and Imagining: What Space for Feminism in Scholarship on Africa?," published in the e-journal *Feminist Africa*,[17] can be linked to the programmatic ambitions associated with the social movement orientation of Black women activists in Germany today: in both contexts, the Black women's movement as a critical collective is facing the question "What spaces are imaginable?" in order to effect change and apply transformative impulses to society as a whole.

In envisioning the spaces needed to effect long-term change, two objectives have proved to be of key importance: first, determining reflexive courses of action when interacting with the state; and second, determining the content, and thus the direction and envisioned quality, of epistemic change. Determining that epistemic change is of vital importance is not sufficient; the conditions for that change and the actual content of the change required must also be determined. Considering the long-term impact of social movement work requires a clarification of the links between the sites of social mobilization on the one hand and wider societal contexts on the other. Specifically, a positive but also critical relationship with the state (Spivak) and with the mainstream (Pereira) must be developed.[18] This actually contextualizes epistemic change as facilitated by its influence both within and outside mainstream contexts, powerfully shaped by a mode of interaction that is both positive and deeply critical.

The movement's increased orientation toward content can be illustrated on several levels. A more recent and promising analytical perspective is the attempt to employ the symbolic potency of decolonization strategies across disciplines to effect new epistemic developments. Decolonization is an increasingly debated approach. There are diverse understandings of what its target should be. Two of these seem especially fitting for the situation of epistemic productions by Black women activists that revolve around the contested themes of Blackness and belonging: first, understanding decolonization as the interruption of an (exclusive and canonized) focus on texts authored and authorized by the West,[19] and second, understanding it as a substantial shift of focus away from the imperial center.[20] Since whiteness in the symbolic order is seen to constitute the center of knowledge, this center, according to Linda Tuhiwai Smith, needs to be reconfigured. Using these perspectives on decolonization with the aim of facilitating epistemic change, the specific perspective of the Black women's movement has developed alongside the orientation toward breaking out of dominant projections. Hegemonic knowledge systems around Blackness (as well as around gender and sexuality as intricately linked to Blackness) have tended to be deeply implicated in a form of projection in which Blackness is marked and scrutinized to actually produce constructions of whiteness. These constructions tend to make whiteness the standard (knowledge-based whiteness, democratic whiteness, progressive whiteness, charitable whiteness, aestheticized whiteness, cultured whiteness, nationalized whiteness). The impetus of the decolonization project in this case entails, as Smith puts it, "breaking (free of) the penetration and surveillance" of the (white) Western gaze. With regard to epistemic production, confronting the violent hegemonic order means—in my understanding—quite literally shifting analytical energy *away* from arguing against racialized constructions, which in any case say more about the white self via its marking and marketing of the Black subject. Rather, decolonization entails focusing on the logic *behind* these dominant projections. Furthermore, it entails laying open the processes that facilitate the projection—in the same way that Bourdieu proposes that one should lay open the subtle processes by means of which *male* dominance is constructed and reconstructed daily. Smith makes it clear that she is not calling for a boycott of Western texts. Rather, she suggests that new standards be discussed and agreed upon that would ensure that epistemic production engages with its implication in oppressive orders and knowledge systems. Epistemic production therefore requires accountability for balance. Acknowledging the non-neutrality of epistemic production, as well as practicing and applying critique to our own academic production, is crucial to the building of this balance. Breaking the dominant patterns of projection also implies attentiveness to intersectional analyses. In the context of the Black women's movement it requires a commitment to breaking out of a mode of social movement history that trivializes the *movement work* of women activists. Social movement history often attributes "notable deeds" to male subjects. The perspective pursued by Black women activists in Germany resolutely refuses to consider male activity as the standard and takes the agency of women very seriously. This perspective therefore "gives back" symbolic weight to the agency of women.

Sharing Knowledge versus Sharing Information: Changing Experiences

In search of inspiration, Black women activists in Germany are looking more intensely at the framework of African feminist thought.[21] Critical knowledge produced in the context of African gender studies by African feminist and gender activists is gaining relevance, as transnational perspectives and globalized knowledge distribution facilitate access to their debates and perspectives. Referencing knowledges that are being produced away from (and outside of) the hegemonic center of the West is another advance in the project of decolonization. Using African social thought as an analytical tool is regarded as a form of *symbolic action* that *changes* the way in which knowledges from African contexts have been reduced to the status of "native informants/information" within hegemonic knowledge orders. This supports Smith's proposal to share knowledge rather than sharing information.[22] Sharing knowledge is perceived to entail a deeper commitment than merely consuming information. It involves engaging deeply with the power-critical analyses produced in everyday contexts. Within a critical pedagogy of decolonization, access to alternative knowledges can deeply influence action and the direction of social movement work. Epistemic change is not an empty term, as this project illustrates. Epistemic change is deeply committed to changing (Black) people's outlooks and perspectives and—most importantly—as a consequence changing the quality of our experiences.

NOTES

Maureen Maisha Eggers, "Knowledges of (Un-)Belonging: Epistemic Change as a Defining Mode for Black Women's Activism in Germany," was first published in *Hybrid Cultures—Nervous States: Britain and Germany in a (Post)Colonial World,* ed. Ulrike Lindner, Maren Möhring, Mark Stein, and Silke Stroh (Amsterdam: Rodopi, 2010): 189–202. It is reprinted here by permission of Editions Rodopi b.v. (Amsterdam and New York).

1. Ekpenyong Ani, Jasmin Eding, Maisha M. Eggers, Katja Kinder, and Peggy Piesche, "Transformationspotentiale, kreative Macht und Auseinandersetzungen mit einer kritischen Differenzperspektive—Schwarze Lesben in Deutschland," in *In Bewegung bleiben: 100 Jahre Politik, Kultur und Geschichte von Lesben,* ed. Gabriele Dennert, Christiane Leidinger, and Franziska Rauchut (Berlin: Querverlag, 2007), 164–67.
2. Gayatri Spivak, "Not Really a Properly Intellectual Response," interview by Tani E. Barlow, *Positions: East Asia Cultures Critique* 12, no. 1 (2004): 141–43.
3. Charmaine Pereira, "Between Knowing and Imagining: What Space for Feminism in Scholarship on Africa?," *Feminist Africa* 1 (2002): 9–33.
4. Pierre Bourdieu, *Masculine Domination,* trans. Richard Nice (Cambridge: Polity, 2001), 134.
5. Ani et al., 165.
6. The (historicized) presence of prominent Black activists such as trade unionist Fasia Jansen, who survived the Third Reich in the concentration camp Neuengamme, preceded the organized movement and is to a certain extent acknowledged in various histories of resistance in Germany.

7. Guy Nzingha St. Louis, *Gedichte einer schönen Frau* (Berlin: Gudula Lorez, 1983).
8. Paulette Reed-Anderson, *Rewriting the Footnotes: Berlin and the African Diaspora* (Berlin: Ausländerbeauftragte des Senats, 2000).
9. Peggy Piesche, "Black and German? East German Adolescents before 1989: A Retrospective View of a 'Non-Existent Issue' in the GDR," in *The Cultural After-Life of East Germany: New Transnational Perspectives*, ed. Leslie Adelson (Washington, DC: American Institute for Contemporary German Studies [AICGS], 2002), 37–59.
10. Linda Tuhiwai Smith, *Decolonizing Methodologies: Research and Indigenous Peoples* (London: Zed, 1999), 6, 33. The term "Black Australia" is an example of a powerful signifier of oppositional identity devised by Aboriginal activists.
11. Gayatri Spivak, interview by Kerry Chance and Yates McKee, April 24, 2001, http://ccs.ukzn.ac.za/files/chanceandmckee.spivak.pdf.
12. Bourdieu, 21, 133. The term "gentle violence" refers to processes that allow violence to be internalized so that the direct application of violence is replaced by the self-activating (self-infliction) of violence. Bourdieu thus speaks of a complex agreement with the system of violence in question.
13. Spivak, interview by Barlow, 152.
14. The transnational project BEST: Black European Studies (at the Universities of Mainz and Massachusetts) has assembled and systematized a large body of work in this emerging field (www.best.uni-mainz.de/modules/Informationen/index.php?id=13).
15. The exhibition *Generation ADEFRA* was held at the Museum Europäischer Kulturen in Berlin-Dahlem from September 2006 to October 2006. *Homestory Deutschland* is a joint project of the ISD and the Bundeszentrale für politische Bildung and has been a traveling exhibition since 2006.
16. The artist in question is Mark Medlock. For example, "Mark Medlock gewinnt *DSDS* 2007," www.dsds-superstar.de/2007/05/05/mark-medlock-gewinnt-dsds-2007/ (no longer available).
17. Pereira.
18. Spivak, interview by Barlow, 141; Pereira, 12.
19. Edward Namisiko Waswa Kisiang'ani, "Decolonizing Gender Studies in Africa" (paper presented at CODESRIA conference on African Gender in the New Millennium, Cairo, April 7–10, 2002), http://codesria.org/IMG/pdf/KISIANGANI-1.pdf.
20. Smith, 34, 39.
21. For instance, by drawing on online resources such as the e-journal *Feminist Africa* and the website of CODESRIA.
22. Smith, 16.

2

Inspirited Topography

Haunting Survivals and the Location of Experience in Black German Traditions of Knowledge and Culture

NICOLA LAURÉ AL-SAMARAI

sie sind die betroffenen und ich bin extrem, was auch immer sich ihrer betroffenheit entzog, war meine chance, am leben zu bleiben.

[they are concerned and I am too extreme; whatever escaped their concern was my chance to stay alive.]

—Guy St. Louis, "14. nov. 1994"

People of color, women of color, queers of color have a history with, around, and in Germany. We were, we are, and we will be . . . at home.

—Olumide Popoola and Beldan Sezen, *Talking Home*

Some time ago I had the pleasure of conversing with an Afro-German architect about the significance of spirituality in creating and imagining autonomous Black German cultural spaces. We spoke about the now seemingly taken-for-granted achievements of a hard-won communal persistence, thought about whether different forms of Black German cultural expressions are borne forth by a certain spirit (*Geist*), and asked how this specter haunts a mode of knowledge characterized by and consisting of diverging and extremely contradictory voices and experiences. Indeed, our conversation transformed into an *inspirited* dialogue, since the spirit of our thinking already illuminated the murky paths of our mental journey, opening up a re/visionary space wherein spirituality did not take the form of a denigrated, superficial, and esoteric appetizer in an elaborate meal of cultural cannibalism but, rather, could be re/defined and re/located as the main course in Black diasporic, and especially in Black German, concepts of resistance.

That I was able to rely upon such an autonomous conversational space reminded me of the varying becomings and transmutations of Black German cultural production, of the emergent and ever-shifting multifaceted strategies of culturo-historical negotiations found in theoretical writings, autobiographies, poetry, and visual arts as well as the specific lines of traditions that were founded upon these structures. These traditions not only voice important sites of resistance against racist violence, exclusion, and the ongoing zealous dismembering and erasure of a Black German presence and historicity, but also are the outcomes of sometimes directly and sometimes loosely connected, transformatively creative impulses that enable Black Germans to reticulate their histories and presences within autonomous narratives. This historical emplotment is anchored by an expressive counter-intelligence and encodes the empowering inscription of a re/visionary counter-history and counter-memory that Houston Baker Jr. describes as "spirit work."[1]

Spirit work animates the powerful striving of historical and contemporary root-taking into a multivoiced and constantly shifting soundscape. Cultural producers play a special role in the ongoing emplotment of a self-defined Black subjectivity, which is principally marked by the interplay of sound and motion, memory and reclamation, reconfiguration and recontextualization. In their theoretical and artistic imaginary these cultural producers create distinct articulatory practices, thus redefining social, political, and cultural/historical fields of representation within white as well as Black diasporic contexts, often in radical ways. As part of an emerging cultural topography, these practices stand at the center of the inspirited topography I would like to conjure in this essay. I am particularly interested in the specific framings and issues, places and voices, continuities and fractions that disrupt and negotiate the violent omnipresence of white dominance and house [*beheimaten*] Black German presences within their own time-space.[2]

"in the beginning was the word"[3]: Reclaiming Black German History

In the context of subjugated communities it is quite unusual to be able to date so precisely both the pivotal break from historical dispossession and the move toward a self-determined historicity. Moreover, in a Black German context—which differs from the collective experience of oppression Black people have faced in the Americas and in other parts of the world that has brought forth many single voices rooted in it—only the consciously established chorus of isolated voices makes collectivity visible and audible. Although published in 1986, the pathbreaking anthology *Farbe bekennen: Afro-deutsche Frauen auf den Spuren ihrer Geschichte*[4] still remains one of the most important milestones of coming to terms with history and the structural paradigm shift suggested by its editors.

Conceptualized as a collage in the form of a monograph, *Farbe bekennen* attempts to weave together and establish an interior chronology for the deeply fragmented and actively erased contours of Black German history. The vital dialogue between May Ayim's historical research, the autobiographical sketches of Afro-German women from different generations, the numerous photographs and poems, and the two transcribed conversations between several participants juxtaposes differing modalities of experience, knowledge, and articulation. As readers we are confronted with the discursively and emotionally challenging communicative strategies of emerging counter-narratives and counter-memories. Furthermore, given the violent amnesia surrounding the history of German colonialism in academic historiography and public discourse, the inclusion and discussion of its intellectual, cultural, and quotidian consequences for the lives of several generations of Black German women proves that the echoes of Germany's colonial past cannot be muted as easily as the German mainstream would like. *Farbe bekennen* lays bare the skeleton of a dismembered colonial experience that shaped and still continues to inflect multilayered cultural cartographies in which dominant and subjugated historicities echo in and against each other, that has inscribed the bodies of Black and white men and women, and that inseparably intertwines Black and white German pasts and presents. Consequently, *Farbe bekennen* bears witness to a violently hierarchical encounter and relationship without which neither Black nor white German histories are thinkable.

By giving voice to a painful historical moment through a set of diverse Black and predominantly female perspectives, *Farbe bekennen* serves as an originating leap that enabled many other such endeavors. Its multivocal text valiantly attempts to overcome the imposed discontinuity of a buried history so as to no longer passively suffer from it, while also testifying to the complex beginnings of a diasporic presence in Germany and a counter-historiographical space with radically new discourses, including the then literally unthinkable analysis of dominant *rassischer*[5] (racial) social structures, dynamics, and patterns of perception. Furthermore, the decidedly collaborative intergenerational memory-work of the editors created a representational and imaginative architecture in which neglected and annihilated *lived* experiences of Black German people could find a home. The empowering ethico-epistemological principle of concretized experience as a central criterion of meaning-making[6] relocated the marginality of Black Germans so that it no longer represented a site of loss and deprivation but rather transmogrified into and was appropriated as a site of resistance.[7] The liberatory movement from silence to speech, from margin to center—identified by bell hooks as "talking back"—which in its first steps insisted on creating a name for itself, is nothing other than the historical process of Black-subject-becoming. Thus, designations such as "Afro-German" or "Black German" do not represent the outcome of mere semantic games but disfigure hegemonic naming and classificatory strategies. The necessity of a neologism to vocalize the reconcilability of Germanness and Blackness—animating, in the most literal sense, this fraught nexus through its own historical sound—amplifies the powerful effects of a white imaginary that in its infinitely eloquent speechlessness eradicates Black German existence even in the subterranean recesses of the German language.

Inhabiting language in a world of fixed differences where Black people, both symbolically and in everyday life, are conscripted to the realm of sub- or nonhuman and repeatedly consigned to their "proper place" in the racial order of things initially signified the willful appropriation and positioning of a newly minted Black "self" against a white "other." This evolving *tradition of strategic demarcation* safeguarded marginality as a space of survival and cultural retreat while simultaneously initiating—in Glissant's terminology—"processes-of-bringing-into-relation"[8] with other Black time-spaces all over the world. As an emergent form, diasporic thinking in the German context not only required flexible positionalities to transgress seemingly fixed borders and crude phantasms of racialized national belonging but also became an integral part of a multivocal internal and global call-and-response among subjugated individuals and communities. In *Farbe bekennen* the sisterly presence of African American poet Audre Lorde provides a source of inspiration and strength by excavating the hidden interconnections between different modalities of diasporic multirootedness. In a transatlantic dialogue Lorde encourages Black Germans to define themselves, to share their (hi) story with other Black people / people of color and to imagine forms of communality that are attentive to the careful preservation and strategic use of differences as fundamental conditions of possibility.

This daring vision has since been framed and further explored by numerous Black activists, artists, and scholars in Germany who—with their tireless grassroots work, their cultural, intellectual, and theoretical input, and their well-grounded political practice—have contributed to conceptualizing and establishing communal permanence and to bringing into being a vibrant, by now comprehensive body of thought. The many journeys to transform a once nearly impassable cultural terrain into an inhabitable "intervening space" and to become part of a "revisionary time"[9] are oftentimes initiated and undertaken by Black German feminists and queers who, borrowing a phrase from Peggy Piesche, keep venturing "to undig and to dig over,"[10] to put pieces together and put them up for discussion. Which is just another way to say: to map and to remap.[11]

"contemplating being Me"[12]: Autobiographical and Poetic Blueprints

Against the white background of dominant racist images, words, sounds, and formations of fantasy, and in view of a specifically Black German tension between individual isolation (*Vereinzelung*) and a fragmentary collective memory as well as expropriated materio-cultural inscriptions, the confidence in and reference to lived individual experience opens up a space to assert and verify the existential and spiritual dimensions of uniqueness and personhood. To become the author of a (hi)story, to speak instead of being spoken, means to mentally take possession of it and—always a conscious or unconscious political act of self-representation—to imbue it with authority.[13] The authorizing authorship articulates itself as an *autobiographical impulse* that shapes and permeates the creative expressions of Black Germans. Its inscription—although too readily perceived as such—represents far more than a mere deconstructive commentary on a preexisting formation. It is first and foremost a cultural strategy of survival in marginality, which brings together Black German *fictions of selfhood*[14] to generate connections between them and to privilege and set in motion the unseen and often intangibly personal.[15] It also creates the foundation for a counter-memory that, through the conduit of Black experience-based intellectual and artistic strivings, carves out a space in a counter-discursive world of its own. The concomitant multilayered overlapping of diverging life-worlds (*Lebenswelten*) "behind the actual / between the lines / under the surface"[16] does not excavate a coherent counter-narrative where polyphony flows into a harmonic consonance but a narrative from which springs a fragmented, plural, and necessarily contradictory cultural reservoir of diasporic expressivity.

Its dissonant sound can be heard most clearly in the now voluminous archive of autobiographies by Black Germans.[17] Since the authors cannot fall back on the luxury of a safety net of historical continuity, they are forced to inscribe their stories into the abyss of invisibility and silence. Consequently, these texts are "accounts of . . . self-learning"[18] as well as conscious acts of personal memory-work and hence *performative events* that somehow negotiate and reconfigure white master-discourses. The survival of "invisibly bloody childhoods"[19] undergirds and shapes these autobiographies as a leitmotif. Invariably the texts narrate racist violence against which the autobiographical subjects have to physically defend themselves or develop a "layer of callus on the eardrum"[20] just to stay sane; they talk about individual becomings and consciousnesses in a destructive white world, which is ostensibly populated by "only one reality, only one truth";[21] they note the necessity of filling a cultural interstice with a self for which there simply is "no prefabricated format, which 'mono-culturals' often wield so lightly and utilize at the expenses of others";[22] and they think about how to make peace with one's past in order to imagine freedom beyond the confines of mainstream success.[23] They speak of a world that expects people of color to "shut up, keep quiet, behave nicely," in which "they neither disturb nor draw any attention to themselves and, please, do not make any demands"[24]—a world where Black identity is "defined and normalized completely by the exterior world, i.e., in which the 'I' receives its value only through antithetical demarcations—'non'-white / 'non'-German."[25]

We encounter these exclusionary strategies of normalization in significant white male and female pre-texts, which resonate loudly within the Black autobiographical texts and are thus important because their at times piercing noise makes audible the still normative presentness of a *rassischer* discourse of colonial derivation. The commonplaces of this discourse—contrary to Michelle Wright's assertion[26]—should certainly be termed anti-Afro-German, *because* Black Germans and Germans of color are incessantly represented and positioned as "Others-from-without" and *because* the *intentional* individual and collective expulsion effectively effaces a Black German being in the past as well as in the present.[27] Against the background of such an eradicated history, whiteness in Black autobiographies does not appear so much as a pleasantly chatted-about abstract category but rather manifests most clearly as the Black experience of violence (*Schwarze Gewalterfahrung*). In their writings the authors attempt to lend meaning to this all-encompassing and mobile state of being, which materializes as a consolidation of powerful social dislocations and fragmented temporalities (*Un-Orte und Un-Zeiten*).[28] Since these individual experiences are differently coded in each text, it is key to develop critical readings from a Black perspective that eschew the hitherto-dominant exoticizing, voyeuristic, and pseudo-humanist discourses of concern (*Betroffenheit*) as well as the tendency to judge either the "literary quality" of the autobiographical texts or whether they re/produce "positive" or "negative" images. Instead the challenge lies, according to Gina Dent, "not in policing the areas over which our gaze may trespass, but, rather, in making clear that what we reveal there are the effects of that gaze."[29] Thus the contradictory and conflicting "effects" of Black German looks can appear as complex *Heimsuchungen*[30] of a traumatized history that allow us to enter an intellectual *tradition of autobiographical negotiation.* Furthermore, freeing the autobiographies from their discursive isolation and reading them as *speaking to each other* constitutes their entirety as a perpetually expanding intergenerational and symphonically vocal archive, which is not only important for vigilant encircling of the diverse gendered experiences of Black subjects. As the exhibition project *Homestory Deutschland: Schwarze Biografien in Geschichte und Gegenwart* (Homestory Germany: Black biographies in past and present)[31] has convincingly proven for more than a decade, such an archive also, in the course of establishing a counter-historiography, provides the condition of possibility for making re/memory usable as a powerfully effective communal re/source.

While Black German autobiographies recount individual long-term stories, which due to the mostly solitary grappling with repressive social conditions are centered on the experience of isolation, poetic art as an expressive form with a momentary character marks a different space of survival and life. Audre Lorde vividly reminds us that poetry is not a luxury for Black people / people of color but a vital necessity of existence, where meaningful action springs from learning "to bear the intimacy of scrutiny and to flourish within it."[32] In the Black German context this necessitates a radical and visionary discovery of the self, which simultaneously works as a performative act of invention (*Selbsterfindung*) in the manner described by Olumide

Popoola and Beldan Sezen in the preface to their anthology *Talking Home:* "Like so many others *we* had to find and write the words *our*selves *we* so desperately needed. Words that helped *us* to deal with *our* experiences in Germany, that made *us* visible, that let *us* be."[33] Finding such words enables artists to leave the gray zone of a permanent racist state of emergency, to "give name to the nameless so it can be thought,"[34] and, in a language "that turns around like an echo / that bursts morning into leaves,"[35] to create a world where pain and happiness are shared, beauty is celebrated, visions are elaborated, and concepts of communality are tested.

By interweaving nets of "common ways, new cross-roads" with moments "of entering, en/coun/tering, ex/changing / de/part/uring,"[36] Black German poetry represents an important form of imaginative memory-work and consciousness-raising. Although personal experience provides an initial and important inspiration, the consequences of its lyrical compacting intensification (*Ver-Dichtung*) map an altogether different topography. Projects like the journals *afro look* and *Afrekete* (both founded in 1988); the first collection of poetry by Black Germans, *Macht der Nacht* (Power of night, 1991/1992); the anthologies *Talking Home* (1999), *May Ayim Award* (2004), and *Arriving in the Future* (2014); the collaboration of MCs in groups like Advanced Chemistry (founded in 1987), Brothers Keepers, and Sisters Keepers (both founded in 2001); or the rap/dance stage play *Coloured Children* (1997) stem from a *tradition of collaborative writing/speaking* that fuses individual perspectives in a larger concert of crosscurrents and discontinuities. Such transformative movements not only embed the distinct voices in a communal harmonics but also convert the isolated dismembered "I" into a recallable and multiply relational "us," inaugurating, in Kobena Mercer's words, a "communifying process."[37] This process makes it possible to reunite the dispersed parts of the self as well as to connect the multitude of Black presences to that "borderless and brazen" place "where my sisters are / where my brothers stand / where / our / FREEDOM / begins."[38]

With its transgressions and delimitations the spirit of such an "*Überlebenskreativität*" (creativity of survival)[39] initiates a healing process that burrows into the interiority of words. If, as Édouard Glissant states, "the imposition of a history that is not self-created can make you sick, then an imposed language can also lead to disease,"[40] this history is articulated in and therefore has to be seized and transformed. Conquering language, however, is not an easy venture because "white language / Black thought"[41] are not compatible at times. Therefore the "acquisition of verbal virility"[42]—regulation number six from the sharp-witted pantomimic *Anleitung zum schwarzen Profil* (Instruction manual for Black profiling) by Elke Jank—constitutes a prerequisite in the striving for a collective expression. This particular striving Glissant describes as "forced poetics"—forced because "a need for expression confronts an inability to achieve expression"[43] in order to render effable matters pertaining to subjugated groups. The Black German word, like any other oppressed utterance, must pave its way, albeit through nomadic detours, into self-expression, for which it needs inventive word scratchers who assume the task of dis-estranging (*ent-fremden*) German semantics by infusing these with an obstinate sense of self (*Eigen-Sinn*). Dismantling and deterritorializing the dominant use of language through contextual migrations, transmutations, or remodelings,[44] as well as the sense of "how to tame the German language with its consonant clusters, declinations and complex sentences without sacrificing flow or rhythm,"[45] provides the strategic and energetic potential base for the development of artistic skills in word and rhyme. These skills are also used to interrupt and dialogize hegemonic German monolingualism with the sound of multiple tongues, which allows less conflicted modes of artistic expression,[46] or, as in the hexilingual rap "Polyglott Poets," brings together the multiple roots of Black German reality.[47]

These shifting creolizations offer a distinctly Black German mode of signifying and are not limited to linguistics, at least not to a restrictive definition thereof. They can be found in the borrowing and mixing of aesthetic styles and narrative traditions,[48] thus rendering novel geopoetic territories decipherable. Within these self-defined spaces preassigned meanings of "origin" and "descent," of "home" and "exile," of "belonging" and "out-of-placeness" become invalid, for they unfurl into lively glocalized versions of a diasporic expressivity[49] with completely new imaginative convergences. As seen in the volumes *blues in schwarz weiss* and *nachtgesang* by poet May Ayim, the German text corresponds to Ghanaian Adinkra symbols that stem from Ashanti oral culture and traditionally serve as abstract signs of warning, encouragement, or advice.[50] These symbols constitute a parallel visual text that is tightly interwoven with Ayim's written words. Both texts densify into a missive that makes visible "related distances / distant relations / between continents" of an emerging "at home in transit"[51] while also slyly eluding visibility by opaquely coding it as *Heimat in Bewegung* (home in motion).

"Manifesting a visible existence": Positionings of Black German Visual Artists

Black German visual art becomes imperative in a society in which the "experience of visibility, the world of gazes and being looked at by others, constitutes one of the central aspects of how racism is lived and received,"[52] in which the right to look represents a primarily white and predominantly male privilege, and in which these historically sedimented, asymmetrical-looking relations institute scopic domains infused with unequal power relations. Although visual artists like Marc Brandenburg, Yvonne Buntrock, Christina Grotke, Manou Holzner, Ika Hügel-Marshall, Stephen Lawson, Guy St. Louis, Raja Lubinetzki, Nzitu Mawakha, Sandrine Micossé-Aikins, Ingrid Mwangi, Sabina Odumosu, Ricky Reiser, and Daniel Kojo Schrade[53] and filmmakers/screenwriters like Fatima El-Tayeb, Oliver Hardt, John A. Kantara, Branwen Okpako, and Pierre Sanoussi-Bliss[54] have created their own spaces of articulation in their paintings, drawings, photographs, collages, sculptures, multimedia installations, and films, their work, although partly recognized, is still excluded from broader public discussion. Clearly this omission is far from coincidental, given that claiming what W. E. B. Du Bois called the "second sight" of Blackness in word and image occurs in a highly contested cultural territory and fundamentally queries the supremacy of the white master-gaze, especially its violent conscriptions of racialized difference. In their work Black German visual artists "return the look," thus confronting the colonial roots of hegemonic gazes as well as their sense of direction that stipulates "one group glances but remains invisible, while the 'Others' are fixed as objects of the gaze."[55] Lastly, they negotiate the results of this fixation that re/produces an imaginary overflowing with racist images and renders the conquered peoples and bodies of "the rest of the world" as a mythic fantasy of an imperial omnipotent eye.

Within these hegemonic and controlling "scopic regimes of modernity," as Michele Wallace defines them,[56] visual artists attempt to find access to a tradition they have been denied. It is of special importance in the Black German context that they want "their work grounded in an analysis of historical and cultural predicaments," their cultural productions embedded "in a historical and contemporary framework,"[57] and their practices understood as an important moment of working through the past in order "to remember our people no matter where they come from."[58] Viewed against the backdrop of multiple forms of unnaming Black historicity and its attendant stories of (non)belonging, "processes of bringing-into-relation" the invisible or unspeakable—words not (yet) uttered or stories no longer narratable—and "our many belongings, now spread all over the world, which we can draw upon, but which we also have to seek out, identify and reconnect ourselves,"[59] establish a *tradition of visual memory-work.* Located amid a deeply fragmented Black German time-space, this memory-work is characterized by a creative praxis that relates and relays two spheres: the disarticulation of Black German experience from its placement in a system of racist figurations of the white German cultural imaginary and its rearticulation within a new diasporic framework that bears witness to the difference and diversity of this experience.[60]

The figural self-renewal accompanied by the symbolic reclamation of Black pasts and presents envisions a space of visibility that allows for the telling of complex stories about "normal people, people just like us"[61]—Black stories told from a Black perspective about "things fundamentally imbalanced, displaced."[62] The effects of these imbalances and displacements alongside normative axes of power like racism or hetero/sexism as well as historical and contemporary memory-gaps constitute reality as a dense matrix, challenging artists to embark on a journey between history and fiction, art and ritual, and Western and non-Western influences in which they appropriate and recontextualize elements of an established or enforced culture to estrange, recode, or ensnare them in new contexts of meaning.[63] Works such as the collage *Bitte nicht füttern!* (Please do not feed!) by Yvonne Buntrock, which thematizes the *Völkerschauen;*[64] Stephen Lawson's wooden sculpture *Schwarze deutsche Eiche (Die nächste Generation)* (Black German oak [The next generation]); or the *Afronaut Series* by Daniel Kojo Schrade illuminate a flexible map that allows the tracing of hidden historical fissures and the visualizing of them as autonomous geopolitical readings in their interleaving and amalgamation of putatively incompatible contexts.[65]

Cinematic texts such as *Alles wird gut* (Everything will be fine), *Zurück auf los!* (Return to go!), and *Tal der Ahnungslosen* (Valley of the innocent)[66] grapple arrestingly with these fissures, taking on a particularly important role in the still noticeable lack of Black German fiction as instantiations of narrative literature.[67] These films narrate, respectively, the adventurous detours of two Black West German women from different backgrounds finding each other, the *Lebenskünstlertum*[68] of a gay, HIV-positive *Ossi* (East German) who dreams of a singing career performing old GDR songs, and an

East German police officer's search for her lost résumé. The humorous and thoughtful introspections concerning Afro-German lives and interpersonal entanglements lay open the oftentimes highly grotesque absurdity of normative societal rules and at the same time develop a public space that renders a constantly mutating multivocal Black presentness (*Gegenwärtigkeit*) representable. Black queer filmmakers in particular, through their perspectives and their choice of subjects and main characters, offer vital strategic positionings that encircle diverse and divergent aspects and overlappings in the multiple axes of marginalization. Consequently, they interrupt and dialogize prevalent heteronormative patterns of perception and, as Kobena Mercer concludes, "insofar as they speak *from* the specificity of such lived experiences they overturn the assumption that minority artists speak *for* the entire community."[69]

The conscious and multilayered conceptual desedimenting of Black identities also provides a starting point for conceptualizing the emancipation of Black bodies from the overdeterminations of white racist and sexist discourses. Black British visual artist Keith Piper's question about what kind of visual language is appropriate to the tension between colonial conquest / enslavement / rape and murder / the violent fetishizing of Black bodies and representations "beyond the suffering image"[70] is also of critical importance for Black German artists. For Stephen Lawson, for instance, giving Black bodies back their beauty and discreteness avoids covetous hostile takeovers. Lawson's sculpture *Mask Dancer / Mask of the Intermingling Minds*—a woman in motion wearing a mask and giving herself a constantly changing face in different times and different movements—embodies this approach in a special way, since neither the mask nor the face it covers ever becomes tangible, thus producing a protective opacity that defines its own location. It should come as no surprise, then, that Lawson describes his works as "Trojan horses" bodying forth unhomely stories and, if placed somewhere, estranging a formerly familiar place.

By refusing white fantasies of control and authority, by "unearthing, remembering and making visible absent texts,"[71] the historically situated image work of Black artists reveals a landscape in the visual *present tense* that enables them to draw from the global archive of diasporic expressivity and (re)connect the multitude of dispossessed Black German spatiotemporal experiences with other Black time-spaces. The globally relayed relatedness of cultural translation has to bridge enormous distances and gaps, for which some artists—Lawson and Buntrock, for example—use the binding power of storytelling, which bespeaks their desire to be located within these storytelling traditions. Reclaiming this Black cultural tradition, which represents a foundational building block in the establishment of autonomous survival spaces, not only enables these artists to visually encode their memory traces but also gives the ancestors and the communal elders back their old/new roles as spiritual guides and keepers of history. In the Black German context the reimagining/rememory of an "ancestral legacy"[72] is literally of re/visionary significance: it conjoins the legacy of a scarcely accessible yet existent intergenerational historical (dis)continuum with an idea of historical rootedness that grounds it, and vice versa.

Black German word scratchers' and visual artists' creative articulations, in the form of manifold *Heimsuchungen,* enunciate a nomadic aesthetics that consciously discards conjurings of discreteness and boundedness and critically synthesizes and creolizes cultural elements. It thus strives for a communal memory "[that] evokes mosaic images and sounds, and invades everyday existence."[73] As a *memorial perpetuum mobile* marked by particular strategies of talking and looking back, these artistic constellations welcome the challenge of "putting-into-relation" (Black) worlds. Moreover, their interlaced tactile textu(r)ality inaugurates a Black German cultural topography taken hold of and transformed into a (un)homely abode of spirits: a life-world as *continued existence* (*Über/Lebensraum*) filled with the syncopated polyphony of Black experiences, which are linked by and bound to the force of *spirit work.*

Translated by Alexander G. Weheliye

NOTES

This essay is a revised version of my article "Inspirited Topography: Über/lebensräume, Heim-Suchungen und die Verortung der Erfahrung in Schwarzen deutschen Kultur- und Wissenstraditionen," in *Mythen, Masken und Subjekte: Kritische Weißseinsforschung in Deutschland,* ed. Maureen Maisha Eggers, Grada Kilomba, Peggy Piesche, and Susan Arndt (Münster: Unrast, 2005), 118–34. I would like to thank Tazalika te Reh for fundamentally inspir(it)ing the framing of this essay, Yvonne Buntrock and Stephen Lawson for conversations and the permission to publish some of their thoughts, and Regina Stein and Markus Schmitz for suggestions and materials.

I am indebted to Alexander G. Weheliye for his careful translation and for being the great intellectual companion he is.

1. Houston A. Baker Jr., *Afro-American Poetics: Revisions of Harlem and the Black Aesthetic* (Madison: University of Wisconsin Press, 1988), 5.
2. In the context of this article the term "time-space" defines an animated site: through the re/construction of an autonomous counter-history a deeply fragmented and disintegrated Black German temporality and locality can be re/possessed and provided with continuity. The striving for continuity should in no way be misread as a linear fixation of a minoritarian historicity but marks a development that enables Black Germans to re/create the multiply cut relations between historical and contemporary places, times, and dispersed Black presences.
3. May Ayim, *blues in schwarz weiss: gedichte* (Berlin: Orlanda, 1995), 15.
4. See *Farbe bekennen: Afro-deutsche Frauen auf den Spuren ihrer Geschichte,* ed. Katharina Oguntoye, May Opitz, and Dagmar Schultz (Berlin: Orlanda, 1986); trans. Anne V. Adams in cooperation with Tina Campt, May Opitz, and Dagmar Schultz as *Showing Our Colors: Afro-German Women Speak Out* (Amherst: University of Massachusetts Press, 1992).
5. The terms "*Rasse*"/"*rassisch*" are rendered in German throughout. Although it is customary in Germany, I do not consider the replacement of the German terms by the seemingly less problematic English terms "race"/"racial" in academic or public contexts very helpful, because that actively disavows and veils German racial formations by virtue of linguistic displacement. The use of the English terms locates race and racism elsewhere and, in the process, serves as a protective shield against the manifold ways in which race thoroughly permeates Germany's history and present political configuration. I follow El-Tayeb, who states: "Acknowledging that '*Rasse*' does not exist as a biological reality cannot . . . become a commonplace just by avoiding any reference to concepts based on '*Rasse.*' On the one hand, avoiding such concepts ignores the enormous political and economic inequalities that derive from the social effectiveness of racial hierarchies and means that structural racism cannot be adequately analyzed. On the other hand, avoiding such concepts negates the potential for resistance of social group identities that formed as a reaction to racism." Fatima El-Tayeb, "Begrenzte Horizonte: Queer Identity in der Festung Europa," in *Spricht die Subalterne deutsch? Migration und postkoloniale Kritik,* ed. Hito Steyerl and Encarnación Gutiérrez Rodríguez (Münster: Unrast, 2003), 138n1.
6. Patricia Hill Collins, *Black Feminist Thought: Knowledge, Consciousness, and the Politics of Empowerment* (New York: Routledge, 1991), 209.
7. bell hooks, "marginality as a site of resistance," in *Out There: Marginalization and Contemporary Culture,* ed. Russell Ferguson (Cambridge, MA: MIT Press, 1990), 341.
8. Édouard Glissant, *Poetics of Relation,* trans. Betsy Wing (Ann Arbor: University of Michigan Press, 1997), 95. For Glissant "relation" is an open totality of movement—"it is the boundless effort of the world: to become realized in its totality, that is, to evade rest" (ibid., 171–72).
9. Homi Bhabha, *The Location of Culture* (London: Routledge, 1994), 7.

10. "Peggy Piesche," in *Homestory Deutschland: Schwarze Biografien in Geschichte und Gegenwart,* catalog commissioned by Initiative Schwarze Menschen in Deutschland/ISD Bund (Essen: Margreff Druck und Medien, 2006), 137.
11. For almost a decade, these intellectual efforts along with their results and output have noticeably fallen by the wayside. While current international research trends give rise to the impression that talking *about* Black German matters increasingly replaces work *with* Black German approaches, the situation in the German academy indicates an alarming consolidation of white power structures. (For recent developments in Germany, see https://blackstudiesgermany.wordpress.com/community-statement-black-studies-an-der-universitat-bremen-deutsche-version/.) In order to reemphasize Black German approaches and to bring to the fore their complex contextual embedment, i.e., a Black German body of thought, the following list of selected references aims to provide relevant material for historicizing and reintegrating theoretical discussions and analyses. The below-mentioned anthologies have been coedited by or contain writings of Black German activists and scholars. For a better overview, the list is in chronological order: "Geteilter Feminismus: Rassismus, Antisemitismus, Fremdenhaß," *beiträge zur feministischen theorie und praxis* 27 (1990); *Entfernte Verbindungen: Rassismus, Antisemitismus, Klassenunterdrückung,* ed. Ika Hügel, Chris Lange, May Ayim, Ilona Bubeck, Gülsen Aktas, and Dagmar Schultz (Berlin: Orlanda, 1993); *Schwarze Frauen der Welt: Europa und Migration,* ed. Marion Kraft and Rukshana Shamim Ashraf-Khan (Berlin: Orlanda, 1994); May Ayim, *Grenzenlos und unverschämt* (Berlin: Orlanda 1997); *AufBrüche: Kulturelle Produktionen von Migrantinnen, Schwarzen und jüdischen Frauen in Deutschland,* ed. Cathy S. Gelbin, Kader Konuk, and Peggy Piesche (Königstein/Taunus: Ulrike Helmer, 1999); *Spricht die Subalterne deutsch? Migration und postkoloniale Kritik,* ed. Hito Steyerl and Encarnación Gutiérrez Rodríguez (Münster: Unrast, 2003); *TheBlackBook: Deutschlands Häutungen,* ed. ADB Köln/cyberNomads (Frankfurt/M: IKO, 2004); *Mythen, Masken und Subjekte: Kritische Weißseinsforschung in Deutschland,* ed. Maureen Maisha Eggers, Grada Kilomba, Peggy Piesche, and Susan Arndt (Münster: Unrast, 2005); *re/visionen: Postkoloniale Perspektiven von People of Color auf Rassismus, Kulturpolitik und Widerstand in Deutschland,* ed. Kien Nghi Ha, Nicola Lauré al-Samarai, and Sheila Mysorekar (Münster: Unrast, 2007); *de-platziert! Interventionen postkolonialer Kritik,* ed. Nadine Golly and Stephan Cohrs (Berlin: wvb, 2008); Noah Sow, *Deutschland Schwarz Weiß: Der alltägliche Rassismus* (Munich: Goldmann, 2008); Nana Adusei-Poku, "Pop-Porn, Feminismus im Käfig?," *Style and the Family Tunes,* 2010, 70–79; Maureen Maisha Eggers, "Knowledges of (Un)Belonging: Epistemic Change as a Defining Mode for Black Women's Activism in Germany," in *Hybrid Cultures—Nervous States: Britain and Germany in a (Post)Colonial World,* ed. Ulrike Lindner, Maren Möhring, Mark Stein, and Silke Stroh (Amsterdam: Rodopi, 2010), 189–202 (chapter 1 in this volume); Grada Kilomba, *Plantation Memories: Episodes of Everyday Racism* (Münster: Unrast, 2010); Fatima El-Tayeb, *European Others: Queering Ethnicity in Postnational Europe* (Minneapolis: University of Minnesota Press, 2011);

Wie Rassismus aus Wörtern spricht: (K)Erben des Kolonialismus im Wissensarchiv deutsche Sprache, ed. Susan Arndt and Nadja Ofuatey-Alazard (Münster: Unrast, 2011); Sandrine Micossé-Aikins, "Not Just a Blackened Face" (December 4, 2013), http://www.textures-platform.com/?p=3169; Maureen Maisha Eggers and Sabine Mohamed, "Schwarzes feministisches Denken und Handeln in Deutschland," in *Feminismen heute: Positionen in Theorie und Praxis,* ed. Yvonne Franke, Kati Mozygemba, Kathleen Pöge, Bettina Ritter, and Dagmar Venohr (Bielefeld: transcript, 2014), 57–76. A plurality of Black German positions is also provided by the online dossiers http://www.bpb.de/gesellschaft/migration/afrikanische-diaspora/ (from 2004) and https://heimatkunde .boell.de/dossier-schwarze-community-deutschland (from 2006). For recent queer/feminist approaches of Black people and people of color, see, for example, http://femoco2013.jimdo.com/; http://maedchenmannschaft.net/tag/schwarzer-feminismus/; http://streit-wert.boellblog.org/2011/10/12/katja-kinder/; and http://www.derbraunemob.de/, all with additional links.

12. Cinnamon Sandjon, "sinnend ICH sein," in *May Ayim Award: Erster internationaler schwarzer deutscher Literaturpreis 2004,* ed. Peggy Piesche, Michael Küppers, Ekpenyong Ani, and Angela Alagiyawanna-Kadalie (Berlin: Orlanda, 2004), 87.
13. Anne McClintock, " 'The Very House of Difference': Race, Gender, and the Politics of South African Women's Narrative in *Poppie Nongena,*" in *The Bounds of Race: Perspectives on Hegemony and Resistance,* ed. Dominick LaCapra (Ithaca, NY: Cornell University Press, 1991), 198. Working through Edward Said, McClintock states "that the word *author* itself springs from the same etymological root as *authority* and is attended by potent notions of engendering, mastery, and property."
14. In this context "fiction" designates the creative process of reconstructing and/or reimagining the Black self autobiographically and/or poetically.
15. Houston A. Baker Jr., *Workings of the Spirit: The Poetics of Afro-American Women's Writing* (Chicago: University of Chicago Press, 1991), 39.
16. Ayim, *blues in schwarz weiss,* 51.
17. Within the last two decades, Black German autobiographical writings have provided important cross-epochal reference points that, albeit highly individual, lay bare the evidently putative contradiction between drastic historical changes in twentieth-century Germany and racist continuities as firm as ever. For autobiographies of Black Germans born prior to 1945, see, for example, Hans J. Massaquoi, *Destined to Witness: Growing Up Black in Nazi Germany* (New York: Morrow, 1999); Theodor Wonja Michael, *Deutsch sein und Schwarz dazu: Erinnerungen eines Afro-Deutschen* (Munich: dtv, 2013); Marie Nejar, *Mach nicht so traurige Augen, weil du ein Negerlein bist: Meine Jugend im Dritten Reich* (Reinbek bei Hamburg: Rowohlt, 2007); Gert Schramm, *Wer hat Angst vorm schwarzen Mann: Mein Leben in Deutschland* (Berlin: Aufbau, 2011). For autobiographies of Black West Germans—many of whom are sports, music, or entertainment celebrities—see, for example, Kevin-Prince Boateng, *Ich, Prince Boateng: Mein Leben. Mein Spiel. Meine Abrechnung* (Kulmbach: Plassen, 2015); Harald Gerunde, *Eine von uns: Als Schwarze in Deutschland geboren* (Wuppertal: Peter

Hammer, 2000) (though written by her white German husband, this biography of Bärbel Kampmann was authorized by her and is therefore mentioned here); Jimmy Hartwig, *"Ich möcht' noch so viel tun . . .": Meine Kindheit, meine Karriere, meine Krankheit* (Bergisch-Gladbach: Bastei Lübbe, 1994); Ika Hügel-Marshall, *Daheim unterwegs: Ein deutsches Leben* (Berlin: Orlanda, 1998); Charles M. Huber, *Ein Niederbayer im Senegal: Mein Leben zwischen zwei Welten* (Frankfurt/M: Scherz, 2004); Steffi Jones, *Der Kick des Lebens: Wie ich den Weg nach oben schaffte* (Frankfurt/M: Fischer, 2007); Günther Kaufmann, *Der weiße Neger vom Hagenbergl* (Munich: Diana, 2004); Samy Deluxe, *Dis wo ich herkomm: Deutschland Deluxe* (Reinbek bei Hamburg: Rowohlt, 2009); Mark Medlock, *Ehrlich* (Munich: pendo, 2007); Thomas Usleber, *Die Farben unter meiner Haut: Autobiographische Aufzeichnungen* (Frankfurt/M: Brandes & Apsel, 2002). For autobiographies of Black East Germans, see, for example, André Baganz, *Lebenslänglich Bautzen II: Als Farbiger in der DDR* (Berlin: Westkreuz, 1993), revised edition published as *Endstation Bautzen II: Zehn Jahre lebenslänglich* (Halle [Saale]: Mitteldeutscher Verlag, 2010); ManuEla Ritz, *Die Farbe meiner Haut: Die Antirassismustrainerin erzählt* (Freiburg: Herder, 2009); Detlef D! Soost, *Heimkind—Neger—Pionier: Mein Leben* (Reinbek bei Hamburg: Wunderlich, 2005); Abini Zöllner, *Schokoladenkind: Meine Familie und andere Wunder* (Reinbek bei Hamburg: Rowohlt, 2003). Some of these autobiographies are discussed in chapter 3 of this volume.

18. Edward Said, *Beginnings: Intention & Method* (New York: Columbia University Press, 1975), 358.
19. Audre Lorde, "Gefährtinnen, ich grüße euch," in *Farbe bekennen,* 14.
20. Hartwig, 36.
21. Hügel-Marshall, 17.
22. Huber, 9.
23. Soost, 220.
24. Hartwig, 38.
25. Peggy Piesche, "Identität und Wahrnehmung in literarischen Texten Schwarzer deutscher Autorinnen der 90er Jahre," in *AufBrüche,* 198.
26. Michelle M. Wright, *Becoming Black: Creating Identity in the African Diaspora* (Durham, NC: Duke University Press, 2004), 191.
27. Contemporary dominant refusals to perceive Black Germans and Germans of color in general as nothing other than "Others-from-without" by positioning them as "*Ausländer*" (foreigners) or "*Fremde*" (non-natives) can partly be read as an outcome of repressed historical/discursive events, especially the campaigns about the Afro- and Asian-German Rhineland children in the 1920s and the discussions about Black West German children born immediately after 1945. Despite their relatively small numbers, both groups were constructed as threats to the purity of the German nation. This underscores the deep entrenchment of historical narratives grounded in a persistently *völkisch*-national framework by which the imagined racial homogeneity of the white German community was and is reconstituted. The reified idea of "*Fremdrassigkeit*" (being of foreign race), first conceptualized in the vehement colo-

nial debates about race-mixing and the "*Mischlingsfrage*" (mulatto question) during the twentieth century's first decade, predetermined all subsequent perceptions of Black Germans as a genuinely *internal* "problem" that needed to be "solved" accordingly: either through forced sterilization during the Third Reich, or by various plans of "voluntary" emigration in the 1950s, or via recent, mainly discursive displacements. Indeed, these active efforts to expel historical and contemporary generations of Black Germans from the German "*Volkskörper*" (body politic) are based upon and at the same time re/formulate an explicit and frequently violent "anti–Black German discourse" against "Others-from-within" that is densely encoded in contradictory and shifting lines of reasoning. Hence, it marks multilayered histori(ographi)cal disjunctions that necessitate vigilant excavation and reconnection. See Tina Campt, *Other Germans: Black Germans and the Politics of Race, Gender, and Memory in the Third Reich* (Ann Arbor: University of Michigan Press, 2004), 31–62; Fatima El-Tayeb, *Schwarze Deutsche: Der Diskurs um "Rasse" und nationale Identität 1890–1933* (Frankfurt/M: Campus, 2001), 178–200; Reiner Pommerin, *Sterilisierung der Rheinlandbastarde: Das Schicksal einer farbigen deutschen Minderheit, 1918–1937* (Düsseldorf: Droste, 1979), 71; Yara-Colette Lemke-Muniz de Faria, *Zwischen Fürsorge und Ausgrenzung: Afrodeutsche "Besatzungskinder" im Nachkriegsdeutschland* (Berlin: Metropol, 2002), 188; and Nicola Lauré al-Samarai, "Neither Foreigners nor Aliens: The Interwoven Stories of Sinti and Roma and Black Germans," in *Women in German Yearbook* 20, ed. Ruth-Ellen Boetcher Joeres and Marjorie Gelus (Lincoln: University of Nebraska Press, 2004), 167–73.

28. For a more detailed discussion of this aspect, see Nicola Lauré al-Samarai, "Unwegsame Erinnerungen: Auto/biographische Zeugnisse von Schwarzen Deutschen aus der BRD und der DDR," in *AfrikanerInnen in Deutschland und Schwarze Deutsche—Geschichte und Gegenwart,* ed. Marianne Bechhaus-Gerst and Reinhard Klein-Arendt (Münster: Lit, 2004), 200–206.
29. Gina Dent, "Black Pleasure, Black Joy: An Introduction," in *Black Popular Culture: A Project by Michele Wallace,* ed. Gina Dent (New York: New Press, 1998), 7.
30. Although "*Heimsuchung*" is correctly translated as "visitation," the "interior" meaning of the composite noun "*Heim-Suchung*" is "searching for home," but at the same time it expresses connotations of haunting, trial, and unhomeliness in Bhabha's sense. All these resonating layers are part of how I understand and use it.
31. *Homestory Deutschland* was commissioned by the Initiative Schwarze Menschen in Deutschland/ISD Bund in 2005. It is conceptualized as a collective self-portrait, displaying biographies of twenty-seven Black women and men, all of whom have lived in Germany during the past three centuries. The exhibition contains pivoting panels that have portrait pictures on one side and personal stories on the other. To find out about "the story behind the face," the viewer turns the panel. As a parallel to the turning of the panels, which requires visitors to physically interact with the biographees, the pages of the catalog need to be separated for the personal stories to become visible. For more information, see http://www.homestory-deutschland.de/. For a detailed analysis of the exhibition project, see also Nicola Lauré al-Samarai, "Diasporisches

Denken, ex-zentrisches Kartografieren: Grundlegungen der Wechselausstellung *Homestory Deutschland,*" in *Kunst und Politik: Jahrbuch der Guernica-Gesellschaft,* vol. 13, *Museum und Politik—Allianzen und Konflikte,* ed. Anna Greve (Göttingen: V&R unipress, 2011), 97–113.

32. Audre Lorde, "Poetry Is Not a Luxury," in *Sister Outsider: Essays and Speeches* (Freedom, CA: Crossing Press, 1984), 38.
33. Olumide Popoola and Beldan Sezen, eds., *Talking Home: Heimat aus unserer eigenen Feder: Frauen of Color in Deutschland* (Amsterdam: blue moon, 1999), 1 (emphasis added).
34. Lorde, "Poetry," 38.
35. Raja Lubinetzki, *Der Tag ein Funke: Aus dem Tagebuch des Logik Verfalls* (Berlin: Janus, 2001), 30. German original: "Die Sprache, die sich umdreht, wie ein Echo / die den Morgen belaubt."
36. Eleonore Wiedenroth, "Vorwort," in *Talking Home,* 6. German original: "So entsteht ein neues Netz, gemeinsame Wege, neue Wegkreuzungen, Orte der Be/geh/ung, der Be/geg/nung, des Mit/ein/ander Aus/tauschens, des Auf/bruchs."
37. Kobena Mercer, *Welcome to the Jungle: New Positions in Black Cultural Studies* (New York: Routledge, 1994), 11.
38. Ayim, *blues in schwarz weiss,* 61.
39. Popoola and Sezen, 1.
40. Édouard Glissant, *Le discours antillais* (Paris: Éditions du Seuil, 1981), 358. Passage omitted from English translation.
41. (Do), "Weisse sprache," *Afrekete* 3 (1989): 13.
42. Elke Jank, "Schwarz-weise Spitzen: Anleitung zum schwarzen Profil," *Afrekete* 3 (1989): 22–24.
43. Édouard Glissant, *Caribbean Discourse,* trans. J. Michael Dash (Charlottesville: University of Virginia Press, 1989), 120.
44. Piesche, "Identität," 201.
45. Kofi Yakpo a.k.a. Linguist, "'Denn ich bin kein Einzelfall, sondern einer von vielen': Afrodeutsche Rapkünstler in der Hip Hop Gründerzeit," in *TheBlackBook,* 334.
46. Eleonore Wiedenroth, "Ain't no gap," in *Talking Home,* 9.
47. Yakpo, 334.
48. See, for example, Philipp Khabo Koepsell, *Die Akte James Knopf: Afrodeutsche Wort- und Streitkunst* (Berlin: Unrast, 2010), a bilingual collection containing "Read-only-Poetry, Spoken Word texts and Rap." Therefore, most of the texts are intended for performance. See http://jamesknopf.blogspot.de/p/uber-das-buch.html.
49. See, for example, *Arriving in the Future: Stories of Home and Exile,* ed. Asoka Esuruoso and Philipp Khabo Koepsell (Berlin: epubli, 2014). Presented as "an anthology of poetry and creative writing by *Black writers in Germany*" (cover blurb, emphasis added), the collection prioritizes an intercontinental collaborative approach by interweaving a Black German experience with dissimilar yet corresponding Black

experiences. It thus contributes to redefining and redimensioning a geopolitically situated yet *inter*diasporic context—that is, Germany.

50. Ablade Glover, "Adinkra Motive," in *blues in schwarz weiss*, 129.
51. Ayim, *blues in schwarz weiss*, 29.
52. Tobias Nagl, "Fantasien in Schwarzweiß—Schwarze Deutsche, deutsches Kino," in *TheBlackBook*, 298.
53. For further details regarding artists' statements and productions, see http://www. marcbrandenburg.de/; https://heimatkunde.boell.de/2006/05/01/visual-artist-yvonne-buntrock; http://www.atelier-lawson.de/; Nzitu Mawakha, *Daima: Images of Women of Colour in Germany* (Münster: edition assemblage, 2013); http://www.mwangi-hutter.de/art/portfolio_files/Mwangi%20Hutter_portfolio.pdf; http://www.danielkojoschrade.com/. For detailed discussions, analyses, and theoretical contextualizations of Black (German) visual art, see, for example, Sandrine Micossé-Aikins, "Codes of Color: Sprechen und Schweigen im postkolonialen Kunstbetrieb Deutschlands und/oder Die Kunst, Tabus zu besprechen" (master's thesis, Universität der Künste Berlin, 2008); Sandrine Micossé-Aikins, "Kunst," in *Wie Rassismus aus Wörtern spricht*, 420–30; *The Little Book of Big Visions: How to Be an Artist and Revolutionize the World*, ed. Sandrine Micossé-Aikins and Sharon Otoo (Münster: edition assemblage, 2014); Yvette Mutumba, "Afrospheres in the German Art Scene," in *Re/Positionierung: Critical Whiteness/Perspectives of Color*, ed. Neue Gesellschaft für Bildende Kunst (Berlin: Eigenverlag, 2009), n.p. For critical considerations regarding politics of representation and curatorial practices in the visual field, see, for example, the contributions of Nana Adusei-Poku, http://www.nana-adusei-poku.com/news/bio-publications/; Belinda Kazeem, Nicola Lauré al-Samarai, and Peggy Piesche, "Museum, Space, History: New Sites of Political Tectonics" (June 2008), http://eipcp.net/transversal/0708/kazeemetal/en; and Yvette Mutumba and Teimaz Shahverdi, "Über Grenzgänge im kulturellen Schaffen" (December 2012), https://heimatkunde.boell.de/2012/12/18/ueber-grenzgaenge-im-kulturellen-schaffen.
54. For further details regarding artists' statements, see, for example, http://www.oliver-hardt.com/; http://www.kantara.de/; Barbara Kosta and Fatima El-Tayeb, "Everything Will Be Fine: An Interview with Fatima El-Tayeb," in *Women in German Yearbook* 18, ed. Patricia Herminghouse and Ruth-Ellen Boetcher Joeres (Lincoln: University of Nebraska Press, 2002), 31–44; and http://www.filmportal.de/person/branwen-okpako_4c0acea015c147ed90879713ceaeab5c.
55. Nagl, "Fantasien," 298.
56. Michele Wallace, *Dark Designs & Visual Culture* (Durham, NC: Duke University Press, 2004), 341.
57. Christiane Della, "Schwarze KünstlerInnen in Zeiten der Globalisierung," in *TheBlackBook*, 331.
58. Yvonne Buntrock (painter), interview by author, October 2, 2004.
59. Stephen Lawson (sculptor), interview by author, August 17, 2004.

60. Abdellatif Khayati, "Representation, Race, and the 'Language' of the Ineffable in Toni Morrison's Narrative," *African American Review* 33.2 (1999): 1.
61. Fatima El-Tayeb and Angela Maccarone, *Alles wird gut: Das Film-Buch* (Berlin: Orlanda, 1999), 4.
62. Buntrock.
63. Coco Fusco, *English Is Broken Here: Notes on Cultural Fusion in the Americas* (New York: New Press, 1995), 33.
64. "Human zoos," also called "ethnological expositions," were nineteenth- and twentieth-century public exhibits of human beings. These displays emphasized the cultural differences between "traditional" non-Western peoples and "enlightened" Western publics and were predicated on unilinealism, scientific racism, and Social Darwinism.
65. For in-depth considerations, see "Experimentelle (Frei)Räume: Materielle Realitäten von Künstler/-innen of Color. Roundtable: Fatima El-Tayeb, Stephen Lawson, Daniel Kojo Schrade, Hito Steyerl," in *re/visionen,* 323–36.
66. *Alles wird gut,* directed by Angelina Maccarone, written by Fatima El-Tayeb (Multimedia/Norddeutscher Rundfunk, 1997); *Zurück auf los!,* directed by Pierre Sanoussi-Bliss (Pro-Fun Media, 2000); *Tal der Ahnungslosen,* directed by Branwen Okpako (teamWorx Produktion für Kino und Fernsehen, 2003).
67. Recent fictional writings, such as the novellas *the things that I am thinking while smiling politely* (Münster: edition assemblage, 2011) and *Synchronicity—the original story* (Münster: edition assemblage, 2014) by Sharon Otoo, the play *Also by Mail* by Olumide Popoola (Münster: edition assemblage, 2013), and *Contrapunctus,* the novel by Michael Götting (Münster: Unrast, 2015), have started to fill this narrative lack.
68. Literally translated "life-artist," someone who pieces together his living from various activities that, collectively, bring in just enough money to live. No office, no suit, no boss, no rules. [Astonishingly, German has a word for such people, English doesn't.—Trans.]
69. Mercer, 213 (emphasis in the original).
70. Keith Piper in discussion of Black artists, *Black Atlantic* events, Berlin, fall 2004.
71. Keith Piper, "Sind nicht alle Räume transkulturell?," in *Der Black Atlantic,* ed. Haus der Kulturen der Welt (Berlin: HKW, 2004), 287.
72. Toni Morrison, "Rootedness: The Ancestor as Foundation," in *Black Women Writers (1950–1980),* ed. Mari Evans (Garden City, NY: Anchor Press/Doubleday, 1984), 343.
73. Teshome H. Gabriel, "Thoughts on Nomadic Aesthetics and the Black Independent Cinema: Traces of a Journey," in *Out There: Marginalization and Contemporary Cultures,* ed. Russell Ferguson, Martha Gever, Trinh T. Minh-ha, and Cornel West (Cambridge, MA: MIT Press, 1990), 402.

3

Self-Assertion, Intervention, and Achievement

Developments in Contemporary Black German Writing

DIRK GÖTTSCHE

In her pathbreaking study *Becoming Black: Creating Identity in the African Diaspora* (2004), Michelle Wright maintains that the "inability on the part of white Germans to understand so simple a concept as one being both Black *and* German is most likely unique to the Afro-German experience."[1] Faced with "a racist discourse directed at Africans rather than Afro-Germans," she argues, Black Germans are perceived as "Others-from-without," rather than as "Others-from-within" like "the Black in Britain, France, and the United States."[2] Here I ask to what extent Wright's analysis, which draws on pioneering feminist Black German writings from the 1980s and 1990s, holds true for the much larger and more diverse range of Black German literature published since then. I begin by briefly outlining early works of Black German literature that have become canonical within the field. I then turn in more detail to the postmillennial diversification of Black German discourse: the cross-mapping of memory discourses relating to diasporic history, colonialism, and National Socialism, and new approaches to Black German identity in narratives of personal achievement. The last section analyzes recent developments that demonstrate new confidence in Afro-German identity while also reinforcing now-established traditions of cultural critique and diasporic politics. These texts engage with dominant themes in German cultural debate while also introducing postcolonial and transnational frames of reference into contemporary German literature. As I show, the reflection of Afro-German experience in Black German writing makes a significant contribution to the "postcolonial project"[3] of "decolonizing the mind"[4] and hence to the cultural transformation of German society through minority intervention.

Writing Back: The Emergence of Black German Diasporic Discourse

The authors discussed in this essay represent four generations of Black Germans: survivors of National Socialism; the postwar generation, typically with African American fathers and white German mothers; the children of mostly African fathers born in West and East Germany during the 1960s and 1970s; and some younger authors born during the late 1970s and 1980s whose work already reflects the experience of modern transnational multiculturalism. The rise of Black German literature therefore epitomizes cultural shifts as much as demographic developments. Small numbers and the cultural legacy of colonialism meant that the first postwar generation of Black Germans did not begin to write about their experiences and to engage in diasporic politics until the cultural revolution of 1968 and subsequent feminist, alternative, and multicultural movements had provided the cultural framework for such antiracist self-assertion. Like the parallel rise of African migrants' literature, the beginnings of Black German writing are linked to West German countercultures, left-wing anticolonialism, and the influence of African American cultural politics.

The beginnings of Black German literature are marked by anthologies that combine personal accounts of Black German experience with research into the history of colonialism and the political fight against racism. The seminal collection *Farbe bekennen: Afro-deutsche Frauen auf den Spuren ihrer Geschichte* (*Showing Our Colors: Afro-German Women Speak Out,* 1986, trans. 1992) testifies in particular to the inspirational role of the African American feminist writer and critic Audre Lorde. Moving beyond "just articulating their victimization," the Black Germans in this volume sought to "expose the origins of their victimization and in the process challenge and redefine German cultural identity,"[5] for which "the African American experience served initially as a central point of reference."[6] *Farbe bekennen* also pioneered historical inquiry into Black German history and the memory of Germany's forgotten implication in European colonialism, combining May

Opitz's research into the history of Africans in Germany with life-writing (autobiographical narratives, essays, and interviews) representing three generations of Black German experience. Gisela Fremgen's volume . . . *und wenn du dazu noch schwarz bist: Berichte schwarzer Frauen in der Bundesrepublik* (. . . and if, in addition, you are also Black: Reports from Black women in the Federal Republic, 1984)[7] similarly combines autobiographical accounts with a focus on German colonialism and racism. Intervening in German discourses about national identity and "decolonizing the mind," the blend of identity discourse and cultural politics established by *Farbe bekennen* was to gain renewed significance after German reunification in 1989, when violence against Black Germans, migrants, and refugees was rife and neo-Nazism and right-wing ideas were gathering strength.

The literary works of leading Afro-German activist and performance artist May Opitz, coeditor and principal author of *Farbe bekennen,* also give expression to Afro-German self-assertion, the exploration of transatlantic African diasporic culture, and the fight against continuing German racism from a feminist perspective. Born in Hamburg in 1960 to a Ghanaian father and a German mother and raised in foster care, May Opitz (who later claimed her father's name, Ayim) stands out in Black German literature as the only literary writer of this early phase and a poet of significant standing whose work has inspired other Afro-Germans. Her seminal collection of poems, *blues in schwarz weiss* (*Blues in Black and White,* 1995, trans. 2003), and two posthumous publications—the poetry of *nachtgesang* (Nightsong, 1997) and a collection of essays and interviews, *Grenzenlos und unverschämt* (Borderless and brazen, 1997)—reflect the themes and concerns of her academic and political work.[8] The poems address the hardship of coping with racist othering and exclusion; engagement with the African culture of her father's Ghana, where she traveled twice; fascination with African diasporic discourse and culture in America and the Caribbean; and outspoken criticism of exoticist stereotypes about Africans and resurgent racism in Germany. "distant ties" gives particularly poignant expression to the challenges of growing up Black in white West Germany, summarizing this diasporic condition in the metaphor of a shifting home of transnational dimensions, of "displacement, exclusion, and internal conflict":[9] "distant ties / connected distances / between continents / on the road at home."[10] Other poems use humorous satire to expose residual racism and colonialist stereotypes in mainstream white German society (e.g., "afro-german I" and "afro-german II") or pay homage to key figures in the African

American movement, such as Martin Luther King Jr. ("The Time Thereafter") and Audre Lorde ("Soul Sister"), or to African diasporic history ("Blues in Black and White"). References to African American blues and Asante art are part of an "intercultural dialogue" that enables reappreciation of Afro-German "textured identity," paving the way toward "a broadened definition of German identity."[11] Ayim's poetry thus displays affinities to anglo- or francophone postcolonial aesthetics and recalls similar approaches in some African migrants' writing from the same period, such as El Loko's *Der Blues in mir* (The blues in me, 1986), Kolyang Dina Taiwé's . . . *dann ist das Herz verwundet: Eine Begegnung der Kulturen* (. . . then the heart is wounded: An encounter of cultures, 1997), and Daniel Mepin's novel *Die Weissagung der Ahnen* (The prophecy of the ancestors, 1997).[12]

The same pattern informs Black German autobiographies such as *Daheim unterwegs: Ein deutsches Leben* (At home on the move: A German life, 1998)[13] by Ika Hügel-Marshall, born in 1947 to a white German mother and an African American soldier. Using Ayim's poem "entfernte verbindungen" as her epigraph, Hügel-Marshall presents her life as a story of racist experience and late self-assertion in the context of the feminist Black German movement of the 1980s. Having been told from an early age that "blacks are stupid, backward, primitive, . . . shifty, dangerous, pitiful,"[14] the little girl wishes to be white and tries "to ignore [her] blackness" (48). Not until 1986 does Hügel-Marshall identify openly as a Black German and engage in the campaign against German racism and for the acknowledgement of Black German history. This self-assertion includes the discovery of the transatlantic African diaspora, which transcends the traditional confines of German identity: "Black history is my history too, and in that I include the story of blacks in Africa, America, and Europe. . . . I have more than just a single reference point" (110). Her new self-confidence thus has a postcolonial dimension modeled on African American cultural politics.

Diasporic Identity and "Multidirectional Memory"

In his study of Holocaust memory "in the age of decolonization," Michael Rothberg examines the transnational interaction between discourses about colonialism and the Holocaust to argue that "collective memory" is "*multidirectional*": it is "subject to ongoing negotiation, cross-referencing, and borrowing."[15] Black German writing offers further evidence for Rothberg's theory by cross-mapping the historical memories of African diasporic history, German colonialism, National Socialism, and, more recently, the demise of the German Democratic Republic. The examples discussed in this section give particular prominence to the "productive, intercultural dynamic"[16] of such multidirectional interaction between African diasporic discourse and Holocaust memory.

Eine von uns: Als Schwarze in Deutschland geboren (One of us: Born Black in Germany, 2000), Harald Gerunde's biography of his late wife, Bärbel Kampmann, combines the memory of Black German history with the critical memory of National Socialism and German colonialism, contextualizing Kampmann's life in a multidirectional network of collective memory discourses. Again following the conceptual framework of *Farbe bekennen,* this biographical novel blends this specifically German postcolonial discourse with a diasporic concept of Black German identity as cross-cultural construction and a narrative technique that adapts West African ideas for a postcolonial aesthetic. Although not a piece of Black German writing in the literal sense (since Gerunde is white), *Eine von uns* illustrates how the need for self-assertion against the daily experience of exclusion gave rise to a diasporic identity despite the absence of an obvious postcolonial situation. The novel presents the life of Kampmann, the daughter of a German mother and an African American soldier, as the story of a girl who is made to feel different by the racist perceptions and concepts of the Germans around her. Born in 1946 and raised in Bielefeld as the only Black child in town, she is confronted with experiences of discrimination and racism both in the "structures and institutions" of West German society and in German postwar "culture as a whole"—for instance, when her mother tries to bleach her skin or straighten her hair.[17] The "development of what I call 'my Black consciousness'" (152) begins only after a first, failed marriage and a career change in the wake of West Germany's cultural liberalization after 1968, when university study, an interest in African American cultural politics, and Kampmann's friendship with Jean-Claude Diallo, a political refugee from Guinea, pave the way for new self-confidence as a Black German. Rediscovery of her father and her African American family, US citizenship, and a trip to Guinea in 1994 complete this history of diasporic self-assertion as Kampmann refuses to remain a victim.

The reconstruction of Kampmann's family history and its historical context serve to illustrate the transnational and transcultural frames of reference in Black German history as a whole, in particular the slave trade and African

American suffering and resistance. This cross-mapping of biographical and historical inquiry is reflected in one of the novel's leitmotifs, the interconnectedness of supposedly private lives in transnational social networks that ultimately represent the history of humankind: "Bärbel's story as I'm telling it here is not private, nobody is private, only he or she him or herself and nobody else. Everybody is always all the others. And Bärbel's story takes place on several continents in several centuries" (8). This multidirectional network underpinning Black German "textured identity"[18] also includes the critical rediscovery of German colonialism in the family history of Kampmann's German mother. Her German grandfather turns out to have fought as a marine in the colonial war against the Nama and Herero in Namibia (as well as serving in China), enabling the novel to cross-stitch the memory of African diasporic history with the memory of Germany's own colonial history, a theme of growing significance in German literature since the later 1990s.[19] This rediscovery also allows the biography to explore connections between German colonialism and National Socialism, in which Kampmann's mother's family is also deeply implicated. Linking the Herero genocide, Auschwitz, and postunification violence in one history of German racism, *Eine von uns* cross-maps these memory discourses in ways established by Hannah Arendt.[20]

A third line of postcolonial inquiry is associated with Kampmann's journey to Guinea in search of her presumed African roots. Kampmann redefines herself in African diasporic terms. In line with postcolonial concepts of cultural identity as "a complex, on-going negotiation"[21] and construction, however, the African "origin" of an individual Black German can no longer be verified; it can only be "invented" in a process of cross-cultural self-assertion. As in Hügel-Marshall's *Daheim unterwegs,* such Black German empowerment introduces a cross-cultural dimension in embracing African American and African culture in its response to German ethnocentrism; it is, in Bhabha's words, "both transnational and translational."[22] This is also in evidence in the postcolonial aesthetic of Gerunde's novel. The narrative technique of weaving together biography, diasporic critique, and postcolonial inquiry is modeled on West African textiles with their "polyrhythmic" patterns of motivic "transitions, repetitions, parallels, repetitions, digressions, and unexpected contrasts" (Gerunde, 8, 79). This postcolonial aesthetic is in turn linked to a cross-cultural ethic of dialogue and mutual respect: "Read reality as text, read your difference as a text that God, before whom you are all called to account, has revealed to you!" (9). As a complex "text," the reality of Black German experience requires appreciation of difference and multiperspectivist representation, including the cross-mapping of (post)colonial and Holocaust memory.

However, the most prominent example of linking Black German experience to the critical memory of National Socialism is certainly Hans J. Massaquoi's autobiography *Destined to Witness: Growing Up Black in Nazi Germany* (1999), written in English but a huge best seller in Germany, where, under the title *"Neger, Neger, Schornsteinfeger!": Meine Kindheit in Deutschland* ("Negro, Negro, chimney sweep" [a German children's rhyme]: My childhood in Germany),[23] it helped to put Black German history on the map far beyond the limited readership of other Afro-German publications. This autobiography is transnational in both its origin—Massaquoi was born in Hamburg in 1926 as the son of a white German mother and the grandson of Liberia's first consul general in Germany—and its impact: it was given significant media coverage and was successfully adapted for prime-time television.[24] Managing to survive National Socialism and the Allied bombardment of Hamburg, Massaquoi went on to meet his father and his African family in Liberia in 1948 before realizing his dream of emigrating to the United States in 1950, where he became a journalist and eventually managing editor of the renowned African American magazine *Ebony*.[25] *Destined to Witness* belongs to both American and German literature and challenges the concept of national literatures in ways similar to African migrants' writing in German.

Massaquoi's emphasis is on the critical memory of National Socialism from a Black German perspective. After his African family's return to Liberia in 1929, Massaquoi and his mother move to a working-class area of Hamburg, where he is exposed to racism, to "hostile stares and insulting remarks,"[26] to which he initially responds—like Hügel-Marshall and Kampmann almost thirty years later—by attempting "to remain as inconspicuous as possible" (50). His self-assertion as a Black teenager in Nazi Germany begins with his fascination with the Black American star athletes Joe Louis and Jesse Owens in 1936 and his involvement in the oppositional Swingboy movement in late 1930s Hamburg.[27] After the war he becomes "an active participant, observer, and reporter of the greatest social and political movement of the century—the black struggle for racial equality waged during the fifties, sixties, and seventies in the United States, in colonial Africa, and in the West Indies" (3). Returning to Germany as a journalist, he thinks rather prematurely in 1966 that "the former Third Reich . . . had ceased to be a 'white' nation," while in 1997 "the alarming rise in hate crimes and the proliferation of a variety of neo-Nazi groups with racist agendas" in postunification Germany raises new concerns (435–36). Massaquoi's sequel, *Hänschen klein, ging allein . . . : Mein Weg in die Neue Welt* (Little Hans went alone . . . [a German children's song]: My journey to the New World, 2004), is even more critical, linking racist experience to the memory of German colonialism (including the Herero genocide) and to Black German persecution and survival under National Socialism. But Massaquoi also takes an interest in Black self-assertion reflected in Black success stories in German sports, television, film, and music,[28] a topic that came to the fore in Black German writing at the very time that the sequel was published.

It is useful to compare Massaquoi's autobiography with the account of another Black German Nazi survivor, Marie Nejar's *Mach nicht so traurige Augen, weil du ein Negerlein bist: Meine Jugend im Dritten Reich* (Don't look so sad because you're a little Negro: My youth in the Third Reich, 2007). Nejar was born in Hamburg in 1930, the daughter of a sailor from Ghana and the granddaughter of a Creole from Martinique. Her early years have much in common with Massaquoi's: support from Hamburg's cosmopolitans and German non-collaborators enables her to survive the Nazi regime and the Allied bombing raids, even as racist responses alert her to her otherness: "My first conscious memories are connected to my dark skin."[29] Like Massaquoi, the little girl shares her peers' Nazi enthusiasm and struggles to understand why she is not allowed to join in. Participation in Nazi film productions such as *Münchhausen* (1943) and *Quax in Afrika* (1945/53), however, allows the teenager to escape the reality of the regime and World War II through the "parallel universe" of a cinematic "world of appearances" (116). Only much later does she realize "that the Blacks in the films of the Nazi period were exploited to support the ideology of the National Socialists" (104). Nejar thus provides personal evidence for this much-discussed theme in recent postcolonial historiography.[30]

After the war Nejar resists opportunities to emigrate to Ghana and embarks on a career as a Black pop star modeled on the "cliché of the cute 'chocolate kid'" (210). Finding herself typecast along exoticist and racist lines, she trains as a nurse in 1958. Her account thus echoes Massaquoi's in combining the memory of National Socialism with the memory of Black German history and self-assertion, but it reflects a very different identity discourse. Despite her consistent criticism of racial stereotyping, Nejar draws a clear line between her cultural identity as a German and Africans: "I just wasn't an African, as things from daily life indicated again and again" (236). Using imagery similar to that of African migrant writers Luc Degla and Jones Kwesi Evans in their assessments of the cultural identity of contemporary Afro-German children,[31] she claims, paradoxically, "I am whiter than white. Yes, my skin color is black, but that is just external, internally I am no different from any of my white friends and neighbors" (Nejar, 238). Nevertheless, Nejar's autobiography is open to a "contrapuntal reading"[32] that highlights the postcolonial dimension in her family history, including transnational mobility and migration that link Africa, the Caribbean, Germany, and Riga, where her Creole grandfather first worked.

Gert Schramm's highly significant autobiography *Wer hat Angst vorm schwarzen Mann: Mein Leben in Deutschland* (Who's afraid of the Black man [a German children's game]: My life in Germany, 2011), the only memoir by a Black German concentration camp survivor, offers a very different perspective on the cross-mapping of Black German experience and the memory of National Socialism and the Holocaust. It is also distinguished by its links between these themes and Schramm's ambivalent memories of the German Democratic Republic, since Schramm, born in Erfurt in 1928 to a white German mother and an African American of Cuban background, moved between East and West after the war, making the unusual decision to return to the GDR in 1964. After an initial confrontation with the Nazi system in 1941, Schramm is imprisoned and sent to the Buchenwald concentration camp in October 1943 at the age of only fourteen, where he survives thanks to the Communist-led underground, while his father is presumed to have died at Auschwitz. After liberation in 1945 he therefore swears that he will commit his life to the struggle "against fascism and for another, a better world."[33] This overview cannot do justice to Schramm's powerful memoir, which remembers Black German suffering and self-assertion during the Nazi period, in postwar East and West Germany, and in the context of resurgent right-wing violence after German unification; written from a working-class perspective and also from the perspective of Black antifascism (259), the memoir provides a nuanced account of the different attitudes of white Germans. Unlike Nejar, Schramm explicitly frames his memoir as a critical intervention into postunification German cultures of memory, writing as an active member of the committee of former concentration camp inmates at Buchenwald and expressing his dissatisfaction with the politics of memory in postunification Germany and at Buchenwald in particular (253). Unlike

Massaquoi's memoir, the discursive frames of reference here are therefore German cultures of memory, postunification discourse, and international antifascism rather than African or African American culture or modern transnational multiculturalism. Schramm's harrowing experiences and his politicized cultural critique distinguish this memoir sharply from the autobiographies published by younger Black German authors since the late 1990s.

Black German Diversity and Achievement

Their self-confident approach to Black German identity align Massaquoi and Schramm with recent Afro-German autobiographies by art world and media professionals who focus on Black German achievement and integration. Departing from the model of Black German writing represented by *Farbe bekennen,* life-writing from the late 1990s already suggests a shift toward Afro-German authors "performing" the "subjective normality" of their lives.[34] Performative normality, at times extending to a mainstreaming of Afro-German experience, plays a significant role in postmillennial Black German literature, moving beyond a discourse of victimization and challenging the perception of Black Germans as "Others-from-without." At the same time, Black German writing has become more diverse since the millennium, with growing evidence that this diversification is linked to the multicultural transformation of German society since the 1980s (despite its serious ongoing problems).

A transitional text in terms of both generation and identity discourse, and one that illustrates the link between diversification and multiculturalism, is Thomas Usleber's *Die Farben unter meiner Haut: Autobiographische Aufzeichnungen* (The colors beneath my skin: Autobiographical notes, 2002). Usleber's account differs from earlier African diasporic discourse by giving Black German self-assertion an individualist and multicultural direction. Born in 1960 to a German-Hungarian mother and an African American soldier, Usleber grew up in provincial Lower Palatinate and joined the city of Frankfurt's administration as an adult, ultimately working in the office of multiculturalism. Endorsing Hügel-Marshall's autobiography in terms of racist experience,[35] Usleber tells a similar story of racist "discrimination and humiliation," "rejection and injustice" (2, 28). His self-assertion in the face of racist exclusion, however, takes an individualist and ethical turn, reflecting his belief in "justice, equality of opportunity, and Christian neighborly love" (30) based on personal recognition and respect: "I didn't seem to belong to the Germans because of my skin color and to any other community because of my German upbringing and my German language. Thus for me identity could only mean finding my own independent identity beyond assumptions on which most others could rely upon from the outset" (44). Insisting that his identity is "much more colorful" than his "brown" skin and that there are far more "commonalities" than "differences" between German and non-German cultures (141, 127), Usleber's individualism clearly draws on a multicultural frame of reference. This individualism does not mean, however, that his autobiography is apolitical. Usleber questions ethnic concepts of German identity and promotes the multicultural transformation of German society. Rather than adapting African diasporic cultural politics, he highlights the discovery of his American Indian ancestry as yet another instance of multiculturalism and compares the histories of his German-Hungarian mother's family and his African American father's family as examples of one global history of migration (12).

An intermediate position in the transition from narratives of self-assertion in the face of racist experience to stories of achievement and integration is also marked by the actor Günther Kaufmann's autobiography, *Der weiße Neger vom Hasenbergl* (The white Negro from the Hasenbergl, 2004). Another representative of the immediate postwar generation of Black Germans born to white German mothers and African American soldiers, Kaufmann narrates his rise from a working-class childhood in Bavaria to success as an actor noted for his work with film director Rainer Werner Fassbinder and on stage and television. This achievement is set against a series of incidents illustrating the daily racism in (South) German society to which he was exposed from childhood. And in some of his acting he is expected, like Nejar, either to reproduce the German cliché of the primitive African or, at the other extreme, to contribute to antiracist productions whose racial theme, he feels, hits too close to home.[36] Kaufmann summarizes the predicament of his experience in the following assessment of his work at a theater in Vienna in 1983–1984: "Celebrated in an anti-racist play as a Black star—threatened and reviled as a Black person" (202).

Fellow actor Charles M. Huber, well-known for his role as a detective in the popular German television series *Der Alte* (The old man, 1984–1997), goes a significant step further in giving Black German experience a multicultural turn. His memoir, *Ein Niederbayer im Senegal: Mein Leben zwischen zwei Welten* (A Lower Bavarian in Senegal: My life between two worlds, 2004), recasts the diasporic Germany–United States–Africa triangle in the context of the cultural revolution of the late 1960s and takes the exploration of African roots to an unprecedented level. In a book that devotes a section to the defining experience of Senegal and Gambia, Huber's discussion of Afro-German and German-African cross-cultural identity formation reads in parts like an inversion of African memoirs of migration to Germany that tell complementary stories of cross-cultural self-assertion and hybridization.[37] Huber was born in Munich in 1956, the son of Senegalese diplomat and occasional actor Jean-Pierre Faye and a white professional woman who left his education up to her mother in Lower Bavaria, where Huber experienced traumatizing ostracization for being "Black and illegitimate to boot."[38] His account of his youth in Munich charts his troubled path toward Black German awareness in the context of colonial stereotypes, until he embraces the hippie movement's promise of freedom and identifies with the African American civil rights movement, reinventing himself as a "German Black Panther" (202). He succeeds in breaking away from drug addiction and personal crisis only when he departs for Senegal in search of his father; there he discovers that he has binational siblings in Paris, Stockholm, and Senegal as part of the transnational network of an "African, postcolonial family of intellectuals" that includes Senegal's president-poet Léopold Sédar Senghor (73, 89). Huber is one of the few Black German authors to discuss postcolonial conditions explicitly (3, 252) and the only one to call himself a "German African" (8), his text echoing some recent African migrants' writing in its multidirectional transnational reach.

Authors of East German origin give expression to the shifts in contemporary Black German literature quite differently than do those from the West, since East Germany did not experience the multicultural transformation that began in West Germany during the 1980s. Autobiographies with an East German background and written from a postunification perspective instead often combine an examination of Black German history and experience with a critical reassessment of the German Democratic Republic, where an official socialist internationalism masked really-existing racism.

The most prominent example is the autobiography *Schokoladenkind: Meine Familie und andere Wunder* (Chocolate child: My family and other miracles, 2003) by journalist Abini Zöllner, born in 1967 in East Berlin to a German-Jewish mother and a Nigerian journalism student. Having escaped the "latent discrimination" directed at "people of color in smaller towns or even villages" by growing up in Berlin,[39] Zöllner does not make German racism a major theme, and her ironic accounts of multicultural politics in postunification Berlin, where she was asked to report about "my life as a colored person in the GDR" (192), suggest wariness about ideological antiracism as another source of potential stereotyping. This does not, however, prevent Zöllner from noting the racist legacy in East Germany—where she was expected, for example, to become "a good sportsperson or musician" because of her African "blood" (102)—or from critiquing the "positive discrimination" (104) that benefited her early career as a dancer, speaker, and actor, when East German authorities used her to demonstrate their commitment to internationalism. *Schokoladenkind* thus does not follow the established pattern of *Farbe bekennen;* the focus is instead firmly on the normal problems of adolescence in East Germany and on the transforming impact of German unification. Zöllner's emphasis on private and family life reflects a strategy of normalization in the representation of Black German experience.

Schokoladenkind is in many ways the earliest example of mainstreaming the Black German experience. Its detachment from African diasporic politics is underlined by Zöllner's assessment of her father and his Nigerian culture. With its "zillions of traditions, zillions of borders, zillions of cultures," Nigeria is presented as quintessentially multicultural (92). Nevertheless, Zöllner portrays Nigeria's multiculturalism stereotypically as "a big mess" and reaffirms German clichés of contemporary Africa as political chaos and exotic paradise, blessed with "oil and peanuts" but blighted by "corruption and poverty" (92). Zöllner's own identity is clearly constructed as (East) German rather than Black German, African, or multicultural; her father's African roots and culture are not hers, and her mother's German-Jewish descent seems equally marginal. The passage devoted to her Jewish great-grandparents' death in Nazi Germany and the survival of her mother's immediate family in Chinese exile is not part of a wider reflection on German-Jewish history and heritage. The postunification narrative of successful arrival in Western society overrides postcolonial and post-Holocaust concerns.

A more critical combination of postunification narrative and Black German achievement can be found in the autobiography *Heimkind—Neger—Pionier: Mein Leben* (Ward of the state, Negro, pioneer: My life, 2005) by dancer and choreographer Detlef Soost, a successful dancing coach in contemporary German entertainment and television casting shows. Born in East Berlin in 1970 to a white German mother and a medical student from

Ghana, Soost was raised in a children's home from the age of eight. Unlike Zöllner, Soost is exposed to racism and stereotyping during his early childhood in a working-class district, and the stigma of being a ward of the state reinforces his shame at feeling "different and inferior"[40] long before his violent "first encounter with racism" in a political sense in 1988, on the eve of the GDR's demise (132–33). His book also provides poignant illustration of the problems facing East Germans in their transition to Western society, as Soost's teenage career as a fashion model and dancer was thrown into crisis by his encounter with Western capitalism until he was able to establish a reputation as a dancing coach in the late 1990s.

This story of personal achievement is presented from the point of view of critical self-reflection.[41] In retrospect, Soost interprets his constant "pressure to prove myself" and his addiction to "status and recognition" as the unconscious result of his experience as a Black German, his shame at being different driving him forward as though he was "in flight from my past" (11, 127, 162). The turning point from victimization to self-assertion is marked by the teenager's discovery of dance as a mode of personal expression in Black culture (74), which initiates a more far-reaching discovery of African diasporic discourse and of his wider African and Black German family, as in earlier Afro-German autobiographies from the West. He feels like he has finally arrived by becoming part of this transnational family and community. This symbolic acknowledgement of African diasporic identity is underlined by the book's open ending, as Soost flies to Ghana for a reconciliation with his father and an exploration of his African "roots." His story of Black German self-assertion and achievement thus returns to core elements of the Black German discourse pioneered in *Farbe bekennen,* albeit from the perspective of contemporary German multiculturalism and postunification memory.

Narratives of achievement, however, are by no means exclusive to Afro-German authors from East Germany. Following Kaufmann's and Huber's example, quite a few sport, music, and television celebrities from West German and Austrian backgrounds have published recent autobiographies that fit this mold. In *Der Kick des Lebens: Wie ich den Weg nach oben schaffte* (The kick of life: How I made it to the top, 2007), Steffi Jones, born in Frankfurt in 1972 of white German and African American parentage, contrasts her success as a leading figure in German women's soccer with her elder brother's descent into drugs and crime. Soccer star and actor Jimmy Hartwig, a cancer survivor of white German and African American descent born a generation earlier in 1954 in Offenbach, published two memoirs, *"Ich möcht' noch so viel tun . . .": Meine Kindheit, meine Karriere, meine Krankheit* ("I'd still like to do so much . . .": My childhood, my career, my illness, 1994) and *Ich bin ein Kämpfer geblieben: Meine Siege, meine Krisen, mein Leben* (I remained a fighter: My victories, my crises, my life, 2010). The trained nurse Freddy Sahin-Scholl, born in 1953 to white German and African American parents, tells the story of his success as a popular singer in *Der Mann mit den zwei Stimmen: Vom Waisenkind zum Star* (The man with two voices: From orphan to star, 2011). Austrian television host Arabella Kiesbauer, born in 1969 to a white German actor and an engineer from Ghana, builds her memoir *Mein afrikanisches Herz* (My African heart, 2007) around a trip of self-exploration to Ghana in 2007. These publications[42] reflect the growing presence of people of African descent in German public life and call for new ways of conceptualizing recent Black German experience. Although their individual approaches vary, they display strategies of performative normality that have little connection with the diasporic politics of the Black German movement and echo Zöllner in mainstreaming Black German experience.

"A New Approach": Continuities and Developments

Such accounts of achievement epitomize the diversification of Black German literature since 2000 and the growing presence of Afro-German voices in German public discourse, but celebrity memoirs are only one strand in the field. African diasporic cultural criticism has also gained new momentum, and works by authors born during the late 1970s and 1980s have emerged from the changing context of contemporary multiculturalism. There are now clear signs of an established tradition of Black German writing that is reflected in recurring themes and in textual references to pioneering early works such as *Farbe bekennen* and May Ayim's poetry. Contemporary Black German writing builds on the achievements of the 1980s and 1990s while at the same time moving in new directions. The tragic mode of the blues—as in Ayim's *blues in schwarz weiss* or, in the parallel tradition of African migrants' writing, El Loko's *Der Blues in mir*—has given way to often self-confident performative "negotiations"[43] of difference and "emplacement"[44] in a German society in transformation that requires "a new approach."[45]

The most striking example of this tonal shift is Noah Sow's book *Deutsch-*

land Schwarz Weiß: Der alltägliche Rassismus (Germany Black and white: Everyday racism, 2008). This remarkable publication by a Black German musician and media personality of white German and West African origin, born and raised in Bavaria, is neither fiction nor life-writing but a critical study and in parts a practical guide that uses "enlightenment" to contribute to "real social changes"[46] in the perception and position of Africans and Black Germans. Sow explores and exposes structural, institutional, and subliminal instances of racism, as well as "stereotyping and exoticization" (35) more generally, in the media, in advertising, in children's literature, and crucially in contemporary German language usage. Her conviction "that far-right racism can only exist because there's racism in the social mainstream that hasn't been dealt with" prompts literary "anti-racism training" (226–27) that makes for revealing and often unsettling reading.

This critique of German racism includes another reminder of German colonial history, the colonial "anthropological expositions," the Herero genocide, and links between colonialism and National Socialism (83–99) as well as a brief summary of Black German history since antiquity, now extending to the memorialization of the Black German movement's pioneering phase during the 1980s and 1990s (99–102, 128–29, 305–7). A defining stylistic feature that contrasts strikingly with the tone of early Black German writing is the book's use of wit, humor, and irony. Setting the tone, Sow's critical exploration is prefaced by a "Prologue: My Own Background" (13–15), in which Sow reverses the established discursive hierarchy between Europe and Africa by writing about Germany, Bavaria, and her German grandmother in a style used in traditional (colonial) discourse to talk about "primitive Africa" and its "natives." This use of irony and humor as a weapon of performative self-assertion and strength defies victimization much more confidently than did the writing of the postwar generation.

This style also distinguishes Sow's *Deutschland Schwarz Weiß* from Manu-Ela Ritz's similarly themed *Die Farbe meiner Haut: Die Antirassismustrainerin erzählt* (The color of my skin: The antiracism trainer tells her story, 2009). While Ritz's critique of German racism also contains an educational element, her "book about racism," a "theme of her work, her life, and her suffering,"[47] is far more personal. It combines various forms of life-writing (autobiography, interviews, essays) with poetry and the outline of a drama in addressing traumatizing early experiences of racism as well as strategies of empowerment (a term she uses in English [118]). Born in provincial East Germany in 1969 to a

Kenyan student and a white German mother who offered her up for adoption, Ritz offers a harrowing account of East German racism similar to Soost's and combines Black German history with fairly bleak memories of German unification before turning to her achievements as a scriptwriter and antiracism trainer. Her account of traumatic early memories, emblematically titled "Forgotten Memories or Remembered Forgetting" (22), sarcastically exposes the GDR's "postulated, propagated friendship of the peoples" as a mere mask of "really-existing racism" (48). In her highly ambivalent assessment, revolutionary slogans of unification such as "We are the people" and "We are one people" sound more like a threat than a promise (46, 48). *Die Farbe meiner Haut* thus reinforces Wright's assessment of Black Germans as perceived "Others-from-without." Including the sketch "Homestory Deutschland," a play about "300 years of Black German history" (159), and closing with May Ayim's poem "afterword,"[48] Ritz's book is even more explicit than Sow's in revitalizing the tradition of Black German writing established by *Farbe bekennen,* while also putting those beginnings in historical perspective.

The Black German struggle against residual German racism in an increasingly multicultural society is also in the background of the only fully fictional text discussed in this section, the novel *Schanzen-Slam* (2009) by Victoria B. Robinson, a journalist and writer of African American and white German parentage born in 1980. *Schanzen-Slam,* whose title refers to rap and poetry competitions in the Sternschanze quarter of Hamburg, chronicles the adventures of three German women in their twenties as they try to find their place in society and their partners in life. Rather than putting Black cultural politics center stage, *Schanzen-Slam* breaks with the potential pitfalls of minority literature; with its laid-back style and youthful theme, its references to pop culture and the creative writing scene, it could just as well be seen as an example of recent German pop literature. It is indicative of the postmillennial shifts in Black German literature that Robinson's narrative demonstrates the normality of being German and Black. For example, the reader only learns by implication that Lea is a Black German when the text mentions her "Afro" hairstyle and her indignation about "the sexualization of Black people."[49] This indirect mode of characterization undercuts stereotypical representation, while the narrator also emphasizes Lea's political objections to "cultural appropriation" (192): "Lea liked to talk about 'normal' people when she meant Black people and whenever she was upset that some white person or other 'stole' out-of-context cultural symbols that they didn't even understand" (20). The text endorses Lea's criticism, prefacing the novel with a dedication to "the sisters and brothers who have prepared the way. / Yes we are walking indeed!" (4), an obvious reference to African diasporic culture and the Black German movement. At the same time, however, inverted commas and a touch of humor in relevant passages put excessive radicalism into perspective. Crucially, Robinson does not construe Black characters as victims or as better people. The Lea strand of the novel, for example, deconstructs the Black male idol of her dreams (dreadlocks included). The critical points of reference are introduced through the back door: "But when Lea talked about 'postcolonial criticism' and 'whiteness as a category of analysis' she [Tine] always felt like a dumbbell" (85). Passages such as this one reference postcolonial cultural critique and point in a humorous way to Germany's "backwardness" in overcoming residual racist legacies, but they also mark a hiatus between relevant critical theory and social practice.

A related strategy of reconceptualizing Afro-German identity in a multicultural and transnational context can be seen in *Dis wo ich herkomm: Deutschland Deluxe* (That's where I come from: Germany deluxe, 2009) by Samy Deluxe (Samy Sorge), a highly successful star in the German hip-hop scene since his first hit album in 2000. Written in casual conversational style, this publication is an unusual form of life-writing that combines autobiographical narrative ("My Story" [11]) with cultural essayism in themed chapters that range from the self-reflection of Afro-German identity (e.g., "Who Am I," "Father's Day," "Superhero") to more general commentary on topics such as drugs, success, the hip-hop lifestyle, or the transition from adolescence to adulthood. Many of the chapters match the titles and themes of the raps on Deluxe's CD *Dis wo ich herkomm* (March 2009). At one level the book can be seen as the artist's response to the controversy sparked by the perceived nationalism of the CD's title song, which challenges his audience to move from a "Fuck politics!" attitude to sociopolitical engagement in a multicultural society—"a new approach," which is presented, however, in the controversial terms of "national pride," "our Germany," "the new Germany" (20, 22; CD). Deluxe's involvement with the antiracist hip-hop project Brothers Keepers and with numerous other activities, as well as the cultural criticism of his raps and essayism, puts his commitment to the struggle against racism in Germany and for the advancement of disenfranchised minorities beyond doubt; but his book's subtitle, *Deutschland Deluxe,* epitomizes a cross-stitching of diasporic and national discourses that is unprecedented and challenges the established frontlines of cultural politics in Germany. His "analysis of my own development, particularly with reference to this Germany in which we live" (11), works toward an Afro-German identity discourse that has moved through African American diasporic culture to explore a different, specifically German vision of "good cohabitation" between people from different ethnic backgrounds in a society that is becoming "more and more colorful, more and more mixed, more and more open, culturally too—at least in the big cities" (29, 33).

In its autobiographical dimension, *Dis wo ich herkomm* looks back at defining experiences in Sorge/Deluxe's life, from his childhood and youth in Hamburg, through his career as a pioneer of German-language hip-hop, to his new role as a father and man of thirty who seeks to reconcile the rebel culture of hip-hop with civic responsibility, happiness, and success. Deluxe was born in 1977 to a Sudanese father and a white German mother, and his Afro-German experience replicates some established tropes, such as "this oppressive feeling of not belonging, of being unwanted" (22); feeling, like Usleber, that he is "too white for the Blacks and too Black for the whites" (16–17); being addressed as a foreigner (23, 62); and the (largely unsuccessful) attempt to ascertain his "African roots" (60) by visiting his father in Sudan at the age of sixteen. But, unlike Afro-Germans of earlier generations, he is brought in contact with African diasporic culture from an early age due to the multiculturalism of 1980s and 1990s Hamburg, while his later return to the city reflects his disillusionment with the culture of violence, chauvinism, and consumerism in African American rap. Nevertheless, the critique of racism plays a central role in Deluxe's account, including brief references to German colonialism and National Socialism and to Massaquoi and Sow (29, 22, 115). Arguing "that racism is not German, European, or Western" (49) and citing racism in Sudan as an example, Deluxe's confidence in social transformation through positive examples contrasts sharply with Sow's radicalism, suggesting a strategy of engagement and dialogue rather than confrontation in addressing residual racism. In a sense, however, the idea of presenting an Afro-German biography as a "Germany book" (69) is radical in itself; it is provocative both to left-wing antinationalism and to traditional racialized notions of German citizenship that rule out the multicultural nation that Deluxe endorses. Deluxe therefore takes the discourse of performative normality in recent Afro-German writing to a political level.

Conclusion

Black German writing has clearly developed significantly since the 1980s. Arguably it was the shared experience of racially motivated othering and exclusion that inspired Germans of African descent but with very diverse ethnic, cultural, and social backgrounds to voice their experience in literature and to work toward an African diasporic community and culture in Germany. Recent publications confirm the success of this new departure in German literary history by their growing numbers and by intertextual references that demonstrate the establishment of a diasporic tradition. The postmillennial diversification of Black German writing, however, also indicates shifts in discourse and tone toward increased self-confidence and new engagement with mainstream culture. Self-assertion in the face of residual German racism and critical intervention into German debates about national identity continue to play a crucial role, but narratives of achievement and performative normality also suggest new confidence in Black German identity within a transforming multicultural society, in particular in authors born since the later 1970s. While the perception of Afro-Germans as "Others-from-without" continues to be a defining issue, literary responses now vary between "'performing' the diaspora"[50] and staging fuller "emplacement"[51] in a more multicultural society.

This shift in discourse goes along with generational transitions, reflecting growing multiculturalism, increased global mobility and communication, and new transnational frames of cultural reference. At the same time Black German literature remains predominantly autobiographical; Ayim's poetry and Robinson's novel seem to be exceptions. Feminist in its origins, "Afro-German literature" was seen as "primarily women's literature" as recently as 2005.[52] In light of the autobiographies of Massaquoi, Schramm, Kaufmann, Huber, Sahin-Scholl, Soost, and Deluxe, this no longer holds true, but outside the line of celebrity memoirs, Black women authors still predominate. Finally, even if Black German literature has developed traditions that give it a degree of coherence, boundaries are blurred not just with African migrants' literature and transnational works such as Massaquoi's *Destined to Witness* but also with German mainstream literature. Robinson's *Schanzen-Slam* presents itself as "pop literature" rather than Black German literature, Deluxe's *Dis wo ich herkomm* primarily targets hip-hop fans, and Gerunde's *Eine von uns* gestures toward mainstream novels that engage with the Afro-German experience, such as Eva Demski's *Afra* (1992) or Peter Henisch's

Schwarzer Peter (2000). Seen together, these texts (and the fact that some of them run into several editions) demonstrate the presence of the Black German voice in contemporary German literature.

NOTES

Dirk Göttsche, "Self-Assertion, Intervention, and Achievement: Developments in Contemporary Black German Writing," is an abridged version of Göttsche's article "Self-Assertion, Intervention and Achievement: Black German Writing in Postcolonial Perspective," *Orbis Litterarum* 67 (2012): 83–135. It is reprinted here by permission of the editors.

1. Michelle M. Wright, *Becoming Black: Creating Identity in the African Diaspora* (Durham, NC: Duke University Press, 2004), 191.
2. Ibid., 190–91. For a discussion of the problems of applying the concept of African diaspora to the experience of Black Germans, see Clarence Lusane, *Hitler's Black Victims: The Historical Experiences of Afro-Germans, European Blacks, Africans, and African Americans in the Nazi Era* (New York: Routledge, 2002), 37–38; and Tina Campt, *Other Germans: Black Germans and the Politics of Race, Gender, and Memory in the Third Reich* (Ann Arbor: University of Michigan Press, 2004), 171–81.
3. Homi K. Bhabha, *The Location of Culture* (London: Routledge, 1994), 171.
4. Ngugi wa Thiong'o, *Decolonising the Mind: The Politics of Language in African Literature* (London: James Currey, 1994).
5. Leroy Hopkins, "Writing Diasporic Identity: Afro-German Literature since 1985," in *Not So Plain as Black and White: Afro-German Culture and History, 1890–2000*, ed. Patricia Mazón and Reinhild Steingröver (Rochester, NY: University of Rochester Press, 2005), 183.
6. Tina Campt, "Reading the Black German Experience: An Introduction," *Callaloo* 26, no. 2 (2003): 289.
7. Gisela Fremgen, ed., *... und wenn du dazu noch schwarz bist: Berichte schwarzer Frauen in der Bundesrepublik* (Bremen: Edition CON, 1984). Also see Olumide Popoola and Beldan Sezen, eds., *Talking Home: Heimat aus unserer eigenen Feder: Frauen of Color in Deutschland* (Amsterdam: blue moon, 1999).
8. May Ayim, *blues in schwarz weiss: gedichte* (Berlin: Orlanda, 1995); May Ayim, *Blues in Black and White*, trans. Anne V. Adams (Trenton, NJ: Africa World Press, 2003); May Ayim, *nachtgesang: gedichte* (Berlin: Orlanda, 1997); May Ayim, *Grenzenlos und unverschämt* (Berlin: Orlanda, 1997). Also see Jennifer Michaels, "'Fühlst du dich als Deutsche oder als Afrikanerin?': May Ayim's Search for an Afro-German Identity in Her Poetry and Essays," *German Life and Letters* 59 (2006): 500–14.
9. Stefanie Kron, *"Fürchte Dich nicht, Bleichgesicht!": Perspektivenwechsel zur Literatur afro-deutscher Frauen* (Münster: Unrast, 1996), 137.

10. Ayim, *Blues in Black and White,* 42.
11. Karein K. Görtz, "Showing Her Colors: An Afro-German Writes the Blues in Black and White," *Callaloo* 26, no. 2 (2003): 307, 314.
12. See Dirk Göttsche, "Deutsche Literatur afrikanischer Diaspora und die Frage postkolonialer Kanonrevision," in *Postkolonialismus und Kanon,* ed. Herbert Uerlings and Iulia-Karin Patrut (Bielefeld: Aisthesis, 2012), 327–60.
13. Ika Hügel-Marshall, *Daheim unterwegs: Ein deutsches Leben* (Berlin: Orlanda, 1998). The English translation has the very different but equally telling title *Invisible Woman: Growing Up Black in Germany,* trans. Elizabeth Gaffney (New York: Continuum, 2000). The German title cites a line from May Ayim's poem "entfernte verbindungen"; see Hopkins, 199.
14. Hügel-Marshall, *Invisible Woman,* 54. Subsequent references are given parenthetically in the text.
15. Michael Rothberg, *Multidirectional Memory: Remembering the Holocaust in the Age of Decolonization* (Stanford, CA: Stanford University Press, 2009), 7, 3.
16. Ibid., 3.
17. Harald Gerunde, *Eine von uns: Als Schwarze in Deutschland geboren* (Wuppertal: Peter Hammer, 2000), 145–46. Subsequent references are given parenthetically in the text.
18. Görtz, 307.
19. See Dirk Göttsche, "Der neue historische Afrika-Roman: Kolonialismus aus postkolonialer Sicht," *German Life and Letters* 56 (2003): 261–80; Dirk Göttsche, *Remembering Africa: The Rediscovery of Colonialism in Contemporary German Literature* (Rochester, NY: Camden House, 2013).
20. See Rothberg; Dirk Göttsche, "Colonialism and National Socialism: Intersecting Memory Discourses in Post-War and Contemporary German Literature," *Gegenwartsliteratur: A German Studies Yearbook* 9 (2010): 217–42.
21. Bhabha, 2.
22. Ibid., 172.
23. See Hans J. Massaquoi, *Destined to Witness: Growing Up Black in Nazi Germany* (New York: Morrow, 1999), and Hans J. Massaquoi, *"Neger, Neger, Schornsteinfeger!": Meine Kindheit in Deutschland,* trans. Ulrich Wasel and Klaus Timmermann (Bern: Fretz & Wasmuth, 1999). The English and German versions are not entirely identical: some chapters are reversed in order, and each version has chapters that are missing from the other version, although the German translation is slightly shorter than the English original. Differences between the two versions reflect attention to the cultural context of their publication, i.e., to the knowledge and typical associations of their respective American and German readers. Massaquoi's sequel, *Hänschen klein, ging allein . . . : Mein Weg in die Neue Welt,* trans. Ulrich Wasel and Klaus Timmermann (Frankfurt/M: Scherz, 2004), to date appears not to have been published in English.
24. See *"Neger, Neger, Schornsteinfeger!": Ein Leben in Deutschland,* after the autobiography by H.-J. Massaquoi, directed by Jörg Grünler (ZDF/ATF, 2006); Lusane, 36.

25. See Frank Mehring, "'Nazi Jim Crow': Hans Jürgen Massaquoi's Democratic Vistas on the Black Atlantic and Afro-Germans in *Ebony*," in *Germans and African Americans: Two Centuries of Exchange*, ed. Larry A. Greene and Anke Ortlepp (Jackson: University Press of Mississippi, 2011), 141–65, on links between Massaquoi's memoirs and the cultural criticism of *Ebony*.
26. Massaquoi, *Destined to Witness*, 18. Subsequent references are given parenthetically in the text.
27. On the Swingboys in Hamburg, see Lusane, 204–6.
28. See Massaquoi, *Hänschen klein*, 89–111.
29. Marie Nejar, with Regina Carstensen, *Mach nicht so traurige Augen, weil du ein Negerlein bist: Meine Jugend im Dritten Reich* (Reinbek bei Hamburg: Rowohlt, 2007), 29. Subsequent references are given parenthetically in the text.
30. See Wolfgang Struck, *Die Eroberung der Phantasie: Kolonialismus, Literatur und Film zwischen deutschem Kaiserreich und Weimarer Republik* (Göttingen: V&R unipress, 2010).
31. See the prose sketch "Bounty" in Luc Degla, *Das afrikanische Auge* (Schwülper: Cargo, 2007), 69; Jones Kwesi Evans (with Kai Schubert and Robin Schmaler), *Ich bin ein Black Berliner: Die ungewöhnliche Lebensgeschichte eines Afrikaners in Deutschland* (Freiburg: Herder, 2006), 214–25.
32. Edward W. Said, *Culture and Imperialism* (London: Vintage, 1994), 78.
33. Gert Schramm, *Wer hat Angst vorm schwarzen Mann: Mein Leben in Deutschland* (Berlin: Aufbau, 2011), 121, 126. Subsequent references are given parenthetically in the text.
34. Natasha A. Kelly, "'Sie sind afro-deutsch? . . . Ah, ich verstehe': Zur Entstehung eines neuen deutschen Literaturgenres," *Mont Cameroun: Revue africaine d'études interculturelles sur l'espace germanophone* 6 (2009): 94.
35. See Thomas Usleber, *Die Farben unter meiner Haut: Autobiographische Aufzeichnungen* (Frankfurt/M: Brandes & Apsel, 2002), 26. Subsequent references are given parenthetically in the text.
36. See Günther Kaufmann (with Gabriele Droste), *Der weiße Neger vom Hasenbergl* (Munich: Diana, 2004), 197. Subsequent references are given parenthetically in the text.
37. See Dirk Göttsche, "Colonial Legacies and Cross-Cultural Experience: The African Voice in Contemporary German Literature," *Edinburgh German Yearbook* 1 (2007): 159–75; Dirk Göttsche, "'Eine eigene Mischung aus Identität und Kultur': Afrikanische Migrantenliteratur in deutscher Sprache zwischen Diaspora und Transkulturalität," *Mont Cameroun: Revue africaine d'études interculturelles sur l'espace germanophone* 6 (2009): 29–51; Dirk Göttsche, "Cross-Cultural Self-Assertion and Cultural Politics: African Migrants' Writing in German Since the Late 1990s," *German Life and Letters* 63 (2010): 54–70.
38. Charles M. Huber, *Ein Niederbayer im Senegal: Mein Leben zwischen zwei Welten* (Frankfurt/M: Scherz, 2004), 36–37. Subsequent references are given parenthetically in the text.

39. Abini Zöllner, *Schokoladenkind: Meine Familie und andere Wunder* (Reinbek bei Hamburg: Rowohlt, 2003), 102. Subsequent references are given parenthetically in the text.
40. Detlef D! Soost (with Anne Ascher), *Heimkind—Neger—Pionier: Mein Leben* (Reinbek bei Hamburg: Wunderlich, 2005), 58. Subsequent references are given parenthetically in the text.
41. On Zöllner's and Soost's memoirs as stories of achievement, see also Ekpenyong Ani, " 'Say it loud!': Afro-diasporische Lebensgeschichten im deutschen Kontext," *Dossier "Schwarze Community in Deutschland,"* ed. Maureen Maisha Eggers, Heinrich-Böll-Stiftung 2006, http://www.migration-boell.de/web/diversity/48_583.asp.
42. Steffi Jones (with Broka Herrmann), *Der Kick des Lebens: Wie ich den Weg nach oben schaffte* (Frankfurt/M: Fischer, 2007); Jimmy Hartwig, *"Ich möcht' noch so viel tun . . .": Meine Kindheit, meine Karriere, meine Krankheit* (Bergisch-Gladbach: Bastei Lübbe, 1994); Jimmy Hartwig, *Ich bin ein Kämpfer geblieben: Meine Siege, meine Krisen, mein Leben* (Berlin: Siebenhaar, 2010); Freddy Sahin-Scholl, *Der Mann mit den zwei Stimmen: Vom Waisenkind zum Star* (Munich: Irisiana, 2011); Arabella Kiesbauer, *Mein afrikanisches Herz* (Munich: Piper, 2007).
43. Bhabha, 2.
44. Campt, *Other Germans,* 7.
45. Samy Deluxe (with Götz Bühler), *Dis wo ich herkomm: Deutschland Deluxe* (Reinbek bei Hamburg: Rowohlt, 2009), 22. Subsequent references are given parenthetically in the text.
46. Noah Sow, *Deutschland Schwarz Weiß: Der alltägliche Rassismus* (Munich: Goldmann, 2008), 9. Subsequent references are given parenthetically in the text.
47. ManuEla Ritz, *Die Farbe meiner Haut: Die Antirassismustrainerin erzählt* (Freiburg: Herder, 2009), 11–12. Subsequent references are given parenthetically in the text.
48. Ayim, *Blues in Black and White,* 167–68.
49. Victoria B. Robinson, *Schanzen-Slam* (Berlin: Anais, 2009), 35, 23. Subsequent references are given parenthetically in the text.
50. Wright, 196.
51. Campt, *Other Germans,* 7.
52. Hopkins, 183.

4

After the German Invention of Race

Conceptions of Race Mixing from Kant to Fischer and Hitler

ROBERT BERNASCONI

You tell me that hitler
Is a mighty bad man.
I guess he took lessons
From the ku klux klan.
—Langston Hughes, "Beaumont to Detroit: 1943"

In this essay, I sketch the history of German anxiety about race mixing between Blacks and whites, especially white Germans. I focus primarily on scientific (*wissenschaftlich*) thinking about race mixing because it is in this context that one is best able to locate German racism within its broader international context. Since the end of the Second World War there has been a concerted effort to isolate certain strands of German racial thinking in order to save the reputation of the Western intellectual tradition as a whole. For example, Herder and Fichte were often castigated, whereas Kant was protected, even though Kant can be said to have invented the scientific concept of race to mark allegedly permanent inheritable characteristics.[1] I shall break with this tendency and place the intellectual origins of German racial thinking during the Nazi era in a broader context. However, to make this topic manageable in the brief space allowed me, I will in the last part of this essay focus on Eugen Fischer. Fischer is a natural focal point for a study of the scientific perception of Black Germans because of both his groundbreaking work on race mixing and his role in the sterilization programs of the 1930s.[2]

I must begin, however, with Adolf Hitler. Hitler took full advantage of the emotional antipathy many Germans felt toward race mixing. That antipathy had been heightened as a result of the so-called Black Horror: the occupation of the Rhineland by Black soldiers from France's colonies after the First World War and the mixed-race population that resulted from their presence there.[3] In the 1920s Hans Günther, a widely read author on racial issues, had called for state regulation to prevent that group from propagating further.[4] Hitler referred to the Black Horror in *Mein Kampf* (1925) when he called the French "the most terrible enemy." He wrote of the French:

> This people, which is becoming more and more negrified, constitutes in its tie with the aims of Jewish world domination an enduring danger for the existence [*Bestand*] of the white race in Europe. For the contamination [*Verpestung*] by Negro blood on the Rhine in the heart of Europe is just as much in keeping with the sadistic thirst for vengeance of this hereditary enemy of our peoples as is the ice-cold calculation of the Jew thus to begin bastardizing the European continent at its core and to deprive the white race of the foundations for a sovereign existence through infection with lower humanity.[5]

I shall not try to make sense here of Hitler's theories or of his attempt to connect his concern with race mixing between Blacks and whites with his belief that the Jews were plotting world domination. However, it is important to recognize that the fear of racial contamination that Hitler drew on to incite hatred was widespread elsewhere, especially in the United States, and had the support of many in the scientific community.

Hitler complained about Germany's history of inattention to racial hygiene. Insofar as his point was that Germany was not as involved in eugenic programs as the United States or most countries in Northern Europe, he was right (see *Mein Kampf* 446, trans. 403). For example, Germany was among the last of the major nations to adopt a sterilization program, although once it had done so, it pursued the program with unusual efficiency.[6] Whereas most eugenic programs were directed against allowing the insane or those designated as sexually depraved to breed, Hitler believed that breeding programs should also be directed toward racial purity. He thought that intermixing resulted in both a physical weakening of the higher race, including a diminishment of the power to propagate, and a mental deterioration. The racially mixed person was congenitally conflicted: "In all critical moments in which the racially unified being makes correct, that is, unified decisions, the racially divided one will become uncertain, that is, he will arrive at half measures" (442, trans. 400). Hitler planned to take advantage of the fact that there were still in Germany a significant proportion of "unmixed stocks of Nordic-Germanic people whom we may consider the most precious treasure for our future" (442, trans. 400). Evoking the language of Social Darwinism, Hitler declared that race mixing was the concern of the state because it had implications for "the mutual struggle for existence" (443, trans. 400). He even castigated missionaries in the belief that they would turn "healthy, though primitive and inferior" Hottentots and Zulu Kaffirs into "a rotten brood of bastards" (446, trans. 403). None of these ideas was new, but fear generated by the existence of the so-called Rhineland Bastards gave Hitler a ready audience for his views.[7]

Concern over race mixing predated the introduction of the scientific conception of race and marked it from the outset. When in 1775 Immanuel Kant presented the first scientific definition of race, he appealed to the possibility of race mixing to secure the distinction between races and species.[8] He used Buffon's rule, according to which fertility across generations established that the parents were of the same species, to attack polygenesis, the belief that there was more than one human species. To explain how the different races arose from one original pair but, once formed, became permanent, Kant posited the existence in the original human being of four germs (*Keime*) representing the four races, such that the actualization of one of these germs, through interaction with the climate, excluded further changes except through race mixing. According to Kant, specifically *racial* characteristics were those that mixed-race children inherited in equal proportions from their parents. Skin color was his primary example because it was so visible, but any permanent inheritable characteristics that were shared equally among the offspring of race mixing fit that description. Nevertheless, even if the possibility of race mixing was what necessitated the category of race and differentiated it from species, Kant believed that the existence of races was an indication that race differences belonged to the design of providence. This meant that race mixing was against nature.[9]

The idea that race mixing was also socially unwise because it compromised the clear boundaries between the races became widespread among North Americans once chattel slavery took on a racialized form.[10] However, a new argument against race mixing was introduced in the nineteenth century. The earliest occurrence of it that I have found is in Friedrich Ludwig Jahn's *Deutsches Volkstum,* written in 1810 in the aftermath of Prussia's defeat by Napoleon. Jahn asserted that "hybrids among animals have no genuine capacity for reproduction and in the same way mixed peoples have as little propensity for surviving as a nation."[11] He believed that the original human race was extinct but judged that the races that had since been formed in its place should be preserved. To cultivate a fear of race mixing among his readers, Jahn turned to the "Hottentots" (or Khoikhoi). He praised their harmless nature but at the same time warned against the devilish nature of the mixture created when Boers and "Hottentots" reproduced together.[12] The products of this union, called "Bastards" or "Basters," were brought to the attention of the European public by the French traveler François Le Vaillant, who made two visits to South Africa.[13] Jahn's use of Le Vaillant illustrates how a few passing comments in a travelogue could fuel European prejudices. The likely source of Jahn's warning about the devilish nature of the Basters is a remarkable passage in Le Vaillant about their readiness to assassinate their masters and to commit "acts of treachery" almost daily in their plantations.[14] But there is nothing in Le Vaillant about their lack of fertility. Indeed, he says the opposite, warning that they are multiplying so fast that they might soon dominate.[15]

Race mixing had its advocates, even among extreme racists like Christoph Meiners, who in his essay from 1790, "Von den Varietäten und Abarten der Neger," argued in favor of it: "The progressive improvement of African blood through continual new mixing with European blood, as has also been shown in all similar cases in other parts of the world, confirms the pleasant prospect that Europeans, not merely through their mastery and enlightenment, but also above all through their mixing with other less noble peoples, can contribute and have contributed to the completion and happiness of the latter."[16] (However, in other contexts Meiners favored racial purity for the Germans and even appealed to the purity that the Spanish had maintained from the Moors as a precedent.)[17] Attitudes supportive of race mixing persisted well into the 1830s in standard works like James Cowles Prichard's *Researches into the Physical History of Mankind.*[18]

Even in Jahn's immediate circle, not everyone shared his suspicion of race mixing. Over fifteen years before Arthur de Gobineau's *Essai sur l'inégalité des races humaines* (Essay on the inequality of the human races) appeared in 1853, Wolfgang Menzel posited a "law of nature" concerning race mixing that operated throughout history.[19] However, his law pointed in an entirely different direction from that of Gobineau. Gobineau believed that there was no civilization to which the white race did not contribute, and that race mixing was another precondition of civilization, even though it was also the source of the decline of civilizations.[20] By contrast, Menzel argued in 1835 that Christianity and civilization would be fully victorious as a consequence of a universal mixing of the colored and white races (88). He claimed that if ten whites and ten Blacks mixed together, after eight generations they would all be white (84–85). To be sure, Menzel did not completely overturn the whole logic of purity: "Mixing itself is only a transition, a form that again disappears, with purity as the aim" (160).

Jahn's claim that race mixing impacted fertility remained only a marginal consideration until the 1840s. Only then was race mixing no longer understood as producing offspring that were midway between the parents, but instead as generating a population that was inferior, physically and/or morally, to both parent races. Honoré Jacquinot, a zoologist who had circumnavigated the globe with Jules Dumont d'Urville, claimed to be "the first to signal this sterility of the metis of the human species."[21] However, Jacquinot was beaten to the punch by Josiah Nott, a physician from Mobile, Alabama, who, more than anyone else, was responsible for the revival of polygenesis in the mid-nineteenth century. In 1843 Nott published an article in the prestigious *American Journal of the Medical Sciences* that maintained: "The Mulatto a Hybrid—probable extermination of the two races if the Whites and Blacks are allowed to intermarry." Drawing on an anonymous essay in the *Boston Medical and Surgical Journal* that argued that those of mixed race should be understood as being the carriers of a disease, Nott insisted that race mixing led to a decrease in fertility.[22] Nott's arguments had a broad impact on the leading natural historians of his day, including Louis Agassiz at Harvard and Paul Broca, founder of the Société d'Anthropologie de Paris.

By the end of the nineteenth century, with the advent of Darwinism, Nott's polygenistic framework seemed antiquated. Nevertheless, his anxieties about race mixing remained widespread and were confirmed by statisticians. For example, Frederick Hoffman, who was born in Germany but emigrated to the United States at the age of nineteen, argued in *Race Traits and Tendencies of the American Negro* that mulattoes were more susceptible to disease and an early death than were pure whites or pure Blacks. Anticipating appeals to the need for *Lebensraum,* Hoffman suggested that when whites needed more space, they would not hesitate to attack "races who prove themselves useless factors in the progress of mankind."[23] At about the same time in Germany, Otto Ammon made a study of military recruits in Baden on the basis of which he warned that, except in special cases where both parents were close to the pure original German types to which they belonged, such as the round-headed and the long-headed Germans, the offspring of race mixing were liable to be annihilated in the struggle for existence.[24] These attitudes, which were quite widespread, prepared the way for the genocides of the twentieth century, including that of the Herero.[25]

The whole tenor of the discussion was changed in 1913 when Eugen Fischer wrote *Die Rehobother Bastards und das Bastardierungsproblem beim Menschen* (The Rehoboth mongrels and the mongrelization problem in humans), which English, American, and German scholars considered to be the first genuinely scientific study of racial mixing.[26] Fischer studied an isolated community of the Basters or Bastards that Le Vaillant had observed 130 years earlier and found them "healthy, strong, and very fertile."[27] The specific moral and physical consequences predicted by Nott had not been realized. Nevertheless, Fischer still opposed race mixing, basing his argument in part on the idea of a hierarchy of races: "Without exception every European people (including those peoples that derive from Europe) that has absorbed the blood of inferior races—and only dreamers can deny that Negroes, Hottentots, and many others are inferior—had paid for this absorption of those lesser elements by spiritual and cultural decline" (302). Whereas Fischer rejected the idea that hybrid populations would inevitably decline of their own accord, he conceded that they would not fare well in the struggle for existence and faced extinction. In company with Social Darwinists like Ammon, Fischer maintained that, under conditions of competition, the Rehoboth Bastards would inevitably decline; they should be protected only as long as their continued existence could be considered useful (302). Fischer concluded that if there was even a slight possibility that race mixing was damaging "our race," then it should be prevented. Ethical and legal norms had to be subordinated to the task of the preservation (*Bestand*) of the race (303).

This still left open the question of the conditions under which a mixed-race population might constitute a biological danger to others that outweighed its utility. Fischer's adoption of Gregor Mendel's theory of inheritance becomes significant here, and it should be remembered that Fischer claimed to be the first to apply Mendel to the study of the human races in a concerted way (101). Mendelism broke with the widely held conviction that mulattoes shared equally the racial characteristics of their parents. To be sure, the general phenomenon to which Kant and subsequent theorists had pointed was confirmed: the offspring of two different races *tended* to have characteristics roughly midway between the parent races, in this case the Boers and "Hottentots" (305).[28] However, before Mendel there was no good explanation of why two light-skinned mulattoes might have a dark-skinned child. Mendel's theory explained this and also the fact that, as Fischer observed, the Rehoboth Bastards exhibited a remarkable variety of characteristics. But whereas Fischer presented his book as a scientific refutation of the claim that race mixing led to a lack of fertility and was so understood by scholars at the time, a few years later he somewhat surprisingly suggested that in all probability the mixing of Northern Europeans and Negroes led to a decrease in fertility.[29] Anxiety over the so-called *Rheinlandbastarde* (Rhineland mongrels) perhaps helps to account for the change. Fischer expressed similar views in the context of Hitler's initial racial policies: "Is a sacrifice too great when saving a whole people is at stake?"[30]

As Fischer's ties to Mendelism strengthened, his opposition to race mixing was placed on a different footing from that of his predecessors. In a 1916 essay, Fischer stated the crucial innovation for the application of Mendel's laws to humanity: a new inheritable variation, once introduced, cannot be bred out of the population. It can always recur after a gap of several generations, and so can be eliminated only with the death of those who carry it.[31] Applied to the effects of race mixing, this refuted the widespread idea, already illustrated with reference to Menzel, that those effects could be undone, thereby allowing restoration of a lost racial purity. Even if the Mendelian trait was no longer visible, it was still present and could easily reappear several generations later. At the end of the nineteenth century the proper response to the perceived biological danger of race mixing was thought to be isolating this group from the white population (except for a "reintegration" of those of mixed race into one of the two parent races as the proportions changed) and, if one believed Hoffman and others, waiting for them to die out in the struggle for existence. With the rediscovery of Mendel's theories at the beginning of the twentieth century, one could no longer believe in a progressive restoration of an original pure race. There was now a scientific account of how, as a result of light-skinned mulattoes passing, a white parent might be surprised by a dark-skinned child; the stuff of novels was also material for the scientists. Other supposedly racial characteristics of a more fundamental nature, like lower intelligence or moral depravity, might also recur unexpectedly. In the United States, this resulted in the introduction of the "one-drop rule" in 1924.[32] In Germany, there was a strong interest in North American theorists like Madison Grant, who not only advocated sterilization as a means for racial improvement but also saw "passing for white" as a threat to the white race.[33] Clearly sterilization would not be a viable policy to address racial mixing in the United States, but in Germany such an intervention was still possible, if the political will could be found. Hitler provided that will.

The impact of Mendel's laws of differentiation is certainly visible in Hitler's race thinking. Indeed, Fischer may have been one source of Hitler's understanding of Mendelism. It seems that during Hitler's time in Landsberg Prison, he read the second edition of *Human Heredity,* a book with essays by Erwin Baur, Fritz Lenz, and Eugen Fischer.[34] In any case, in his so-called *Second Book,* dictated in 1928, Hitler expressed the belief that, because of its increasingly strict immigration policies, the United States had a stronger racial pool on which to draw than did Europeans. Furthermore, he maintained that, among Europeans, the average quality of the English was higher than that of the Germans. This, Hitler explained, was why the Germans needed a racial policy based on the best science, which meant Mendel's laws of differentiation. Such a policy would acknowledge that the first- or even the second-born would not necessarily reflect the most racially valuable side of the two parents. It was thus necessary to maximize the number of offspring and allow the struggle for survival (*Lebenskampf*) to select the best of them.[35]

Nevertheless, certain consequences of Mendelian theory did not suit some of the racial prejudices fostered by National Socialism. Mendel's theory of inheritance made it clear that a race was not defined by its original character; some characteristic introduced from one population could penetrate the whole of another population. Hence William Bateson, the British naturalist, wrote: "In the light of Mendelian knowledge the discussion whether a race is pure or mixed loses almost all significance."[36]

Whereas Jahn's contemporary Ernst Moritz Arndt had argued in 1815 that the Germans were one of the few European races that were pure and thus free of the decay brought about by race mixing, Rudolf Virchow's exhaustive study, for example, had debunked that idea.[37] In the 1920s even the more popular racial theorists like Hans Günther conceded that the Germans were far from racially pure.[38] This was the source of their racial anxiety. Günther admired how the United States had established laws to control propagation, lamenting that "the feeling of responsibility towards the coming generations will for a long time yet not be awakened in Europe to the same degree as in the United States."[39] In his position as director of the Kaiser Wilhelm Institute of Anthropology, Fischer advised that the Germans did not need to pursue a policy of racial purity at all costs. On February 1, 1933, he gave a widely publicized lecture under the title "Rassenkreuzung und geistige Leistung" (Racial crossbreeding and intellectual achievement) in which he insisted that crossbreeding and not racial purity was the most important factor in the emergence of high culture, so long as the races concerned had the appropriate endowments or capacities.[40] Indeed, the day before Hitler took power, Fischer insisted, in a formulation that was reminiscent of Gobineau, that the Nordic race accomplished its highest achievements when it was mixed with races that were not significantly inferior to it. By contrast, "where it has remained most pure, the Nordic race has brought forth no great cultural achievement."[41] It has been speculated that Fischer was removed from his position as head of the Society for Racial Hygiene in June 1933 because of this, but it did not stop him from playing an important role both in the development of Nazi racial policy[42] and also in its execution, including authorizing one of his assistants, Dr. Wolfgang Abel, to conduct a statistical survey of the *Rheinlandbastarde.*[43] In 1937 he served on a commission whose tasks included identifying the African ancestry of the *Rheinlandbastarde* with a view to their sterilization.[44] Although it was apparently outside the legal parameters of the Nazi Sterilization Law, 385 of the mixed-race children were sterilized.[45]

Fischer had long supported sterilization as a way to address the spread of hereditary diseases. Whether he saw the *Rheinlandbastarde* in those terms is not entirely clear. His early work had shown that mulattoes were not as great a threat as Nott had thought them to be, but his Mendelism led him to believe that, once racial intermixing was introduced into a population, its legacy could not be addressed effectively except by sterilization.

I have shown that although the scientific idea of race was German in origin, it was not in Germany but above all in the United States that the biological argument against race mixing was developed and pressed. It is increasingly recognized that German ideas of eugenics were in large measure taken over from the Anglo-Saxon countries, but it is still not widely appreciated that crucial components of the German idea of race more generally—including horror at the thought of German "blood" being "contaminated," as Hitler put it, by "Negro blood"—had their source outside Germany. Kant was against race mixing because it was against nature, but he did not believe that the survival of a people depended on its racial purity. However, that idea was widely held in the second half of the nineteenth century and at the beginning of the twentieth century, and to promote it attempts were made to convince people that they felt revulsion at the very thought of race mixing. The feeling that there was a problem of race mixing between Blacks and whites was widespread in the United States and in those European countries that had a much longer history of colonial occupation than Germany had. This was why it proved so easy to evoke sympathy for the Germans in the United States and Britain on account of the Black Horror.[46] To understand why the "Black Horror" proved such a successful rallying cry in Germany in the 1920s and why it led to the sterilization of a number of the *Rheinlandbastarde* in the 1930s, one must look beyond specifically German ideas about Black people and take a much broader view.

NOTES

1. Robert Bernasconi, "Who Invented the Concept of Race?," in *Race,* ed. Robert Bernasconi (Oxford: Blackwell, 2001), 11–36.
2. *Race after Hitler Other Germans: Black Germans and the Politics of Race, Gender, and Memory in the Third Reich Not So Plain as Black and White: Afro-German Culture and History, 1890–2000,* ed. Patricia Mazón and Reinhild Steingröver (Rochester, NY: University of Rochester Press, 2005), 87–90; and especially Fatima El-Tayeb's important study *Schwarze Deutsche: Der Diskurs um "Rasse" und nationale Identität1890–1933* (Frankfurt/M: Campus, 2001), 82–83.
3. See Reiner Pommerin, *Sterilisierung der Rheinlandbastarde* (Dusseldorf: Droste, 1979). For a brief overview in English, see Rosemarie K. Lester, "Blacks in Germany and German Blacks," in *Blacks and German Culture,* ed. Reinhold Grimm and Jost Hermand (Madison: University of Wisconsin Press, 1986), 113–34. For an example of the literature the controversy spawned, see Heinrich Distler, *Das deutsche Leid am Rhein: Ein Buch der Anklage gegen die Schandherrschaft des französischen Militarismus* (Minden in Westfalen: Köhler, 1921).

4. Hans F. K. Günther, *Rassenkunde des deutschen Volkes,* 9th ed. (Munich: Lehmann, 1926), 146.
5. Adolf Hitler, *Mein Kampf* (Munich: Franz Eler, 1942), 704–5; *Mein Kampf,* trans. Ralph Mannheim (Boston: Houghton Mifflin, 1971), 624. Subsequent references are given parenthetically in the text.
6. On the connection between American eugenics and racism in National Socialism, see Stefan Kühl, *The Nazi Connection: Eugenics, American Racism, and German National Socialism* (Oxford: Oxford University Press, 1994).
7. See also Alfred Rosenberg, *Der Mythos des 20. Jahrhunderts* (Munich: Hoheneichen, 1935), 646–47; *The Myth of the Twentieth Century,* trans. Vivian Bird (Newport Beach, CA: Noontide Press, 1993), 425–26.
8. See Robert Bernasconi, "True Colors: Kant's Distinction between Nature and Artifice in Context," in *Klopffechtereien—Missverständnisse—Widersprüche? Methodologische Perspektiven auf die Kant-Forster Kontroverse,* ed. Rainer Godel and Gideon Stiening (Paderborn: Fink, 2012), 191–207. The continuity with Kant is shown in the way that Fischer confirmed the idea that the investigation of race mixing was critical to the investigation and identification of racial properties. See Fischer's "Das Problem der Rassenkreuzung beim Menschen," in *Verhandlungen der Gesellschaft Deutscher Naturforscher und Ärzte,* ed. Alexander Wittig (Leipzig: Vogel, 1913), 73.
9. Immanuel Kant, "Über den Gebrauch teleologischer Principien in der Philosophie," *Werke* (Leipzig: Modes und Baumann, 1838–1839), 7:166–67; "On the Use of Teleological Principles in Philosophy," trans. John Mark Mikkelsen, in Bernasconi, *Race,* 42. See further Robert Bernasconi, "Kant as an Unfamiliar Source of Racism," in *Philosophers on Race,* ed. Julie K. Ward and Tommy Lott (Oxford: Blackwell, 2002), 145–66.
10. Robert Bernasconi, "The Logic of Whiteness," *Annals of Scholarship* 14, no. 1 (Spring 2000): 75–91.
11. Friedrich Ludwig Jahn, *Deutsches Volkstum* (Leipzig: Reim, 1817), 20.
12. Ibid., 166.
13. As Raymond Howgego dryly observes, Le Vaillant's notes shed "little light on his route or the peoples he encountered," as he seems to have been largely concerned "with the bird life and the shape of the women's buttocks." See *Encyclopedia of Exploration to 1800* (Potts Point: Harden, 2003), 625. For the broader context, see Nicholas Hudson, " 'Hottentots' and the Evolution of European Racism," *Journal of European Studies* 34, no 4 (2004): 308–25.
14. François Le Vaillant, *Voyage de Monsieur Le Vaillant dans l'intérieur de l'Afrique par le Cap de Bonne-Espérance dans les Années 1780, 81, 82, 83, 84, et 85* (Paris: Leroy, 1790), 2:133–35; *Travels into the Interior Parts of Africa by the Way of the Cape of Good Hope in the Years 1780, 81, 82, 83, 84, and 85,* translator unknown (London: Robinson, 1790), 2:135–37.
15. Le Vaillant, 133; trans. 134–35.
16. Christoph Meiners, "Von den Varietäten und Abarten der Neger," *Göttingisches Historisches Magazin* 6 (1790): 642–43. See also Susanne Zantop, "The Beautiful, the

Ugly, and the German," in *Gender and Germanness*, ed. Patricia Herminghouse and Magda Mueller (Providence: Berghahn, 1997), 21–35.

17. Christoph Meiners, "Über die Natur der Germanischen und übrigen Celtischer Völker," *Göttingisches Historisches Magazin* 7 (1791): 124.

18. "Mixed breeds are very often produced superior in almost all their physical qualities to the parent races, and particularly with so much vigour of propagation, that they often gain grounds upon the older varieties, and gradually supersede them." James Cowles Prichard, *Researches into the Physical History of Mankind*, 3rd ed. (London: Sherwood, Gilbert and Piper, 1836), 1:146; *Naturgeschichte des Menschengeschlechts*, trans. Rudolph Wagner (Leipzig: Voss, 1840), 1:184.

19. Wolfgang Menzel, *Geist der Geschichte* (Stuttgart: Liesching, 1835), 84. Subsequent references are given parenthetically in the text.

20. Arthur de Gobineau, *Essai sur l'inégalité des races humaines*, Oeuvres 1, ed. Jean Gaulmier (Paris: Gallimard, 1983), 173, 342–48; *The Inequality of Human Races*, trans. Adrian Collins (London: Heinemann, 1915), 36, 208–10. Fischer referenced Ludwig Schemann's *Gobineaus Rassenwerk* (Stuttgart: Frommann, 1910) in his *Sozialanthropologie und ihre Bedeutung für den Staat* (Freiburg: Speyer und Kaerner, 1910), n20. See also Fischer's letter to Schemann of January 16, 1910, quoted in Peter Weingart, Jürgen Kroll, and Kurt Bayertz, *Rasse, Blut und Gene* (Frankfurt/M: Suhrkamp, 1992), 99.

21. Honoré Jacquinot, *Zoologie* (Paris: Gide, 1846), 2:91–92, cited in Claude Blanckaert, "Of Monstrous Metis?," in *The Color of Liberty: Histories of Race in France*, ed. Sue Peabody and Tyler Stovall (Durham, NC: Duke University Press, 2003), 49.

22. Philanthropist, "Vital Statistics of Negroes and Mulattoes," *Boston Medical and Surgical Journal* 27, no. 10 (October 12, 1842): 168–70, and Josiah C. Nott, "The Mulatto a Hybrid," *American Journal of the Medical Sciences* 6 (1843): 252–26. Both are reprinted in *Race, Hybridity, and Miscegenation*, ed. Robert Bernasconi and Kristie Dotson (Bristol: Thoemmes Continuum, 2005), 1:1–3, 6–14.

23. Frederick Hoffman, *Race Traits and Tendencies of the American Negro* (New York: American Economic Association, 1896), 328–29.

24. Otto Ammon, *Die natürliche Auslese beim Menschen* (Jena: Fischer, 1893), 315.

25. Dan Stone, "White Men with Low Moral Standards? German Anthropology and the Herero Genocide," *Patterns of Prejudice* 35, no. 2 (2001): 33–45. For a more general view of the background, see Robert Bernasconi, "Why Do the Happy Inhabitants of Tahiti Bother to Exist at All?," in *Genocide and Human Rights*, ed. John K. Roth (New York: Palgrave Macmillan, 2005), 139–48. One should remember the colonial context of Fischer's study and the war the Germans fought against the Hereros. See Jürgen Zimmerer, "War, Concentration Camps and Genocide in South-West Africa: The First German Genocide," in *Genocide in German South-West Africa: The Colonial War of 1904–1908 and Its Aftermath*, ed. Jürgen Zimmerer and Joachim Zeller (Pontypool: Merlin, 2008), 41–63. However, the Basters sided with the Germans. See Jon M. Bridgman, *The Revolt of the Hereros* (Berkeley: University of California Press, 1981), 25.

26. *Genetics and Eugenics The Mulatto in the United States Race and the Third Reich: Linguistics, Racial Anthropology and Genetics in the Dialectic of Volk*, 74.

27. Eugen Fischer, *Die Rehobother Bastards und das Bastardierungsproblem beim Menschen* (1913; repr., Graz: Akademische Druck und Verlagsanstalt, 1961), 302. Subsequent references are given parenthetically in the text.
28. See also Eugen Fischer, "Die Rassenunterschiede des Menschen," in Erwin Baur, Eugen Fischer, and Fritz Lenz, *Grundriß der menschlichen Erblichkeitslehre und Rassenhygiene* (Munich: Lehmann, 1923), 1:93; *Human Heredity*, trans. Eden Paul and Cedar Paul (London: Allen, 1931), 127–28.
29. Eugen Fischer, *Rasse und Rassenentstehung beim Menschen* (Berlin: Ullstein, 1927), 127; Hermann Werner Siemens, *Grundzüge der Vererbungslehre, der Rassenhygiene und der Bevölkerungspolitik* (Munich: Lehmann, 1926), 70; *Race Hygiene and Heredity*, trans. Llewellys F. Barker (New York: Appleton, 1924), 103.
30. Eugen Fischer, "Erbe," *Mein Heimatland: Badische Blätter für Volkskunde, Heimat- und Naturschutz* 21, no. 5–6 (1934): 150.
31. Eugen Fischer, "Die Rassenmerkmale des Menschen als Domestikationserscheinungen," *Zeitschrift für Morphologie und Anthropologie* 18 (1916): 281. See also "Rassenentstehung und älteste Rassengeschichte der Hebräer," *Forschungen über das Judentum* 3 (1938): 121–22.
32. There is some controversy among historians as to when the states adopted the so-called one-drop rule, but contemporaries privileged Virginia's "Act to Preserve Racial Integrity," passed in 1924. Earnest Sevier Cox called it "the most perfected legal expression of the white idea." See Earnest Sevier Cox, *White America* (Richmond, VA: White America Society, 1925), 393.
33. Madison Grant, *The Passing of the Great Race* (New York: Scribner, 1919), 53; *Der Untergang der großen Rasse*, trans. Rudolf Polland (Munich: Lehmann, 1925), 46; and *The Conquest of a Continent* (New York: Scribner, 1933), 285; *Die Eroberung eines Kontinents*, trans. Elza Mez (Berlin: Metzner, 1937), 161. The translation of the second of these books included a preface by none other than Eugen Fischer.
34. Fritz Lenz, "Die Stellung des Nationalsozialismus zur Rassenhygiene," *Archiv für Rassen- und Gesellschaftsbiologie* 25 (1931): 302. See also Baur, Fischer, and Lenz.
35. Gerhard L. Weinberg, ed., *Hitlers zweites Buch* (Stuttgart: Deutsche Verlags-Anstalt, 1961), 125–27; *Hitler's Second Book*, trans. Krista Smith (New York: Enigma, 2003), 109–12.
36. William Bateson, "Heredity," *Annual Report of the Board of Regents of the Smithsonian Institution*, 1915, 388.
37. Rudolf Virchow, "Gesamtbericht über die von der deutschen anthropologischen Gesellschaft veranlassten Erhebungen über die Farbe der Haut, der Haare und der Augen der Schulkinder in Deutschand," *Sämtliche Werke* 45, ed. Christian Andree (Hildesheim: Olms, 2009).
38. E. W. Arndt, "Fantasien zur Berichtigung der Urtheile über künftige deutsche Verfassungen," *Schriften für und an seine lieben Deutschen* (Leipzig: Weidmann, 1845), 2:376; Hans F. K. Günther, *Rassenkunde des deutschen Volkes* (Munich: Lehmann, 1923), 186.

39. Hans F. K. Günther, *Rassenkunde Europas* (Munich: Lehmann, 1926), 200; *The Racial Elements of European History,* trans. G. C. Wheeler (New York: Dutton, 1927), 246.
40. Eugen Fischer, "Rassenkreuzung und geistige Leistung," as reported in *Magdeburger Zeitung,* no. 123 (August 3, 1933), 6, cited by Niels C. Lösch, *Rasse als Konstrukt: Leben und Werk Eugen Fischers* (Frankfurt/M: Lang, 1977), 232–33. Similar views were expressed by Fischer's collaborator and former student Fritz Lenz in *Grundriß der menschlichen Erblichkeitslehre,* 1:429; trans. *Human Hybridity,* 692. See also the attempt to reconcile Fischer's relatively positive assessment of the Rehoboth Bastards with his position on race mixing in Bernhard Gessler, *Eugen Fischer (1874–1967)* (Frankfurt/M: Lang, 2000), 93–98.
41. Eugen Fischer, "Rassenkreuzung und geistige Lieferung," *Internationales Ärztliches Bulletin,* March/April 1936: 35, cited by Robert Proctor, *Racial Hygiene: Medicine under the Nazis* (Cambridge, MA: Harvard University Press, 1988), 40. It has been suggested that Fischer was the first significant German anthropologist to acknowledge Gobineau. See Benoît Massin, "De l'anthropologie physique libérale à la biologie raciale eugénics-nordiciste en Allemagne," *Revue d'allemagne* 25, no. 3 (1993): 394. On Fischer's relation to Schemann, see Hans-Walter Schmuhl, *The Kaiser Wilhelm Institute for Anthropology, Human Heredity, and Eugenics, 1927–1945* (Berlin: Springer, 2008), 112–14.
42. On the controversy surrounding Fischer's removal, see Lösch, 231–53. According to Weindling, Fischer's name was temporarily struck from the list of associate editors of Alfred Ploetz's *Archiv.* See Paul Weindling, *Health, Race and German Politics between National Unification and Nazism, 1870–1945* (Cambridge: Cambridge University Press, 1993), 508. This is not reflected in the title pages of the journal, but the 1936 issue contains an unusual portrait of Fischer by Ploetz that appears to be a public plea for his cooperation. See Alfred Ploetz, "Lebensbild Eugen Fischers," *Archiv für Rassen- und Gesellschaftsbiologie* 30 (1936): 85–87. Fischer was one of a group of leading educators, also including Martin Heidegger, who pledged their allegiance to Hitler in a document that was roughly translated into four other languages. Fischer took the occasion to emphasize unity of blood. See *Bekenntnis der Professoren an den deutschen Universitäten und Hochschulen zu Adolf Hitler und dem nationalsozialistischen Staat* (Dresden: Limpert, 1933), 9–10.
43. Benoit Massin, "The 'Science of Race,'" in *Deadly Medicine: Creating the Master Race,* ed. Dieter Kuntz (Washington, DC: United States Holocaust Memorial Museum, 2008), 96–97.
44. Pommerin, 78.
45. Sheila Faith Weiss, *The Nazi Symbiosis: Human Genetics and Politics in the Third Reich* (Chicago: University of Chicago Press, 2010), 101; Schmuhl, 296–99. On this and the close relation of German and American eugenicists, see Clarence Lusanne, *Hitler's Black Victims* (New York: Routledge, 2003), 129–43.
46. See Iris Wigger, "'Black Shame'—The Campaign against 'Racial Degeneration' and Sexual Degradation in Interwar Europe," *Race & Class* 51 (2010): 33–46, and *Die "Schwarze Schmach am Rhein"* (Münster: Westfälisches Dampfboot, 2007).

5

Counterfeit Money / Counterfeit Discourse

A Black German Trickster Tale

TOBIAS NAGL

Let us begin by the impossible.
—Jacques Derrida

Research into the history of the Black diaspora in Germany, perhaps even more than similar scholarship in France or the United Kingdom, has always been confronted with a complex epistemological framework of visibility and invisibility. Moments of absence, discontinuity, loss, and even scale have all contributed to making the subjective dimensions of its object of study almost invisible. This invisibility not only results from the repression of the place of the German shores of the Black Atlantic in dominant historiographies and the corresponding marking of Black bodies as "Others-from-without"[1] through political and discursive apparatuses of racial formation, but must also be understood as an effect of the particular temporality and ruptures through which a Black German subjectivity has historically emerged. As Tina Campt points out with respect to the contemporary Afro-German politics of memory: "Unlike other 'settlers' in Germany, Black Germans have no originary collective migration or displacement (either voluntary or forced) with which they can identify or trace their existence. This population traces their history primarily to a number of individual journeys of Blacks over two centuries from different nations."[2]

Accordingly, historical scholarship has made the documentation of these contested individual presences a main objective, chiefly in the form of biographical accounts that can often be retrieved only from official records.[3]

The scarcity of these documents, their ruptures, and the absence or tragic loss of important firsthand narratives that could help us better understand the emergence of historical Black German subjectivities at the dawn of and within modernity further complicate this endeavor and are among the primary problems the historian of Black German modes of articulation encounters. The moral-juridical treatise *De iure Maurorum in Europa* (On the rights of Moors in Europe) by Wilhelm Amo, the Ghanaian German early Enlightenment philosopher, must be considered lost, as must the novels and plays the Black German actor Louis Brody wrote in the late 1920s, according to evidence from both the *Crisis* and the *Völkischer Beobachter*.[4]

But even where we can recover empirical traces of agency and subjectivity from the archive or are in the position to collect oral memory narratives, we still have not overcome the perhaps even more pressing questions of subalternity on a methodological and theoretical level. There is no immediate access to a subaltern consciousness, as Gayatri Spivak reminds us, and forms of subaltern articulation are neither transparent nor easily readable as expressions of a logically presumed, self-identical subject of enunciation.[5] Rather, they flicker between different poles of subjugation and subjectivation, split, highly positioned, bearing traces of what W. E. B. Du Bois has described as the "peculiar sensation" of a "double consciousness."[6] What we might need, then, I would suggest, is not just additional evidence of the mere historical existence of a Black presence in Germany but readings and reading strategies of the historical records we already have that are theoretically more nuanced and are willing to address these issues openly.

What I am trying to do, therefore, is not so much develop a cohesive historical narrative of Black political agency and consciousness in the Weimar era (which would be difficult enough in its own right). Following Walter Benjamin, who argued (against Ranke) that "the history that showed things 'as they really were' was the strongest narcotic of the [nineteenth] century,"[7] I will rather try to outline a *nonlinear* reading of archival fragments that brings the German past into a *constellation* with our postcolonial present—a constellation through which the emergence of a *historical* Black German subjectivity might, to quote Benjamin again, "be seized only as an image which flashes up . . . in a moment."[8]

In this essay I examine how Black Germans, mainly former colonial subjects, articulated claims for citizenship, rights, and recognition vis-à-vis a scopic regime that forced them to look at themselves "through the eyes of others"[9] and a political regime that denied them full citizenship in the aftermath of the Versailles treaty. At the same time, I show how they subverted both othering and ordering regimes that reduced them to what Giorgio Agamben, following Hannah Arendt's reflections on the implications of the question of statelessness, has recently described as "bare life."[10] Although they often possessed German passports, were raised in German missionary schools, and even identified themselves as German, they were considered neither Germans nor citizens of the Allied powers but were forced to dwell in between juridical categories while facing the constant threat of deportation.

In drawing on an array of "diasporic resources"[11] and counter-histories as well as using strategies of mimicry and masquerade, these "flashes" of an emerging Black *German* subjectivity in the Weimar era that I am trying to retrieve from the colonial archive not only counterfeited nationalist discourses quite effectively but also defined a Black German consciousness in the context of both the "Black Atlantic" and the nation-state and thus challenged, interrupted, and disturbed received racialized notions of Germanness and narratives of the nation from *within*. All these issues become nowhere so obvious as in the story of Wilhelm Munumé and Peter Makembe, two tricksters who were involved in one of the most fascinating, mysterious, and maybe even poetic crime-plots of the Weimar Republic.[12]

It is not without irony that Munumé and Makembe had starred as extras in the German colonial epic *Ich hatt' einen Kameraden* (I had a comrade), shot by Conrad Wiene on Berlin studio lots in 1926.[13] The only feature film of that era to address colonial revisionist claims directly, it recapitulated the outbreak of World War I in German East Africa, using Black actors to embody the already mythical figures of the "loyal Askari" who had courageously fought on the side of their German colonial masters. In one memorable sequence, a group of Askari gather and salute the German squadron leader, who asks them if they are willing to defend "unseren deutschen Mutterboden" ("our German mother soil") in Africa. One of the Askari, probably played by Munumé, steps forward and replies: "Herr Major, wir sind Deutsche!" ("Major, we are Germans!") Although colonial propaganda in the Weimar era relied heavily on the ideological trope of former colonial subjects desiring the return of their former masters, such forms of Black identification with notions of Germanness turned into a rather dangerous supplement to German nationalist discourse when uttered *in* Germany.[14]

The night *Ich hatt' einen Kameraden* premiered in Hamburg during a huge propaganda event, the so-called Reichskolonialwoche (Reich colonial week), a police squad broke into the apartments of Wilhelm Munumé and Peter Makembe in Berlin. The evidence resulting from the raid was overwhelming. Among the confiscated items were a counterfeit British five-pound note, two bottles of printer's ink, eight different passports issued to Makembe, several printer's rollers for counterfeit money, an address list of other African migrants in Berlin, British work reports issued to the names of Smith and Johnson, a passport issued to the name of the British seaman Johnson Smith, fourteen sheets of notepaper with the mysterious imprint "King Bondongulo of Accra, Gold Coast of West Africa," and postcards printed with a photo of Munumé and a long poem. Three days later the major newspapers reported on the incident and declared that the police had been alarmed by reports about two "elegantly dressed Negroes with cosmopolitan manners" who had placed strange orders at several printers in Berlin, claiming they were acting on behalf of a King Bondongulo of Accra. Makembe and Munumé had been working as actors and possessed German passports, the police declared, but now it seemed likely that they actually were "international rascals."[15]

Neither Munumé nor Makembe had started their careers as counterfeiters or actors, although the capacity to act, to counterfeit identities, and to wear masks must have been as useful for Black migrants then as it is today. But who were they then?

Peter Makembe migrated to Germany from Cameroon during the colonial period; he taught as a language instructor at the University of Hamburg from 1912 to 1919 and founded an import company for tropical fruit. He functioned as a treasurer for the Afrikanischer Hilfsverein (African aid association), an early political organization of Black migrants in Germany, and also cosigned a petition directed at the Reichstag in which former colonial subjects expressed their support of Cameroonian claims for national self-determination after the war, recalling the violent atrocities of German rule.[16] Makembe must have been a man who not only had difficulty enduring humiliations but also was courageous and tenacious enough to fight injustices. Born in 1892 in Duala and educated in German schools, he is probably best described as a member of the class of assimilated "almost the same but not quite" colonial subjects that Homi Bhabha, following V. S. Naipaul, termed "mimic men."[17] Considering Bhabha's influential remarks on the subversive effects of colonial mimicry, which take the question of education as their starting point, the story of how and when Makembe first became notorious is all the more remarkable.

In 1914 Makembe tried to sue a shop clerk who had addressed him with the informal second-person singular form "du" instead of the formal "Sie." In his court testimony, Makembe explained that his German teachers had told him that as an adult he would be addressed in this formal manner of speech. The legal representation at the court thus was forced to address if and how an "educated Negro" should be formally recognized. What a provocation this was becomes quite clear in light of the reaction of the right-wing *Deutsche Tageszeitung*: "Would it not be best not to raise a species of educated Negroes?" Mimicry as a form of counterfeiting or "doubling," as Bhabha argues, "repeats the fixed and empty presence of authority by articulating it syntagmatically with a range of differential knowledges and positionalities that both estrange its 'identity' and produce new forms of knowledge, new models of differentiation, new sites of power."[18] In other words, since subaltern mimicry has the power to double or repeat the authority of discourse, this authority is displaced and appears, at least momentarily, to be defective or lacking.

Wilhelm Munumé also had gained some notoriety prior to his arrest in the summer of 1926. Born in Cameroon in 1897 and a German resident since 1913, he had run a clothing store in Wiesbaden and got by as a traveling artist and actor. In 1921, as the Wiesbaden police later informed their colleagues in Berlin, he had distributed postcards for a living, which had "glorified his check frauds and his person." The manner of his trickery, however, clearly elucidated "what a clever lad" he was. Using the name "John Black," he had passed himself off as a representative of "the Negro republic of Liberia" when meeting with German banks and manipulated exchange rates with counterfeit Liberian ads in the financial newspapers. Munumé well knew how to play to the white gaze for his own purposes. In October 1924 Munumé had given a "patriotic" speech in a Rhineland bar and spent thirty days in prison after being arrested by French occupation forces. His bravery, however, did not make him a hero in the eyes of the nationalist German bureaucracy, which assumed that he had initiated this conflict only to receive financial aid from the colonial authorities, as many African migrants did at that time. Munumé nevertheless found a way to capitalize on his experiences: he turned to literature, leaving us with a poem titled "Opfer des deutschen Vaterlands" (Sacrifice / victim of the German fatherland), which, I would argue, might be considered the inaugurating moment of Black German postcolonial writing. Distributed on commercial postcards bearing Munumé's photographic portrait, the text read:

Look at him, he stands there sternly,
Wilhelm Munumé from Duala.
Cultivated by Germans
Thus France felt his Germanness too.

Thirty days he suffered abuse and pain;
His only sin, being "A German."
He fought for German honor,
Suffered hunger and thirst in a dank cell.

On 10.20.24 in the restaurant "Mother Angel"
In Wiesbaden it was, where Piat, the French scoundrel!
Seized him, who with bold courage
Stood up for Germany, Munumé spoke well.

Yet Piat, the Special Commissar,
He had in truth one more victim!
They hit him hard, to the quick
But the German-Cameroonian suffered in silence, no blood

May he be a shining example to all,
In a land where Germanness is still considered holy.
His father too stood forty years ago,
Loyally helping the Germans in Africa-land.

He, son of a chief, scorned as a "boche,"
Is expected to kneel before French colors!
He did not do it, loyal to the death.
He knows only one thing, Germanness is the command.

Though his skin be black, as German born,
Chosen as an example for us "whites."
German man, German woman, your most holy duty,
Forget not Munumé from Cameroon.

He suffered for you too, he is well worth it.
Though he be homeless, you have hearth and home.
Support him well, the German man,
So that he can again rebuild anew.

There will once more come a day when the nation will need
Wilhelm Munumé, the German son.
He stands for German-Cameroon, he still wants to see again
German colors flying once more in Africa.

[Seht ihn Euch an, streng steht er
Wilhelm Munumé aus Duala.
Den haben Deutsche kultiviert
Drum hat auch Frankreich sein Deutschtum verspürt.

Dreißig Tage litt er Mißhandlung und Pein;
Seine einzige Schuld "Ein Deutscher" zu sein.
Er hat für Deutschlands Ehre gestritten,
Hunger und Durst in dumpfem Kerker gelitten.

Am 20. 10. 24 im Restaurant zur "Mutter Engel"
In Wiesbaden war's, da Piat, der Franzosenbengel!
Ihn stellte, der mit keckem Mut
Für Deutschland eintrat, Munumé sprach gut.

Doch Piat, der Spezial-Kommissar,
Er hatte ein Opfer mehr, fürwahr!
Man schlug ihn hart, wohl bis aufs Blut
Doch der Deutsch-Kameruner litt schweigend, kein Blut.

Als leuchtendes Vorbild sei allen bekannt,
wo noch Deutschtum heilig gilt im Land.
Auch sein Vater vor vierzig Jahren stand.
Treu helfend den Deutschen im Afrikaland.

Er, Häuptlingssohn, als Boche verschrien,
sollt' so vor französischen Farben sich knieen!
Er tat es nicht, getreu bis zum Tod.
Er kennt nur eins, Deutschtum ist Gebot.

Ist auch schwarz seine Haut, als Deutscher geboren,
so ward er uns "Weißen" als Vorbild erkoren.
Deutscher Mann, Deutsche Frau, Eure heiligste Pflicht,
Vergesset Munumé aus Kamerun nicht.

Er litt auch für euch, er ist es wohl wert.
Er heimatlos, ihr habt Heimat und Herd.
Unterstützet ihn gerne, den deutschen Mann
damit er von neuem aufbauen kann.

Es kommt einst ein Tag, da braucht die Nation
Wilhelm Munumé, den deutschen Sohn.
Deutsch-Kamerun vertritt er, er will es noch sehen,
Daß in Afrika Deutsche Farben einst wehen.]

Writing *in* German, Munumé is also writing *his* Germanness both in linguistic and semantic terms. "Germanness" is his "command"; he is "the German man" and "German born." Writing both in German and on Germanness can thus be conceived as an attempt to write himself (and a Black German subject of enunciation) into history and existence as well as into the nation. Such an identity claim, however, is in no way "authentic" or unproblematic, not even in the poem itself. Munumé writes about himself in the distancing third-person form, through the eyes of a collective white audience looking at an image, being permanently confronted with what we might describe in Fanonian or Du Boisian terms as the "gaze from the place of the other" ("*Look* at him").

Although this racializing visual regime affects him negatively ("*Though* his skin be black"), both Munumé's literary subject and his photograph counter this gaze with physical and mental strength ("he stands there *sternly,*" holding himself up as a "model" for whites). At the same time, it is precisely this "strength" that marks him as German—as becomes obvious in the French gaze that "senses" his "Germanness" immediately. Not only are Blackness and Germanness conceived as *not* contradictory ("Though his skin be *black,* as *German* born"), but Munumé's subject also blurs racial boundaries when he takes up a white point of view in the next, remarkable line: "Chosen as an example for *us* 'whites.'" Who is this "us," we might ask—or better: into what kind of collective is it *turned* when appropriated by Munumé? Is this shift articulating a moment of alienation or a transformation of both the subaltern subject and the nation? And why is "whites" marked, and thus put under erasure through quotation marks, and the blackness of his skin is not?

Munumé also makes references to German colonial history that seem to argue for the return of the former colonial masters. At the same time, this memory of German colonialism is linked to an experience of trauma and homelessness. He reminds his readers not to forget *him* and his suffering, yet he also reminds *them* of the German colonial past that uncannily returns through his diasporic presence like a revenant or specter ("Though *he* be homeless, *you* have hearth and home"). It is suggestive to read Munumé's literary rendering of his homelessness and assertion of belonging in the way Homi Bhabha understood Freud's notion of the *un-heimlich:* as a blurring of the boundaries that separate the familiar and unfamiliar, the "homely" and the "unhomely," center and periphery. It is this *un-heimlich* space or gap *in* which and *through* which Munumé enunciates an emerging Black German subject position. "The unhomely moment," as Bhabha writes about subaltern "literatures of recognition," "relates the traumatic ambivalences of a personal, psychic history to the wider disjunctions of political existence."[19]

The trial against Munumé and Makembe started in January 1927. The evidence collected by the police was damning but also revealing of how ingenious the two were. Although their white German business partners occasionally became suspicious, Munumé and Makembe finally succeeded in having 700 five-pound notes with a "Bank of England" imprint produced by a Berlin printer. Confronted with information provided by the Bank of British West Africa that there were no records of King Bondongulu, they played the anti-British card, arguing "that the British tried to thwart the independent action of the natives by any means necessary and simply denied the existence of King Bondongulu." It must have been their "elegant manners," the detective superintendent later assumed, that had enabled the two to get away with their lies so easily and to deceive the petty employees who had involuntarily become accessories to the crime.

Like Joan Riviere's phallic women who put on "womanliness as a masquerade"[20] to hide their power, Munumé and Makembe also knew how to wear the "mask of Blackness." At the printers where the counterfeit money was finally printed, Makembe performed a song-and-dance number with the effect, as the employee who did the job meekly stated in evidence, "of distracting me." During the trial, Munumé relied on similar strategies of returning the white gaze. Confronted with a witness who claimed to have recognized him as the person who had tried to trade in a fake note at an exchange booth, Munumé replied with a cheeky grin: "There are many Negroes in Berlin who look the same to a white person."

Munumé's and Makembe's tale, however, is not just about trickery or counterfeiting both money and discourses; it can also tell us something about solidarity and the diasporic relatedness of the Black community in Weimar Berlin. When these two tricksters could not refute the evidence brought against them during the trial, Munumé declared that they had acted on behalf of a Black seaman and that some of the items confiscated in his apartment belonged to a certain Ernest Banks, an international artist and actor who was traveling from country to country and had been a member of the "Chocolate Kiddies." This might appear to be simply yet another diversion in this already mysterious case, but there is strong evidence that Munumé and Makembe were not the lone operators they claimed they had been. Munumé's defense not only testifies to the transnational connections of Germany's Black community at that time and the importance Black seamen and traveling African American artists had in establishing such a communicative network across the "Black Atlantic," but the trial took place with the strong participation, as the *Berliner Börsen-Zeitung* put it, of "the Black compatriots" of the accused.[21]

Quite fascinating in this respect is an extremely enigmatic, coded letter written by Richard Ekamby, a Black German migrant who had just moved to Braunschweig, and addressed to Munumé and the "gentlemen of the Duala people in Berlin." Using language full of religious symbolism, Ekamby thanks the members of Berlin's Black community who had supported him during his stay and then declares that he is waiting for a sign for collective action: "I am also awaiting what is to come, to shed light on how things look in the distance. We all want to serve, if called upon. I want to help. This is good for us all, if we excel in goodness. If this happens, do send an update immediately."

Munumé and Makembe were found guilty and sentenced, respectively, to three years and one and a half years in Berlin-Plötzensee. But even in prison they would not cease to "agitate." Starting in January 1927, they wrote a series of petitions and pleas for clemency that are among the most interesting documents of Black German writing we have from that era. As addressees, Munumé and Makembe picked high-ranking politicians such as Field Marshall General Paul von Hindenburg and the chancellors Hermann Müller and Gustav Stresemann. Using the self-conscious tone of diplomatic negotiations, Munumé presented himself as a kind of politician and, as he put it, member of the Black "intelligentsia" who had always supported "German-Cameroonian cooperation" and worked for the "education of young German Negro citizens" ("*deutsche Negerbürger*").

The claim for citizenship, time and again, played a crucial role in his letters, and he expressed the issue repeatedly in formulations such as "*deutsche*

Neger Bürger" (German Negro citizens), "*Deutschneger*" (German Negroes) or "*deutsche Negerreichsbürger*" (German Negro citizens of the Reich). The construction of a counter-historical memory of the German colonial past was a central device in his endeavor. Munumé rhetorically referred to the greatness of German rule and the sacrifices Black German soldiers had made on the African battlefields, yet he also recounted colonial atrocities and the attempts of Black German "organic intellectuals" or, to use his own word, "academics" to sue representatives of the colonial administration in German courts, ranging from the famous case of Mpundo Akwa[22] to the interventions of Rudolf Duala Manga Bell and Ngosi Din. In a remarkable passage in his letter to Chancellor Müller, Munumé proudly relates the Black German struggle for recognition to a larger temporal and geographical framework of Black emancipation: "You will give us German Negro citizens complete equal rights, as the American president Abraham Lincoln did for his Negro citizens in 1862."

After Makembe's release from prison he was considered "stateless," and the German police attempted to deport him to Cameroon. But Makembe deserted the steamer during its stop in Rotterdam and returned to Berlin, again working as an actor. Having served his sentence, Munumé, like many other Black Germans in the early 1930s, entered into the German Communist Party's sphere of influence and delivered public speeches during the international campaign against the "legal lynching" of the "Scottsboro boys," linking the racism of the US legal system to his experiences in the colonies. Although we still do not know who Wilhelm Munumé and Peter Makembe really were, their tale might inspire us to seize hold of a memory of a Black German past "as it flashes up at a moment of danger."[23] But that is only one way of ending this messianic Black German trickster tale, which perhaps does not have an ending at all. In January 1932, after trading in counterfeit Canadian checks, two Black German men were arrested in Antwerp who claimed to be representatives of Haile Selassie I . . .

NOTES

1. Michelle M. Wright, *Becoming Black: Creating Identity in the African Diaspora* (Durham, NC: Duke University Press, 2004), 8.
2. Tina Campt, "Reading the Black German Experience: An Introduction," *Callaloo* 26, no. 2 (2003): 289–90.

3. Katharina Oguntoye, *Eine afro-deutsche Geschichte: Zur Lebenssituation von Afrikanern und Afro-Deutschen in Deutschland von 1884 bis 1950* (Berlin: HoHo Verlag Christine Hoffmann, 1997); Hans Werner Debrunner, *Presence and Prestige: A History of Africans in Europe before 1918* (Basel: Basler Afrika Bibliographien, 1979); Peter Martin, *Schwarze Teufel, edle Mohren: Afrikaner in Bewußtsein und Geschichte der Deutschen* (Hamburg: Hamburger Edition, 1993).
4. See my "Louis Brody and the Black Presence in German Film before 1945," in *Not So Plain as Black and White: Afro-German Culture and History, 1890–2000,* ed. Patricia Mazón and Reinhild Steingröver (Rochester, NY: University of Rochester Press, 2005), 109–35.
5. Gayatri Chakravorty Spivak, "Can the Subaltern Speak?," in *Marxism and the Interpretation of Culture,* ed. Cary Nelson and Lawrence Grossberg (Champaign: University of Illinois Press, 1988), 271–313.
6. W. E. B. Du Bois, *The Souls of Black Folk,* ed. Brent Hayes Edwards (Oxford: Oxford University Press, 2007), 8.
7. Walter Benjamin, *The Arcades Project,* ed. Rolf Tiedemann, trans. Howard Eiland and Kevin MacLaughlin (Cambridge, MA: Harvard University Press, 1999), convolute N 3, 4, 463.
8. Walter Benjamin, "Theses on the Philosophy of History," *Illuminations,* ed. Hannah Arendt, trans. Harry Zohn (New York: Schocken, 1969), 255.
9. Du Bois, 8.
10. See Giorgio Abamben, *Homo Sacer: Sovereign Power and Bare Life,* trans. Daniel Heller-Roazen (Stanford, CA: Stanford University Press, 1998). For Arendt's important analysis of "The Decline of the Nation-State and the End of the Rights of Man," see *The Origins of Totalitarianism* (San Diego: Harcourt Brace Jovanovich, 1973), 267–302.
11. Jacqueline Nassy Brown, *Dropping Anchor, Setting Sail: Geographies of Race in Black Liverpool* (Princeton, NJ: Princeton University Press, 2005), 42.
12. See also Andreas Selmeci and Dag Henrichsen, *Das Schwarzkommando: Thomas Pynchon und die Geschichte der Herero* (Bielefeld: Aisthesis, 1995), 28ff; Manfred Mahlzahn, "The Black Captains of Köpenick: A Story of 1920s Berlin," in *Berlin—Wien—Prag: Moderne, Minderheiten und Migration in der Zwischenkriegszeit,* ed. Susanne Marten-Finnis and Matthias Uecker (Bern: Lang, 2001), 91–106; Eve Rosenhaft, "Afrikaner und 'Afrikaner' im Deutschland der Weimarer Republik: Antikolonialismus und Antirassismus zwischen Doppelbewusstsein und Selbsterfindung," in *Phantasiereiche: Zur Kulturgeschichte des deutschen Kolonialismus,* ed. Birthe Kundrus (Frankfurt/M: Campus, 2003), 282–301.
13. For a film-historical assessment of the production and reception context, see my book *Die unheimliche Maschine: Rasse und Repräsentation im Weimarer Kino* (Munich: text + kritik, 2009), 479–520.
14. What I am referring to here is the gap between a projected "desire" for German rule based on fantasies of Black "lack" or inferiority that made former colonial subjects into the subjects and agents of colonial revisionism and identification

with German citizenship as a claim for rights and participation in the nation and its wealth.

15. "Gauner aus dem Mohrenlande," *Berliner Lokal-Anzeiger,* August 2, 1926.
16. Leroy T. Hopkins, "Zwei schwarze Unternehmer im Deutschland der Weimarer Zeit," in *Zwischen Charleston und Stechschritt: Schwarze im Nationalsozialismus,* ed. Peter Martin and Christine Alonzo (Hamburg: Dölling & Gallitz, 2004), 67–72.
17. Homi Bhabha, "Of Mimicry and Man: The Ambivalence of Colonial Discourse," in *The Location of Culture* (London: Routledge, 1994), 85–92.
18. Bhabha, "Signs Taken for Wonders," in *Location,* 119–20.
19. Bhabha, *Location,* 11.
20. Joan Riviere, "Womanliness as a Masquerade," in *Formations of Fantasy,* ed. Victor Burgin, James Donald, and Cora Kaplan (New York: Methuen, 1986), 35–44.
21. "Macombe und Munumé, die Abgesandten des Negerkoenigs Bondongulo," *Berliner Börsen-Zeitung,* January 23, 1927.
22. See Elisa von Joeden-Forgey, ed., *Mpunda Akwa: The Case of the Prince from Cameroon: The Newly Discovered Speech for the Defense by Dr. M. Levi, Münster* (Hamburg: Lit, 2004).
23. Benjamin, "Theses," 255.

6

Black Voices on the "Black Horror on the Rhine"?

CHRISTIAN ROGOWSKI

On May 24, 1921, an open letter titled "*Die deutschen Neger und die 'schwarze Schmach'*" (German Negroes and the "Black disgrace") appeared in the *Berliner Zeitung am Mittag*. The presence of Africans on German soil, in the context of the deployment of French colonial troops (primarily from North and West Africa) in the Rhineland in the wake of World War I, had triggered a vehement propaganda campaign against what the German press came to call the "*schwarze Schmach*" or "*schwarze Schande*" (Black disgrace).[1] This anti-Black propaganda inspired a degree of racially motivated resentment among white Germans that made life difficult for people of African descent living in the unoccupied parts of the country. Barraged with allegations that brute savages were marauding through the German heartland, the Berlin letter states, Germans were no longer willing to distinguish between the occupying African troops and "German Negroes," primarily subjects from Germany's erstwhile colonies in Africa, leading to acts of racially motivated violence against innocents: "Our appeal is occasioned by the following incident: about two weeks ago, one of our compatriots was assaulted on the street by passers-by and severely beaten up; the people had taken him for one of the Blacks from the occupied territory."[2] Written on behalf of the Afrikanischer Hilfsverein (African aid association), founded in 1918 in Hamburg as the first self-help organization for people of African descent living in Germany,[3] the letter was signed by Louis Brody.

Born in 1892 as Ludwig M'bebe Mpessa in Duala, then part of the German colony Cameroon, Brody had come to Germany in the 1910s and found employment in the film industry, quickly establishing himself as an actor in countless films.[4] Brody's letter exposes the contradictions underpinning German racial attitudes toward Black Africans in the context of Germany's sudden and involuntary decolonization. In particular, Brody addresses the *Askari* myth, the image of indigenous troops who helped General Paul von Lettow-Vorbeck remain undefeated in East Africa and whose bravery and loyalty were tirelessly cited as evidence of Blacks' alleged gratitude for the supposedly benevolent nature of German colonial rule:[5] "Besides, we have to remind the Germans that Lettow-Vorbeck did not conduct war in Africa on his own, but that indigenous people participated as well and risked their lives on behalf of the German flag."[6] In the wake of the empire's collapse, Brody points out, the achievements of indigenous people and their alleged loyalty to the German cause were erased, as all Blacks were portrayed as brute and uncontrollable savages. The emotionally charged climate of a "culture of defeat,"[7] riddled with hurt national pride, paranoid status anxieties, and self-pitying resentment, had occasioned in white Germans, Brody suggests, a racially charged reluctance to differentiate between very different people of African descent. To Brody, the Germans involved in anti-Black propaganda were unwilling or unable to consider Black Africans as subjects in their own right, as human beings with distinct personal stories and histories.

Brody's intervention raises the subject of Black responses to the propaganda campaign against what internationally became known as the "Black Horror on the Rhine"[8]—a campaign waged by various German government branches, numerous official and semiofficial organizations, and a range of groups and individuals across the political spectrum.[9] Simple as this subject may seem, it involves a plethora of methodological questions of both a conceptual and a practical nature. In what follows, I will briefly address these fundamental questions before discussing documents from the various Black constituencies potentially involved in responding to the "Black Horror" campaign. I will also note instances in which both adversaries in the conflict, the French as well as the Germans, employed—or seemed to employ—Black voices in what has been labeled a "memory war" (*guerre de mémoire*) following World War I.[10]

As concerns the Black constituencies involved in the constellation, we need to distinguish between at least four partly overlapping and interconnected groups. First, there are the French colonial troops who were directly targeted by the German propaganda efforts. Hailing from Northern and sub-Saharan West Africa (as well as Madagascar and Indochina), they were, for the most part—and somewhat disingenuously—lumped together indiscriminately as Blacks by the Germans.[11] The second group consists of Black Africans residing in Germany during the propaganda campaign. They became the targets of racist attacks fueled by the anti-Black fervor unleashed by the campaign. For reasons of space I will not be able to address two more groups that took an active interest in the debates: francophone African intellectuals and artists of the period (residing mainly in France), and representatives of the African American intelligentsia in the United States and the public sphere they defined within their own Black communities.

To what extent is it possible to assume a unified Black perspective on the issues raised by the anti-Black propaganda campaign even among and between the four, or more specifically two, groups identified above? How do these groups fit into the matrix of the "Black Atlantic,"[12] the constellation that tends to define Blackness for African Americans, the shared memory of the experience of forcible displacement, slavery, and racial oppression known as the Middle Passage?[13] Is the experience of forcible recruitment and deployment on foreign soil that the French colonial troops underwent comparable to the collective trauma of the Middle Passage? There is evidence that to a certain extent this may indeed be the case: suddenly removed from their families and their known environment without any sense of where they were heading, the West African recruits were often subjected to harsh discipline in the French military (including floggings and psychological abuse), disorientation (including fear of enslavement), and illness (due to exposure to harsh climate), not to mention the harrowing experience of trench warfare.[14] Yet, given the range of ethnicities and cultures and of historical and political circumstances surrounding the recruitment of various generations of colonial soldiers, are we perhaps succumbing to an "African mystique,"[15] constructing a false and essentializing sense of Black identity when we view very different sets of experiences through the unifying lens of the concept of a Black diaspora?

If the memory of the Middle Passage, or of its colonial partial analogue, is crucial to the self-definitions of people of African descent as Black, how do Black Germans, who shared neither the former nor, in most cases, the latter experience, fit into this overall picture?[16] Does the designation Black perhaps erase the numerous and complex differences between individuals and groups even among the various constituencies we seek to address? Is it legitimate to include among Blacks people from Northern Africa who may not define themselves as Black at all? Likewise, can we assume that the many different ethnic groups in sub-Saharan Africa would or did consider themselves Black? Or are we running the risk of blurring the same kinds of distinctions and differentiations that were erased in the German propaganda efforts aimed indiscriminately at the French colonial troops? In other words, are we perhaps replicating racist forms of discourse by using blanket terms such as Black when speaking of very different individuals and populations and very different sets of experiences? At the same time, we must respect the efforts of individuals who, during that period and later, sought to define a sense of selfhood and pride in their identity as Blacks precisely through recourse to the notion of a shared African heritage that crossed national, cultural, social, historical, and geographical borders. It is with these cautionary concerns that I proceed.

In attempting to reconstruct how the French African troops experienced the racist propaganda campaign directed against them, we encounter obstacles that are nearly impossible to overcome. To begin with, newspapers published in the occupied territories were heavily censored, as were newspapers brought in from unoccupied Germany. Black African troops deployed in the Rhineland did not, of course, speak German and were mostly illiterate, so they would not have read the accusations leveled against them even had such newspaper reports made it through. The *tirailleurs sénégalais* ("Senegalese riflemen"—the designation used for all West African troops, even those hailing from beyond the borders of Senegal proper) were usually segregated from the white French population and had long been kept separate from white French military units.[17] Moreover, as a rule the West African troops were taught only rudimentary French (so that they could follow the commands of their white French officers), meaning they had limited if any access to information appearing in the French press. Yet as early as October 1919, French authorities reported that their colonial troops took offense at being referred to as "*Neger*" (Negro) or "*Schwarzer*" (Black) by the Germans.[18] Whether the French here were reporting objections actually raised by the troops or whether they were primarily warning the German media to back off from racist discourse is not altogether clear. We know that even within the French colonial troops there existed a "racial hierarchy" of sorts, with North Africans from Algeria and Morocco eager to disassociate themselves from sub-Saharan Africans they considered racially inferior and "uncivilized."[19]

According to the official report of US General Henry T. Allen of the Rhineland High Commission, only about five thousand "Black" troops were stationed in the Rhineland, a tiny minority out of the more than one hundred thirty-five thousand French West African troops deployed in the European war theater.[20] Partly in response to the international echo generated by the onslaught of German protests, the French authorities actually withdrew most sub-Saharan African troops by the summer of 1920,[21] before the German propaganda campaign kicked into high gear. We must therefore assume that few of them actually became aware of the extraordinary venom that their presence on German soil unleashed in countless publications. Their experience of their German sojourn, it would appear, consisted mainly of encounters with the German civilian population.

While some Black soldiers certainly experienced racially motivated resentment in the Rhineland, there are no indications that relations between the Black African troops and the German population in the occupied territories were any worse than those involving white Frenchmen, although of course this varied according to local circumstances.[22] In the bishopric of Speyer, for instance, the troops from Madagascar were actually quite popular: mostly Christians, they worshiped alongside the Germans in the same churches.[23] In Worms, one of the places in which West African troops stayed the longest (until the end of May 1920, when they were withdrawn after a sojourn of over a year), only a few complaints of sexual assault or physical abuse involving Black soldiers were reported. The mayor of Worms, in an official report of June 1920, acknowledged that, on the whole, the African French soldiers had displayed "good discipline."[24] The intense propaganda pouring in from unoccupied Germany may actually have made things worse, inciting Germans to racially motivated acts of violence, such as assaults on Moroccans in Worms after the West African troops had left, which prompted the mayor to travel to Berlin in early June of 1920 in hopes of halting the German propaganda campaign.[25]

In their often haphazard efforts to refute German accusations of sexual mayhem and brutal savagery, French authorities frequently employed "Black" voices, sometimes with curious results. For instance, on May 31, 1920, the semiofficial daily in the occupied zone, *L'Écho du Rhin,* published a sarcastically titled piece, "Lettre d'un 'sauvage' donnant une leçon de civilisation aux Allemands" (Letter from a "savage" giving a lesson in civilization to the Germans), in which Domba Maoulé, a soldier from Niger, expresses shock over having witnessed Germans, men and women, bathing outdoors in the nude. The alleged letter, reproduced in the grammatically and orthographically faulty pidgin French known as *petit nègre* (enhancing the impression of authenticity), culminates in a proclamation of the writer's sense of modesty and propriety: Maoulé asks how the French can allow such scandalous behavior among the Germans that would be unthinkable in Niger.[26] In an intriguing twist, he accuses the Germans of sexual impropriety and the very lack of "civilization" they impute to the Black Africans.

French military authorities and the French press eagerly published pronouncements allegedly written by individual *tirailleurs*.[27] Since most West African soldiers were illiterate and knew little if any French, authorities would provide form letters that the soldiers "signed," often without knowing what the letters actually contained.[28]In these letters the soldiers profess their loyalty and gratitude to *la grande nation* and their amazement at the achievements of French civilization, such as electricity, trains, and indoor plumbing. They do not fail to mention the fair and benevolent treatment received from the white authorities: "We are doing fine in France: [we are] well lodged, well fed, and I am not bored: on the contrary, I am proud to belong to the army of the French, who are treating us just like the *toubabous* [white soldiers]."[29] Even if such prefabricated professions of patriotic fervor and military loyalty, aimed at convincing a domestic and international audience of the baselessness of the German charges, were made with the knowledge and consent of the colonial soldiers, they can hardly count as authentic testimonials. They are couched in the language of loyalty preformulated by the French authorities and do not give us a sense of the soldiers' lived experience. We have no access to their experience other than through multiple filters—linguistic, ideological, political, and cultural—since the *tirailleurs* had no political agency or any direct access to public media. Their situation is thus subject to the complex dynamics of subjugation and domination encapsulated by Gayatri Spivak in the famous question, "Can the Subaltern Speak?"[30]

Whatever public pronouncements the French colonial soldiers ostensibly made, such statements were instrumentalized according to a "paternalistic politics of acculturation"[31] to counteract the German charges, and emphasis was placed on the soldiers' adaptability and discipline and the progress they had made toward achieving European sophistication, turning them into examples of the success of the French "civilizing mission."

Thus the German propaganda stereotype of Blacks as "brute savages" was replaced with its opposite, a version of the "good savages" myth. French historian Jean-Yves Le Naour has argued that this infantilizing depiction of Blacks as "good children"—*grands enfants,* desexualized, obedient, and deprived of any agency—actually partakes, in inverse form, of the same racism the Germans deployed.[32]

If the French authorities instrumentalized "Black" voices in overtly positive terms, in the German media "Black" voices—or so it seemed—appeared in diametrically opposed fashion. Here, the focus was to show how much the French were allowing the savagery of their "Black" subjects to run rampant. In May 1923, for instance, the *Rheinischer Beobachter* featured a report titled "Across the Colony" by a certain Mohamed ben Mohamed, allegedly a soldier from Morocco, that featured sardonic comments on the "Africanization of the Rhineland" by the French. Released from four years of German captivity, the writer expresses his sense of delight, upon entering occupied Koblenz, to find "African conditions" pertaining there, where *boches* (the French derogatory term used for Germans) can no longer prevent him from defecating in the railway compartment as he pleases. Likewise, after indulging his sexual whims in the bordellos of Trier, where two of the six women who pressed charges against him ended up dead, he is looking forward to receiving the "Paris Medal of Culture." The author's homesickness is assuaged by the fact that the French have permitted him and his cohorts to set up their straw huts in the "boring squares" of the occupied German cities.[33] The article exhibits many characteristics of official German propaganda, disseminated by people like Alfred von Wrochem and Paul Rühlmann, that casts the French Rhineland occupation as a "colonization" of Germany.[34] With its vitriolic polemics, the article squarely appeals to white solidarity: Mohamed's account supposedly reveals that the French are breaching a basic civilizational contract by relegating a fellow European nation to the status of colonial subjects. Moreover, in evoking the specter of colonization, the article mobilizes deep-seated German racialized fears: if Germans are turned into colonial subjects dominated by Blacks, their status as whites is at stake.

Such racist diatribes are easily diagnosed as paranoid products of an incensed German propaganda machine. That judgment is not so easy in the case of *Die schwarze Welle* (The Black wave), a 1925 book bearing the imprint of a certain Afim-Assanga. Subtitled *Ein Negerroman* (A Negro novel), the book purports to be a translation of writings by a man from French Sudan who was forcibly recruited into the French colonial army. It describes how he worked as a forced laborer on the construction of a trans-Saharan railroad that was to link France's North African territories with its sub-Saharan colonies, giving ample opportunity to illustrate the extreme callousness and brutality France displayed toward its West African colonial subjects. During the final year of World War I, Afim-Assanga is deployed in the European theater, where he is wounded. After the war, he is assigned to join the French colonial troops that were to occupy the Rhineland in Germany (although his actual service there is not described).

Throughout the book, the first-person narrator employs extended interior monologues to chronicle the emergence of a Black militant consciousness in Samory, his protagonist. Samory, chief of the Mande tribe, is the son of the (historically real) rebel chief Almamy Samory Touré, whose successful military resistance to French colonial rule (prior to his defeat in 1898) had earned him the moniker the "African Alexander [the Great]."[35] Spurred by his experience of abuse and oppression and by his sexual desire for white women, young Samory comes to hate the French, and all whites, as "hereditary enemies of his race" (26) and begins to devise plans for an uprising: the newly established railway will help funnel African rebels into the European metropole, where they will launch a vengeful bloodbath. In establishing a transportation infrastructure in their colonies, the narrative suggests, the French are unwittingly providing their disgruntled colonial subjects with the means to undermine white supremacy and launch an all-out racial war.

Afim-Assanga's narrative is framed by four distinct types of text, all designed to lend an aura of authenticity. The first such framing device is an introduction by Fritz Oswald Bilse. Bilse introduces Afim-Assanga's text as a "*document humain* der schwarzen Rasse" ("human document of the Black race") (vi) and describes his role as editor and translator as that of fashioning a cohesive narrative out of often fragmented and incomprehensible jottings-down written in pidgin French (v). This allegedly reconstructed and streamlined narrative is followed by what purport to be excerpts from the translated transcripts, complete with gaps and conjectures regarding ostensibly illegible parts of the manuscripts. To further enhance the text's credibility, a note by a notary public from Regensburg, J. R. Dengler, reassures the reader that these excerpts indeed correspond to Afim-Assanga's manuscript. The whole thing is rounded off by an afterword titled "Tatsachen zur Negerfrage" (Facts on the Negro question), in which a certain Ludwig Schneyer points out that

Afim-Assanga's musings concerning the future of Black-white relations are sadly all too true: the book, Schneyer argues, confirms that France is frivolously endangering delicate racial hierarchies by including Africans in its military force and bringing them into the European theater. Schneyer registers stirrings of Black racial consciousness in moderates like W. E. B. Du Bois and René Maran, as well as a rising pan-African militancy in Marcus Garvey and South African Black nationalism, that—in conjunction with the disastrous influence of Islam and Bolshevism—will spell trouble for white supremacy. France's imprudent assimilationism puts bees into Blacks' bonnets concerning civic equality and political sovereignty. By giving Blacks access to potential positions of power, France will be responsible for unleashing the "Black wave" that threatens to engulf Europe in racial warfare. It is up to Germany, defenseless but vigilant, to shoulder the burden of "securing the future of the entire white race" in the heart of Europe (191).

Die schwarze Welle features a series of episodes bearing a striking resemblance to another famous "Negro novel," *Batouala: Véritable roman nègre* (1921) by René Maran from Martinique, which caused controversy in France due to its critical assessment of French colonialism.[36] Maran's novel (mentioned by Schneyer in his afterword) was the first work by a Black francophone author to receive the Prix Goncourt, the prestigious French literary award. The structural parallels may not be the only reason to doubt the authenticity of *Batouala*'s purported German "counterpart."[37] More important, perhaps, are numerous narrative and thematic inconsistencies in *Die schwarze Welle:* the first-person narrator seems to be oddly well informed about the people he encounters (their names, positions, backgrounds, ideas, etc.) and about political and historical facts beyond his immediate experience. Moreover, his comments often directly mimic main tenets and tropes of German anti-French and anti-Black propaganda. For instance, the narrator supposedly overhears French officials discuss the "real" objective of their colonial enterprise—to gain "hegemony over Europe" (21). Likewise, he describes a tribal wake at which the sacrifice of three former slaves leads to a cannibalistic orgy of "blood lust" (65). The novel contains numerous racist generalizations about the "Negro," with statements like: "Yet because Samory is a Negro, he is also immeasurably vain" (74). Afim-Assanga/Bilse's Samory is sexually licentious, insensitive to physical punishment, and politically hotheaded—quite in line with contemporary German anti-Black stereotypes. His militantly pan-African rhetoric of impending racial warfare, it would seem, directly echoes the German racist diatribes of Schneyer's afterword, rather than the other way around. The trope of "Black waves" of African soldiers that gives the book its title had already appeared in the revisionist World War I memoirs of German field marshall Paul von Hindenburg, *Aus meinem Leben* (From my life, 1920).[38]

Die schwarze Welle employs an ostensibly Black perspective to articulate German racialized fears associated with the emerging processes of potentially violent decolonization, and akin to the more general, gendered post–World War I fears analyzed by Klaus Theweleit in his famous *Male Fantasies*.[39] The book's particular historical and cultural interest in the context of the "Black Horror" controversy lies in how it instrumentalizes these racialized fears and turns them against France and its supposedly imprudent imperial politics. By purporting to let Blacks speak for themselves, the text claims to unmask the "real" racial dynamics underpinning the contemporary Franco-German conflict.

That both the French and the Germans would seek to enlist supposedly "authentic" Black voices in support of their cause may indeed attest to the significance both sides attributed to the "symbolic power of the African discourse."[40] But who, we must ask, could actually speak for the Black African troops themselves? The two main autobiographical records that chronicle an early-twentieth-century West African perspective sadly do not provide us with any information about the German sojourn of the *tirailleurs sénégalais*. The celebrated autobiographical novel *Force-Bonté* (1926), by Bakary Diallo from Dagana (Senegal), describes the author's military sojourns in Morocco and France, but Diallo was not deployed in the German occupation.[41] The posthumous two-volume autobiography by Amadou Hampâté Bâ from Mali, *Amkoullel, l'enfant peul* (1991) and *Oui, mon commandant!* (1994), chronicles his service in the French colonial authorities after World War I, but for health reasons Bâ was not recruited into the colonial army.[42] Thus neither account helps us reconstruct crucial aspects of "the lived reality of the war for the African masses whose perceptions of their experiences were never recorded."[43]

All the same, (some) Blacks never were entirely without agency or voice in the web of European colonial and imperial politics. The figure of Blaise Diagne, the first Black African deputy in the French National Assembly, illustrates the many ironies, tensions, and contradictions to which African efforts to advance Black African interests were subjected. Representing the four so-called *communes* of Senegal (coastal districts that enjoyed French citizenship, rather than status as colonies), Diagne played a major role in expanding and strengthening the French colonial *force noir* in the wake of initiatives proposed by General Charles Mangin. Diagne, a member of the privileged, educated colonial elite, advocated military service for his African cohorts in hopes that paying the "*impôt du sang*" ("blood tax") for France would help colonial Black Africans gain respect and recognition, eventually leading to full legal and civic rights of citizenship.[44] Diagne prevailed over the explicit objections of the Governor-General of French West Africa, Joost Van Vollenhoven, who feared that the colonial peasant societies would face economic collapse if thousands of young men, their most valuable labor force, were withdrawn, and who resigned in protest over the recruitment initiative.[45] In the spring of 1918, Diagne conducted a much-publicized tour through French West Africa, accompanied by considerable pomp and circumstance,[46] that resulted in the recruitment of some seventy-seven thousand Africans for the French war effort.[47] And in December 1918 it was Diagne who persuaded French prime minister Georges Clemenceau to deploy Black troops in the occupied Rhineland. Diagne hoped that the service of the Africans on European soil would enhance their status with the French authorities and considered it a prestigious assignment that would pay "symbolic homage" to the African troops.[48] Clemenceau initially objected—partly for fear that the Africans would not be able to handle the climate, partly because he was worried about a "revolt of the Germans."[49] Ironically, then, a Black African politician was at least partly responsible for the presence of West African troops on German soil and thus—in a sense—for the racist paranoia that ensued.

In 1920 Diagne vehemently opposed the withdrawal of the West African troops from the Rhine, demanding a full integration of the Black units into the French army on equal footing, or, if they were to be removed, the participation of other Allied armies in the occupation.[50] Not only did the French authorities reject such proposals, but they also failed to come up with effective strategies to combat the German propaganda onslaught. Frustrated by the half-hearted and uncoordinated French counterpropaganda efforts, Diagne in early 1922 demanded that an official report (with the findings of various international inquiries) be published and distributed to the entire world to exonerate his fellow Africans, yet his efforts came to naught.[51] Thus the private sector in France took the initiative. The Comité privé d'assistance aux troupes noires (Private committee for the support of Black troops) and the Société anti-esclavagiste de France (French anti-slavery society) collaborated on an extensive collection of materials refuting the German charges.

Compiled and edited by Camille Fidel, the lengthy brochure features an entire section on Black perspectives on the issue. Interestingly, alongside declarations by Black organizations from Belgium and the Netherlands and responses from the US African American community, Fidel reprints in full Brody's protest letter on behalf of Black Germans.[52]

The French antiracist publication thus places the intervention by Brody and the Afrikanischer Hilfsverein into the larger context of a nascent discourse on the Black diaspora in Europe and the United States. In Germany, people of African descent had indeed begun struggling to make their voices heard. On June 17, 1919, for example, Martin Dibobe, as the representative of Cameroonians residing in Germany, submitted a petition to the National Assembly convened in Weimar. The demands of the "32-Point-Paper" included full legal, political, and economic equality for colonial subjects under the terms of Germany's civil law code.[53] Not unlike the Allied delegates at the Versailles treaty negotiations who failed to respond to the interventions submitted by the first Pan-African Congress (held concurrently in Paris in 1919)on behalf of the future fate of the African colonies, the German politicians deliberating the constitution of the fledgling republic were clearly not ready to grant political agency to Africans or to listen to their voices: Dibobe's remarkable document, as well as a similar petition of June 27, 1919, to the Reich Colonial Office, was suppressed and not acted upon.[54] Only abbreviated versions were published, distorting and falsifying the petitions into former colonial subjects' professions of loyalty to the German metropole.

To the best of my knowledge, the letter by Brody and the Afrikanischer Hilfsverein is the only pronouncement protesting the "Black Horror" campaign on behalf of Africans residing in Germany to reach the German public. It is an important document of the emerging forms of self-organization by the Afro-German community in the twentieth century's first decades.[55] Not only does the letter ask Germans to differentiate between former colonial subjects now residing in Germany and the French colonial occupation troops; it also reminds Germans of the obligations they took on themselves in their African colonial venture. Their former colonial subjects, the letter notes, now find themselves in a legal and political limbo—treated by the Allied victors as Germans, they can't return to their respective homelands, yet at the same time the Germans view them as an unwelcome presence associated with national humiliation and defeat: "We therefore ask the Germans to consider that we suffer just as much as they do, and that they not treat us with condescension. In particular, we wish to emphasize that we are not an amoral and savage race, as is generally claimed in Germany at the moment."[56] Grammatically, it is not clear whether the "we" that seeks to challenge the notion of a "savage race" refers only to German Africans or whether it includes French Africans as well. While the letter tries to establish a clear distinction between "German Negroes" and the French colonial troops, it implicitly acknowledges that for most white Germans such a difference does not exist. The "we" thus both disavows and affirms a sense of a common Black identity, a paradoxical gesture that simultaneously rejects and accepts an identity imposed from without.

In a sense, then, the letter by Brody and the Afrikanischer Hilfsverein displays a peculiarly German inflection of the "double consciousness" Paul Gilroy has defined as a key characteristic of the "Black Atlantic." There is of course no guarantee that the text that appeared in the *Berliner Zeitung am Mittag* fully represents what was written or whether it was edited or altered in some way. But even in its existing form, the letter displays a remarkable awareness of the quite literally impossible subject positions imposed on Blacks in postwar Germany, as the country, following an enforced and involuntary decolonization, had suddenly become a "post-colonial state in a still-colonial world."[57]

In the Germany of the early 1920s, fraught with racialized tensions, Blacks had no real public forum to voice their concerns. Yet the racial hysteria fueled by the "Black Horror" campaign drastically impacted their lives. As Theodor Wonja Michael, son of Theophilus Wonja Michael of Cameroon (a signatory to the petition to the National Assembly at Weimar mentioned above), suggests, living conditions for Blacks in Germany before World War I were on the whole not bad: "Before World War I, it was . . . sort of a climate of being pampered. That was actually to change abruptly after World War I."[58] Theodor Michael and many other "racially mixed" children born in Germany in the 1920s were not recognized as Afro-Germans—that is, as Germans of part-African descent—but were assumed to be so-called Rhineland Bastards, the offspring of the French colonial occupation troops.[59] Michael notes that it was the "Black Horror on the Rhine" campaign that "led to an anti-Black atmosphere" in postwar Germany.[60]

The sense of endangerment and ambiguity that permeates the letter by Brody and the Afrikanischer Hilfsverein seems to mark the emergence of a diasporic consciousness, tentative and conflicted, among Blacks in Germany. Before the crisis engendered by war and defeat, the situation of Blacks in Germany differed from that of the "Black Atlantic" in that they had not been subject to forcible removal from their homelands and to slavery or military service abroad but had, like Martin Dibobe, Theophilus Wonja Michael, and Louis Brody, for the most part traveled voluntarily to the metropole for various forms of employment (for instance, in trade, diplomatic service, academia, or entertainment). The defeat of Germany, the collapse of its colonial empire, and the racial hysteria associated with the Rhineland occupation thrust the small Black African minority residing in Germany into a peculiarly postcolonial situation that showed marked similarities with the experience of displacement, disenfranchisement, and racially motivated discrimination to which Blacks were subjected elsewhere. Under the pressure of the "Black Horror" campaign and the racially motivated oppression it triggered, Blacks in Germany began to seek, however tentatively and modestly, a distinctly Black voice of their own in the public arena.

NOTES

This research was supported in part by a grant from the Amherst College Faculty Research Award Program, as funded by the H. Axel Schupf '57 Fund for Intellectual Life. I would like to thank Martin Klimke for help in obtaining some of the materials, Dick van Galen Last for valuable advice, and Manuame Mukasa for useful feedback.

1. See Dick van Galen Last, "Black Shame," *History Today* (October 2006): 14–21; Iris Wigger, *Die "Schwarze Schmach am Rhein": Rassistische Diskriminierung zwischen Geschlecht, Klasse, Nation und Rasse* (Münster: Westfälisches Dampfboot, 2007); Christian Koller, *"Von Wilden aller Rassen niedergemetzelt": Die Diskussion um die Verwendung von Kolonialtruppen in Europa zwischen Rassismus, Kolonial und Militärpolitik (1914–1930)* (Stuttgart: Franz Steiner, 2001).
2. Louis Brody, "Die deutschen Neger und die 'schwarze Schmach,'" *Berliner Zeitung am Mittag*, May 24, 1921.
3. Leroy T. Hopkins, "Race, Nationality and Culture: The African Diaspora in Germany," in *Who Is a German? Historical and Modern Perspectives on Africans in Germany*, ed. Leroy T. Hopkins (Washington, DC: American Institute of Contemporary German Studies, 1999), 1–31; Peter Martin, "Anfänge politischer Selbstorganisation der deutschen Schwarzen bis 1933," in *Die (koloniale) Begegnung: AfrikanerInnen in Deutschland 1880–1945: Deutsche in Afrika 1880–1918*, ed. Marianne Bechhaus-Gerst and Reinhard Klein-Arendt (Frankfurt/M: Lang, 2003), 193–206; Robbie Aitken and Eve Rosenhaft, *Black Germany: The Making and Unmaking of a Diaspora Community* (Cambridge: Cambridge University Press, 2013), 129–31.

4. Tobias Nagl, "Louis Brody and the Black Presence in German Film before 1945," in *Not So Plain as Black and White: Afro-German Culture and History, 1890–2000*, ed. Patricia Mazón and Reinhild Steingröver (Rochester, NY: University of Rochester Press, 2005), 109–35.
5. Stefanie Michels, "Askari—treu bis in den Tod? Vom Umgang der Deutschen mit ihren schwarzen Soldaten," in *AfrikanerInnen in Deutschland—Geschichte und Gegenwart*, ed. Marianne Bechhaus-Gerst and Reinhard Klein-Arendt (Münster: Lit, 2004), 171–86; Stefanie Michels, *Schwarze deutsche Kolonialsoldaten: Mehrdeutige Repräsentationsräume und früher Kosmopolitismus in Afrika* (Bielefeld: transcript, 2009).
6. Brody.
7. Wolfgang Schivelbusch, *The Culture of Defeat: On National Trauma, Mourning, and Recovery* (New York: Metropolitan, 2003).
8. Robert C. Reinders, "Racialism on the Left: E. D. Morel and the 'Black Horror on the Rhine,'" *International Review of Social History* 13 (1968): 1–28.
9. Keith L. Nelson, "The 'Black Horror on the Rhine': Race as a Factor in Post–World War I Diplomacy," *Journal of Modern History* 42, no. 4 (1970): 606–27; Gisela Lebzelter, "Die 'Schwarze Schmach': Vorurteile—Propaganda—Mythos," *Geschichte und Gesellschaft* 11 (1985): 37–58; Jean-Yves Le Naour, *La honte noire: L'allemagne et les troupes coloniales françaises, 1914–1945* (Paris: Hachette, 2003).
10. Marc Michel, *Les africains et la grande guerre: L'appel à l'afrique (1914–1918)* (Paris: Karthala, 2003), 233.
11. Alfred Guignard, "La propagande contre nos troupes indigenes," *Revue de France* 2, no. 6 (1922): 180–84.
12. Paul Gilroy, *The Black Atlantic: Modernity and Double Consciousness* (Cambridge, MA: Harvard University Press, 1993).
13. Maria Diedrich, Henry Louis Gates Jr., and Carl Pedersen, eds., *Black Imagination and the Middle Passage* (New York: Oxford University Press, 1999).
14. Joe Lunn, "Kande Kamara Speaks: An Oral History of the West African Experience in France 1914–18," in *Africa and the First World War*, ed. Melvin Page (London: Macmillan, 1987), 28–53; Joe Lunn, *Memoirs of the Maelstrom: A Senegalese Oral History of the First World War* (Portsmouth, NH: Heinemann, 1999).
15. Hazel Rowley, "A Sort of Homecoming," *Nation*, September 11, 2006, 46.
16. Tina Campt, *Other Germans: Black Germans and the Politics of Race, Gender, and Memory in the Third Reich* (Ann Arbor: University of Michigan Press, 2004).
17. Naija Aarim, "Colored Soldiers and Racial Formation in the Great War: French Racial Attitudes toward American Negro Troops and Algerian 'Tirailleurs,'" *Proceedings of the Annual Meeting of the Western Society for French History* 28 (2002): 283.
18. Bayerischer Staatskommissar, ed., *Die Pfalz unter französischer Besatzung von 1918 bis 1930: Kalendarische Darstellung der Ereignisse vom Einmarsch im November 1918 bis zur Räumung am 1. Juli 1930* (Munich: Süddeutsche Monatshefte, 1930), 56.
19. Le Naour, 172.
20. Martin Süß, *Rheinhessen unter französischer Besatzung: Vom Waffenstillstand im*

November 1918 bis zum Ende der Separatistenunruhen im Februar 1924 (Stuttgart: Steiner, 1988), 166; van Galen Last, 19.

21. Michel, 205.
22. Christian Koller, "Die 'Schwarze Schmach'—Afrikanische Besatzungssoldaten und Rassismus in den zwanziger Jahren," in *AfrikanerInnen in Deutschland,* 155–69.
23. Sally Marks, "Black Watch on the Rhine: A Study in Propaganda, Prejudice and Prurience," *European Studies Review* 13 (1983): 300.
24. Süß, 167.
25. Christian Koller, " 'Afrika am Rhein': Zivilbevölkerung und Kolonialtruppen im rheinischen Besatzungsgebiet der 1920er Jahre," in *Besatzung: Funktion und Gestalt militärischer Fremdherrschaft von der Antike bis zum 20. Jahrhundert,* ed. Günther Kronenbitter, Markus Pöhlmann, and Dierk Walter (Paderborn: Schöningh, 2006), 112.
26. Quoted in Le Naour, 173.
27. Hans-Jürgen Lüsebrink, " 'Tirailleurs Sénégalais' und 'Schwarze Schande': Verlaufsformen und Konsequenzen einer deutsch-französischen Auseinandersetzung (1910–1926)," in *"Tirailleurs Sénégalais": Zur bildlichen und literarischen Darstellung afrikanischer Soldaten im Dienste Frankreichs,* ed. Joachim Schultz and János Riesz (Frankfurt/M: Lang, 1989), 66.
28. L'Angely, "L'armée noire vue par les noirs," *Les annales coloniales* 38 (March 8, 1923): 1.
29. Ibid.
30. Gayatri Chakravorty Spivak, "Can the Subaltern Speak?," in *Marxism and the Interpretation of Culture,* ed. Cary Nelson and Lawrence Grossberg (Champaign: University of Illinois Press, 1988), 271–313.
31. Lüsebrink, 64.
32. Le Naour, 170.
33. Mohamed ben Mohamed, "Quer durch die Kolonie," *Rheinischer Beobachter* 2, no. 22 (May 27, 1923): 343.
34. Jared Poley, *Decolonization in Germany: Weimar Narratives of Colonial Loss and Foreign Occupation* (Oxford: Lang, 2005), 215–29.
35. Afim-Assanga, *Die schwarze Welle: Ein Negerroman,* ed. F. O. Bilse (Regensburg: Habbel & Naumann, 1925), 23. Subsequent references are given parenthetically in the text.
36. René Maran, *Batouala: Véritable roman nègre* (Paris: Michel, 1921).
37. Véronique Porra, *L'Afrique dans les relations francoallemandes entre les deux guerres: Enjeux identitaires des discours littéraires et de leur réception* (Frankfurt/M: IKO, 1995), 104.
38. Lüsebrink, 60.
39. Klaus Theweleit, *Männerphantasien Band 1: Frauen, Fluten, Körper, Geschichte.* (Frankfurt/M: Roter Stern, 1977); *Male Fantasies Volume 1: Women Floods Bodies History,* trans. Stephan Conway in collaboration with Erica Carter and Chris Turner (Minneapolis: University of Minnesota Press, 1987).

40. Porra, 259.
41. Bakary Diallo, *Force-Bonté* (Paris: Rieder, 1926).
42. Amadou Hampaté Bâ, *Amakoulell, l'enfant peul: Memoires* (Paris: Actes Sud, 1991); Amadou Hampaté Bâ, *Oui, mon commandant!* (Paris: Actes Sud, 1994).
43. Lunn, "Kande," 29.
44. Michel, 189.
45. Myron Echenberg, *Colonial Conscripts: The "Tirailleurs Sénégalais" in French West Africa, 1857–1960* (Portsmouth, NH: Heinemann, 1991), 44.
46. Described in vivid detail by eyewitness Bâ, *Amakoulell,* 353–57.
47. Werner Glinga,"Le tirailleur sénégalais: A Protagonist of African Colonial Society," in *Self-Assertion and Brokerage: Early Cultural Nationalism in West Africa,* ed. P. F. de Moraes Farias and Karin Barber (Birmingham, UK: University of Birmingham Centre of West African Studies, 1990), 151.
48. Marc Michel, "Colonisation et défense nationale: Le général Mangin et la force noire," *Guerres mondiales et conflits contemporains* 37 (1987): 38.
49. Michel, *Africains,* 205.
50. Le Naour, 179.
51. Guignard, 184.
52. Camille Fidel, ed., *Die Widerlegung des Beschuldigungsfeldzuges gegen die farbigen französischen Truppen im besetzten rheinischen Gebiet* (n.p.: n.d., ca. 1922).
53. Paulette Reed-Anderson, *Berlin und die afrikanische Diaspora/Berlin and the African Diaspora: Rewriting the Footnotes* (Berlin: Die Ausländerbeauftragte des Senats, 2000), 46–49. See also Stefan Gerbing, *Afrodeutscher Aktivismus: Interventionen von Kolonisierten am Wendepunkt der Dekolonisierung Deutschlands 1919* (Frankfurt/M: Lang, 2010).
54. Adolf Rüger, "Imperialismus, Sozialreformismus und antikoloniale demokratische Alternative," *Zeitschrift für Geschichtswissenschaft* 23 (1975): 1296; Aitken and Rosenhaft, 195–202.
55. Eve Rosenhaft, "Afrikaner und 'Afrikaner' im Deutschland der Weimarer Republik: Antikolonialismus und Antirassismus zwischen Doppelbewußtsein und Selbstfindung," in *"Phantasiereiche": Zur Kulturgeschichte des deutschen Kolonialismus,* ed. Birthe Kundrus (Frankfurt/M: Campus, 2003), 282–301; Martin.
56. Brody.
57. Marcia Klotz, "The Weimar Republic: A Postcolonial State in a Still-Colonial World," in *Germany's Colonial Pasts,* ed. Eric Ames, Marcia Klotz, and Lora Wildenthal (Lincoln: University of Nebraska Press, 2005), 135.
58. *Pagen in der Traumfabrik: Schwarze Komparsen im deutschen Spielfilm,* directed by Annette von Wangenheim(Westdeutscher Rundfunk, 2001).
59. John Kantara, "Schwarz sein und deutsch dazu," *Die Zeit,* April 23, 1998, 66; Reiner Pommerin, *Sterilisierung der 'Rheinlandbastarde': Das Schicksal einer farbigen deutschen Minderheit, 1918–1937* (Düsseldorf: Droste, 1979).
60. *Pagen.*

7

Black "Others"?

African Americans and Black Germans in the Third Reich

MARIA I. DIEDRICH

John A. Williams's novel *Clifford's Blues* (1999) follows the gay African American jazz musician Clifford Pepperidge through his thirteen-year internment in Dachau. One of the novel's defining themes is Clifford's interaction with Black Germans in the concentration camp, such as Dr. Nyassa, a man whose biography perfectly illustrates the intricacies of race in Nazi Germany: not only is he a biologist associated with the notorious Kaiser Wilhelm Institute in Berlin, where Hitler's race legislation was designed, but he is also, according to the racial terminology of the Third Reich, a "*Mischling*"[1] (half-breed), of Tanganyikan-German parentage—and, of fatal consequence, he is married to a white German. This, according to the Nuremberg laws, makes him a "race defiler" (58). In 1939 Pepperidge and Nyassa are joined by the adolescent Pierre Braun. Like Nyassa, the fourteen-year-old is a "*Mischling*"—the son of an African American soldier and a white German woman, one of the so-called Rhineland Bastards (170) whom the regime had submitted to compulsory sterilization in 1937. Though of totally divergent backgrounds and experiences, Pepperidge, Nyassa, and Pierre spontaneously connect *via* their Blackness and the victimization that comes with Blackness in Nazi Germany.

Williams's novel constructs a Black diasporic awareness that is more than the artificial product of an artificial camp situation. He works with images that signify continuity, hence a Black agency particular to Germany, moving the novel beyond the topos of paralyzing victimization. In the conversations between the men, who had never met before Dachau, names of Blacks in the United States and Germany are dropped almost matter-of-factly, evoking a Black diasporic network: there is the African American marine biologist Ernest Just from Howard University, who spent years at the Kaiser Wilhelm Institute in the thirties, until his marriage to Hedwig Schnetzler forced him into exile from what he had begun to embrace as his German haven from American racism;[2] there are memories of Sam Wooding and other jazz musicians touring Germany; and there are dreams of Harlem on Saturday nights, and of the Schwarz-Weiss Verein in Berlin. The prisoners share memories and information configured by their lives as Blacks in Germany, yet their conversation is not one among equals. In all matters pertaining to Black history and Black agency, both Dr. Nyassa and Pierre automatically defer to Clifford as authority, and Clifford in turn embraces this attitude as an expression of respect deriving from his vanguard position as African American in the Black diaspora and as African American sojourner in Europe.

Also published in 1999 was Hans J. Massaquoi's autobiography *Destined to Witness: Growing Up Black in Nazi Germany.* Massaquoi's father was a wealthy Liberian, his mother a white German nurse who remained in Germany with her son when their Liberian family returned to Africa in 1929. After an early childhood in Hamburg surrounded by affluence and protected by his grandfather Momulu Massaquoi's privileged status as consul general to the Weimar Republic, Hans not only was reduced to working-class poverty but also had to deal with being a mixed-race boy growing into young manhood during the Nazi terror. The Nazi regime denounced him as a "*Mischling*"—that is, as both a perversion of nature and a threat to German racial purity, since for the Nazis the mixed-race individual personified, as Tina Campt contends, the dreaded "dissolution of the distinction between whites and Blacks."[3]

Massaquoi's autobiographical narrative shares with Williams's novel the evocation of an atmosphere and racial setting in which life for Blacks was—and Clarence Lusane's *Hitler's Black Victims* confirms this point—relentlessly dangerous. Massaquoi's memoir diverges dramatically from *Clifford's Blues,* however, in that its protagonist's Hamburg is characterized by the absence of a Black diasporic consciousness, by the "lack of shared narratives of home, belonging, and community that," as Tina Campt puts it, "sustain so many other Black communities and on which they draw as 'resources' in numerous ways" (180). Massaquoi constructs himself as a lonely Black German child and adolescent who struggles to survive in a sea of overwhelming and viciously aggressive Aryanness.

Both narratives were published at the end of a decade in which the paradigms of the Black diaspora and the Black Atlantic dominated the ways in which the transnational Black experience was recovered and theorized by international scholarship. Yet that which members of that transnational Black trio can almost spontaneously and immediately rely on in Williams's African American novel surfaces only slowly, almost reluctantly, in Massaquoi's German memories, at fragmented moments within an experience of overwhelming non-connectedness. Massaquoi achieves a continuous diasporic identity only after the war, as a consequence of his encounter with African American GIs, his years in Liberia, and, ultimately, his emigration to the United States and his reinvention as an African American. Massaquoi leaves a Germany that, even after the war, continues to refuse him the still racialized title of German,[4] and he joins that Black diasporic elite which W. E. B. Du Bois in his "Conservation of Races" (1897) had celebrated as the "advanced guard of the Negro people."[5] In so doing, Massaquoi not only acquires a new nationality and community but also implicitly affirms the hierarchy defining this Black diasporic realm.

As my point of reference for my analysis of African American–Black German interactions and their representations during the Third Reich, I will relocate Williams's and Massaquoi's texts within the historical context they evoke. I will use them as a starting point for my attempts to recover the context and reconnect them to the African American narratives of the thirties and forties that reflect on direct interactions of African Americans with Germany during this crucial period in African American and Black German history. My analysis is based on autobiographical and biographical writings, correspondence, and journalism by Marian Anderson, Josephine Baker, Horace R. Cayton, W. E. B. Du Bois, Langston Hughes, Ernest E. Just, Claude McKay, Alain Locke, Jesse Owens, Paul Robeson, John Welch, and others, and my focus will be on the Black diasporic discourse of these texts. The question I raise is not just how the experience of Black Germans / Blacks in Germany relates to that of other Black diasporic populations all over the world (Campt 68), but how members of the most visible and audible Black diasporic community—that is, African Americans, who regard themselves as the diasporic vanguard—reflect on and represent this Black German experience.

Whether we read reports or letters and diaries written while the correspondent was living or traveling in Germany, like Du Bois's in 1936 and Just's throughout the 1930s, or retrospective accounts like Anderson's, Baker's and Cayton's autobiographies and Welch's autobiographical reports for the *Pittsburgh Courier,* what unites the texts is a sense of dread at Hitler's assumption of power, at the Nuremberg laws, at political and racial persecution, and especially at the deadliness of German anti-Semitism. What also unites them, however, is that, as they deplore the ferocious racial policy implemented in the German nation under—or rather, in collaboration with—Hitler, Black Germans or Blacks in Germany are curiously absent.[6] The authors, to a person, evoke an African American sojourner in a Germany they define as white.

This absence of German Blackness from African American narratives is stunning in a historical situation in which Black diasporic awareness permeated the African American media. Beginning in 1919, several Pan-African congresses were staged in major European cities and New York—congresses devoted, as Paul Gilroy argues, to the "dream of a global co-operation among peoples of colour."[7] These international gatherings propagated a vision of Black diasporic relations that were global in scope. African American activists like Du Bois played defining roles in these congresses, and they saw to it that the Black diasporic dream was widely advertised in the African American press. In 1929 the Caribbean writer Claude McKay celebrated this Black diasporic awareness in his novel on Black life in Marseille, *Banjo.*

Since the 1880s, the African American press also had regularly reported on German anti-Black racism—racial policy in Germany's African colonies, the Herero genocide, the racially defined and internationalized "Horror on the Rhine" scare launched by a defeated Germany, the jazz ban and the degenerate art campaigns of the early thirties. In December 1934 Paul Robeson, disgusted at the racial violence he had witnessed during a visit to Germany, publicly renounced his plans to work with Max Reinhardt, and Josephine Baker eventually joined the French Resistance for the same reasons. Yet despite the availability of this information, the public outcry against the implementation of the Nuremberg laws did not result in the African American media or African American intellectuals undertaking a systematic analysis of the systemic quality of German anti-Black racism. It failed to lead to readings that would connect the Herero murder, the "Rhineland Bastards," and the "degeneration" of culture issues and thus arouse concern for the fate of Black Germans under this regime. In fact, the warning voices were balanced, if not silenced, by individual public voices like those of Locke, Du Bois, and Welch, who continued to compare their personal experiences as African Americans in Germany to their everyday lives in the United States—and found life in the United States deficient, relentlessly dangerous, and humiliating.

African American travelers to Germany in the thirties spent most of their time in cities like Berlin, Dresden, Düsseldorf, Frankfurt, Hamburg, and Munich. It was in these urban centers that they must have come across other Blacks staying in Germany: African diplomats, churchmen, scholars, businesspeople; African American scholars, entertainers, and artists; sailors from around the globe; and, finally, Black Germans. Photography of the period shows African American and African musicians, artists, and sailors interacting, and later Black GIs and Black Germans like Massaquoi in the German theater (Campt 3). Yet none of these Blacks made it into African American narratives as individuals or as a group; none of these encounters triggered the question of what would happen to this (unacknowledged) Black non-community in a fiercely racialized country that Horace Cayton, on his first trip to Germany in 1933, decried as an "armed camp of madness,"[8] and that the Robesons, on their last German sojourn before the war, experienced as that "terrible feeling of wolves waiting to spring."[9]

In attempts at explaining this Black German absence in the African American discourse on Germany, the most obvious cause tends to be forgotten: just as there was no Black community in Germany but merely "a diverse group" of Blacks who came "from a wide range of class, ethnic, geographic, and even historical backgrounds,"[10] there was no Black German community in the United States, no audible Black German voices who could have told the Black German story as insiders. Afro-Caribbeans in the United States, African students at historically Black colleges, and African American missionaries to British West Africa guaranteed that the Black community in the United States received a continuous flow of information on Black life in those territories and remained focused on events there. This kind of powerful institutional connection, the physical presence of a considerable number of people who could and would speak up with authority based on experience, was lacking for Black Germans in the United States. They had no voice of their own to tell their story and instead had to rely on African Americans to speak for them, but there were no volunteers.

In 1936 W. E. B. Du Bois spent six months in Germany on a research visit funded by the Oberlaender Trust, an institution founded by the German American Nazi sympathizer Gustav Oberlaender.[11] The weekly reports Du Bois published in the *Pittsburgh Courier* under the heading "Forum of Fact and Opinion" are representative of the absentee discourse that permeated the narratives of those African Americans who entered Nazi Germany in those years. In these columns he constructs himself as a solitary and privileged African American traveler and scholar and, as a consequence of this very definition of self, claims objectivity for himself and his reporting, along with the authority that comes with a respectable personal German biography. Sojourning in a country seething with anti-Semitism and under the lash of the secret police, he portrays himself as interacting constructively with a Germany that is represented as all white. He repeatedly stresses that he personally encountered no racism whatsoever, and that the race prejudice he observed "is not instinctive prejudice."[12] He records no incidents of anti-Black violence, and the only example of anti-Black discrimination is relegated to the periphery.

Du Bois's reluctance to face up to the genocidal racial politics of the Third Reich was no doubt rooted in his special relationship to Germany and German culture dating back to his student days at Berlin's Kaiser Wilhelm University. This scholar's love affair would be replicated by the philosopher Alain Locke and by Ernest Just. The cautious maneuvering of these prominent African American intellectuals throughout the thirties illustrates how easy it was for privileged individuals to become entangled in the dramatically shifting German landscape of the day, where, as Locke's biographer Jeffrey Stewart maintains, "what looked good is suddenly murderously bad."[13] Their writings pay testimony to the power and tenacity of the dream world people construct for themselves as a survival strategy.

Even after returning to the United States in 1937, Du Bois would insist in an interview with the *New Yorker Staats-Zeitung und Herold,* a German-language newspaper, that Blacks in Germany do "not yet face any traces of racial hatred."[14] But who are the "*Neger*" (Negroes) Du Bois evokes in the interview? Is he talking about African Americans, African nationals, Black Germans? We just don't know, for they are almost invisible in his *Pittsburgh Courier* editorials, and in this interview they merge into that anonymous, faceless Blackness in Germany that to the African American observer still appeared unthreatened.

There is one brief reference to anti-Black policy in the *Pittsburgh Courier* columns, however, that might serve as yet another key to our decoding of Du Bois's silencing strategy. Almost in passing, he mentions that "in public dance halls and in the half-world Negroes must be welcomed with care and secretly; police spies would quickly suppress any open commerce."[15] Nazi policy, he admits in this one instance, targets Blacks and tries to exclude them from establishments where people socialize spontaneously and potentially intimately. Yet his report's focus is not on this German policy of racial discrimination but on its ultimate failure—that is, on the German defiance that surfaces in the formulation "must be welcomed with care and secretly." Despite the danger, he insists, Blacks are indeed welcomed by both the owners of the establishments and their customers. Du Bois's "must be welcomed" formula thus stands for a subtle and strategic argumentative move in which he implicitly dissociates the Nazi official from the German everyman. Through this rhetoric of dissociation he can continue to embrace the German *Volk* as potentially and slyly anti-Nazi while relegating Hitler and his henchmen to the realm of the not-representative, the non-German, which he then rejects unconditionally. The episode is transformed into a self-legitimating discourse for his German sojourn and for his love of a German *Volk* and culture that he can thus continue to celebrate as uncontaminated by Nazi ideology.

There is a second, equally disturbing subtext to this episode. Again, as in the *Staats-Zeitung* interview, Du Bois's construction of the "*Neger*" remains anonymous, faceless, while class and social geography move center stage. In a meticulous analysis of this episode, Werner Sollors contends that, by using the word "half-world" in this context, Du Bois implicitly associates the raids against Blacks in Germany with the criminal milieu. Thus relegating the Black customers of these establishments, the victims of this exclusionary policy, to the social periphery, Du Bois implicitly legitimizes the police activities as moves that are beyond race. In this episode, he speaks not as the African American intellectual but as the American bourgeois observer of low life. His distancing gesture becomes expressive of that "game of one-upmanship based on stigmatizing certain sectors of society," of that refusal "to forgo his bourgeois bias against the working class," that Michelle M. Wright has also diagnosed in her pertinent reading of the "On Being Crazy" in Du Bois's *The Souls of Black Folk*.[16]

That bourgeois bias and cultural snobbery could be at the core of Du

Bois's (non)rendering of the Black German experience is further suggested by yet another remarkable omission from his reports. He was traveling a country where the Nazi Party's daily newspaper, *Völkischer Beobachter,* had triumphantly announced the ban on n****r jazz in radio.[17] The Nazi Party, supported by powerful segments of the media, had also launched fierce campaigns against "Degenerate Art" featuring grotesquely racialized images of American Blacks and Jews. Neither campaign made it into Du Bois's columns, nor does he mention any of the Blacks—mostly African Americans—in the German entertainment industry who were targeted by such campaigns. As his scathing criticism of primitivist elements in Claude McKay's 1928 novel *Home to Harlem* testifies, Du Bois refused to associate—and especially refused to be associated—with a milieu he defined as "half-world," and he was reluctant to move outside the elitist social geography he claimed and embraced as his birthright.

In this respect, the Du Bois of 1936 seems to be representative of many African American travelers to Europe who simply enjoyed the privileged position they occupied for the preciously limited time in which they were physically removed from everyday American racial harassment. Omitting Black Germans / Blacks in Germany as potential targets of the Nazis' genocidal theory and praxis from their personal narratives can thus also be read as self-protective: they claim for their individual selves, for this one sojourn, the right to a "vacation," however brief and precarious, from the cruelly racialized American experience. Tina Campt suggests that it is legitimate to read this discourse of absence as an illustration of that "excess of meaning" that Lyotard in *The Differend* identified as the ultimate definer of silence.[18] A cacophony of conflicting motives and objectives not only precluded the interaction of these visitors with the majority of African American entertainers in Germany, as well as with Black Germans, but also prevented analysis and critique of this intricate relationship in their narratives.

The hierarchy between the privileged African American traveler to Germany and the Black German subject, which in this specific German context surfaces as class hierarchy and social bias, can also be identified as operating on a larger scale, in the hierarchical and even hegemonic relationship between African Americans and other members of the Black diaspora that Tina Campt identifies in *Other Germans.* Deciphering "asymmetries of power that exist across and between different Black communities and the very different relationships to diaspora that arise as a result," Campt critiques "the telling role ascribed to Black America," along with the "frequent citation of Black America" in the discourses of the Black diaspora and the Black Atlantic as "an almost privileged site or referent in the trajectory of diasporic cultural, community, and identity formation." She argues that the diasporic discourse emerging from these constructions of an African American exceptionality "refers not so much to a relation of equity than of hegemony" (177–78).

This hegemony permeates the representational strategies that were employed in the African American encounter narratives and the African American media in their reporting on anti-Black German racism and violence. Whether they deplore the slaughter of the Herero people or the tragic fate of the "Rhineland Bastards," the emphasis is on Black victimization and pathology rather than agency, on a victimized Black "Other" in Africa and Europe. This again implicitly and automatically constructs the African American as a model of defiance associated with self-empowerment and agency. African Americans reconfigure themselves as "the vanguard of the Black race, the people most qualified to lead Africa and other members of the diaspora to freedom and prosperity"[19]—Du Bois's "advanced guard of the Negro people."

This hegemony also surfaces in the homogenized "*Neger*" in Du Bois's *Pittsburgh Courier* columns and in his 1937 *Staats-Zeitung* interview, and it dominates John Welch's German reports for the *Pittsburgh Courier* as late as April 1944. The former jazz musician and journalist came to Germany in 1932 as a student and for the next twelve years lived and worked as a musician in Nazi Germany. In his first *Pittsburgh Courier* article he insists: "So far as the Negro in Germany is concerned, it would be unfair to state that he has to suffer to any considerable degree through Hitler's endorsement of racial prejudice." Welch published this statement after he had suffered months of "internment in Bavaria."[20] On the one hand, this all-inclusive positioning of "the Negro in Germany" empowers Blacks in Germany / German Blacks by including them in the larger framework of the Black diaspora subtly promising the watchful solidarity of the more sophisticated African American avant-garde with their fate as fellow Blacks within this paradigm. On the other hand, it "others" these Black Germans: neither Du Bois's nor Welch's text, in its deindividualizing construction of "the Negro," pays tribute to the diversity, complexity, and intricacies that characterize the Black experience in Germany. Perhaps even more importantly, neither reflects critically on the implications of this specific German diversity for African Americans within a larger Black diasporic relationship. Consequently, it becomes almost impossible for these African American sojourners to fully explore what Paul Spickard termed the specific "racial or ethnic dynamics" in the Third Reich "in that place's own terms."[21]

If we look at the records of the period, it seems we can identify only one area in which anything like a Black diasporic connectedness in the African American–Black German context emerges: athletics. For Massaquoi, who reconstructs a childhood characterized by the absence of Black community and memory, the initial boxing match between Joe Louis and Max Schmeling in June 1936 becomes the first instance in which he experiences a sense of Black diasporic connectedness and Black pride. This feeling is almost imposed on the reluctant ten-year-old Hans, who admits to having been a Schmeling fan, by his white German pals. They fuse the German Hans and the African American "Black Bomber" through a strategy of racial "othering" when they insist that Joe Louis "looked exactly like me." Hans appropriates the white German boys' racial "othering" and transforms it into an empowering act of Black self-identification when he embraces a Blackness that suddenly represents strength, skill, and masculinity rather than peripheral inferiority: "It felt wonderful to note the respect accorded to a black man by people who normally felt superior to blacks, and have some of that respect rub off on me. I hadn't enjoyed that feeling of pride in my African ancestry since my grandfather left Germany six years earlier."[22] This sense of belonging and racial bonding does not evaporate with Joe Louis's defeat, and it is there for Hans to rely on when he attends the Berlin Olympics: "Unlike my original feelings towards Joe Louis and Max Schmeling, I never was torn by conflicting loyalties between the black Olympic athletes and the athletes of my motherland. . . . It was clear to me that the black athletes' victories were my victories, that their defeats were my defeats. I immediately felt a surge of pride over the very special kinship that linked me with these men from America."[23] The awareness that the extreme racialization of sports in the Third Reich and in the United States might result in Black diasporic bonding was also expressed in Goebbels's press directive of August 3, 1936: "The racial point of view should not be used in any way in reporting sports results; above all Negroes should not be insensitively reported."[24] But how dynamic, how interactive within the African American–Black German context was that bonding over the Louis-Schmeling matches and the Olympic triumphs?

Lusane documents the African American press's almost unanimous support for the boycott movement against the Olympics following Hitler's accession to power and the Nuremberg laws.[25] They vigorously protested the exclusion of athletes on the basis of race in Nazi Germany and in the United States—Jewish athletes in Germany, and African American and Jewish athletes in the United States. They also warned that African American athletes' safety could not be guaranteed in a Germany that was so brutally racialized. This boycott movement evaporated when leading Black athletes like Jesse Owens, Ralph Metcalfe, and Eulace Peacock opted for participation, arguing that Black victories would serve as the most powerful repudiation of Nazi and US racial theories and practices. The triumphant success of these athletes in Berlin, and the racial pride that surged through the African American community and through those Black Germans whose testimony we possess, proved them right, and even the German media could not help paying tribute to their victories. So much, indeed, that Du Bois, who was in Germany at the time, praised the German press reports for the *Pittsburgh Courier:* "Jesse Owens was lauded and pictured and interviewed. . . . He is without doubt the most popular single athlete in the Olympic Games of 1936."[26] However, neither during the boycott nor when they celebrated Blackness triumphant in Berlin did the African American media raise issues concerning the fate of Black German athletes like Louis Brody-Alcolson / Louis M'bele Mpessa. Were they still able to train for the Olympics in German sports clubs that had banned Jews, Sinti, and Roma? Could they claim membership on the German Olympic team? After all, most had become "*staatenlos*" (stateless) with the Reich Citizenship Law of November 1935. Would they be safe in a country that defined "*Negerblut*" (Negro blood) as non-Aryan and alien?[27]

The absence of these questions from contemporary African American press reports on the Olympics and from interviews, memoirs, and biographies of the participating African American athletes reveals that the relation between African American and Black German participants in the Black diasporic space was still hegemonic. Subsumed under the hegemonizing and generalizing designation "Negroes in Germany," Black Germans in these African American narratives of the German thirties and forties are relegated to a diasporic periphery at best. Consequently, they are denied representation as victims or potential victims of German anti-Black racism, and their specific struggles "go overlooked" (Campt, 189). This representational strategy leaves the exceptionality of the African American experience firmly intact and moves that African American experience center stage within the international Black diaspora.

At the same time, Du Bois's "not yet" formula and Welch's denial that Black Germans / Blacks in Germany suffer "to any considerable degree" show that the African American representation of German anti-Black racism is primarily a strategic one. It focuses less on race in Germany than on the racial situation in the United States and, as Michelle Wright argues in her brilliant reading of identity constructions in the African American diaspora, is firmly rooted in national rather than diasporic frames of reference and their by-definition exclusionary practices.[28] Du Bois's and Welch's insistence that they personally never suffered from German racism reveals the hypocrisy of the (white) American public outcry against the racial implications of the Nuremberg laws and especially German anti-Semitism. Du Bois spelled out this programmatic core of his argument when he lectured at the end of his German sojourn: "It would have been impossible for me to have spent a similarly long time in any part of the United States, without some, if not frequent cases of personal insult or discrimination. I cannot record a single instance here."[29] Welch, after months of internment in Bavaria, and after suffering through the reluctant efforts of the US State Department to liberate African American detainees,[30] reminds his readers in no uncertain terms that there "are certain whites in the South who would look forward with joyful anticipation at duplicating Hitler's process of elimination. The cruellest and most fanatical hatred of the Jew is no greater than that hatred which these people harbour toward the Negro."[31]

Du Bois and Welch, in concert with many other African American voices of the day, unmasked a white American anti-German discourse that merely cast a veil over what Charles W. Mills defines as a universal white racial contract[32] from which Black people all over the world suffered, and which African Americans were experiencing on a daily basis. This was true even during the war years, as illustrated by a headline in the April 8, 1944, edition of the *Pittsburgh Courier* reading "German Prisoners Ate In Station Dining Room In Texas, While Negro Soldiers Were Forced To Accept 'Kitchen Hand-Outs.'" In "Beaumont to Detroit: 1943," Langston Hughes confirmed: "You tell me that hitler / Is a mighty bad man. / I guess he took lessons / From the ku klux klan."[33]

NOTES

1. John A. Williams, *Clifford's Blues* (Minneapolis, MN: Coffee House, 1999), 58. Subsequent references are given parenthetically in the text.
2. Kenneth R. Manning, *Black Apollo of Science: The Life of Ernest Everett Just* (New York: Oxford University Press, 1983), 238–324.
3. Tina Campt, *Other Germans: Black Germans and the Politics of Race, Gender, and Memory in the Third Reich* (Ann Arbor: University of Michigan Press, 2004), 76. Subsequent references are given parenthetically in the text.
4. Heide Fehrenbach, *Race after Hitler: Black Occupation Children in Postwar Germany and America* (Princeton, NJ: Princeton University Press, 2005), 1–45.
5. W. E. B. Du Bois, "The Conservation of Races" (1897), *The Oxford W. E. B. Du Bois Reader,* ed. Eric J. Sundquist (New York: Oxford University Press, 1996), 42.
6. Clarence Lusane, *Hitler's Black Victims: The Historical Experiences of Afro-Germans, European Blacks, Africans, and African Americans in the Nazi Era* (New York: Routledge, 2003), 63–64.
7. Paul Gilroy, *The Black Atlantic: Modernity and Double Consciousness* (Cambridge, MA: Harvard University Press, 1993), 126.
8. Horace R. Cayton, *Long Old Road* (New York: Trident, 1965), 228.
9. Peter Martin and Christine Alonzo, eds., *Zwischen Charleston und Stechschritt: Schwarze im Nationalsozialismus* (Cologne: Dölling und Galitz, 2004), 319.
10. Michelle M. Wright, *Becoming Black: Creating Identity in the African Diaspora* (Durham, NC: Duke University Press, 2004), 194–95.
11. Werner Sollors, "W. E. B. Du Bois in Nazi Germany, 1936," *Amerikastudien/American Studies* 44, no. 2 (1999): 209.
12. W. E. B. Du Bois, "Forum of Fact and Opinion," *Pittsburgh Courier,* December 19, 1936.
13. In conversation with Maria I. Diedrich.
14. "Farbiger bereist Nazi-Deutschland," *New Yorker Staats-Zeitung und Herold,* January 29, 1937. The German reads: "Die Behandlung der Neger zeigt, wie Dr. Du Bois sich ausdrückt, 'noch keine Spur von Rassenhaß.' "
15. *Pittsburgh Courier,* December 19, 1936.
16. Wright, 78.
17. Martin and Alonzo, 269; "Verbot des Niggerjazz im Rundfunk," *Völkischer Beobachter,* Berliner Ausgabe, No. 286, October 13, 1935, 5.
18. Jean-François Lyotard, *The Differend: Phrases in Dispute,* trans. Georges Van Den Abbeele (Minneapolis: University of Minnesota Press, 1988), 16.
19. John Cullen Gruesser, *Confluences: Postcolonialism, African American Literary Studies, and the Black Atlantic* (Athens: University of Georgia Press, 2005), 18.
20. John Welch, "I Lived 12 Years under Hitler," *Pittsburgh Courier,* April 22, 1944.
21. Paul Spickard, ed., *Race and Nation: Ethnic Systems in the Modern World* (New York: Routledge, 2005), 5.

22. Hans J. Massaquoi, *Destined to Witness: Growing Up Black in Nazi Germany* (London: Fusion, 2001), 91–92.
23. Massaquoi, 97.
24. Lusane, 225.
25. Lusane, 119–20, 222–26.
26. W. E. B. Du Bois, "Forum of Fact and Opinion," *Pittsburgh Courier,* October 17, 1936.
27. Lusane, 103–9.
28. Wright, 229–31.
29. W. E. B. Du Bois, "Forum of Fact and Opinion," *Pittsburgh Courier,* December 5, 1936.
30. Lusane, 155–59.
31. John Welch, "I Lived 12 Years under Hitler," *Pittsburgh Courier,* May 6, 1944.
32. Charles W. Mills, *The Racial Contract* (Ithaca, NY: Cornell University Press, 1997).
33. Langston Hughes, "Beaumont to Detroit: 1943," *Common Ground,* Fall 1943, 104.

8

The Motion of Stillness

Diaspora, Stasis, and Black Vernacular Photography

TINA CAMPT

I. Sta·sis:

1. an act or condition of standing or stopping
2. a state of static balance or equilibrium among various forces

Stasis. Stillness? Lack of movement? The cessation or suspension of development or change? Thinking this term in relation to Black European and African diaspora studies more broadly, what might it mean to theorize the politics of diasporic formation through the critical lens of *stasis?*

In *Embodying Black Experience: Stillness, Critical Memory, and the Black Body* (2010), Harvey Young delivers a provocative theory of diasporic formation that challenges us to rethink dominant emphases on movement, migration, and mobility as the primary constitutive forces of the African diaspora. Acknowledging that the forced and voluntary displacements initiated by the Middle Passage and the Atlantic slave trade remain crucially relevant points of departure for understanding Black diasporic communities transnationally, Young proposes a shift in orientation that, I would argue, is at the same time a fundamental shift in vision.

The alternative analytic Young's work proffers is disarmingly simple: an exploration of *stillness.* Examining the implications of the ways in which Black bodies stood still—the ways they were forcibly made immobile or remained willfully stationary—is, for Young, a method of recovering Black bodies from a dissipation that results from an emphasis on their relentless movement and dispersal. As Young explains, "*stillness,* like movement and the body, is an integral and defining part of the Black Diaspora," for, as he contends, "bodies, occasionally densely packed as cargo and often shackled, ... endured the multiple legs and enforced immobility of the Middle Passage journey. ... Contrary to popular belief, movement was not the primary feature of the Middle Passage. ... There was a lot of stillness."[1]

What Young emphasizes is not a notion of stillness as a lack of activity. His accent is instead on stillness as an effortful *action.* For him, the stillness of diaspora is an active state and an exertive *performance.* His most captivating example for this compelling thesis focuses on the stilled Black body in early photographic technology, specifically a radical re-reading of the now-infamous slave daguerreotypes commissioned by Louis Agassiz and photographed by J. T. Zealy.

Commenting on the images of five male figures captured in this series, Young opines:

> I am fascinated by these men because their bodies represent the Middle Passage in a way that inanimate commodities cannot. They dispel the romance of travel narratives and challenge the academic thrall to movement through a seemingly effortless but, undoubtedly, physically taxing

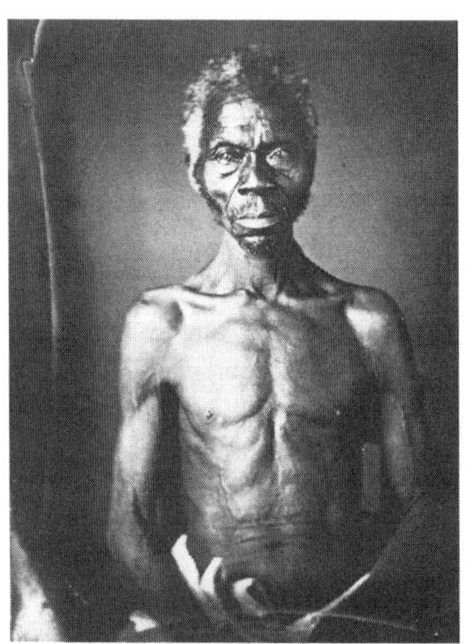

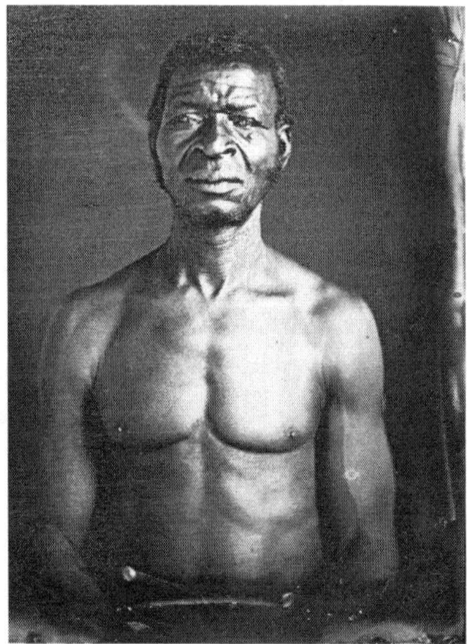

> *performance of stillness.* It is these men who sat and stood still in cells, holds, blocks, and plantations who repeat those prior performances within the studio session. Furthermore, their performance of stillness opens up new possibilities for critical reading strategies and, indeed, positionings for cultural historians and scholars. *Their daguerreotypes . . . succeed in capturing motion. That motion is stillness.* To look at Alfred is to see a person who stood still not for a brief moment, but upwards of a minute. It is to see a person who consciously is *enacting motionlessness* [emphasis added].[2]

The stillness Young identifies as integral to the diaspora is not confined to particular acts of "enforced immobility" restaged in images like Zealy's slave daguerreotypes. He asks us to perceive stillness as a willful cessation of movement. His crucial accent on *performance* is significant, for the "performance of stillness" Young reads in the steely looks of Jack, Jem, Renty, Alfred, and Fassena is an effortful act—an active *stopping* of movement that is itself a form of agential refusal that balances a number of different forces in motion.

What happens when we transfer the insights of Young's conceptual reframing from a focus on the Middle Passage and African American cultural formation to an alternative site of diasporic formation: Germany? What do we see differently when applying the lens of stasis to vernacular images of mundane and quotidian moments in the everyday lives of Black communities in diaspora? How does stillness, and my own refinement of his thesis to the term *stasis,* articulate diasporic formation for a community that was not shaped primarily by the trajectory of rupture and displacement produced by the Middle Passage?

Three boys triangulated among rubble, sculpture, or stone. A structure rises in the background to tower above them—yet diminutive they are not. Chins level and eyes trained directly on the camera, they project poise, propriety, respectability. Below them, three siblings have multiplied to a family of six. A traditional family portrait: matriarch and patriarch, with progeny aligned in front and the youngest babe in arm. The setting is once again stone—unyielding, immobile, monumental. Stone is the canvas that links the palette of these images. Stone and *stillness,* for the figures posed in each seem as immovable as the fundament that serves as their backdrop.

The proud African patriarch pictured here is Ekwe Ngando. Born in 1876 in Duala, Cameroon, he arrived in Germany in 1910 as part of an

Askari performance group that appeared in a spectacle staged in honor of Crown Prince Wilhelm III. His wife and the mother of his children was Ida Kleinfelt, born in 1885 in Silesia. We do not know where they met, or the circumstances of that meeting or of their engagement and future marriage—only that they met sometime between Ekwe's arrival in 1910 and the birth of their first son in 1912. We know as well that they were parents to the children posed in this portrait: their eldest, a son named Ekwin (born in 1912); their daughter Erika (1915); and their sons Mandega (ca. 1917) and Manga (1919).

Do these photographs visualize stillness? Is their stillness defined by or as a lack of motion? What might it mean to conceptualize the stillness imaged in these photos as a form of stasis that is neither stagnation nor motionlessness but instead an effortful *equilibrium* achieved through a labored balancing of opposing forces and flows? It requires us to think of stasis as a kind of motion in suspension: a form of motion held in tension that haunts and animates stillness. It requires us to imagine the *performance of stillness* as an active still*ing* of motion, albeit one that never attains the complete cessation of movement. Extending Young's line of argument and imagination, what would it mean to read these photographs as articulations of diaspora that image stillness as a modality of stasis that is both integral to and constituent of diasporic formation? Unlike Agassiz's anthropological frame, which used the photographic stilling of Black bodies to capture essential racial difference and reduce Blacks to the inhumanity of pure flesh, in these images we see thoughtfully staged portraits of Black bourgeois respectability. How should we engage these very different enactments of stillness?

This is not a family in motion or on the move, though their infant's prominent carriage is evidence of a journey by foot to the staging of this portrait. Their diasporic formation, while it certainly began in migration, is all about staying put. It is fundamentally about stillness, though not the forced immobility described by Young. Young emphasizes the extended physical temporality of stillness necessary to produce a daguerreotypic image, which required its subject to remain motionless for upward of three minutes to produce a non-blurry image. The circumstances of the Ngando portraits certainly minimize this temporality of stillness, yet they similarly generate a visual archive that confronts us with the consequences of diaspora not as movement, but as everyday acts of refusal—refusal to capitulate to the status of outsider, refusal to be made invisible. These acts of refusal transform the family photograph into a site of self-fashioning and performance of complex forms of fugitivity.

The Ngandos' photographic and diasporic stasis must therefore be read as a willful stilling aimed at achieving a complex and delicate balance and equilibrium—their stasis is an act of *diasporic dwelling*. Indeed, it is a practice of diasporic home-making we might consider a kind of *home-o-stasis*. It is an active and effortful practice of balancing multiple flows that produces *motion even in stillness*.

II. Ho·meo·sta·sis:

1. a state of equilibrium or tendency to reach equilibrium, either metabolically within a cell or organism or socially and psychologically within an individual or group
2. a balance in which internal change continuously compensates for external change to keep conditions relatively uniform
3. the maintenance of metabolic equilibrium within a person or social group through a tendency to compensate for disruptive changes

A lone soldier and two trios of military men. Mandenga Ngando wears the uniform of the Reichsarbeitsdienst, while Ekwin Ngando is dressed in that of the Wehrmacht—brothers clad in the uniforms of their fatherland. This very different set of images resonates eerily with those we have just viewed. How do we read them in relation to those taken decades before?

These images offer powerful historical traces that record these individuals' membership in central institutions of the National Socialist military regime. Yet in images like these we see not only a German Wehrmacht soldier but also a soldier sharing leisure time with friends. One photo depicts a member of the Reichsarbeitsdienst on duty and in the company of other men in his unit. It shows not just a man in service but a Black man in the service of the Reich at a time when, we are led to believe, non-Aryans and Black Germans in particular were absent from the social landscape. Like the other images reproduced here, these photos present Black Germans as integrated members of a German society that seems at ease with their partaking in public activities.

50

A mother clutches her son's arm as they beam at the camera. They are posed before a railing against a verdant background of trees, and the softly rippling waters of a lake or pond and a rowboat tethered just below project the placid rhythms of a day in the park. Stillness, stasis, or *homeo*stasis? The image conveys leisure time spent as respite in the midst of wartime turmoil and the enduring presence of daily life in spite of larger events. The spectacle of military display depicted in the images showing members of the corps engaged in their duties contrasts yet coalesces with the less iconic, heroic, or ceremonious aspects of a soldier's life. The snapshots, most likely taken by other soldiers or by friends or family members, differentiate themselves little from numerous others produced by ordinary Germans in this period. The individuals' integration into the larger narrative these photographic practices construct makes race and non-Aryan heritage seem almost a forgotten detail.

As part of a larger archive of Black German vernacular photography, these are photographs taken with the intention of capturing a particular occasion for posterity. Each image clearly displays pride in a loved one in uniform and also the respect and admiration the uniform bestowed on its wearer and, indirectly, on the wearer's family and friends, even in a context where the uniform represented allegiance to a racial regime whose aim was the eradication of non-Aryan Germans, including the individual who wore it. These photographs do not celebrate exceptional events or moments. They articulate instead the stuff of daily life: moments of relaxation, indulgence, or leisure; times when we feel most at ease, most ourselves. While far less formally staged than studio portraits, they are performances of stillness nonetheless. They are enactments that rely not on the props and poses of studio portraiture but on commonly accepted performances of masculinity made visible through their depiction of forms of male bonding and military presentation.

As photos of militarized masculinity, these images function as visual affirmation of national subjects in formation that record their sitters' aspirations to the privileged status reserved for German military manliness. This affecting collection of images of Black Germans in uniform materializes race in ways that are inextricable from gendered embodiments of national belonging. They image Afro-German subjects who emerge in the trappings of nationalized masculinity; yet this nationalist visuality is premised on the concealment, repression, and destruction of the very forms of racial difference the images depict.

These photos are a category of image Laura Wexler describes as "domestic photography," "images [that] may be—but need not be—representations of and for a so-called separate sphere of family life. Domestic images may also be configurations of familiar and intimate arrangements intended for the eyes of outsiders . . . or . . . metonymical references to unfamiliar arrangements . . . intended for domestic consumption."[3] These photos were taken with an intention to connect and out of a desire to image affiliation. They were made quite literally to invoke a "relation." In this way, these images' domesticity both enables and disarms them, inoculating them in ways that render them initially familiar and unremarkable, yet amplifying their impact in the process. Their vernacularity domesticates them by rendering them at once hauntingly sentimental and eerily unsettling. Each image stages military camaraderie as a kinship in arms that the domestic photo addresses to family and extended relations. Such domestic depictions of soldiers as kin move us in a double sense: they stir emotional connection in us, and they move us toward a closer relation to the image or else toward a more distanced estrangement based on the proximity that might have been but must at all costs be avoided.

III. The Motion of Stillness

Three boys pinned down in a fake gun battle. Or perhaps *Winnetou* was a recent bedtime story, and this is instead a game of cowboys and Indians. Fanciful hats sit awkwardly on small heads, with one hat completely unstable and falling forward off the kinky Afro of a young Harry Davis, pictured far left. Lying on their stomachs on a cobblestone courtyard, the boys flatten themselves to the ground, seeking cover from imaginary incoming fire. Smiling ear to ear, arms and guns extended, they are fully in character, dodging bullets and firing back to the "bang-bang" of a fantasy shoot-out.

A "bang-bang" of a different sort. The clash of ten sticks on five snare drums. A children's band: fife and drum corps circa 1935. A line of boys, alternating right to left: drum, flute, drum, flute, drum. The alternating pattern ends left of the bandleader, where the group's smallest members jumble together in disarray. Out in front, third from the left, stands Harry Davis in a pristine sailor suit, with drum at waist. A marching band in full regalia. Was their performance imminent or had it just ended? Perhaps a local parade in celebration of spring. On a sunny day like this in a village like Rüdersdorf, the whole town might be assembled. Parents, friends and neighbors—this band was the embodiment of belonging.

No banging and certainly no music. Quite possibly a lot of fidgeting—but an utter lack of movement was certainly the goal. Mission seemingly accomplished. Twenty-six tamed and docile boys assemble in a group photo under the watchful eye of a schoolteacher. Towering over them center frame, he gazes off into the distance, a sense of satisfaction on his face, seemingly

proud of his supreme accomplishment: successfully corralling this group of boys. Sailor suits and suspenders, offset ears, and, front row far left, a curiously formal trench coat adorn this motley crew. And the tallest among them stands fourth from the right: Harry Davis, impeccable and well kempt, sporting what today would count as a perfectly formed 'flat-top 'fro.'

Orphaned and fugitive images. Fleeting moments, glances into a past at once tangible and ephemeral. A boy and his friends, playing war games with toy guns or making music in a marching band. What unites these photographs is the continuity of groups. Each photo stills a moment of group activity, of children in school or at play. If we read these images together, what do we see? They visualize boyhood through a tableau composed of group constellations that structure the social milieu of a child. A trio of friends, a primary school class, a marching band—these images typify a life entangled in the social networks of everyday life.

The photographs of Harry Davis might be considered "orphaned" to the extent that, as with the other photographs included in this essay, we no longer have access to their owners or producers, the subjects featured in them, or the families of those who witnessed or might authenticate their circumstances. Like the images of the Ngandos, Davis' reclaimed images were displayed in the 2002 exhibition *"Besondere Kennzeichen: Neger"—Schwarze im NS-Staat* ("Distinguishing Characteristics: Negro"—Blacks in the Nazi State) and constituted part of a larger archive of photos of Black German families featured in the "Family Album" that introduces the volume of essays published in conjunction with the exhibit. They are among ten photographs published of Harry Davis, born in December 1921 in Kalkberge, the son of John Davis, a Liberian migrant to Germany, and Hedwig Agnes Erna Pausin Davis. John and Agnes Davis settled in Rüdersdorf just outside Berlin in the late teens or early twenties, where John supported his family through a variety of positions, including minor roles in the fledgling colonial propaganda film industry and as an employee of the shoe shop shown here.

Yet these images of family stability and diasporic stasis/dwelling also enact subtle forms of fugitivity through their capacity to visualize a recalcitrant normalcy in places and settings where it should not be, and to display survival not in heroic or spectacular acts but through participation in life's mundane events. They do so through depictions of domesticity and dwelling that manifest profound statements of refusal through their enactment of the solace and intimacy of such settings and defiantly protective practices of homing and

embrace. Their "stasis" is again a *home-o-stasis* that is not a stoppage of motion but an effortful balancing and coordination of forces of *motion in stillness.* Indeed, we might think of home-o-stasis as one important way of illuminating the forms of diasporic dwelling depicted in this archive of images. For the complex practices of dwelling that characterize the Black German community require acts of balancing and coordination that allow them to claim the status of German subjects and, simultaneously, to articulate equally complicated forms of fugitivity as racialized German subjects of African descent.

IV. Home-o-stasis and the Fugitivity of Home

Rüdersdorf bei Berlin, circa 1937. Several years later another trio of friends congeals, lounging together on a living room couch. "At home" both literally and figuratively, they relax, reassured in each other's presence and in the collectivity formed through that presence. Beer bottles and glasses adorn a side table. These vessels betray the progression of the evening like an hourglass marking the passage of time. These men have had a few and aren't finished yet. They slouch together on the sofa, cigarettes in mouth, mid-drag or mid-sentence, the inhalation of the brown-skinned young man to the left, Harry Davis, suspended in perpetuity.

A moment from now they could be asleep on top of each other, slumbering with one's head in another's armpit, drooling their way through a beer-addled dream world. Equally likely, they could be doubled over in laughter at

a comment from across the room. Regardless of the plotline that transpired later, the affect of this image is undeniably domestic. The body language it captures is familiar, if not familial. It emotes and connotes comfort, intimacy, and proximity. These are friends who are both at home and at home with each other. What other men would dare to practically cuddle on a couch?

Rüdersdorf, circa 1938. Another trio, in a markedly different setting, with a markedly different sensibility. The venue is a workplace, a farm with livestock literally in hand. Rather than conversation, work is in progress: the shearing of sheep, its physical labor momentarily paused. Tufts and piles of wool permeate the image: in the background, in the foreground, under foot and in hand. Soft and fuzzy, wild and unruly, the wool adds texture, tactility, and contrast to the image. This texture seems at odds with the photograph's laconic subjects. The image itself is equally fuzzy, with figures right and left slightly out of focus. But its subjects are certainly not fuzzy—anything but. They are rugged individuals, working men posed with purpose and intent. Indeed, it is difficult to imagine they would be photographed any other way. The closeness of the tight workspace is palpable. Light filters in from behind the camera and through the circular perforations of wall vents in the background. Surely these vents were intended to do nothing more than provide fresh, if minimal, air and ventilation, and their light illuminates nothing, highlighting instead that which is invisible: the air the men breathe, the smell of animals, the aroma of this workplace—an aroma that probably went unnoticed. Working here together day after day, they probably scarcely mentioned it.

As palpable as the smell we must associate with this place are the equally palpable physical sensations that accompany it. The tactility of wool saturates the space and microscopic fibers that certainly filled the air in a room where razors were hard at work on animals we associate with passivity and compliance. A diminutive lamb rests its head at the waist of the center figure. Its shearer strikes a commanding pose, with electric razor in hand and one leg raised, supported by the plank on which the livestock rests. Contrary to his authoritative stance, he, like his colleague to the right, is merely an apprentice. At left, their *Schermeister* or teacher stares at the camera in half profile. At far right, his Black German apprentice, Harry Davis, cradles the next one to be sheared: a black sheep.

Was the irony of this shot intentionally staged or serendipitous? Was its composition a prank or a lighthearted joke? Or did it go completely unnoticed by the photographer and his subjects? Perhaps it was a detail that seemed as unimportant as another overlooked feature of this photo: a beer bottle perched innocently and remotely, yet nevertheless all too prominently, on a ledge in the upper left corner of the frame. Was the black sheep an analogue that visualized the unspoken but unavoidable contrast in this image: the loud silence of racial difference? Does it stand in for the obvious—that which need not (and should not?) be stated? Possibly, but perhaps we should read it both less cynically and less allegorically. Within the tight proximity of this workspace there is either intimacy or animosity. In this photo, presence indicates belonging, for you would not and perhaps could not be there if you did not belong. A common task, a common space, a common masculinity performed in the collectivity of work. Similar to the military enterprise that solidified the three brothers-in-arms, this display of masculinity in labor renders these individuals one in work. But how lasting is the erasure of such barriers? While racial difference may here seem repressed, it was certainly not irrelevant. What this photo makes visible is how labor can create a common world, even for individuals situated very differently within that world or larger society. Like the visual contrast of the black sheep in this photo, it too could neither be erased nor overlooked.

These images of Harry Davis were taken sometime between 1935 and 1939, while he was living as an apprentice on a *Pachthof* or lease farm,

dubbed Grünelinde, that was operated by Wilhelm Thomae on the outskirts of Rüdersdorf. They are part of a larger archive of family photos that show Davis from childhood to earlier adulthood: at play or at rest with friends, shearing sheep and driving a tractor, or assembled at a communal gathering of friends and colleagues.

As a series, the photos chronicle happy times and moments of leisure at different periods in Davis's life. As their archivist notes, images like these depict the place of protection and acceptance Davis enjoyed at the time as one of several apprentices who inhabited a marginal position in the eyes of the Nazi regime.[4] In addition to Davis, a Black German, Thomae also employed two other workers, one of Jewish heritage and one a Communist, whom Thomae sheltered based on his anti-Nazi convictions as a committed socialist.

As compelling as this biographical sketch is, it too gives only a minimal account of what we see. Returning to the question posed at the beginning of this essay, I ask what shifts if we read this image through the lens of stasis, or a more complex notion of home-o-stasis that describes an equilibrium achieved through a delicate balancing of forces that articulates what Young described as a form of diasporic stillness in motion. Here I would suggest we engage these photos through what I will call "the fugitivity of their domestic affects."

V. Fugitivity, Domesticity, and the Haptics of Embrace

This image could have been the postscript to the previous image or the prequel to the living room scene captured in the photo that opened the preceding section. Perhaps the day that ended on a couch in a parlor began hours earlier with the three men standing in the sunshine outside a pub. A send-off for a buddy conscripted to serve, a toast to welcome him briefly home, or possibly a chance encounter or temporary companionship forged through beer. Huddled together shoulder to shoulder, the young men seem poised to raise their glasses, or the glasses may be drifting downward following a group swallow.

Photographed against a backdrop of foliage dangling from a balcony or window box, the proximity of this jovial group is as striking in its physicality as the previous image is. At far right, a young man seems to tug on the lapel of his friend, Harry Davis, whose presence helps constitute this series of images as a set. Second from left, the most ebullient of the five beams widely, about to sip from his glass. At far left, a fifth member completes the group; dressed in uniform, he is a member of a military group we cannot identify from our vantage point, but his casual presence in this configuration attests to the ubiquity of the military in everyday life, for the Third Reich was a thoroughly militarized society where uniforms were a visual norm in the *Biergarten* as well as on the battlefront.

What do we learn by reading these three images together? In fact, their significance materializes only when read in relation to one another and in the spaces between them. Collectively, they tell us that Davis was part of a family, albeit one that was not based on biology or heredity. These images register modes of inclusion and embrace produced through the affects of domesticity and belonging that constituted him as a member of multiple sites of everyday sociality: the workplace, the pub, the garden, the parlor. The figuration of his inclusion in these photos signifies not through the singularity of any one image but instead, serially, as multiples linked by easily overlooked details that constitute them as a set.

The fugitivity of these images' domestic affects emerges in the scenes of intimate gatherings, on the couch or at the pub—scenes that signify and stage friendship through the physical intimacy on display: arms clapped on shoulders, heads resting on shoulders, heads touching other heads, friends huddling together shoulder to shoulder. Viewed singly, each photo stages a narrative that offers an account of a particular event or occurrence. As a set, the images present scenes of youthful camaraderie unified by the continuity of Davis's presence amid multiple social networks of everyday life. What produces their seriality is a domesticity of intimate touches that renders Davis indistinguishable from the norm and produces him as adopted kin in ways that both shelter him from and expose him to a regime that sought his exclusion. These groups of young people are engaged in common activities and thus share purpose and social context. The litany of these configurations portrays Davis as quite popular or at least deeply embedded in the social life of his locale and perpetually surrounded by friends.

Perhaps most striking when looking at the images more closely is the gaze exchanged in the last photo between Davis and the soldier-friend, who stands almost opposite him. His face cast downward, Davis seems to look up to his slightly taller companion and, at the same time, down at the ground. Similar to the photos of Davis on the farm, a slightly older Davis strikes an almost bashful figure here, making us wonder whether he was a willing or recalcitrant photographic subject. Camera shy he obviously was not, though if these images in some way distort this fact, he was, at the very least, clearly the involuntary subject of persistent photographic attention. These were not obligatory family portraits but snapshots—thoughtful yet spontaneous images that capture moments of conviviality for future enjoyment. At least one photographer (though likely more) desired to capture his image, to keep and hold it over and again.

But what's right and what's wrong about the conviviality pictured in the final image? Paradoxically, the presence of the soldier both confirms and disrupts the image's conviviality. His appearance pairs with Harry's consistent visibility as the focal point that underlines the affective power of these images of trios and close-knit groups of friends. While the men share beer, a sunny afternoon, and conversation, the uniform amid these civilians distinguishes their lives from the soldier's life. One member of this group is visibly conscripted to protecting and upholding the rule of the state, and that state is a regime founded on a doctrine of racial purity and productivity and dedicated to Aryan supremacy and domination—which returns us to the image and its affects.

Viewed as a set, what connects these photos as well is, ironically, beer. Even at work, the bottle positioned on the ledge signals break time and the continuation of the modes of conviviality that the other images in this series celebrate more explicitly. Whether in a daily or weekly ritual or in a chance encounter, close friends, first-time acquaintances, and even adversaries can share a beer. Small, mundane details like a beer bottle or a uniform mark the continuities of everyday life in this litany of snapshots of Davis and friends, Davis and colleagues. These photographic depictions of Davis's movement into and out of public and private spaces compose an image of haptic domesticity. They picture employment and industry, leisure and belonging, and even a fluid interaction with members of the military. Our recognition of scenes we might have experienced or witnessed, suffered through or enjoyed, spurs us to conjure narratives that make the images make sense in the absence of personal or biographical authentication and validate the feelings of connection they inspire. The impulse to narrate these photos of intimate everyday relations derives from the sense of attachment and connection that is evoked through the structure of feeling they project and portray.

The tenderness, joy, and connection that structures Davis's placement within the context of each group enunciates relations of intimacy that seem unwavering throughout this archive. These images touch us through the physical touches they depict and the affective relations they solicit: the "touch" of head to head, head to shoulder, arm to shoulder, shoulder to chest. The forms of stillness these images display are stilled moments of embrace. They perform a stop-action movement that establishes physical contact intended to capture the intimacy of adopted kinship. It is an embrace that signifies visually in the multiple forms of embrace these photos image and through what those physical embraces represent: inclusion, acceptance, and protection at a time when the opposite was expected. Yet it is in the seamlessness of these images' depiction of the "touch" of intimate relation and the embrace of adopted kinship that their fugitivity also resides. For the embrace that sustains their relation was the embrace of an outsider turned kin. These images materialize the presence of a racial Other as the ultimate adopted relation—shielded in plain view by friends, neighbors, and coworkers who adopted him as kin and a chosen relation and who buffered scrutiny and potential injury by the state through his inclusion in the tightly woven fabric of community.

Stillness or stasis? Diasporic dwelling as home-o-stasis. I'll conclude by offering these terms for your further consideration and scrutiny. My hope is that this exploration of the motion of stillness and the fugitivity we find in domestic photographs of Black German life in the early twentieth century will bring us closer to understanding some of the politics and potentialities of both vernacular photography and diasporic formation.

NOTES

Sections II–V of this essay were published in chapters 1 and 2 of Tina Campt, *Image Matters: Archive, Photography, and the African Diaspora in Europe* (Durham, NC: Duke University Press, 2012). These sections are reprinted by permission of Duke University Press. The vernacular photographs of Black German families included in this essay are reprinted by permission of Archiv Dr. Peter Martin, Hamburg.

The catalog to his groundbreaking exhibition of these remarkable images, *Zwischen Charleston und Stechschritt: Schwarze im Nationalsozialismus* (Hamburg: Dölling und Galitz, 2004), makes the larger photographic archive publicly available. The slave daguerreotypes are reprinted by permission of the Peabody Museum of Archaeology and Ethnology, Harvard University.

1. Harvey Young, *Embodying Black Experience: Stillness, Critical Memory, and the Black Body* (Ann Arbor: University of Michigan Press, 2010), 42.
2. Ibid., 44.
3. Laura Wexler, *Tender Violence: Domestic Visions in an Age of US Imperialism* (Chapel Hill: University of North Carolina Press, 2000), 21.
4. In an interview reflecting on the Davis family photos, scholar and archivist Peter Martin reads them as visualizing the milieu of integration and belonging in which Davis lived as a member of this closely knit farm community. Martin emphasizes their portrayal of everyday life in the Third Reich as well as the sheltered and protective environment of the farm, which shielded Davis from Nazi scrutiny and potential harm. "It is clear from these photos that he lived a public life. He loved the others [pictured with him] and they were about the same age. They clearly had a close relationship—one sees it in all of the images. They're lounging on the sofa, and he is present at all the family celebrations" (22). Describing one figure, Martin comments: "This was a family event that they celebrated at the farm. It shows that he was present; he was part of the family. And one cannot forget that this was a time in Germany when racism was at its most virulent. They were living on a farm, and in such a farming community one was also able to hide. It was a small community, a community in which one developed close personal relationships very quickly. And this changes things because [in that context] prejudice and the fetish character of such ideas disappear." In addition, Martin also points out the highly modern and successful "model" character of Thomae's farm as both significant and exceptional for the time period. He speculates that it produced important provisions during a period of wartime shortages and restrictions. Martin postulates that this played some role in the farm's ability to shelter both a Black German like Harry and other apprentices who were of Jewish heritage or affiliated with the Communist Party. Peter Martin, audio interview with the author, Hamburger Institut für Sozialforschung, Hamburg, Germany, November 16, 2006. See also Tina Campt, *Other Germans: Black Germans and the Politics of Race, Gender, and Memory in the Third Reich* (Ann Arbor: University of Michigan Press, 2005), 91–100.

9

My 13 Years under the Nazi Terror

MARTHA STARK

INTRODUCTION

by Felicitas Rütten Jaima

In 1949 Martha Stark, born in Nuremberg in 1914 to a white German mother and an African American father, was interviewed by Percival L. Prattis, executive editor of the *Pittsburgh Courier,* at one time the most widely circulated newspaper for Black Americans. Prattis's interview focused on Stark's experiences during the Third Reich, and from May 7 to July 2, 1949, the paper published her story in nine installments under the title "My 13 Years under the Nazi Terror: Amazing, True Life Story of a Negro Girl in Germany Who Fought Hitler—and Won." Stark's account sheds light on the experiences of Black Germans under the Nazi regime, documenting the Nazis' attempt to poison her, her seven-week imprisonment, and their threats to deport her to a concentration camp. Her German stepfather's upper-middle-class background and connections to local Nazi officers protected Stark from many assaults, while the arrival of the American army in Bavaria preserved her from Auschwitz. In this introduction I will situate Stark's experience in the context of other narratives by Black Germans who survived National Socialism. I also will emphasize some important qualities of Stark's account, and I will locate the *Pittsburgh Courier*'s publication of Stark's story within the larger framework of the African American press's treatment of the Third Reich during and after World War II.

In *Hitler's Black Victims,* Clarence Lusane argues that, with the exception of the children born during the Rhineland occupation who were targets of forced sterilization, Blacks as a group were not subjected to systematic discrimination under Nazism. In contrast to Jews and other minority groups, he asserts, Blacks were perceived "neither as a cultural or social community nor as an economic or political community," so their fate depended on capricious, inconsistent, and often local decisions.[1] Tina Campt somewhat similarly maintains that during the Third Reich some Afro-Germans were able to find partial protection within local community networks that "often proved resistant to NS racial ideology and in this way sheltered those Afro-Germans who were seen as part of these communities. . . . The paradoxical effects of this racial state" meant that "some Afro-Germans could . . . enjoy some of its privileges while simultaneously suffering discrimination and persecution."[2] Black German accounts of living under the Nazi regime show how what I call "peripheral inconsistencies" shaped the Black experience in Nazi Germany. In *Showing Our Colors,* sisters Doris Reiprich and Erika Ngambi ul Kuo, daughters of a Cameroonian father and a white German mother, report that under the Nazis they lost their German passports, their apartment, and their jobs; Doris narrowly escaped sterilization when an official took pity on her, then with Erika and her Cameroonian husband joined other Africans and Afro-Germans in the Nazis' colonial film industry. Doris recalled: "They couldn't really liquidate us, but neither did they want to tolerate us."[3] Hans J. Massaquoi, grandson of the Liberian consul in Hamburg, reports in *Destined to Witness: Growing Up Black in Nazi Germany* (2001) that he was repeatedly denied admission to the Hitler Youth, forbidden to pursue secondary schooling, and declared ineligible for the German draft, but he otherwise had no more to contend with from the Nazis than racial harassment. Hans Hauck, one of the survivors of National Socialism whom Campt interviews in *Other Germans,* was able to join the Hitler Youth and the German military (and hence claim his right to German masculinity) but, as the son of an Algerian soldier who took part in the Rhineland occupation, was sterilized in 1935. Also interviewed by Campt, Fasia Jansen, daughter of the Liberian consul (and Massaquoi's aunt), was expelled from dance classes at age thirteen because of her skin color but was then assigned by the Nazis to cook for the female inmates of the Neuengamme concentration camp. Daughter of a Ghanaian father and an Afro-German mother, Marie Nejar recounts in her memoir that she was denied admission to the League of German Girls but became an extra in Nazi propaganda films.[4] Theodor Michael, son of Cameroonian Theophilus Wonja Michael, initially found work with a traveling circus, as a bellhop, and in the Nazi film industry but was eventually sent to a forced-labor camp.[5] Of the written accounts of Black German experience under National Socialism, that of Gert Schramm, son of an African American man who was sent to Auschwitz after he returned to Germany and attempted to marry Gert's mother, is the most harrowing: arrested at age fourteen apparently only because he was Black, Schramm spent over a year in a Gestapo prison before being transported to the Buchenwald concentration camp, which he survived until its liberation because older Communist inmates protected him.[6]

The first account of the Black German experience under National Socialism to see print, Martha Stark's story enriches the historiography of Afro-German experiences during the Third Reich for three reasons. It documents gradually increasing racial discrimination accompanying the rise of the Nazi regime. It highlights inconsistencies in the racial climate with which people of African descent contended after 1933. And it gives us insight into the emergence of a Black diasporic consciousness in Germany. Growing up in a white family without her biological father, Stark recalls in passages not included in this excerpt that until 1933 she "was reared as all Germans are in better-class families," cared for by maids, nurses, cooks, and chauffeurs. Her sheltered, elite upbringing also afforded her the luxury of remaining oblivious to political developments until they directly affected her. Given that Stark was the "bastard" (a word that in German means "mixed-race" as well as "illegitimate") child of an extramarital liaison between her mother and an African American prizefighter, her stepfather's unquestioning devotion to her was remarkable.

As a member of the upper class, Stark's mother raised her daughter to be a "lady," which meant wearing nice dresses, taking dance lessons, and learning proper housekeeping skills. To some degree, gender hierarchies also dominate Stark's story, as she structures her recollections around relationships with male mentors, teachers, and boyfriends. On the other hand, Stark defies the stereotype of the German lady when she describes herself as a rough child who fought with boys and played war games. Refusing to conform to what was expected of the well-behaved German girl, Stark adds that the "use of the word 'black' was always the signal to make my blood boil." She also much preferred academics and sports to housework and was determined to become a doctor of tropical medicine in Africa, a far from feminine career choice and doubtless an indication of her awareness of her racial identity.

At the same time, however, her isolation from other Black Germans deprived her of a sense of connection to others from the African diaspora. Unlike the protagonists in John A. Williams's novel *Clifford's Blues* (discussed by Maria I. Diedrich in chapter 7), Stark did not enjoy a network founded on the shared experience of being Black in Nazi Germany. Not until the late 1930s did she learn about the existence of the so-called Rhineland children, the biracial children fathered by French colonial troops occupying the Rhineland. Though Stark acknowledges discriminatory incidents prior to 1933 when her friends called her "Frenchman," an allusion to the German campaign against the "Black Horror on the Rhine," she insists that "it was only when Hitler arrived that the racial problem became acute in Germany because of the type of propaganda which he broadcast about colored peoples." Against this background, it is significant to note that as early as 1929 one of Stark's Jewish friends fled the country and moved with her family to Israel. Upon her departure she encouraged Stark also to leave the country. Others also pressed Stark to consider emigration. However, she was determined to stay with her parents—even despite her 1931 encounter with Julius Streicher, founder and editor of the Nazi newspaper *Der Stürmer,* who called her a "bastard" and warned, "It's time for us to clean out!"

Apart from her bond with her family, the inconsistency of racial hostilities directed at her may also have contributed to Stark's attitude toward emigration. An incident at a public swimming pool exemplifies how incoherent reactions created an ambiguous atmosphere. After a half-Jewish friend of hers is roughly forced to vacate the pool, a man named Meixner, later revealed to be a "Nazi big shot," demands that Stark leave too. But two of the men who had assaulted her Jewish friend now defend Stark, and the crowd at the pool eventually turns against Meixner, instead encouraging Stark to use the pool as often as she wants, as they had known her for her entire life. On a later occasion, when an SS man tries to prevent Stark and her cousin from occupying a café table, Stark's cousin beats him up, and neither other men in uniform nor civilians intervene. No doubt as a consequence, Stark's own attitudes toward the Nazis were also somewhat inconsistent. Stark's 1931 run-in with Streicher early shattered her regard for the new party, yet after the pool incident she writes a long letter to Streicher to complain about Meixner's behavior, trying, as she explains, "to appeal to his ideals as a National Socialist. Also, I told him that in my opinion men like Meixner made the entire party look bad." Surprisingly, Streicher's right-hand man instructs Meixner to apologize to Stark.

Exposure to such contradictory policies may help to explain why Stark was willing to enter into a romantic relationship with a white lieutenant in the German infantry and was later willing to end the affair so as not to impair his chances for advancement. The relationship may also have grown out of Stark's desire for a sense of belonging to Germany. Campt maintains that for Afro-German females "access to national belonging and Germanness is hindered by gender," whereas for males gender enabled it: "although the Nazi regime attempted to deny the black German male the right to propagate the race, paradoxically, he could still maintain his status as a masculine German subject by fighting for and defending that regime."[7] On the other hand, Campt notes that Fasia Jansen derived her sense of belonging and security from her close ties with family and local networks and attributed her survival to these bonds. Though Stark does suffer various Nazi assaults, her family and local connections repeatedly preserve her from far worse, including a delay in her deportation to Auschwitz.

Despite her ordeals, Stark's account as the *Pittsburgh Courier* presents it to the newspaper's African American readership is one of survival, not of victimhood. Indeed, her perseverance may have been intended to inspire Black Americans in their fight against racism. As well, though the Third Reich stripped Stark of her sense of national belonging, the *Pittsburgh Courier* juxtaposes this loss with the gain of what might be termed the beginnings of a Black diasporic consciousness. Having once strongly identified with her German homeland, Stark seems to feel homeless after the war. Desiring a national identity, she mourns: "I wish I could go home, too." Stark, who prior to the war was unaware even of the existence of other Afro-Germans, appears to find solace in her encounters with African American occupation personnel. African Americans offer her the friendship, support, and protection that the Nazis denied her, and—convinced that many Nazis are still in positions of authority—Stark entreats Allied forces to remain to safeguard the "colored babies" born of postwar romances between white German women and African American GIs. As Percival L. Prattis presents her story, Stark's true allegiances lie with the country people of her biological father: "We believe our readers will be touched by this yearning of a woman, born among the Germans, to be with her own people." "I am proud of it they are my people, too," says Stark in her own words. So it is not surprising that Stark married a Black American GI in July 1949.[8]

In publishing Stark's story, the *Pittsburgh Courier* continued an African

American journalistic tradition of linking America's advocacy of democracy abroad to the struggle for civil rights at home. During World War I the African American press drew analogies between atrocities committed in Europe and violence and discrimination against Black Americans in the United States. Though American officials stressed the racism of their German opponents and their own commitment to democratic values even more strongly during World War II, conditions had not changed much for African Americans. In February 1942 the *Pittsburgh Courier* launched the "Double V" campaign, calling for victory over fascism abroad and over racism at home and protesting policies in the American South and elsewhere very similar to those of Nazi Germany; that campaign was picked up by other Black newspaper editors around the country. After the war, the African American press continued to protest the American military's transfer of racist Jim Crow policies to occupied Germany.[9] This context would have framed Stark's story for the *Pittsburgh Courier*'s readers and also explains the editor's decision to publish her quite lengthy account.

In February 1949 the *Pittsburgh Courier* reported that Prattis was in Europe to "view conditions and get first-hand information of [*sic*] GIs and civilians."[10] He most likely met Stark at this time. In newspaper articles based on information he gathered during his trip, he regrets the state of segregation in the army and points to the central argument driving the Double V campaign when he explains that "the German people cannot fail to question democracy that makes distinctions based on color alone. . . . A tremendous step toward the ideological capture of the German people would be taken if segregation in the United States Army were abolished immediately and completely."[11] In addition, while many German officials pushed for international adoption of the children of German mothers and African American GIs to South Africa and the United States,[12] Prattis endorses the efforts of African American women in Germany to aid "the fitting of the children into the German community," arguing that, "although Germany may not want these 'brown babies,' she is compelled to keep them. . . . After all, they are Germans, regardless of their color."[13]

Of course the term "Afro-German" did not yet exist when Prattis met Martha Stark, yet the logic of his argument indicates that, however much Stark wished to "go home" to America and "be with her own people," he understood that she was a German too, regardless of her color. Pratt's papers in the Howard University archive contain no information about his encounter with

Stark or the process of compiling her story. The account's use of American colloquialisms—"big shot," "son-of-a-gun," "take the bull by the horns"—as well as Stark's quite broken English in the passage he introduces as "almost [her] exact language," suggests that he took some liberties in preparing her story for its presentation to African American readers, but we likely will never know how the two communicated with each other or to what degree his editorial interventions shaped the account. Though Stark ends by promising "You will hear about me again," no further stories about her appeared in the *Pitttsburgh Courier,* and nothing is known about her life after 1949.

Martha Stark's years under the Nazi terror are no more or less extraordinary than the experiences of Massaquoi, Hauck, Jansen, Reiprich, Ngambi ul Kuo, Nejar, Stramm, and Michael. As in their cases, the specificities of location, social networks, class, and gender as well as race influenced how National Socialism affected Stark and how she was able to survive. However, Stark's story is unique in that it was compiled before Afro-Germans began the endeavor of collecting information about their own history and thus does not manifest the intertextual influences of that common project. But the common thread in all these stories is the record they provide of the unpredictability and inconsistency of Nazi racial assaults on Black Germans. Stark's "Amazing, True Life Story of a Negro Girl" provides further evidence of the heterogeneity of the Afro-German experience during the Third Reich, shows how and why Black Germans like Stark found it important to claim their connections with other people from the African diaspora, and provides additional important information to scholars and activists in their ongoing effort to piece together the shards of Black German history.

NOTES

I want to thank Maria Höhn for sharing her knowledge about Martha Stark's story with me and for supporting a younger generation of scholars.

Martha Stark's "My 13 Years under the Nazi Terror: Amazing, True Life Story of a Negro Girl" appeared in nine installments in the *Pittsburgh Courier* from May 7 to July 2, 1949. It is reprinted here by permission of the *Pittsburgh Courier.*

1. Clarence Lusane, *Hitler's Black Victims: The Historical Experiences of Afro-Germans, European Blacks, Africans, and African Americans in the Nazi Era* (New York: Routledge, 2003), 7.

2. Tina M. Campt, *Other Germans: Black Germans and the Politics of Race, Gender, and Memory in the Third Reich* (Ann Arbor: University of Michigan Press, 2004), 21.
3. Doris Reiprich and Erika Ngambi ul Kuo, "Our Father Was Cameroonian, Our Mother, East Prussian, We Are Mulattoes," in *Showing Our Colors: Afro-German Women Speak Out*, ed. May Opitz, Katharina Oguntoye, and Dagmar Schultz, trans. Anne V. Adams in cooperation with Tina Campt, May Opitz, and Dagmar Schultz (Amherst: University of Massachusetts Press, 1992), 62.
4. Marie Nejar, with Regina Carstensen, *Mach nicht so traurige Augen, weil du ein Negerlein bist: Meine Jugend im Dritten Reich* (Reinbek bei Hamburg: Rowohlt, 2007).
5. Theodor Michael, *Deutsch sein und Schwarz dazu: Erinnerungen eines Afro-Deutschen* (Munich: Deutscher Taschenbuchverlag, 2013).
6. Gert Schramm, *Wer hat Angst vorm schwarzen Mann: Mein Leben in Deutschland* (Berlin: Aufbau, 2011).
7. Tina M. Campt, "Family Matters: Diaspora, Difference, and the Visual Archive," *Social Text* 27, no. 1 (2009): 107.
8. P. L. Prattis, "17 Days in Independent India: The First Day—June 1, 1949," *Pittsburgh Courier*, August 20, 1949, 12.
9. For a detailed analysis of the African American press's coverage of Nazi Germany, see Larry A. Greene, "Race in the Reich: The African American Press on Nazi Germany," in *Germans and African Americans: Two Centuries of Exchange*, ed. Larry A. Greene and Anke Ortlepp (Jackson: University Press of Mississippi, 2011), 70–87.
10. P. L. Prattis, "'Brown Babies' Face Dark Future," *Pittsburgh Courier*, February 5, 1949, 1.
11. Ibid.
12. See Heide Fehrenbach's chapter in this volume.
13. P. L. Prattis, "Germany's 'Brown Babies' Must Be Helped! Will You?," *Pittsburgh Courier*, April 30, 1949, 1.

...

MY 13 YEARS UNDER THE NAZI TERROR

Amazing, True Life Story of a Negro Girl

Martha Stark

(As told to P. L. Prattis, executive editor, the *Pittsburgh Courier*)

Installment three

. . .

I made my first contact with one of the Nazis who became very important later during [my] association with Dr. Seidelmann [a mathematics professor who was friendly with my family]. He was Julius Streicher, known as the Jew-hater. Our press box was on one side of the stage and on the other side was the box of the burgomeister [*sic*] or Mayor. One evening, I observed two men sitting in the Mayor's box. They were staring at me as though fascinated. I was disturbed by their gaze.

Between acts, Dr. Seidelmann and I walked out to the foyer to obtain some refreshments. These men, with some others, came for refreshments also, and we almost bumped into them at the buffet. One of the men, stocky, bald-headed and somewhat older than the rest, turned around, looked at me, and then exclaimed to the others in a loud voice: "I'd like to know what that bastard wants in here! It's time for us to clean out!"

Dr. Seidelmann immediately challenged him, as was the custom in those days. He presented his card and demanded the card of the other man. This other man was forced by custom to yield his card to Dr. Seidelmann with the understanding that the two would meet later to avenge the insult offered me. They usually fought with Italian florettes.

The man was Streicher.

His friends began to shove on and others near the buffet ordered him to shut up, reminding him that an opera house was not a beer garden. But he only laughed, nodded at Dr. Seidelmann and me, "I'll see you later." He never showed up to defend his honor.

When I came to myself, Dr. Seidelmann told me: "That man was Julius Streicher, the one who hates Jews. He is the same man who is going to try to run Germany some day. But I would prefer death to living through such shame."

When I returned home that night, I told my parents nothing. I couldn't hurt them. But alone, I found I could not sleep for thinking. We had reached the period when, even in school, there were endless discussions about this new regime, or party, which was promising people heaven and earth. Some of my schoolmates were fascinated when somebody told them everybody from now on would be able to become a field marshal. For everybody, this was something to strive for. But my regard for the new party was shattered in the very beginning. One of the new party's leaders gave me my first lesson.

We prepared for our final examinations that year and, naturally, there was little time left for us to investigate this new party. Still, every week, Jewish families left Nurnberg [*sic*} and Germany forever. Most of them went to England. Later, they went to the United States.

In my grandmother's house, there was a Jewish family. There were four sons older than I. They and the members of my family were good friends and they did much to help my grandmother when she was burdened with three growing children.

One day, two of these four sons called me on the telephone. They insisted, darkly, that they must talk with me. We met in the town and they told me that their family was ready to leave Germany. The father and two sons were going to England and the two other sons wanted to go to northern France. They said to me:

"It is time for you to leave Germany, too, because we have learned that it is going to be terrible in Germany in a short while."

They asked me earnestly to go with them.

I couldn't understand them. I told them:

"I cannot believe anybody would try to bother us. We harm nobody. If we leave, we will appear to be guilty of something. I cannot quit school now either."

After I left them, I felt fear deep within me—not exactly about myself. But I had a feeling of being very much alone because it seemed that everyone I knew well was leaving. These people who had tried to warn me had my very best interests at heart, but I couldn't and wouldn't leave my parents.

Installment four

. . .

I first heard of Adolf Hitler in 1929. During the period from 1919 to 1929, Germany was a very unhappy country. It was on the bottom. It had to suffer hard for losing the first world war. It was the victim of inflation, reparations and the Treaty of Versailles. All of these afflictions upset the people. Seventy per cent were out of work. There were new strikes daily. Crime rates shot up dizzily. This was just the right time for Hitler to sew [*sic*] his seeds of discontent. He moved onto the scene very cautiously at first, apparently preferring to lay the foundations for the structure of his future power by attracting as little attention as possible.

Some of my school mates came one day and told the rest of us that they had heard about a man who was going to free us of everything. I listened to them, but I did not pay too much attention to this kind of talk because it seemed political and we steered clear of politics in my home.

However, one of my friends, a Jewish girl, came to me at just about the same time in 1929 and told me that she was going to have to leave me because her family was going to Jerusalem. She talked to me for a long time and seemed to be trying to tell me more than she really knew. When she finished, she told me that I would remember her and what she had told me. She warned me that I had better find a place to which I could go also. Frankly, at the time, I thought this girl was crazy. Here was one of the first Jewish families to leave. We never heard of them again.

Hitler was just barely discernible on the horizon. Most of us were still living the lives to which we were unaccustomed [*sic*], unaware of the epochal changes which were imminent.

Installment five

Excitement prevailed from the beginning when the Nazi party really took over in Germany in 1932 [*sic*]. There was much more than a political change. The social and economic structure of the nation was visibly and violently affected.

Everybody who worked for the city of Nurnberg [*sic*], or who had a public job, had to show his, or her, birth certificate. The authorities would then have the family line of each individual traced back through three generations in order to find out if there was a Jewish or any other type of "nichtarisch" ancestor.

Under the term "nichtarisch" they included the following peoples: Jews, Armenians, Negroes, Gypsies, Japanese and Chinese. Arabs and East Indians were considered "arisch" or Aryan. They called them the "urarier."

Complexion, or skin color, was not the really decisive factor in determining these classifications. The Nazis worked on a kind of purity of racial blood theory.

Terror seized the people throughout Nurnberg. Jews were hunted down and picked up at night. There were many Germans who sympathized with the plight of these Jews but they were afraid to protest. . . .

In my sports club . . . , all those who were part Jewish had to get out. The Nazis ordered this. When I saw the Jews leave, I began waiting and waiting for the day when I would be told to pack up, too. Nothing happened. But the suspense of not knowing exactly what my status might be was unbearable.

These officials had always been my friends and when I approached them they seemed to get real angry about my case. They told me that the order applied only to Jews, that they were going to stick by me and that everybody wanted me to stay in the club.

Each city had a Nazi headquarters known as the Brown House. The headquarters authorities divided the city into sections and the sections were broken down into blocks. This was a type of organization guaranteed to get the people under control. In the blocks, the Nazis kept under their alert eyes the people who were living close together. In each block there were some Nazi fanatics and they were made the bosses or supervisors.

In the Nazi organization the more lowdown and brutal a person was the higher rank he received. If you met one of your true friends and felt the impulse to talk about the new regime, you were compelled to exercise the precaution of locking all doors and windows and of talking in whispers. This was true because at no time could you be sure that your neighbor, your maid, or even your own brother, was not waiting for a chance to obtain a new stripe and to put you in jail.

I shall always remember the day when I received my first impression as to the kind of men chosen to supervise these concentration camps. In my neighborhood there were two sons in a good family. One of these brothers was of excellent character. When he grew up he obtained a good job and was on the way to making something of himself when the Nazis came. But the other brother, whose name was Heinz, was from the beginning the black sheep, even though the darling of the family. He was expelled from high school. His father gave him a job in his business, but Heinz proceeded to steal 25,000 marks from his own father. Then a friend of his father gave him a job. Heinz also stole from this friend. He acted as though he were born to be a thief.

When the Nazis took over Heinz had left Nurnberg and I had forgotten all about him. One day I was standing at a street car station when somebody slapped me on the shoulder from behind and exclaimed, "Hi, Martha. I'm glad to see you after such a long time."

I turned around and found myself standing in front of a strikingly uniformed SS man. The silver stripes and the silver braid he wore on his uniform told me that he was a high-ranking SS officer. This man was Heinz. He smiled at my bewilderment and surprise and then told me that he had finally made it, that he was one of the leaders in the concentration camp at Dachau.

One afternoon I had gone to the city pool to swim as I was in the habit of doing in the winter time. I met there an old friend of mine, Walter Stein. Walter's father was director of art for the city of Nurnberg but his mother was Jewish. We had scarcely started to swim before four men swam to the point where we were and forced Walter to leave the pool. They told him that he must get out right away, that he was a half Jew and that he had no business being there. Walter started to argue, but these men pushed and shoved him to his locker and compelled him to leave the building.

When Walter climbed out of the pool I followed him. As he and the men argued, I stood aside, speechless. After they had forced him out of the building I dove into the pool again to continue my exercise.

Barely had I hit the water before an elderly man swam up to my side and insisted that I should get out too. He said: "That dirty Jew has left. What about you? Your father was a 'n--r' and you are a bastard. We have no place any more for people like you."

From the manner of his speech I could discern that he was a very low-class man. I retorted: "All right. I'll get out of the pool. But you must go to the lifeguard with me and explain who you are to be ordering people around." To my great surprise two of the men who had chased Walter out of the pool jumped in and grabbed this man who had molested me. Finally, the others in the crowd turned against him and some of the men said, "Let's drown this son-of-a-gun."

They told me that his name was Meixner and that he was a Nazi big shot from the Brown House in Nurnberg. They also told me to come to the pool as often as I wanted, that they had known me since I was a baby.

When I went home that day I locked myself in my room and wrote a long letter to Julius Streicher. I tried to appeal to his ideals as a National Socialist. Also, I told him that in my opinion men like Meixner made the entire party look bad.

Eight days later my mother came to my room. She was excited all over and shaking with fear. She had an envelope in her hand which she told me contained an order for me to come to the Brown House the next morning at 9 o'clock.

As a result, I told her about the episode with Meixner in the swimming pool and about my letter to Streicher. My stepfather was likewise upset about all this and he told me that I was playing with my life. He informed me that he would not let me go to the headquarters by myself. I didn't want him to accompany me, but I could not restrain him.

The Brown House was quite an imposing structure. A man attired in a brown uniform led us upstairs to a large, luxuriously furnished room. A dozen or more men, all in brown uniforms, were in this room. They looked at us, and especially at me, when we came in. The man who entered and whom they saluted was Brigadefuhrer [*sic*] Herzog, right-hand man to Julius Streicher. He asked me if I were the Martha Dannhorn who had written the letter to Streicher. He turned to his men and told them to bring Meixner in. While waiting, he asked me some questions about my schooling and my life in general.

When Meixner arrived Herzog forced him to tell his story. Meixner started again to get nasty about me, but Herzog immediately ordered him to stop and called him a fool in front of all of his fellows. He then ordered Meixner to apologize to me. Meixner was compelled to say that he was sorry. We were then told that we might go.

On the same afternoon that Meixner accosted me in the swimming pool I met a young man. He asked me if he could take me home. He always seemed to be a head taller than anybody else in any group in which he might be. We met several times after he took me home and we took a deep liking to each other. One afternoon he picked me up at school. He was a lieutenant in the infantry.

He and I spent many happy afternoons together. We frequented the cafes on side streets where there were not many people and would while away the hours enjoying our love for each other. I was afraid to tell my parents about my new friend. One of the reasons was because he wore a uniform. The Nazis and their uniforms had spread so much fear that my parents hated everybody in a uniform. But I did tell my old friend, Dr. Seidelmann, who was with me when I first saw Streicher, about my new love. He arranged things so that we had more time to be together.

Installment six

You will recall Dr. Sigmund Seidelmann, I am sure. He is the mathematics professor and music critic who was with me at the opera when Julius Streicher called me a "bastard." Dr. Seidelmann challenged Streicher to a duel and Streicher appected [*sic*] the challenge but he never showed up.

Dr. Seidelmann knew about my new love affair with Hermann Schwarz, the tall young man who waited outside the swimming pool to take me home after I had had an altercation with a Nazi there. Very often, Dr. Seidelmann would meet Hermann and me after the theatre and the three of us would squeeze into Hermann's little car and drive to a wine house where Dr. Seidelmann liked to take a glass of wine before going home.

It was during this period that the opera, "Madame Butterfly," was presented at the opera house. Dr. Seidelmann invited Hermann to sit in his loge with us.

When the curtain was raised for the opening of the opera, I looked across the stage and saw Julius Streicher and several of his cronies in the loge opposite. Streicher simply stared at us. But when the first act was finished, he sent his adjutant[,] a man named Koenig, over to our loge with instructions to have Hermann come to him immediately. Hermann left and followed Koenig with a surprised and bewildered look on his face. When he returned in about ten minutes, he was pale and very nervous.

I asked him what Streicher wanted. He evaded the question.

Nevertheless, I could see and feel that he had been hurt. On the way home after the opera, he stopped the car to talk to me. He asked me if I would like to go away somewhere, maybe to Africa. I didn't know what was on his mind, but inasmuch [*sic*] as Africa had always been a sort of passion with me, I told him I certainly would. I added that that was where I had always wanted to go after I had finished my studies. But he, with real concern, said: "Darling, I mean right now, this year, not after you have finished your studies. We could go there now and I could enlist in the French Foreign Legion."

I was puzzled as to what the connection might be between his going to Africa and enlisting in the French Foreign Legion. He then explained that it was very much in his blood to be a soldier. He said that all the men in his family, as far back as Frederick the Great, had been army men, and that wherever he went, he would have to be a soldier—even in Africa.

One day, not long after that, Dr. Seidelmann gloomily told me he was going to be compelled to join the Nazi party in order to retain his job as a professor.

He had always told us how much he hated the new regime and he wanted to balk against the Nazi pressure, but his girl friend and I persuaded him not to do so. He was very much humiliated by thus having to truckle to the Nazis.

Two weeks later Hermann told Dr. Seidelmann that his commanding officer had transferred him to Ingolstadt. They gave him no explanation with the order.

When Hermann left, I had to promise him that I would visit him as often as possible. He was supposed to be promoted to a captaincy. I and several of his other friends had been preparing to have a party for him.

A few weeks after he had gone, he sent a telegram for me to my girl friend's house. He was insisting that I should come to Ingolstadt the very next day, Sunday. I had to make up some very tall tales to get away without my parents knowing what I was doing. Ingolstadt is ninety miles from Nuernberg by train. Hermann met me early Sunday morning at the station.

We spent a beautiful summer day together, most of it on the Danube. In the late afternoon, we met some of Hermann's comrades, other officers, and we went into a cafe where we could obtain refreshments and dance. While we were all having a jolly party, Hermann's best friend asked me if I would dance with him. After we had been dancing for a short while, this officer asked me if I were very much in love with Hermann. Surprised by the suddenness of the question, and its nature, I told him that I certainly was, that I wouldn't be there if I were not.

He then asked me if I knew why Hermann had been assigned to that small post and why he had not yet been promoted to a captaincy. I did not know and told him so. He said that he would tell me although it hurt him to do so. He reminded me that Hermann was his best friend and that being a soldier was Hermann's real life. He then said that Streicher had berated Hermann for having me for a girl friend and had reported the matter to his commanding officer. That was why he had been transferred and had not been promoted. Hermann, his friend said, did not want to leave me, but if he didn't, he was going to be made to suffer. This friend then said that if I loved him as much as I had said, I would know what to do.

Indeed I did know what to do! I played my part very well until the train had returned me to Nuernberg. Hermann was so nice to me that rest of the day. He brought roses and candy to me at the train. He put me on the train and kissed me. He promised me that he would come to Nuernberg to see me within two weeks.

But when the door was slammed shut and the train had moved off, I was nothing but a bundle of pain—alone again! Hermann wrote me letters. He came to Nuernberg, but I refused to answer when he called for me, or to see him. He went to see my girl friend. I told her to tell him that I had fallen in love with another man. She reported to me that after she had told him that, his face turned white and that he then complained out of his anguish: "How can a person like her be true? There are too many who like her and her temper is too hot for us. But I never thought she would fool me!"

If he had but known how lonesome I was and how bitter I was against my own people, the Germans. It hurt me to my core to realize that he must think ill of me. Until this day, I regret that the impression given him cannot be erased. It is too late. I shall never be able to speak to him again. He was taken prisoner in Russia and never heard of any more.

From that time onward, I gave up all the things which had been a pleasure to me. I did not even go to my club any more. I prepared myself for my last major examination at school.

One Sunday, a group of boys and girls came to my house and asked me to go to the movies with them. I agreed. After seeing the picture, we went to a cafe for some refreshments. I returned home and went to bed early.

In the morning, my maid called me about seven o'clock as usual and I answered to tell her that I was awake and would soon be out. After waiting awhile and seeing that I didn't come out, the maid returned to rouse me again. This time I didn't answer. I was unconscious.

My parents immediately called the family doctor, an elderly man named Fuerter. After he had examined me, he shook his head and told my mother that, in his opinion, I was suffering from a brain tumor. He said that I was almost blind and paralyzed, too. My parents then called in two neurologists, Drs. Dodel and Sandner. After examining me for an hour, they told my mother exactly what Dr. Fuerter had said and added that I might have about fourteen days to live. Dr. Dodel wanted to take me to his clinic and open up my head. But my mother wouldn't let me go.

She began to hug me and to press me to her bosom. While she was doing this, I returned to consciousness and vomited. The doctors had the presence of mind and the intelligence to retrieve my vomit. They rushed it to the hospital for examination. They found that I was poisoned.

I was not able to talk. The police were notified and immediately began an investigation. They searched every place where I had been but they found out nothing. Finally, they concluded that the canned fruit in the bowl from which I had eaten the day before (after going to the movie) was rotten. They brought the owner of the cafe into court. But he had witnesses who stated that they and others ate fruit from the same bowl and that they were not poisoned. So the cafe proprietor was freed.

It is still a mystery to me how I was poisoned.

For fourteen days, I lay half-blind, paralyzed and almost unconscious.

My classmates took their examinations. Fortunately, I obtained permission to take the tests later. Three months afterwards, I did, and I passed.

A new terror broke in those days, a terror that was as puzzling and humiliating to intelligent, sensitive Germans, as it was painful and debasing to its victims. This was the pogrom against the Jews. It broke out one night. The synagogue, a beautiful old sample of Byzantian architecture, was set afire. All the stores owned by Jews were also put to the blaze in the effort of the Nazi mob to destroy them. Men wearing the brown uniforms of the Nazis and armed with hammers and axes, broke into the apartments of all Jews and chopped up the furniture and dishes. From the upper stories, they would drop the most expensive furniture into the streets where their accomplices would mangle it. They took knives and cut the beautiful oriental rugs (used by the Jews for their prayers) to pieces.

A Jewish family, with which we had been very friendly, had a seven-room apartment, richly furnished, near us. When I went to the apartment the next morning to see what might have happened, I found the wife and mother, speechless from shock, sitting on an old wooden box in the middle of her totally destroyed home. Not even a coffee cup was saved.

Her husband had been ordered to report to the Lorenzerplatz at six o'clock in the morning. All male Jews were required to report there, in the center of the city. They marched these Jews out of town to the stadium in long columns and forced them to spend the entire day picking grass. It made no difference if these Jews were old or sick. The sun was burning and many of them fainted, but they were forced to work on their knees without food and water until six o'clock in the evening. Then they were marched four miles back to town. The mob stood on the sidewalk and spat upon these Jews and called them vile names.

From that day onward, every Jew had to wear a big yellow Star of David on his shoulder. Each Jewish business that remained had on the front door a yellow star on a field of black. If anybody tried to purchase anything from a

Jew, he was certain to get into trouble because there were always some people loitering around waiting for a chance to become informers. I know Hitler paid them well for this kind of work.

The Nazi party used to hold a big meeting in Nuernberg every year. They called it the Reichparteitag [*sic*]. From each German town and village a delegation came to Nuernberg. Diplomats from all over the world were also visitors at the time. The city would be decorated beautifully with Nazi flags and emblems and, for weeks before the affair, the Gestapo would institute a strict check of the people—because Hitler and his crowd were coming and they did not went [*sic*] to take any chances with their lives.

One night a cousin of mine, Rudi Denkmier [*sic*], asked me to spend the evening with him in a downtown cafe. When we entered the cafe, it was crowded with visitors to the Reichparteitag. We found a table where only one SS officer sat and tok [*sic*] our places there. But when we sat down he jumped from his seat and told us that it was impossible for him to sit at the same table with a "n--er." I didn't want any trouble and nudged my cousin to leave. But he said: "No, dear. You stay right here. I'll teach this son-of-a-gun a lesson."

He proceeded to knock the SS officer under the table. A large number of civilians crowded up to the scene of action. The SS officer fought back, but he was no match for Rudi. Every time the storm trooper would rise, my cousin would knock him down again. As a final gesture, he kicked the Nazi through the door of the cafe. He fell like a sack on the sidewalk.

All this happened so quickly that everybody was stunned. The other men in uniform, when they observed the attitude of the German civilians, hesitated to come to the aid of their comrade. But I feared that the Nazis might come and put my cousin in jail. However, nobody bothered us as we left and made our way home.

Installment seven

Somewhere in Germany—I wanted to start my studies at the University of Erlangen, now that I had finished nine years' work in the Humanities Gymnasium in Nurnberg. . . . [M]y purpose was to become a doctor, a specialist in tropical medicine, and to go to Africa. I chose the University of Erlangen because of its distinguished reputation and its nearness to Nurnberg.

Erlangen was only twelve miles from Nurnberg and I could go there by bus from my home. However, before entering the university as a medical student, it was necessary to go through a series of preliminary courses and examinations.

One morning in 1934—I remember it as if it were yesterday—I went to Erlangen to matriculate. Some of my schoolmates and young friends who also planned to enter the university accompanied me. We had a joyful time on the bus. When we reached the university, we went straight to the office of the secretary. We were given papers describing the courses we would have to study and a number of forms to fill out.

One of the forms struck me right in the middle of my face. One of the first questions on the form was to determine whether or not you had ever been a member of the Hitler Youth Organization. There were several others designed to disclose whether you had supported different Nazi organizations and programs. But what hit me hardest was a proviso that you must submit a certificate as proof that you were a pure Aryan. If you didn't, the university could not admit you.

For my friends Hans Dorsch and Fred Endress, filling out these forms was easy. But I could see in a minute that I was beaten. The Nazis had me. What could I do about this?

First, I visited my old friend Prof. Sigmund Schmidt and his wife, the ones who had spent so much time in Tibet and the Himalayas and had been so kind to me as a child. I asked them what they thought should be done. We had endless discussions, but we always ended at the same point: there was nothing to be done.

I'll never be able to tell how I made it home after this crushing blow. How could I tell my parents of this new evidence of Nazi infamy? How could I explain to anybody what it meant to me after I had spent nine years working and learning and planning for a future, only to learn that it had all been for naught? How painfully it came to me that other girls, not concerned with studies, had enjoyed themselves, or were now happily married! Because they were so-called pure Aryans, they had a future and I had none.

My parents tried to soften the blow and to cheer me up. My stepfather, who had always done so much for me, did not fail me this time. One of the best friends of our family told me: "Don't waste your time worrying because of this. With my connections and your father's money, we can make the impossible possible."

As a result, I began to study in private.

One day a friend of mine told me that I could go to Budapest in Hungary. It took some time for me to persuade my mother to let me go. But I had promised myself to fight my way and, in a few weeks, I left Nurnberg on my way to Budapest. It is scarcely necessary for me to compare Germany and Hungary. I ran into the same type of obstacles there that I had encountered in Germany. The only difference was that the Hungarians were not as thorough as the German Nazis. They had a nice way of letting you know that they didn't want you—the university was overcrowded, there was no room in Hungarian homes for German students, and more stuff like that. After four days of fruitless asking and begging I was on my way home again.

I continued working and learning day and night. Sometimes a feeling of triumphant satisfaction came over me when I thought of what a surprise that Nazis would have when they learned that I was working in their laboratories at night and on Sundays. One summer, I spent every Sunday, from early in the morning until afternoon, alone in the laboratory with my professor and the cadavers. How many students would have been proud to have had the chance to study thus alone with such a teacher? How many little pure Aryan babies I helped to bring into the private clinic where I studied! I think Streicher would have had a stroke if he had found this out.

In this part of my story, I refrain from using names because many of the persons who were good-hearted enough to help me are still active and on duty. All the Nazis are not gone yet and their party is not dead. If the identity of these persons were learned, the Nazis might still find a way to punish them. I know now that in trying to help me they were toying with their freedom, maybe their lives. I am glad to be able to express here my gratitude to them.

To satisfy my father, I went to a private business school in Nurnberg for a year to study shorthand and typewriting. I did not like this. On the other hand, my mother wanted to make certain that I knew how to do everything around the house. There was a castle near Nurnberg known as Schloss Oberberg. It was owned by a Baron Weisdorf. But the baron didn't use the castle exactly as a home. He operated a sort of domestic science school where housekeeping was taught for a fee. My mother sent me there for seven months. Although the baron charged and you were supposed to be in school, you worked like a dog. Sometimes I would get up at 5:30 in the morning and work until 9 at night. I would be so tired I could scarcely take off my clothes to fall in the bed.

This work did not leave me much time for my other studies. So when I had convinced myself that I knew how to scrub a door and cook a meal, I kissed Baron Weisdorf and his school a happy good-bye.

There was another girl, Cita Wenk, at Baron Weisdorf's castle with me. She was a nice girl, too, and she took a liking to me. Sometimes we would spend an afternoon together. She would always be talking to me about her cousin from Colonia [*sic*] and about his friend, Herbert Stark, whom she found so nice and interesting. One evening, Cita called me up and invited me to her house. She said her cousin Hermon [*sic*] Sodemann was there and that he had brought his friend with him.

Who could blame me for it if I found this young man to my liking? I did not know. I did not have the slightest idea of what Cita's interest might be. I did notice that neither she nor her cousin seemed to enjoy the fact that Herbert and I got along so well from the start. Later, Cita confessed that she had liked Herbert herself. She said she had thought I was not interested in men, that was why she had called me. She thought she was going to have me to entertain her cousin so she would have more time for Herbert.

Herbert worked for the firm of Gebrueder Stollwerck, the largest chocolate manufacturers in Germany. He was a salesman and had been given the Nurnberg territory. He earned good money, but even without the money, it would have been a distinction to work for that firm. He was two years older than I. I liked him because of his gentle manners.

It was about this time that my private teachers informed me that they could go no further with me. They said I needed practical experience in a large hospital. But it was still impossible for me to obtain that.

When I first met Herbert, he was not surprised about me and my color. He told me that there was a camp on the Rhine river in which the Nazis had imprisoned people like me. This was my turn to be surprised. I had not even suspected the presence of many other colored people in Germany. I learned that these of whom Herbert spoke were the children of German women and African soldiers who had stayed in Germany with the occupation forces after the first world war. Even so, it was difficult for me to believe that they were being treated as Herbert described because I thought that only Jews were imprisoned in such camps.

I questioned some friends who lived near where this camp was supposed to be. They confirmed what Herbert had told me and added that some of these prisoners had been killed. They also said that all the Gypsies had been placed in the same concentration camp.

After a while, the liking Herbert and I had taken for each other deepened. I told my parents about him. They invited him to our house. My stepfather, I guess, had a feeling of optimism about me for the first time. One of his dreams had been to find somebody who would be competent to take over his business when he was old. I thought that perhaps if everything went well with Herbert and me, Herbert would be the man. But I wasn't thinking about marriage. There were too many years of hard work and study behind me for me to give up now—with only a little further to go to finish.

My friend, Prof. Schmidt, planned another expedition to Tibet. His plans were complete except for finances. He hoped the Nazis would permit the money to be spent to finance the project as an aid to culture. Prof. Schmidt told me that if he obtained the funds he would take me with him, as a medical student and secretary. With such a prospect in view, how could I have marriage on my mind?

I told Herbert about my plans. He smiled and said that he didn't like women who were too smart. He said that he respected a woman who could keep house and rear children. I laughed, at first, about his arguments, but two months later, I had to yield to them because I was expecting a baby. This was serious. I didn't want to take up this problem with my parents and the other members of my family. I just had to put aside all my plans and wishes for the future. Somehow, I managed it.

Herbert and I prepared for marriage. According to the new Nazi law, each couple which planned to marry was required to go to the City Hall, submit to a physical examination and obtain a permit. Herbert and I went to the City Hall one morning. We had our papers already. But at the first sight of us, the official told me that it was impossible for me to to marry a German man. We told him about the baby and Herbert told him he wanted to marry nobody but me. Then the official informed us that we would have to return the next morning.

This official was a 100 per cent Nazi. He questioned me for more than two hours and wrote down all my answers. Then I had to come another day for a physical examination. When I arrived at 9:30 in the morning, there were four other men there and two nurses in brown Nazi uniforms. I was compelled to take off all my clothes in front of this group, men and women. I felt so ashamed that I told them all what I thought of them, but they only laughed.

Every person who had had any contact with me, my school teachers, cooks, nurses, maids, was questioned about me. They tried to obtain some pretext to send me either to a concentration camp or to an insane asylum. But nobody would furnish them with the kind of information about me that they wanted. They grilled my mother for several hours and insulted her by calling her filthy names.

From that time on, I had to report to the City Hall regularly, so that they could be sure that I had not run away.

One day, I was taken in an automobile to the Gestapo headquarters, "Deutschhaus-Kaserne." Two men led me into a deep cellar and showed me the cells. There was nothing but cement floors and white, blood-stained walls. They told me that I was supposed to stay in one of these cells until my black soul went to hell. I was wearing short sleeves and one of these men pressed a burning cigarette against my arm. When I yelled in pain, they laughed and tried the trick several more times. Then I ignored them and they grew tired of their game.

I still have three spots on my arm where I was burned. They held me in a cell for nearly an hour, playing with their pistols all the time. I almost lost possession of myself because I couldn't figure out what they wanted. I told them that if they wanted to kill me, to go ahead and make it short, but they laughed again and told me no, not now, maybe some other time. They also told me that I had better keep my mouth shut about what I had seen because if I were brought in again it wouldn't be so good for me. Then they released me.

They also treated my boy friend very roughly. They told him that it was shameful for him to be associating with me, but he stuck to me all the same. Some time [*sic*], I wonder how I lived through those terrible days.

One day when I reached the City Hall, I got into trouble with a young man there. He called me such shameful names and treated me so much like a dog that I forgot myself and told him what I really thought of him and of the whole Nazi regime. He called up somebody and I was quickly placed in jail. I spent seven weeks there. They were seven horrible weeks. Every morning a truck would come for me and about thirty other women and girls, usually criminals. We would be taken out to the woods where we were put to work setting trees in the ground.

Installment eight

Somewhere in Germany—Apathy took possession of me when I was released from prison. I had lost my drive, my energy and my will to do. I was spiritless. There was one man to blame for the misery which many suffered in those days. How I wish that I knew how to lay hands on that scoundrel today! I'm sure he is living. Maybe he has changed his name. He may even now be among the American Occupation Forces.

It sickens one to realize what good fortune your former persecutors may be enjoying while you continue to suffer. This man, a Dr. E. Stemp[illegible] had the lives of many at his disposal. The seven weeks I spent in prison put a scar on me. But I think not alone of myself as a victim of Stemp[illegible]. I remember scores of others whose treatment was even worse than mine.

I am sure you remember how the Nazis employed euthanasia to dispose of their enemies and others whom they did not value. Many, many times I saw in the City Hall adults and children who were suffering from mental or physical defects. They were the true victims of this Stemp[illegible].

With one wave of his paw this man consigned them to the gas chamber. It is possible to talk about these experiences now, possible for us and for others who went through them because, we hope, it is all behind us now. But it is impossible for anyone who had to live through this period not to understand what happened.

The crowning insult and humiliation for me came when Stemp[illegible] and his gang informed me that it was necessary for them to determine to what category of race I belonged. The Nazis had divided the so-called races into different categories based on blood percentages. This testing and sampling to determine your category was carried on in Berlin at what was called the "Rassenforschungsamt." I was ordered to go to the capital for the tests.

I went to Berlin, to Hitler's headquarters, to see these scientists who could measure race down to the last percentage point. When I confronted them in their laboratory, they had at hand machines and instruments of all kinds. These were used in the tests. They were enough to frighten anybody.

I was placed in [the] charge of these "race specialists" and ordered to take off all of my clothes. I was placed upon a kind of round table which these men could move in any direction, right or left, up or down. They gathered around and inspected me from every side and angle. They engaged in a long discussion about my fingernails and my toenails. The shape of my head and nose and my ears sent them off on another lengthy comparison of so-called scientific figures and measurements. Bear in mind that while all this was going on, I was pregnant and had been for five months.

After an examination and check-up that lasted four hours, and after three blood tests, these "eminent" scientists came to the startling conclusion that I had 70 percent Negro blood and 30 percent German. They freely acknowledged that my father's Negro blood had been much stronger in determining my racial strain than my mother's.

The distance from Berlin to Nurnberg is four hundred miles. While I was returning home, I opened the door of the train once with the intention of jumping off and ending everything. Life seemed like nothing but pain for me. But before I jumped, I had a vision of my mother standing before me and pleading. I recalled that I was her only child. I restrained myself.

Not long after this, my father received a mysterious visit from a former schoolmate. He was an important man in the Nazi headquarters. After some preliminaries during which my father wondered about the cause of the visit, this man declared that his attitude toward us had always been friendly and that he was risking his job to come to us at this time.

He then told my parents that he could no longer protect me. It seems as though he had been trying to give me a sort of protection from the inside because of his friendship for my father.

That was the first intimation we had ever had that anybody was trying to protect me. He then warned us that the Nazis were planning another pogrom against the Jews and that this time would get me, too. He therefore advised that I should leave Nurnberg as quickly as possible.

I began to laugh hysterically. Through my mind flashed those many occasions when I had had the chance to go away and wouldn't. My idealism had been ill-placed and had led me to place my trust in a class of people who in a very short time had forgotten what it was to be human. I knew then that I was trapped. It would be impossible for me to obtain an official pass to go anywhere. The Nazis would rather murder me. I could not suppress a feeling of hate, hate for the entire human race.

At first, I did not know where I might flee in such a hurry. Then I had an idea. The next morning found me traveling again, with Herbert, my boy friend. I remembered my friends in the little Catholic town of Berching. These friends had been very nice to me and I clung to the hope that they might give me a home. But what was most important to me, I was leaving the territory of the terrible "Gau Franken" Streicher.

When we reached Berching, I visited first the family of Burgermeister [*sic*] Will. Without asking many questions, he helped us to obtain an apartment and told me that, regardless of anything or anybody, I was under his protection.

I notified my parents and they hurriedly purchased sufficient furniture for three rooms and a kitchen. Two days after I fled from Nurnberg, two trucks came to Berching and brought everything necessary to furnish a home for me.

I should have felt better. Anyone who knows what homesickness is can appreciate how I really did feel. I had lived in a big city all my life. Suddenly, I was forced to leave it and to take up residence in a country town a thousand years old. Everything in it made me feel that time had stopped for a thousand years. The quietness and the loneliness almost maddened me.

My parents didn't have time to visit me during the week and my future husband had to travel on his job. In the evenings, after a visit from my parents, when the last train would leave Berching, I couldn't help standing at my window and crying. I was so close to my native city. Yet I could not go home.

But still Herbert and I could not be married because if we did go through a ceremony and the Nazis found out about it, they would put me in jail again for a long time. They had already promised me that.

On June 6, 1938, I gave birth to a ten-pound boy. But my health was so bad, due to all that I had suffered, that I almost died. We could not keep the baby alive. He died after four hours. I had been supposed to go to the hospital, but I didn't do so because I had lost all my confidence in people on the outside and was afraid to leave home. With my child gone, it seemed once again that I had nothing to live for and I was almost hoping to die. For days I lay in bed without speaking to anyone. No one could touch me but my mother. For the first time in his life, my father forgot about his business. Day after day, he would sit on the side of my bed for hours at a time. It hurt me more to see him suffer. After a week, he returned to Nurnberg.

A few days later, in the afternoon, there was the noise of an automobile horn in front of my horn [*sic*]. My mother asked me to look out the window. I left my bed and stumbled slowly to the front of the room. As I parted the curtains and peered through, I saw standing in the street a light green convertible automobile, covered with flowers. Papa called up to the window where I stood and asked me how I liked my Opel! Dear old Daddy! He had worried so much about me that he had bought for me the kind of car I had always wanted to own. It was just the color I desired.

I had this car for myself because Herbert had his own car and a driver. Herbert stayed in the country with me on weekends but during the rest of the week he was traveling on business.

We went to Berching in March, 1938. On Oct. 9, Bergomeister [*sic*] Will said that he was going to take the bull by the horns and marry us. So he did. There was no ceremony because Herbert and I were afraid for knowledge of the marriage to become public.

When the war broke out in 1939, I suppose I was the only person in Germany who was happy about it because I thought that the loss of the war by the Nazis would mean freedom to me. I also thought that if they were busy with a war they would not have so much time to torment me and others.

My husband fought in the war from the beginning until the end. At first he was a lieutenant. Later, he became a captain in a panzer division.

My life was still very lonesome, but in January, 1940, I gave birth to an eight-pound girl, Elke. She was my sunshine. My health remained bad. We never had enough food and we had no sugar nor butter. I couldn't work much so I employed a young girl to help me in the house. She stayed with us for two years.

The Nazis were very quiet at this time. Perhaps I should say that it seemed to me as though they were quiet. I was pestered by only one person. The teacher in the so-called Christian school, and his wife, seemed to never tire of telling people in Berching to have nothing to do with me because I was the same as a Jew. But, inasmuch as the natives of Berching had never known any Jews, the sense of what this couple said was lost upon them.

My, what terrible nights were those when British and American airplanes bombed Nurnberg! We were forced to open our windows and doors to keep them from breaking. The sky would be red from the fire. I could only pray for the lives of my parents. It was impossible to call them on the telephone or to go to see them by train. Telephone and train service were disrupted.

Very often, driven by my anxiety, I would hop on my bicycle and ride the forty-five miles to Nurnberg to see if my parents were still alive. Sometimes my girl friend in Berching would go with me.

Frequently, we would have to jump off our bicycles and seek cover when gunners in enemy planes would take shots at us. Sometimes bullets spattered all around us. Excitement and danger before had made me almost immune to fear. I did not seem to care much if I did get hit. Once when a bullet nearly struck my right foot, I yelled to my girl friend, "That's all right, Maria. I have the will to die anywhere, but I prefer to die a soldier's death before the Nazis put me in some foxhole."

Feb. 7, 1944, I gave birth to a six and one-half-pound girl, Birgit.

My husband usually came home on a fourteen-day furlough, once a year. He fought in Russia and sometimes I was without mail from him for two months. Nevertheless, I was reasonably happy. I had my daughters.

I had another friend in Berching. If at times there were problems I couldn't solve, I could always go to see Heinz Knuefer. He had a drug store in Berching and he was a personal friend of my husband. He came from the same Rhine river section as Herbert. Kneufer [*sic*] was one of the very few Nazis who remained human. He was an idealist.

One day Kneufer told me that everybody was beginning to feel that the Nazis had lost the war and that Allied troops would soon be coming, even to Berching. When I asked him how he obtained his information, he confided to me that he was an SD (Sicherheitsdienst) man. That was just about the same as the Gestapo.

Knuefer then told me, with pain written all over his face, that he had received an order to send me and my girls to Auschwitz, to the concentration camp where many thousands had been put to death in the gas stoves. He said that my marriage had been automatically annulled because Herbert and I had married against the law. Knuefer did his best to delay sending us away.

At this time, the Americans were fighting very close to us. The Nazis were tracking me down, all right, but at night I could hear the big guns of the Americans. Sleep deserted me. Everytime [*sic*] I heard an automobile in the street, or thought that I heard one, I was convinced that the Nazis had come to get me and I was hoping that the Americans would get to Berching first.

Soldiers were returning, deserters from the front lines. They told us that the Nazi Elite Guard was behind the German front line and that members of the Guard were hanging all German soldiers who left the front. Everybody seemed to know that it was fruitless to keep on fighting.

Herbert by this time had been transferred to the Rhine.

Knuefer came to me again. He was terribly upset. He said that the Nazis were putting pressure on him, that the authorities at Auschwitz had complained because my children and I had not reached there according to orders. Knuefer wrang his hand as though in great perplexity. He said that he could allow me to stay in Berching no more than one more week. He seemed to pray with me that the Americans would come.

And then the Americans arrived! Happiness and fear possessed me. I was happy because I knew that I owed my life and the lives of my children to them. I shared the general fear. We had been propagandized. We had been poisoned against these Americans, all of us. We therefore distrusted our liberators. We dug holes in the ground and buried our little food, our black bread, our flour and our beans. We hid our rugs and paintings and everything else we were afraid these Americans would take.

The first Americans to reach Berching came in tanks. They were followed by infantrymen, colored and white. I cowered behind my window curtains and looked into the street. I knew not what to expect. But the children were not so full of fear. They went out and met the conquerors. My own fears were relieved a bit when the children returned with chocolate and candy, gifts from these soldiers.

The colored soldiers left town shortly. When my girl, Elke, saw the first colored soldier, she was also quite curious. She asked me if his color was due to the fact that he had not washed. That was the same old question.

My husband was held prisoner for about twelve weeks at Kreutznach [*sic*] on the Rhine. He came home broken in body and soil [*sic*]. I did not place all the blame on him when I discovered that since we had met and married, not only had time passed, but we had changed also. Our temperaments and our natures were different.

Now, more than ever, my energy had returned. I felt charged to make a new start in life. But Herbert seemed beaten up and tired of everything. We just did not seem to be able to get along together. Nevertheless, we still respected each other and continued to be good friends.

I begged Herbert for my freedom and we obtained a divorce in July 1946. I did what seemed impossible in the eyes of my family. There had been no divorces among any of our relatives. Herbert returned to his home on the Rhine. I was left with the responsibility of taking care of my two children and myself—because Herbert had nothing with which to support me and I did not even want him to do so.

Installment nine

Somewhere in Germany—Not long after the Americans came, I had a chance to learn how good they were, particularly the colored Americans. I did not return to Nurnberg to live because, by this time, after all the bombings and the bombardment, it was impossible to find an apartment. I did go to Nurnberg frequently to see my family.

But I am going to tell you a secret. I went there because I liked the colored soldiers. They were the first of my people I had met. They were a kind [illegible] to a sort of heartache I felt all the time. I couldn't [illegible] much when I was all among the Germans, but when the young men came along, I felt like I was meeting old friends, who were living in the place in which I should have belonged. . . .

There is one soldier, particularly, whom I wish to thank for all he did for us. His home was in Louisiana and we called him Johnny. If he reads my story in The Pittburgh [*sic*] Courier, I hope he'll realize that we remember him and are grateful to him.

During the war, my automobile stood in the garage all the time because we were forbidden to drive cars. Only the Nazis were allowed to use automobiles. The German Army took the tires and inner tubes from all our cars. In 1946, I had a hard fight to retrieve my license. That was because of the way things are in Germany, even today. The Nazis are still alive. The only difference is that they are quieter and less aggressive.

They seem to be biding their time. Many have changed their names, but in their hearts they have not changed. Now, as before, life remains difficult, more difficult for some of us who were not Nazis than for some of the Nazis themselves. In the section of Germany where I live, most of the key positions are held fy [*sic*] former Nazis. I know them. When will they be taken out of authority and given the punishment they deserve? I can't help thinking about how I suffered for THIRTEEN LONG YEARS while the Nazis were living the good life. But I still have to suffer, more than my persecutors. I didn't receive more food and clothing after the war and I lost my money just like all other Germans.

After the money which I had for myself and my children was gone, I obtained a job in Nurnberg doing office work. My father's business had been ruined by the war like many others. But it was not easy for me to get up at 5 o'clock in the morning, drive my car forty-five miles to Nurnberg in the cold German winter and return in the evening, cold and tired. I was forced to keep a maid to care for my children. Six months ago, I lost the job I had because this concern had lost orders and was compelled to reduce its staff. I am still searching for another job.

Nevertheless, I am grateful for the fact that I am never lonesome now like I was formerly. I have met new friends who have become very dear to me. One of those who have tried to help me is Capt. Elisha McNair. He is a chaplain with the American forces and the kind of a man a chaplain should be. He is busy from morning until evening at the military post, but he is never too tired to come to the aid of someone who needs his help. Hundreds of Germans have called on him for aid. Also, there was Mrs. Mildred Allison of New Orleans and her husband, Jimmy. I spent many happy hours in their home. Finally, there was Mrs. Marie Kenner of Kansas City. She made me feel like a sister. But all, except Chaplain McNair, have left me, gone home.

[EDITOR'S NOTE: In concluding this story, Mr. Prattis uses almost the exact language of Mrs. Stark. It reveals her thinking in German and gives the reader a clearer picture of how she thinks. We believe our readers will be touched by this yearning of a woman, born among the Germans, to be with her own people.]

I wish I could go home, too. All I know, once a prizefighter from the States came to Germany on a tour, and it was my true father. If he is still alive or not, God knows. But I will tell you, Daddy, anywhere, I love you and I thought about you lots of times. And when I was mad about you sometime, because you left me over here, when I met your people in 1945, I beg your pardon, and I am proud of it they are my people, too. My life here was under what you can call "lucky circumstances" because not many children find a stepfather like I had.

Did you ever think about all the colored babies we have over here right now? Pretty soon it will be a problem to us colored people anywhere. It should be done something to keep them from trouble like I had. I didn't want to say that colored soldiers have more babies over here than whites ones, but who recognizes the white babies? The Germans naturally are not happy about these brown infants. Our daily prayer in Germany should be, "God, let the allied troops so long in Germany until we get an international law or something like that to protect us."

Now I have talked to you about everything, and I will tell you what more wishes I have. I read in our paper that Bing Crosby is going to visit Germany this year. Why doesn't come King Cole and Joe Louis? Everybody listen to King Cole's music and he got many friends among the Germans, too. And who's boy's heart, inclusive mine's, too, beat not faster, if we hear about Joe Louis? And I need not to talk about the Army over here.

How it sound when I tell you I would like it when you write to me sometime? Maybe you have some questions about over here and I will answer in The Pittsburgh Courier.

And now, so long. You will hear about me again.

The End

10

Black Occupation Children and the Devolution of the Nazi Racial State

HEIDE FEHRENBACH

This essay explores how attention to Black occupation children fathered by Allied troops of color and born to white German mothers figured in the devolution of the Nazi racial state.[1] Informing this analysis is an insistence that we begin to consider two key postwar developments—namely, democratization and racial reconstruction—in tandem as mutually informing processes. The transition away from Nazi racial practice and understanding was hardly abrupt. Rather, this was a protracted social process lasting at least into the 1960s. It was through the articulation of social policy regarding abortion, adoption, schooling, and integration of these youth into the workforce that questions of German racial redefinition after 1945 were worked out.

Postwar responses to Black occupation children represent a formative moment in the racial reconstruction of postfascist Germany. Military occupation between 1945 and 1949 produced some 94,000 occupation children. However, official and public attention fixed on a small subset, the so-called *farbige Mischlinge* or "colored mixed-bloods," distinguished from the others by their Black paternity. Although they constituted a small minority of postwar German births—numbering only about three thousand in 1950 and nearly double that by 1955—West German federal and state officials, youth welfare workers, and the press invested the children with considerable symbolic significance.

The years after 1945 were constitutive for contemporary German racial understanding, and postwar debates regarding "miscegenation" and "*Mischlingskinder*" were central to the ideological transition from National Socialist to democratic approaches to race. The term "*Mischling,*" in fact, survived the Third Reich and persisted well into the 1960s in official, scholarly, media, and public usage in West Germany. But its content had changed: rather than refer to the progeny of so-called mixed unions between Jewish and non-Jewish Germans as it had during the Third Reich, it came to connote the offspring of white German women and foreign men of color.[2] Thus "*Mischling*" remained a racialized category of social analysis and social policy after 1945, as before. But the definition of *which* races had mixed, as well as the social significance of such mixing, had fundamentally changed.

Contact Zones: The Social Meaning of Military Occupation

The radically altered conditions that confronted Germans in 1945 helped shape the terms of social and ideological revaluation following National Socialism's demise. The postwar reformulation of notions of race in Germany was not a purely national enterprise, however, but an international and transnational one as well, as defeat brought military occupation and the victorious Allies' mandate for Germans to denazify and democratize themselves, their society, and their polity. The first decades after the war were dominated by debates regarding self-definition as contemporaries grappled with the question of what it would mean to be German after Hitler and the Holocaust.

Debates about national self-definition necessarily involved confronting issues of race, since Germany was occupied by the multiethnic armies of enemy nations. Former racial subordinates—whether Jews, Slavs, North Africans, or African Americans—now occupied a position of political superiority due to their membership in the Allied forces. The occupation challenged Germans to function within a context that was radically *postfascist* in terms of social composition and political authority, if not yet in terms of ideological disposition or social policy.

Initially, the most explicit postwar discussions of "race" occurred in response to interracial sex and reproduction between German women and Allied soldiers of color. This was accompanied by an emerging unwillingness among German officials to speak openly about Jews in racialized terms—although anti-Semitism certainly persisted in informal private interactions, in jokes and stereotypes, and even in anonymous exchanges on public transportation or desecrations of Jewish cemeteries.[3]

Practices of segregation and anti-Black racism within the American occupation forces also helped shape racial ideology after 1945. This does not mean that postwar Germans learned anti-Black racism from American occupiers. After all, Germans had a long tradition of such bigotry that predated and was intensified by Germany's short stint as colonial power prior to 1918 and shorter stint as National Socialist power between 1933 and 1945. Rather, informal contacts between occupier and occupied—along with the discriminatory policies of the US military toward its minorities and the tense relations among occupation soldiers of differing ethnicities—affected how Germans perceived and received American political and social values after 1945. Although the American military government in Germany emphasized official efforts to denazify and reeducate the German public, "race" barely figured in formal reeducation programs (beyond the legal language against discrimination that ultimately entered West Germany's *Grundgesetz* [Basic law] in 1949). As a result, racial reconstruction in early postwar Germany primarily resulted not from official Allied pronouncements or programs but more spontaneously from Germans' interaction with and observation of the social and racial dynamics of occupation.

The United States defeated and occupied Germany with a Jim Crow army in 1945, and the hierarchical values of racial segregation affected social dynamics and perceptions of the American occupation, both among American soldiers and between American occupiers and Germans. In particular, interracial fraternization between African American GIs and white German women elicited zealous rage and frequent incidents of verbal and physical abuse from white GIs. In intelligence debriefings of US troops returning from overseas in 1945, for example, numerous white officers and soldiers denounced interracial dating by Black GIs abroad as the primary cause of racial violence in the military. In Germany, it was treated as an unbearable provocation. White GIs harassed German women in the company of Black GIs and physically assaulted the men. American military police forcibly excluded Black GIs from pubs, in effect imposing racial segregation on German establishments, as Maria Höhn has shown.[4] Where segregation broke down, violent brawls, serious injury, and even murder could result. White American hostility toward sexual relations between African American troops and German women in Germany persisted for decades but was especially vehement and violent during the late 1940s and 1950s—the years during which desegregation of the US military was accomplished. Moreover, it was assiduously reported in the German press and no doubt served to justify violence against Black GIs by German men, which was less frequent but not unheard of.[5] Although white Americans and Germans drew on distinct national-historical idioms of race, they agreed upon the necessity to "defend" white manhood and police white women.[6]

In the public behavior of US troops in Germany, troubled American race relations were on display for all to see. Germans absorbed the *postwar* lesson, inadvertently taught by their new American masters, that democratic forms and values were consistent with racialist, even racist, ideology and social organization. German understandings of the content of "democratization" were conditioned by the racialized context within which it was delivered. As a result, military occupation initially reinforced white supremacy as a shared value of mainstream American and German cultures.[7]

Counting "Coloreds," Documenting Difference: Toward a Postwar Taxonomy of Race

German defeat and the influx of occupation forces ended a decade of prescribed Aryan exclusivity in white German women's heterosexual relations. The restrictive, state-mandated Aryanized sex of the Third Reich gave way to a broader range of choice in social relations and sexual partners.[8] By early 1946 the first "occupation children" were born. German officials and social policy came to focus on the implications of consensual sex between occupying soldiers and native women in the Western zones. Evidence from southern Germany suggests that in addition to American GIs, German women also chose French occupation soldiers—including those from Algeria, Morocco, Tunisia, and French Indochina—as lovers, bore their children, and in some cases married them and emigrated.[9] Despite this broader range of social interaction, American soldiers attracted the lion's share of Germans' attention and aggression.

In an early 1950s survey, for example, German social workers asked German women why they had become involved with Black troops. Similar questions were not posed to women involved with white foreign troops.[10] While almost half of those surveyed expressed an intention to marry their Black beaus, German and American officials could not accept that interracial relationships were based upon genuinely mutual love and desire. As a result, the women consorting with Black GIs were accused of wanton materialism and moral deficiency and were characterized as mentally impaired or asocial, or as prostitutes.[11] In many cases, women found in the company of African American GIs were remanded to VD treatment clinics, jails, or workhouses, where they could be held for a few days or for many months.[12]

After 1949, moral assumptions about women in interracial relationships continued to influence how the perceived problem of biracial occupation children was formulated in the Federal Republic. Through the 1950s, German commentators of various political viewpoints insisted that these children should not be made to suffer for their mothers' "sins." The high number of births in Bavaria alarmed state officials there, and they sought in vain to negotiate with the American military government regarding the children's citizenship status. Ultimately, all occupation children, including those of color, were grudgingly extended German citizenship—but only after Allied military government officials made it clear that they would not entertain paternity suits or grant citizenship to their troops' foreign-born, out-of-wedlock offspring.[13] Since marriage between GIs and German women, while legally permissible by late 1946, was virtually impossible for Black soldiers due to racial biases inherent in the screening process, such interracial marriages remained rare, rendering most Black occupation children "illegitimate." By closing off the possibility of emigration, this policy ensured that the children and their mothers would remain German citizens on German soil.[14]

As a resident minority population of citizen-minors, Black occupation children attracted increased official and academic attention with the end of military occupation and the founding of the West German Federal Republic in 1949. From the turn of the 1950s, social and scientific debates about the meaning of race—and its implications for postwar West German society—focused insistently upon these children. Such debates not only invoked but also reconstituted German understandings of race by revising racial classifications, often with reference to contemporary American race relations and social science.

By 1950 West German federal and state Interior Ministry officials explicitly constructed the postwar problem of race around skin color and even more narrowly around Blackness. That year, they surveyed state and municipal youth offices to determine the number and living arrangements of so-called *Negermischlingskinder*. Because the survey was limited to West

German states formerly occupied by the French and Americans and drew on a simplified appraisal of the racial and ethnic composition of those occupying armies, it established a postwar preoccupation with color/Blackness in bureaucratic record-keeping and in official and public discourse regarding the reproductive consequences of defeat and occupation. Furthermore, this schematic racial binary—with its categories for national paternities on the one hand and colored paternity, or "*farbige Abstammung*," on the other—set a precedent for a subsequent federal census of all occupation children in the Federal Republic.[15] In creating one explicitly racialized yet denationalized category keyed to "color," the 1954 census effectively de-raced the offspring of Soviet paternity and rendered Jewishness invisible, implicitly coding the occupation children of these formerly racialized groups "white." As a result, the attribution of racialized identities previously and lethally targeted by the German state before 1945—whether Jewish, Slavic, or "Mongoloid/Asiatic"—disappeared from official record-keeping on postwar reproduction. What remained were distinctions of nationality on the one hand and Blackness on the other.

Postwar Germans' telescoped focus on Blackness was also evident in a number of anthropological studies of "*Mischlingskinder*" in the 1950s. During the first half of the decade, two young German anthropologists, Walter Kirchner and Rudolf Sieg, independently undertook studies of Black German children ranging in age from one to six. Assisted, respectively, by Berlin's youth and health offices and by Christian social welfare organizations in West Germany, Kirchner and Sieg minutely recorded the children's skin color, lip thickness, and hair texture; the breadth of their noses, shoulders, chests, and pelvises; the length of their limbs and torsos; the shape of their dental bites; and the circumference of their heads and chests. In keeping with the earlier practice of German ethnographers and racial scientists, Kirchner appended photographs of the children to his work. Both anthropologists analyzed the children's medical and psychological records as well as their social, family, and moral milieu and subjected the children to intellectual and psychological exams. The point of these exercises was to establish the extent to which "*Mischlingskinder*" deviated from the white norm (Kirchner) and to account for the children's "anomalies" (Sieg).[16]

In exploring the somatic, psychological, and behavioral effects of "racial mixing," both anthropologists drew on the earlier work and methodologies of German racial scientists and eugenicists Eugen Fischer, Wolfgang Abel, and Otmar Freiherr von Verschuer (along with Americans Charles Davenport and Melville Herskovits). Beginning in the 1910s, Fischer pioneered an early study on racial mixing based upon the "Rehobother bastards"—the children of German fathers and Khoikhoi (or "Hottentot") mothers—and concluded that "racial crossing" led to "degeneration" or, at best, the inheritance of "disharmonious traits." Fischer continued his work into the Nazi years. Joined by Abel and others, he conducted racial examinations of the so-called Rhineland Bastards (the biracial German children of French African occupation troops and German women born after World War I) and later of Jews, providing scientific expertise for the Third Reich's increasingly radical program of eugenic engineering that culminated in forced sterilization and murder.[17]

Though beholden to the work of Fischer and others, the anthropological studies of the 1950s departed from that literature in small and self-conscious ways, reworking aspects of the Nazi-era paradigm in search of a morally acceptable postwar alternative. In its attention to the effects of race mixing, Kirchner's postwar work clearly continued his predecessors' tendency to think within a racist eugenicist paradigm. But what *is* peculiarly postwar is his choice of subject: the Black "*Mischlingskind*." This was not a logical choice in demographic terms. The vast majority of Black occupation children resided in the southern states of mainland West Germany. Kirchner's study was based in Berlin, where fewer than two percent (about eighty) of the children were located.[18] A focus on Jewish children or on so-called *Russenkinder,* the colloquial term for German children of Soviet paternity in the first years after the war, would have yielded a larger sample.[19] But there is no indication that Kirchner ever considered such a study, and that is precisely my point. It was politically impossible to contemplate studying Jewish children or "*Russenkinder*" after the death camps, the Nazi defeat, and the onset of the Cold War.[20] The postwar political situation influenced the postfascist study of race and the delineation of racial categories in Germany.

Kirchner's and Sieg's studies were also symptomatic in their exclusive emphasis on a subset of Black occupation children, namely those of African American paternity. Kirchner, for example, examined the medical records and social welfare and school reports of fifty "colored mixed-blood children" in Berlin ranging in age from one to twenty but focused his analysis on a subgroup of twenty-three children, aged one through five, of "American Negro" paternity. Similarly, Sieg had access to children of Algerian, Moroccan, and American paternity but deliberately excluded all but the latter from his study. This deliberate focus on Black American paternity and the post-1945 circumstances of conception allowed these anthropologists to render a relatively rosy picture of the physical, mental, and emotional health of postwar "*Mischlingskind*" as compared to the supposedly more negative impact of Moroccan paternity on "Rhineland Bastards" after the First World War. In accounting for the absence of serious disease among postwar "*Mischlingskinder*," both Kirchner and Sieg credited the relative health and wealth of Black American GIs. Unlike North African soldiers after 1918, who "presumably represented a thoroughly unfavorable selection" in eugenic and material terms, African Americans were assumed to have few serious maladies, in part because "Negros" were defined as mixed-race rather than pure-blooded Blacks and had ample resources with which to provide for their offspring.[21]

This assessment made all the difference for the children. Neither anthropologist found significant deviations in the health, intelligence, or emotional disposition of postwar "*Mischlingskinder*" when compared to their white counterparts. However, they did note certain developmental, physical, and behavioral characteristics that they attributed to the children's "Negroid biological inheritance" and that clearly echoed the stereotypes handed down by previous generations of racial scientists. For example, Kirchner and Sieg cited a disposition for respiratory disease (due to maladjustment to the European climate); abnormalities of dental bite; long legs; lively temperaments; a marked joy in movement, including dance; and well-developed speaking abilities, with particular talents for rhythmic speech, rhyme, and imitation. Although the children were described as open to social contact, they also were declared willful, impatient, uncooperative, and at times given to strong, although not necessarily ungovernable, impulses.[22]

As regards the children's mothers, Kirchner judged their influence as generally beneficial, which, he argued, was not the case with the earlier "Rhineland Bastards," who were alleged to have suffered disproportionately from psychopathologies. Following earlier racial scientists, Kirchner blamed that interwar generation's poor mental health on the miserable genetic stock of their "asocial" mothers, who were deemed a "particularly negative" type of woman. "In the case of Berliner '*Mischlinge*'" born after 1945, he judged that "no such factor presented itself." As Sieg put it at the end of his study: "No detrimental consequences of bastardization were perceptible among *our* '*Mischlingskinder*.'"[23]

Ultimately, then, postwar anthropologists arrived at a less negative assessment of "race mixing" and "*Mischlingskinder*" by reading the contemporary episode in relation to earlier historical experience. Their upbeat prognostications rested on evaluating the distinct national and gender dimensions of each case: "our '*Mischlingskinder*'" presented fewer problems than those of the past because they were fathered by healthy, wealthy "American Negroes" rather than diseased and uncultivated Africans and were born to caring lower-class mothers rather than asocial lunatics.

Finally, the postwar anthropological studies differed significantly from their precursors in their focus on social environment and its potentially mitigating effect on racial inheritance. While Kirchner and Sieg detected a tendency for hotheadedness, impulsiveness, and disobedience among "*Mischlingskinder*," they also declared that these supposedly inherited racial qualities could be tempered by the positive influences of attentive mothers, childhood friendships, and a well-disposed public. The markers of "race," that is to say, were not destiny.[24] If Kirchner and Sieg agreed with earlier anthropologists that racial difference persisted in the biology and psychology of their subjects, Kirchner's innovation was to permit the possibility of social solutions to the purported "problems of race."

In sum, official surveys and anthropological studies of "*Mischlingskinder*" of the 1950s articulated a revised taxonomy of race that would spur new social policy initiatives. In the process, West German official, academic, and media reports constructed a unitary origin for Black occupation children. By consistently representing them as offspring of Black American soldiers, such reports erased the actual national affiliation of the more diverse paternity by Allied soldiers. By the 1950s, "race" in West Germany was embodied in the "*Mischlingskind*" and linked to America. German censuses and scientists had conceived a putatively "new" and peculiarly postwar problem of race.

In this sense, postwar West German definitions of race paralleled those of the postwar United States. For over the course of the 1930s and 1940s, American social scientists softened the differences among whites of European origin (including, in particular, Jews) to a cultural one and conceived of these groups in terms of "ethnicity." Race, as a concept, continued to be employed but was reduced to the radically simplified terms of the Black-white binary (or, at its most articulated, the Black-white-yellow triad), redrawing the lines of meaningful difference according to stereotypical phenotype.[25] The result was a confluence of the broad forms of racial taxonomy in West Germany and the United States.

International Adoption and Racialized Notions of Kinship

As early as 1947, the African American press covered the story of Germany's "brown babies."[26] Interested parties on both sides of the Atlantic were intent on pursuing Afro-German children's "proper" placement. Discussions revolved around issues of national belonging and racial fit. In West Germany, the children were typically imagined as "*Heimkinder,*" or unwanted institutionalized children, despite the fact that barely ten percent resided outside of families.[27] Ignoring actual demographics, most West German authorities viewed the children as a social problem and advocated international adoption as the preferred solution.

Adoption by African Americans—described as "families of their own kind"—struck German social welfare authorities as a fitting solution, since most Germans were unwilling to adopt children from perceived inferior biological or moral backgrounds. Under the Nazi regime, such adoptions by "Aryan" Germans had been legally prohibited in 1939 for "offending the public interest," and existing adoptions deemed "undesirable" could be terminated by the state.[28]

Concerns about heredity and racial-biological factors persisted after 1945 and discouraged adoptions of biracial children by white German couples. The American military government in Germany did nothing to counter this response. In fact, when German officials asked for clarification on adoption law in 1948, the American Legal Affairs Branch responded that it had not abrogated the Nazi-era law but found it "politically and ideologically neutral" (the British and Soviets ruled otherwise). Racial restrictions in forming German families attracted little American attention after 1945 because the assumptions underlying such policy were similar to the principles and practices informing adoption in America, where whites cleaved to whites, Blacks to Blacks, and Jews to Jews. Consideration of race in creating elective families through adoption was therefore not viewed by American officials as necessarily Nazi or even undemocratic.[29]

Shortly after the end of military occupation, West Germans liberalized their adoption law. This was done not to encourage ethnic diversity within the German family but to facilitate the adoption of white (mostly ethnic

German) children who had been separated from their parents or orphaned in the war.[30] Concurrently with adoption law reform, West German officials continued to seek ways to offload the costs and care of Black German children. In 1951, federal Interior Ministry officials pursued negotiations with representatives of the US Displaced Persons Commission to press for the adoption of Black occupation children to the United States using nonquota visas available for war orphans. Strikingly, German officials expressed interest in including in their plan children who had *not* been surrendered for adoption, even if they were currently living in German families and would end up in orphanages in the United States.[31] However, while hundreds of adoptions of Afro-German children to the United States did ensue, most appear to have been voluntarily arranged by the mothers.

Adoptions of Afro-German children to the United States were encouraged and pursued by African American civilians at home and in the US military in Germany as well. From the late 1940s into the 1950s, the African American press in particular spread the word about the plight of unwanted "half-Negro" children abroad. The *Pittsburgh Courier* and Baltimore *Afro-American* published appeals to their predominantly Black readership, urging them to send special CARE packages to "brown babies" and their unwed German mothers.[32] The NAACP and the Urban League also lobbied on behalf of Afro-German children, invoking them to chastise the American government and military leadership about its reluctance to engage in civil rights reform. The NAACP, for example, pointed out that the "problem of the children" was due to prejudicial official policies that didn't permit Black GIs to marry their white German girlfriends.

However, the NAACP and Urban League also expressed doubts about whether adoption into an American culture of virulent anti-Black racism would be in the children's best interests. As Lester Granger of the Urban League put it: "Colored children in . . . Georgia, for example, . . . are much worse off than colored children in Germany."[33] In 1952, Walter White of the NAACP issued press releases praising West Germany's decision to integrate schools without regard to race, noting with irony that the former fascist foe surpassed the democratic United States in racial tolerance and equality. In addition, by the mid-1950s, increasing numbers of Americans began adopting Amerasian children. Published exposés of these children's appalling living conditions in Japan and Korea made Germany's treatment of Afro-German children appear beneficent and broad-minded by comparison. As a result, American youth welfare workers—Black and white—increasingly questioned whether intervention on behalf of Germany's "brown babies" was necessary or advisable.[34]

Black Americans in West Germany saw things differently. Mrs. Mabel Grammer, occasional correspondent for the Baltimore *Afro-American* and wife of a US warrant officer based near Mannheim, observed the miserable economic conditions of some of the children and their mothers in West Germany and actively sought Black adoptive parents. Publicizing the children's plight and working closely with local German public and religious youth offices and orphanages, she facilitated up to seven hundred adoptions between 1951 and 1953 and remained active into the 1960s. Grammer received assistance from West German authorities, who preferred adopting the children to Americans—and especially African Americans—both for reasons of racial "fit" and to release German taxpayers from the costs of the children's care.[35]

Although West German state and local officials eagerly cooperated with Mrs. Grammer through most of the 1950s, even permitting proxy adoptions, by late decade they began to have second thoughts. Economic recovery fueled more domestic German adoption requests, albeit for white children. Since white German children were also eagerly sought for adoption by white Americans, German federal officials began to demand more stringent regulation of international adoptions to keep such "desirable" progeny at home in the Federal Republic.[36]

As a result, the late 1950s marked a retreat from transatlantic adoptions. When it came to Afro-German children, however, West German authorities offered a different rationale for discouraging US adoptions. To explain their policy shift, the federal ministries generalized from the case of "Otto." Charging that the boy suffered severe emotional trauma after being placed with an African American family, German ministry memos warned against similar future placements because of both the child's shock at, and inability to adjust to, an all-Black adoptive family and neighborhood and the child's subjection to racial segregation and Jim Crow laws in the United States. Since white German families were still not adopting biracial children in significant numbers,[37] the preferred destination for such children became Denmark, where, German commentators curiously insisted, racial prejudice was nonexistent.[38]

By the early 1960s, international adoptions of Black German children to Denmark outpaced those to the United States.[39] In contrast to the troubling reports on adoptive Black German children in the United States, West

German officials and social workers painted a picture of easy integration in Denmark due to the elevated class background of the parents and their assured cultural competence in easing the children into a Danish context. Denmark was portrayed in terms of cultural similarity: it was like Germany, only better, since prospective Danish parents seemed "more broad-minded about the children's origins." Moreover, German psychologists concerned with the children's emotional development in the segregated United States now described Danish mothers as more culturally compatible and less overbearing than the "Black mammies" who, a decade before, had been seen as "natural" nurturers to the children.[40] By claiming to act in the children's best interests, the West German state cultivated its role as protector and used its experience in international adoptions to provide a critical comparative perspective on the social progress of American and German democracies. Within a decade and a half of Nazi defeat, West German officials could claim a moral victory when it came to race relations and declare the provisional period of postwar racial reeducation closed.

Integration . . . and Its Limits

By the turn of the 1960s, as the oldest of the postwar cohort of Black German youth concluded their education, the public and official focus shifted from the question of "where the children most properly belonged" to the issue of integration into the West German economy. Historically low unemployment aided this process. These were, after all, the early years of the "guest worker" program, when some major West German industries began to import southern European and, later, Turkish workers to address a growing labor shortage. As Black German teens joined the workforce, municipal and state employment offices tracked their movements and reported the ready cooperation of West German employers in providing training and jobs, as well as the teenagers' unbiased absorption into working life. Press reports, official memos, and academic assessments projected the image of a stable and prosperous democracy whose bureaucrats and employers operated according to principles of social equality and economic rationality. In brief order, integration was declared a success—but only because integration was defined and pursued in *exclusively economic* rather than more broadly social terms.[41]

While social policy interest in Black German children subsided by the early 1960s in West Germany, sporadic media attention continued and centered on two general themes. The first concerned the alleged social progress and economic privilege accorded Blacks in Germany by the 1970s; the second concerned the allure of Black female sexuality. Press coverage took the form of follow-up stories purporting to answer the question of how "the Germans with dark skin" were faring since they'd reached adulthood. While noting examples of prejudice and racist epithets Black Germans had weathered during their young lives, the articles were upbeat and self-congratulatory. In large measure, this was the result of media proclivity to profile performers, personalities, and sports figures—in short, celebrities whose careers contrasted sharply with the mundane blue- and pink-collar work performed by most young Black Germans but who were nonetheless treated as representative of the entire postwar cohort of German "*Mischlingskinder*." For example, magazines highlighted the achievements of Jimmy Hartwig, who grew up in miserable circumstances in Offenbach to become a star of the 1860 Munich soccer club, and of Georg Steinherr, who had to learn to protect himself from bullies as a child and put his resulting "aggressiveness" to good use as a professional boxer.

By the 1970s, the West German magazine *Quick* borrowed the American phrase "Black is beautiful" to report on the various ways that biracial German women benefited from the current mode and marketability of their Black skin. *Quick* showcased Nicky, "a poor orphan child, abandoned by her parents," now transformed into a stunning long-legged temptress (and featured in a full-page magazine photo), who worked in a Munich boutique and turned men's heads as she walked down the street. Rosi, who as a child tried to scrub her "dark skin clean" after being cruelly ridiculed by classmates, was now a fashion model earning a lucrative income thanks to her "dark, exotic" looks. Such magazine articles betrayed a voyeuristic fascination with Black female physicality and sexuality and incessantly invoked these as a powerful stimulant of white male desire.[42] Illustrated weeklies ran racy photo-essays that promised an intimate peek into the personal lives and sexual relationships of Black German women and white German men. Interracial sex was titillating and therefore profitable for the print media.[43] However, there were limits. Relationships between Black German men and white German women did not become the subject of magazine features. That particular gendering of interracial unions apparently offended the boundaries of social acceptability and marketability in the 1970s—even for the West German tabloid press.[44]

One aspect of postwar German reconstruction to receive scant attention is the issue of continuity and rupture in social norms regarding sexual relations between white Germans and ethnic minorities. Indeed, 1945 did not disturb the prerogatives of white German men to engage in non-matrimonial, non-reproductive sexual relations with women perceived as racial others. These liaisons, while not openly condoned by the German majority, were nonetheless tolerated. By the 1970s, in the wake of the American civil rights and Black Power movements, interracial relationships appear to have become increasingly attractive to socially progressive, politically radical German men seeking to advertise their cosmopolitan taste and antiracist credentials, and therefore their irrepressibly un-German hipness.[45]

Afro-German women, on the other hand, suffered from their cultural image as sex objects. Carole, a child care worker in her twenties featured in a 1975 article in the *Neue Illustrierte Revue,* noted that before she could reconcile herself to a relationship with her white German lover, she needed to overcome the "I-just-want-to-seduce-you-complex" that she had internalized at a younger age in relation to white men. (This was likely not made any easier by the way her lover described his first impression of Carole: "I thought, 'What a pretty exotic bird!' I was not averse to the usual little adventure.") Another magazine reported, in an article inexplicably titled "Skin color is no problem," that a young Afro-German woman attempted suicide after a one-night stand with a white partner.[46] In addition, a Black German woman who came of age in the 1960s has described being repeatedly subjected to explicit unwanted sexual advances by male acquaintances and strangers on the street. As a child, she was lectured by the nuns raising her that she—as a Black girl—would need to choose between a future as a Christian missionary and life as a prostitute. To them, her race rendered her inherently more sexualized and morally abject than her white counterparts at the orphanage. However, media reports on Afro-Germans through the late 1970s did not focus on such feelings of debased objectification, profound alienation, and worthlessness produced by social interactions and cultural representations so relentlessly cued to notions of "racial difference."[47]

Social and Epistemic Consequences of West Germany's Retreat from "Race"

Following the defeat and international condemnation of National Socialism, West Germans made Afro-German children integral to their postwar process of national rehabilitation and social redefinition, albeit as *objects* of social policy. Unlike other minority groups in postwar Germany, Black

German children were minors with German citizenship and therefore under German—rather than Allied or UN—control, unlike surviving Jews and other displaced persons. This allowed German officials to conflate issues of race with juvenile stewardship; whatever the policy proposed, Germans claimed to be working in the "best interests" of the child rather than the state.

In the early 1960s, having exhausted the children's use as advertisement of West Germany's successful democratic transformation, official and public attention to the children sharply subsided, and they receded as an object of social policy. One significant step in this direction was the resistance encountered by federal Interior Ministry officials when in 1960 they ordered West German states to conduct another survey of the numbers of "*Mischlingskinder*" in their jurisdictions. The state cultural minister of Schleswig-Holstein refused outright, citing both pragmatic concerns (such as understaffing) and legal principle (such as the constitutional prohibition on singling out individuals on the basis of race). While these objections came from a state with a miniscule Black population, the rebuke effectively nullified the Interior Ministry's postwar practice of keeping separate statistics on Black children.[48]

As a result, official and public discussions regarding the role of race *within* the Federal Republic subsided. As "*Mischlingskinder*" disappeared as a racialized object of social policy, the use of the word *Rasse* and reference to things "racial" were rendered taboo, at least as applied to contemporary German society. In effect, the postwar problem of race, which had been narrowly focused on the problem of the postwar "*Mischlingskind*," was declared solved by public officials and the media once the oldest cohort had been integrated into the workforce. Afterward, the Federal Republic embraced an antihistorical fantasy of harmonious ethno-racial homogeneity among its national citizenry.

The 1960s initiated a new era, continuing to this day, in which difference and its perceived social disruptions have been transferred to the bodies, beliefs, and cultures of Germany's immigrant populations.[49] Since then, discriminatory behavior and violence in Germany have been commonly interpreted as motivated by "xenophobia" or hatred of *foreigners*. This response is an interpretative act with significant social effects: it casts the problem as a contemporary one born of an uncomfortable period of adjustment issuing from the end of the Cold War, the demise of socialism, the ensuing surge of immigration, and the growth of Islamic radicalism. That is, it locates the problem's *origins* as *external* to the German nation and German history, rather than treating the problem as connected to a longer, complex native history of racism and notions of race.

The refusal to speak the name of "race" has not extinguished either racialized notions of difference or expressions of racism in Germany in the decades since 1945. What it has done, until recently, is to deprive German minorities of a critical analytical lens and language with which to effectively confront and counter everyday experiences of social exclusion—and, as importantly, to compare these across ethnic identification. For decades, Germans who grew up as postwar "*Mischlingskinder*" thought their problems were personal ones due to individual inadequacies of appearance, intellect, or morality. Only as adults, and increasingly since the 1980s, have they come to recognize the problem of "race" as historical, structural, and sociological—as a persistent, powerful ideological presence that has shaped their lives despite who they are as individuals. Since the 1990s, invoking "race" and attending to instances of "racism" has allowed Black Germans to join with other minorities—of Turkish, African, Arabic, Asian, Latin American, and Jewish heritage—to compare shared experiences of discrimination, violence, and social marginality and to cooperate in pursuing social equality and justice within Germany.[50] Acknowledging the continuing social and cultural valence of "race" in contemporary Germany need not serve to embolden racism or neofascism. Rather, it can—and has—produced the political and epistemological *possibilities* for exposing and eradicating ethno-racial hatred and violence through the efforts of cross-group coalitions. In this sense, reclaiming "race" as a category of analysis and action has been politically enabling, socially progressive, and historically illuminating. German minorities have begun to put this lesson to good use. It is time for scholars of Germany to learn from their experiences and follow suit.

NOTES

Heide Fehrenbach, "Black Occupation Children and the Devolution of the Nazi Racial State," first appeared in Rita Chin, Heide Fehrenbach, Geoff Eley, and Atina Grossmann, *After the Nazi Racial State: Difference and Democracy in Germany and Europe* (Ann Arbor: University of Michigan Press, 2009). It is reprinted here in abridged form by permission of the University of Michigan Press.

1. For a more expansive analysis and detailed discussion of evidence, see Heide Fehrenbach, *Race after Hitler: Black Occupation Children in Postwar Germany and America* (Princeton, NJ: Princeton University Press, 2005).

2. Fatima El-Tayeb, *Schwarze Deutsche: Der Diskurs um "Rasse" und nationale Identität 1890–1933* (Frankfurt/M: Campus, 2001); Lora Wildenthal, "Race, Gender, and Citizenship in the German Colonial Empire," in *Tensions of Empire*, ed. Frederick Cooper and Ann Laura Stoler (Berkeley: University of California Press, 1997), 263–83. On this shift, see Fehrenbach, chapter, 3.
3. Frank Stern, *The Whitewashing of the Yellow Badge: Antisemitism and Philosemitism in Postwar Germany*, trans. William Templer (Oxford: Pergamon, 1992).
4. See Maria Höhn, *GIs and Fräuleins: The German-American Encounter in 1950s West Germany* (Chapel Hill: University of North Carolina Press, 2002).
5. Alexander Perry Biddiscombe, "Dangerous Liaisons: The Anti-fraternization Movement in the US Occupation Zones of Germany and Austria, 1945–1948," *Journal of Social History* 34, no. 3 (2001): 611–47.
6. The transcript of interviews can be found in the US National Archives, College Park (NACP), Record Group (RG) 107, Civ. Aide to Sec'y. of War, Entry 189, Box 265, Technical Intelligence Reports. See also Walter White, *A Rising Wind* (Garden City, NY: Doubleday, 1945), for descriptions of white violence toward Black GIs in wartime Europe and the United Kingdom; and E. T. Hall Jr., "Race Prejudice and Negro-White Relations in the Army," *American Journal of Sociology* 52, no. 5 (March 1947): 401–9. For a discussion of interracial tensions among US servicemen in 1950s West Germany, see Höhn, 95–108; Johannes Kleinschmidt, "Besatzer und Deutsche: Schwarze GIs nach 1945," *Amerikastudien* 40, no. 4 (1995): 646–65; Biddiscombe; and Timothy L. Schroer, *Recasting Race after World War II: Germans and African Americans in American-Occupied Germany* (Boulder: University of Colorado Press, 2007).
7. See Fehrenbach, chapter, 1.
8. Not all sexual contact between the "liberators and liberated" was elective. For a discussion of the social experience and national mythology of rape in and after 1945, see Atina Grossmann, "A Question of Silence: The Rape of German Women by Occupation Soldiers," in "Berlin 1945: War and Rape: 'Liberators Take Liberties,'" special issue, *October* 72 (Spring 1995): 43–63 (see the other essays in this issue as well, especially those by Helke Sander and Gertrud Koch); Norman Naimark, *The Russians in Germany* (Cambridge, MA: Harvard University Press, 1995); Atina Grossmann, "Victims, Villains, and Survivors," *Journal of the History of Sexuality* 11, no. 1–2 (2002): 306–7; Marlene Epp, "The Memory of Violence," *Journal of Women's History* 9, no. 1 (1997): 58–87; Robert G. Moeller, *War Stories: The Search for a Usable Past in the Federal Republic of Germany* (Berkeley: University of California Press, 2000), 51–87; Ingrid Schmidt-Harzbach, "Eine Woche im April: Berlin 1945—Vergewaltigung als Massenschicksal," *Feministische Studien* 2 (1984): 51–65; Annemarie Tröger, "Between Rape and Prostitution," in *Women in Culture and Politics: A Century of Change*, ed. Judith Friedlander, Blanche Wiesen Cook, Alice Kessler-Harris, and Carroll Smith-Rosenberg (Bloomington: Indiana University Press, 1986), 97–117; and Elizabeth Heineman, "The 'Hour of the Woman,'" *American Historical Review* 101 (1996): 354–95. On rape by Black soldiers, see Fehrenbach,

chapter 2, and the somewhat problematic study by J. Robert Lilly, *Taken by Force: Rape and American GIs in Europe during World War II* (New York: Palgrave Macmillan, 2007).

9. Staatsarchiv Augsburg, Versorgungsamt (VA) Lindau, 1946, Einzelfälle. Also Luise Frankenstein, *Soldatenkinder: Die unehelichen Kinder ausländischer Soldaten mit besonderer Berücksichtigung der Mischlinge* (Munich: W. Steinebach, 1954), 29.
10. Frankenstein, 16–19, 23–24; Höhn; Fehrenbach, chapters 1–2.
11. NACP, RG 306, United States Information Agency (USIA), Research Reports on German Public Opinion, Box 9, Report C-1, "Assessment of Troop-Community Relations," 30–32; Vernon W. Stone, "German Baby Crop Left by Negro GIs," *Survey* 85 (November 1949): 579–83; Frankenstein, 23. Also Hermann Ebeling, "Zum Problem der deutschen Mischlingskinder," *Bild und Erziehung* 7, no. 10 (1954): 612–30; Rudolf Sieg, *Mischlingskinder in Westdeutschland: Festschrift für Frédéric Falkenburger* (Baden-Baden: Verlag für Kunst und Wissenschaft, 1955), 9–79; Gustav von Mann, "Zum Problem der farbigen Mischlingskinder in Deutschland," *Jugendwohl* 36, no. 1 (January 1955): 50–53; Hans Pfaffenberger, "Zur Situation der Mischlingskinder," *Unsere Jugend* 8, no. 2 (1956): 64–71; Herbert Hurka, "Die Mischlingskinder in Deutschland," *Jugendwohl* 37, no. 6 (1956): 257–75.
12. Stadtarchiv Nürnberg, C88/I Pflegeamt/Allgemeine Akten 1908–1993, No. 5, 7, 13; Schroer.
13. After 1949, with the founding of the West German state, German officials unsuccessfully pursued American GI fathers of out-of-wedlock "occupation children" for child support. American authorities refused to permit US soldiers to appear before German courts, and when German women attempted to press paternity suits, soldiers were suddenly shipped back to the United States. Although cast as economic grievances, official German pursuit of child support from American soldiers also represented an attempt to reign in the underregulated social and sexual behavior of foreign troops, subject them to German law, and reestablish the prerogatives of native German men in domestic public and private life.
14. US National Archives and Records Administration, College Park, Maryland (NARA-CP), Office of Military Government, United States (OMGUS), Circular 181. For small sample numbers of marriage applications by African American GIs and German women, see Stone and Frankenstein.
15. Statistisches Bundesamt Wiesbaden, "Statistische Berichte: Die unehelichen Kinder von Besatzungsangehörigen im Bundesgebiet und Berlin (West)," no. VI/29/6, October 10, 1956.
16. Walter Kirchner, "Eine anthropologische Studie an Mulattenkindern in Berlin unter Berücksichtigung der sozialen Verhältnisse" (PhD diss., Free University of Berlin, 1952), 10, 49; Sieg, 10–11. Sieg received permission from the Central-Ausschuβ für die Innere Mission and from the Caritas Verband to conduct his examination of "*Mischlingskinder*" in their orphanages (*Kinderheime*) located in the regions of Bremen/Bremerhaven, Heidelberg/Mannheim, Kaiserslautern, Mainz/Wiesbaden, Nuremberg, and Stuttgart (16). For a compatible analysis, see Tina Campt and

Pascal Grosse, "'Mischlingskinder' in Nachkriegdeutschland: Zum Verhältnis von Psychologie, Anthropologie und Gesellschaftpolitik nach 1945," *Psychologie und Geschichte* 6, no. 1–2 (1994): 48–78.

17. Carola Sachse and Benoit Massin, *Biowissenschaftliche Forschung an Kaiser-Wilhelm-Instituten und die Verbrechen des NS-Regimes: Informationen über den gegenwärtigen Wissenstand* (Berlin: Max-Planck-Gesellschaft, 2000); El-Tayeb; Reiner Pommerin, *Sterilisierung der Rheinlandbastarde: Das Schicksal einer farbigen deutschen Minderheit 1918–1937* (Düsseldorf: Droste, 1979). See also chapter 4 of this volume.

18. In total, 4,776 "children of colored paternity" were recorded in the 1955 census. Of these, the most resided in Bavaria (1,681), Baden-Württemberg (1,346), Hesse (881), and Rheinland-Pfalz (488). The balance were scattered among Nordrhein-Westfalen (151), Bremen (95), [West] Berlin, (72), Lower Saxony (51), Hamburg (10) and Schleswig-Holstein (1). Statistisches Bundesamt, 9. These numbers do not include children who had already been adopted abroad by the mid-1950s.

19. Atina Grossmann, "Trauma, Memory, and Motherhood: Germans and Jewish Displaced Persons in Post-Nazi Germany, 1945–1949," *Archiv für Sozialgeschichte* 38 (1998): 215–39; Grossmann, "Victims, Villains, and Survivors"; Yehuda Bauer, *Out of the Ashes: The Impact of American Jews on Post-Holocaust European Jewry* (Oxford: Pergamon, 1989). On "*Russenkinder,*" see W. Karin Hall, "Humanity or Hegemony: Orphans, Abandoned Children, and the Sovietization of the Youth Welfare System in Mecklenburg, Germany, 1945–1952" (PhD diss., Stanford University, 1998), 146–61.

20. As Atina Grossmann notes, demographer and population policy expert Hans Harmen (whose career spanned the Weimar, Nazi, and postwar years) commissioned a "social hygiene research report" on the "hard core" of Jews still resident in the Föhrenwald displaced persons (DP) camp in 1957, several years after administration of the DP camps had passed into official West German hands. However, the study targeted adults and was based on a total of one hundred questionnaires, interviews, and home visits; unlike Black German children, the subjects voluntarily participated in the study and were not subjected to physical-anthropological or psychological testing. See Grossmann's essay in Rita Chin, Heide Fehrenbach, Geoff Eley, and Atina Grossmann, *After the Nazi Racial State: Difference and Democracy in Postwar Germany and Europe* (Ann Arbor: University of Michigan Press, 2009), 55–79.

21. Kirchner, 12, 35; Sieg, 27.

22. Kirchner, 40–49; Sieg, 25–62. Note that these same attributes were mentioned in 1954–1955 school reports on the children ordered by the federal Ministry of the Interior.

23. Kirchner, 61, 35; Sieg, 65, emphasis added.

24. Arguing that the "psychical" legacy of racial inheritance need not be an insurmountable burden, Kirchner concluded by urging that "everything possible be done" to improve the living conditions of the children (Kirchner 62).

25. On shifts in US understandings of race, see Matthew Frye Jacobsen, *Whiteness of a Different Color: European Immigrants and the Alchemy of Race* (Cambridge, MA: Harvard University Press, 1999); Matthew Pratt Guterl, *The Color of Race in America,*

1900–1940 (Cambridge, MA: Harvard University Press, 2001); and Eric Goldstein, *The Price of Whiteness: Jews, Race, and American Identity* (Princeton, NJ: Princeton University Press, 2006).

26. Coverage in the *Chicago Defender* and the Baltimore *Afro-American* began in 1947; by 1948 the *Pittsburgh Courier* also ran stories on "brown babies" in Germany, as did *Ebony* by the turn of the 1950s.

27. In part the origin of this social imaginary was the popular West German film *Toxi* (a top-ten box office hit in 1952), which scripted the general fate of Black occupation children as abandoned, unwanted, and institutionalized. See Fehrenbach, chapter 4, for a discussion of this movie and its broader impact.

28. Edmund C. Jann, "The Law of Adoption in Germany," Typescript, Library of Congress, Law Library, Foreign Law Section (Washington, DC, 1955). Nazi amendments included "Gesetz über Vermittlung der Annahme an Kindesstatt vom 19.4.1939," the text of which appeared in *Reichsgesetzblatt* I, 795; commentary on the law can be found in *Deutsche Justiz* (1939): 701. Other relevant laws included "The Law to Change and Supplement the Regulations on Family Relations and to Regulate the Legal Status of Stateless Persons" of April 14, 1938, and "The Marriage Law of July 6, 1938." These laws were preceded in the fall of 1935 by the "Law for the Protection of German Blood," which prohibited sexual relations or marriage between "Aryan" Germans and "Jews, Negroes, or Gypsies [Sinti and Roma] or their bastards." For an English overview of German legislation on adoption through the early postwar period, see Jann.

29. The Americans did allow adoptive parents or children to petition for the reinstatement of adoptions that were terminated against their will by German authorities between 1933 and 1945. Jann, 4; Helmut Glässing, *Voraussetzungen der Adoption* (Frankfurt/M: Alfred Metzner, 1957). On the US response, see Archiv des Diakonischen Werkes der Evangelischen Kirche Deutschlands (ADW), Central-Ausschuß-West (CAW), 843. On American adoption practices, see E. Wayne Carp, ed., *Adoption in America: Historical Perspectives* (Ann Arbor: University of Michigan Press, 2004), and Barbara Melosh, *Strangers and Kin: The American Way of Adoption* (Cambridge, MA: Harvard University Press, 2002).

30. In 1948 Bavaria, for example, the justification for the amendment of the state adoption law invoked the "great losses of many families due to the war and the availability of a huge number of orphans," arguing: "It is also especially important to think of such cases in which people, married with children, desire to adopt children of relatives, friends, or neighbors, above all from the eastern regions [of the former German empire (Ostgebieten)] whose parents were killed in the war or its aftermath. Often it is the illegitimate child of a fallen son one wants to adopt." Bayerisches Hauptstaatsarchiv (BayHStA), Staatskanzlei (StK), 130324, "Rechtsausschuss, Antrag aus der Ausschusssitzung vom 5. November 1948." In August 1950, the Bundestag passed a temporary modification of the adoption law ("Gesetz zur Erleichterung der Annahme an Kindes statt") to allow German families with children to adopt. This law was renewed in 1952 to extend to 1955. ADW, CAW, 843, Deutscher Bundestag, 1. Wahlperiode 1949, Drucksache Nr. 3931.

31. Bundesarchiv Koblenz (BAK), B153/342, "Vermerk" to Dr. Rothe, May 25, 1951.
32. Yara-Colette Lemke-Muniz de Faria discusses these initiatives in *Zwischen Fürsorge und Ausgrenzung: Afrodeutsche "Besatzungskinder" im Nachkriegsdeutschland* (Berlin: Metropol, 2002), 102–3.
33. "Meeting of the Committee to consider . . . the Immigration of . . . German Orphans of Negro Blood," Jan 29, 1951, NAACP papers, Reel 8: Group II, Box G11, "Brown Babies, 1950–58."
34. Walter White press release, September 18, 1952, NAACP, Reel 8: Group II, Box G11, "Brown Babies, 1950–58."
35. For a detailed discussion of Mabel Grammer's activities, the response of the International Social Service, and the shifting policy of West Germans, see Fehrenbach, chapter 5, and Lemke-Muniz de Faria. For a discussion of the experiences of Black Germans who were adopted to the United States as children or moved there as adults, see the film documentary *Brown Babies: The Mischlingskinder Story,* dir. Regina Griffin, 2010.
36. Heinrich Webler, "Adoptions-Markt," *Zentralblatt für Jugendrecht und Jugendwohl* 42, no. 5 (May 1955): 123–24. Also BAK, B153: Bundesministerium für Familien- und Jugendfragen, File 1335, I-II, "Material über Probleme des Internationalen Adoptionsrechts"; Hauptstaatsarchiv Stuttgart (HStAStg), Akten des Innenministeriums, EA2/007: Vermittlung der Annahme an Kindesstatt, II, 1955–66; Franz Klein, "Kinderhandel als strafbare Handlung," *Jugendwohl* 37, no. 3 (1956): 95; ADW, Hauptgeschäftsstelle (HGSt), 1161, "Kurzbericht über die Sitzung . . . am 12. Juli 1955 im Bundesministerium des Innern"; BayHStA, Ministerium des Innen (MInn) 81906.
37. ADW, HGSt 3949, Auszug aus dem Bericht über die Tätigkeit der Adoptionszentrale für den Verwendungsnachweis, Zuschuss 1961 and 1963.
38. BAK, B153: Bundesministerium für Familien- und Jugendfragen; HStAStg; Webler, 123–24; Franz Klein, "Zur gegenwärtigen Situation der Auslandsadoption," *Unsere Jugend* 9 (1955): 401–8; Klein, "Kinderhandel," 95.
39. ADW, HGSt 3949. Also BAK, B189/6858: File: Besatzungs- und Mischlingskinder —Allgemein.
40. Ebeling; Klaus Eyferth, "Die Situation und die Entwicklungsaussichten der Neger-Mischlingskinder in der Bundesrepublik," *Soziale Arbeit* 7, no. 11 (1958): 469–78; and Klaus Eyferth, Ursula Brandt, and Wolfgang Hawel, *Farbige Kinder in Deutschland* (Munich: Juventa, 1960).
41. Eyferth remained the exception to this trend. BAK, B149: Bundesministerium für Arbeit und Sozialordnung, no. 8679; BayHStA, MInn 81126, press clippings on "*Mischlingskinder,*" 1960–61; BayHStA, Ministerium für Unterricht und Kultus (MK) 62245, "Volksschulwesen Negerkinder"; Hessisches Hauptstaatsarchiv, Abt. 940/77; Elly Waltz, "Mischlinge werden jetzt Lehrlinge," *Münchner Merkur,* July 9–10, 1960; "Farbige Lehrlinge—wieder sehr gefragt," *Münchner Merkur,* March 15, 1961; Klaus Eyferth, "Gedanken über die zukünftige Berufseingliederung der Mischlingskinder in Westdeutschland," *Neues Beginnen* 5 (May 1959): 65–68.
42. "Wiedersehen macht Freude," *Quick,* April 28, 1963, 38; "Toxi: Alle Menschen sind

nett zu mir," c. 1964, no periodical title given, photo essay filed in Stiftung Deutsche Kinemathek, Berlin, Nachlass R. A. Stemmle; "Die 'Toxis' sind erwachsen—und haben Heiratssorgen," *Welt am Sonntag*, March 26, 1967, 6; Ruth Bahn-Flessburg, "Sie haben die gleichen Chancen wie die Weißen: Auf der Suche nach den farbigen Besatzungskindern," *Unsere Jugend* 20 (1968): 295–303; Ruth Bahn-Flessburg, "Die Hautfarbe ist kein Problem: Farbige 'Besatzungskinder'—Vierzehn Lebensläufe," *Frankfurter Allgemeine Zeitung* (1968, filed in ADW, HGSt 3949, 295–303); "Adam und Eva: Ein Mädchen wie Toxi fand sein Glück an der Elbe," *Neue Illustrierte Revue*, February 10, 1975, 47–50; "Die Deutschen mit der dunklen Haut," *Quick*, November 3–9, 1977, 82–89. Two serialized novels featuring Black German teenaged girls were also published in West German magazines in the early 1960s. See Ursula Schaake, "Meine schwarze Schwester," *Revue*, no. 42 (Christmas 1960) through no. 15 (April 9, 1961); Stefan Doerner, "Mach mich weiß, Mutti!," *Quick* 16, no. 17 (April 28, 1963) through no. 27 (July 7, 1963). For an early study of representations of Blacks in the West German press, see Rosemarie K. Lester, *Trivialneger: Das Bild des Schwarzen im westdeutschen Illustriertenroman* (Stuttgart: Akademischer Verlag H.-D. Heinz, 1982).

43. For example, "Adam und Eva"; see also my analysis in Fehrenbach, 176–79.
44. Rainer Werner Fassbinder's film *Ali: Fear Eats the Soul*, released in 1974, was a provocative exception and certainly not widely seen in Germany at the time.
45. In a somewhat surprising omission, Dagmar Herzog does not discuss interracial sex and its social, political, or symbolic significance in post-1945 Germany in her book *Sex after Fascism: Memory and Morality in Twentieth-Century Germany* (Princeton, NJ: Princeton University Press, 2005). On the New Left's use of exoticized Black bodies in political representation, see Quinn Slobodian, "Radical Empathy: Third World Politics in 1960s West Germany" (PhD diss., New York University, 2008).
46. "Adam und Eva," 47–48; Bahn-Flessburg, "Die Hautfarbe."
47. This last example is from a personal acquaintance. See also Karen Thimm and DuRell Echols, *Schwarze in Deutschland* (Munich: Protokolle, 1973); Gisela Fremgen, *. . . und wenn du dazu noch schwarz bist: Berichte schwarzer Frauen in der Bundesrepublik* (Bremen: Edition CON, 1984); May Opitz, Katharina Oguntoye, and Dagmar Schultz, eds., *Showing Our Colors: Afro-German Women Speak Out*, trans. Anne V. Adams in cooperation with Tina Campt, May Opitz, and Dagmar Schultz (Amherst, MA: University of Massachusetts Press, 1992); and Ika Hügel-Marshall, *Daheim unterwegs: Ein deutsches Leben* (Berlin: Orlanda, 1998), and its English translation, *Invisible Woman: Growing Up Black in Germany*, trans. Elizabeth Gaffney (New York: Continuum, 2001).
48. BayHStA, MInn 81094, "Mischlingskinder," 1960–61.
49. For an expanded discussion of this issue, see Chin et al., *After the Nazi Racial State*, especially chapters 3 and 4.
50. Tina Campt, "Afro-German Cultural Identity," *Callaloo* 26, no. 2 (2003); Francine Jobatey, "*afro-look*: Die Geschichte einer Zeitschrift von schwarzen Deutschen" (PhD diss., University of Massachusetts, 2000).

11

Making African Diasporic Pasts Possible

A Retrospective View of the GDR and Its Black (Step-)Children

PEGGY PIESCHE

It has been more than two decades since the fall of the Berlin Wall and the beginning of the end of the Cold War, yet now-unified Germany still struggles with the legacy of its forty-year division. To be sure, debates have changed over time as a consequence of politicians' priorities, shifting media emphases, and public engagement. However, questions regarding the historical contextualization of the GDR[1] remain at the center of debates about contemporary issues in post-unification Germany. Within these debates, most news outlets foreground the GDR's failed policies and their ramifications for contemporary society. Strikingly, the debates focus primarily on questions of memory, belonging, identity, and exclusion.[2] However, apart from the troubling fact that the GDR is treated as an isolated historical unit seldom juxtaposed to West Germany, of most significance for the direction of these arguments is their insistence on portraying the GDR as a homogeneous *white* country. Emigration (of its own population) rather than immigration is taken to characterize the GDR, and East German history is portrayed as if Black history did not belong to it.[3] Thus, not surprisingly, the politics of integration in the GDR are portrayed as the default reason for the widely voiced assertion that East Germans are incapable of becoming citizens who eventually internalize democracy. The most recent debates—regarding PEGIDA,[4] the Alternative für Deutschland,[5] or general political discussions concerning the European crisis of responding to an evolving/emerging global refugee movement—reveal that the earlier search for a "non-biased view" deriving from an "unfalsified recollection of the GDR"[6] is still unsuccessful.[7] Lutz Rathenow examines this dilemma in his review of *Geschichte der Opposition in der DDR* by Ehrhart Neubert:

> After the fact, the GDR grows more and more different. For some it disappeared without a sound—others can't hear anything but the post-GDR sound. All this takes place against the background of the West being mercilessly demystified. From the last escape route or the eternal enemy that gave life meaning, the West mutated into the sheer never-ending drudgery of everyday life. In the battle for supremacy in commemoration, from which supremacy in the interpretation of history is supposed to follow, unprotected facts, irritations, and material are important.[8]

Since the GDR's collapse, many attempts of this kind have been made. Post-GDR historiography in particular has focused on the inefficient economic system, which resulted in the insufficient output of GDR society, ecological problems, and the totalitarian surveillance of the population. These circumstances brought about an atmosphere of uncertainty that, one might argue, manifested itself in the deeply rooted fear of its citizens.[9] Jan Behrends and Patrice Poutrus emphasize the connection between this economic argument and a certain depiction of East Germans and racialized violence: "During the last few years, the public as well as the scholarly debate concerning this issue has been dominated by explanations that related the high level of violence against foreigners and other minority groups mainly to the hardships brought about by the process of economic transformation from state socialism to market economy."[10] Rathenow's skepticism regarding the possibility of non-biased views suggests that the GDR cannot be understood from its end, but only from its beginning.

Although scholarly studies concerned with ethnic minorities in the GDR have been rare in recent decades, a rather ambivalent notion of visibility of Blackness in Germany can generally be noted. Aesthetic works of marginalized groups have been analyzed with an emphasis on linguistic innovations and intertextuality, especially in reference to hybrid cultures and canon formation. Additionally, the potential exclusionary effects of social conditions have been analyzed, and "self"-"other" relations in a so-called multicultural Germany have been evaluated.[11] It can be maintained that research on minorities, and sometimes even multiculturalism, on the one hand and research on the GDR on the other have developed as two mutually exclusive niches.[12] This essay challenges these mutually exclusive frameworks of analysis by focusing on an aspect of GDR history and culture that has been largely ignored by scholarship. A Black German minority began to emerge in the GDR in the early 1960s. This transpired against the backdrop of GDR policies regarding migration and foreigners, and Black Germans were strongly affected by crucial tensions between the ideal claims and lived effects of these policies. The analysis presented here will therefore illuminate both the social histories and the cultural discourses that emerged from this nexus.

A Socialism of Difference

Those rare yet important works dealing with foreigners in the GDR and their "complex reality" (Runge) as early as the 1990s warrant mention here. In her 1990 study titled *Ausland DDR: Fremdenhass* (Foreign country GDR: Hatred of foreigners), Irene Runge provided the first survey of multi-ethnic circumstances in the GDR—including the naming of those circumstances.[13] Building on Runge's findings, Sabine Kriechhammer-Yagmur and Brigitte Proß-Klapproth edited the 1991 volume *West Meets East,* which examines the practical application of the GDR's policy toward foreigners and its legal bases.[14] In 1993 an extensive collection of interviews depicted the personal experiences of contract workers in the publication *Schwarz-Weiße Zeiten: AusländerInnen in Ostdeutschland vor und nach der Wende: Erfahrungen der Vertragsarbeiter aus Mosambik* (Black and white times: Foreigners in East Germany before and after unification: Experiences of contract workers from Mozambique).[15] In a 2000 article titled "Historische Untersuchungen der Fremdenfeindlichkeit in den neuen Bundesländern" (Historical investigations of xenophobia in the new German states), Patrice Poutrus, Jan Behrends, and Dennis Kuck issued an urgent call for intensive discussion of the GDR's failed integration policies and their ramifications for post-unification Germany.[16] This necessary discussion has yet to take place.[17]

Beyond the question of foreigners, the situation of Black Germans whose social and cultural socialization took place in the GDR must also be assessed, especially with respect to the question of whom GDR citizens designated as their "other."[18] A 1995 poll of Black Germans from the GDR examined this group's socialization process for the first time, giving special attention to those born between 1961 and 1970. Using that information, Jeanette Sumalgy discusses the position of Black German adolescents in the GDR in the context of the country's school system and the situation of binational families.[19] According to her study, the adolescents in question did not receive any positive support from their social environment during crucial periods of their personal development and identity formation. Combined with this lack of support, the fact that an identity was often insistently imposed on these adolescents from without proved to be a significant liability in their search for personal identity.

In the GDR's relatively homogeneous and closed society, Blacks were presumed to be exotic, foreign, and different—patterns of attribution similar to those occurring in other countries. To be associated with such attributes meant also to be regarded as part of "another" society, definitely not part of the GDR but rather foreigners whose stay was limited. Black children and adolescents who were citizens of the GDR, however, had a special position in GDR society. They spoke German, had German names, usually lived in white German families, and took part in everyday German life. The black color of their skin made them special, while the context of their lives seemed to attest to their successful integration. Yet a look at their fathers' situations—in the beginning only Black men were allowed into the country, a point to which I shall return—demonstrates that the socialism of difference, as I will call it, with all its racist stereotypes, had a great impact on both majority and minority cultures. These effects then shaped the lives of children in significant ways.

Kathrin Schmidt's novel *Die Gunnar-Lennefsen-Expedition* (1998) focuses on a GDR family to reveal the entire spectrum of problems associated with guest workers in the GDR. A somewhat ironic passage from the novel reveals key features of the text:

> . . . a little anxiety about the black and white child's future. . . . There've been substantial numbers of differently colored people even in W. for the past few years. They came here from Cuba to learn various trades. . . . From Algeria, to coil hoses in the municipal rubber plant. And there were Vietnamese women in the laundry, after it had lost all its workers from the county prison when they were pardoned.
>
> In the schools children were soon encouraged to be afraid of foreigners, especially of dark men from Algeria, who shopped in Intershops and stalked blond women, if the teacher was to be believed. And who didn't believe her! Indeed, it was the Algerian men who dared to enter the local women and left little brown children behind in increasing numbers, finally attracting the attention of the citizens of W. The Cubans drank a lot . . . , but kept to themselves, at least so it seemed, while no city resident had ever seen the Vietnamese women carrying out everyday tasks, nobody even knew where they lived. Once the Algerian workers in the automobile factory went on strike. . . . This so outraged the townspeople . . . that one day the dark workers began to pack their bags and were replaced by a tamer bunch.[20]

Schmidt develops a creepily pleasant picture of the GDR in the 1970s and subsequently describes a female awakening, the gift of a history to a yet unborn child. Most of the novel's fictional living conditions can be traced in official documents as well, which is remarkable enough, but of key interest here is that the novel's language continually reverts to the racist patterns of designation addressed above. The widespread use of the term "black and white" is itself underwritten by a hegemonic view of hybridity.

Fraternal Aid and Solidarity Agreements

Under the auspices of solidarity agreements between the GDR and the so-called "young nation-states," only men came to the GDR, initially to work or study there, beginning in the late 1950s.[21] Whether they came as students or to assist the GDR's economy depended on the ideological status of their country of origin. If that country had—after having gained independence in the course of the Cold War—decided to lean toward a Western market-based economy, the chance of being admitted to study in the GDR (mostly in medicine or engineering) was very good. This was because the education of the future intelligentsia had to be paid for in foreign currency (meaning US dollars). The GDR bore all related costs for workers from socialist countries, which could be used for propaganda purposes as an expression of solidarity. But citizens of socialist countries who were admitted to the GDR had to accept that they could work only in the production sector rather than pursuing university studies. Thus a two-class system developed in which the country of origin often clearly indicated whether a particular foreigner was studying or working. People from Ghana, Nigeria, Zambia, and Iraq mostly came to study. In contrast, people from Angola, Mozambique, Egypt, Ethiopia, Kenya, Vietnam, and Cuba went into socialist production and took up an apprenticeship as a worker. Members of this latter group were usually employed in areas where workers were in short supply, especially the textile and chemical sectors and precision mechanics, including the assembly of radios and razors. These workers represented a simple economic calculation; even at the beginning of the 1980s there were still approximately 180,000 foreign workers who provided necessary services to the GDR. The importing of low-wage workers was, therefore, not limited to West Germany, although the numbers of guest workers were significantly higher there.

Treaties signed by the relevant governments determined who came.

Depending on the treaty, foreigners were allowed to stay for three to six years, and rotation was strictly enforced.[22] From the middle of the 1970s onward, about half of these temporary immigrants were female. It had become increasingly difficult to hire foreign contract workers over the years, and incidents like the recall of a group of Algerians after riots in 1977 (to which the passage in Schmidt's novel alludes) grew more frequent. Because of these difficulties women were allowed into the country. The relevant treaties defined the contract workers (male and female) as a distinct group subject to collective legal restraints, which included:

payment of twelve percent of the worker's salary to the government of the home country;

no possibility of bringing over other family members;

immediate deportation in case of pregnancy (treaties with Cuba, Vietnam, Mozambique, and Zambia included this passage, which was not revoked until 1989);

immediate deportation should political activity fall outside previously established frameworks (membership in political parties and the formation of political organizations were prohibited);

mandatory membership in the GDR's official labor union and payment of membership fees (including solidarity surcharges);

and centralized accommodation in shared quarters.[23]

Even participation in personal activities such as cultural events, recreational pastimes, and educational pursuits was circumscribed according to specific guidelines, which were adjusted from group to group. With respect to labor law, governmental treaties included passages stating that contract workers could not claim retirement pensions or any type of worker's compensation in case of disability. Monthly payments of sixty marks to the pension fund and sixty months of work at a job requiring such payments were, however, absolute prerequisites for residency status.[24]

Foreign newcomers subjected to these requirements experienced the shock of having left the often multifaceted family structures of home to come to a country in which the lack of integration programs meant immediate personal and social isolation. Citizens of the GDR had only limited access to information about the cultural, economic, and political situation of the foreigners among them, and objective evaluation was difficult if not impossible. Solidarity with the "oppressed peoples of the world" was taught as part of the GDR's patriotic educational curriculum.[25] In most cases, this was no more than propagandistic sloganeering because there was extremely little active exchange, something that would have demanded everyday encounters, travel, and the transmission of information. Encounters with other cultures in public life (or even preparation for living together with other cultures) were impossible outside the GDR and not envisioned inside the GDR. On the contrary, they were actively prevented. Students and their teachers (including tutors) had to sign a statement that they would not establish any contacts with their foreign colleagues beyond what was necessary to meet technical and organizational requirements. Certain "old limitations of thought"[26] were therefore not just passed along but even revived within a new iconographical framework with national and socialist components.[27]

In contrast to the situation in West Germany, foreign students and workers in the GDR were unable to establish a sense of community with their compatriots because they were dispersed throughout the country, split into small groups, and housed in quarters separate from the local inhabitants. The social volatility that developed within these quarters is described by Kriechhammer-Yagmur and Proß-Klapproth: "Working and living conditions, the potential for conflict in the cramped residences due to various ethnic rivalries produced a feeling of homelessness, a loss of inner stability, a falling away of security, as well as uncertainty and fear of contact."[28] Important aspects of foreign workers' and students' systems of social orientation that could have strengthened personal identity were entirely missing. GDR leaders liked to blame foreigners themselves for racism and xenophobia, claiming that their cultural differences and unwillingness to integrate into GDR society were responsible for social tension.[29] In a few cases foreigners did manage to establish contact with locals, sometimes resulting in close relationships; however, multi-ethnic couples were not legally entitled to a shared place of residence, and marriage was often impossible because of the treaties already mentioned. This lack of legal entitlement also meant that these foreigners had no right to take legal action or object to governmental decisions. A foreigner could, according to Paragraph 6 of the third *Ausländergesetz* (foreigners' law) of the GDR (1979), lose his or her right of residence at any time, or it could be limited in duration as well as geographically. The government was not obliged to provide reasons for such actions.[30]

Children of Solidarity in White German Everyday Life

Kathrin Schmidt's novel again comes to mind:

> There had once been great hopes for the daughter . . . but then she came back pregnant from the city where the university was. Her parents took her in and renovated a small room in the attic. They were almost looking forward to their grandchild. From the day the baby was born the girl's parents walked the streets of W. with their heads bowed. The child was not the usual color and its hair was frizzy. The child is now growing up in a pressure cooker, two godmothers dressed prettily in camouflage occasionally pretend like they wish the child only the best.[31]

Children in such cases mostly grew up with only one parent, usually the mother, or they were adopted. The mothers, who had defied governmental, social, and family rules and limits by initiating a relationship with a foreigner and giving birth to a Black child, often fought in vain for the right to marry their partners. Official permission was required but was almost always denied. When refusal was impossible, the civil servant in charge tried to convince the women not to marry by pointing out the situation in the partner's home country and the advantages of socialism. Mostly nineteen to twenty-three years old,[32] from the working class as well as from the intelligentsia, and in a secure position because they were employed, these women also confronted prejudice and massive resentment, which can be attributed to myths whose construction was encouraged: "We had also been warned against having a child because it would lower productivity. . . . Anyway, we're sitting in the cafeteria when a female student came in with a stroller. We were already smiling. Then a colored child stuck his head up and grabbed for something and we all had to laugh. . . . They say they are all lusting after women . . . ; they are much more dangerous and driven by their libido." (These are the words of an anthropology student in the Schmidt novel.)[33] Curricular materials reinforced these myths. The book *Völker, Rassen, Kulturen* (Peoples, races, cultures) consigns the earth's peoples to different races and appearances, in the case of "other races" describing allegedly typical features such as body weight and bodily proportions.[34] This notion of "*Rassenkunde*" (racial science) is underscored by the book's cover, where a dancing and singing Black man folkloristic in appearance seems to emphasize that only "others" are relegated to races.

A personal situation that often entailed hostile encounters with the social environment, an assumed lack of self-knowledge, and insecurity, as well as ignorance and disinterest from the other side, was characteristic of the social conditions that Black children experienced, in contrast to mainstream GDR society, where strong family ties obtained. The study undertaken by Jeanette Sumalgy showed that forty-eight percent of these children grew up with their biological mother and an adoptive father. Almost eighteen percent had only a biological mother, while roughly the same percentage had an adoptive father and an adoptive mother. Four percent grew up with a German grandmother, and only thirteen percent were raised by their biological parents, one Black and one white.[35] The high percentage of those who grew up with no Black parent, coupled with their lack of recognition in public discourse, especially intensified the gaps in personal orientation with which Black Germans contended. Sometimes they experienced this as a severe crisis. According to the Sumalgy poll, two-thirds of those questioned said that they did not have a supportive person to talk to about their experiences of violence and exclusion and resulting problems. Their families were usually not seen as providing an adequate basis for the construction of their identity. The same individuals felt that they had fallen into a lacuna between school and their parents' house because of their Blackness.

Moreover, the mostly negative associations and clichés attached to the term "Black" hindered a positive identification with the "other" parent's origin. Eighty percent of those polled acknowledged having received only very limited information about African and Asian history, literature, music, media, and travel. They perceived that as another deficiency that prevented them from coming to terms with their situation and developing positive self-esteem. Although the books of Kwame Nkrumah, Frantz Fanon, W. E. B. Du Bois, and Alex Haley were available in the GDR, resources for adolescents in the process of individualization and identity formation were overall rather poor and often problematic.

The Village Called Africa

The GDR had high ambitions for its children's publications, as a 1975 statement by a Berlin children's book publisher reveals: "Socialist children's literature is internationalist. It is indebted to the watchword of the Communist Manifesto: Proletarians of all countries, unite! But presenting the entire world in a children's book also means that our children's literature does not evade problems. It addresses contradictions in order to help resolve contradictions. Literature opens up wide to life. Only in this way can it have an effect on life."[36] But the effect of countless children's books as well as movies and comics was more often detrimental, confronting children and adolescents with a(n) "other" history mostly in the form of stereotypes. Karl May's image of the Indian was not only preserved in the GDR's "Indian films" starring Serbian actor Gojko Mitic but also reactivated in books for young readers such as *Der Garten des Indianers* (The garden of the Indian), the Indian fairy tales of Edith Klatt, or Kurt Kauter's *Flieg Kondor Tupac Amaru* (Fly condor Tupac Amaru),[37] in which Tupac Amaru, a descendant of European colonizers and therefore a member of the ruling class, becomes "the hero of liberation for the Indios of Latin America, like Thomas Müntzer in our country."[38] In the illustrated textbook *Kinder in Afrika* (Children in Africa, 1969), the image of an entire continent and its inhabitants is so marginalized in comparison to the small European country GDR that finally only animals in the GDR offer evidence of that ominous Africa from which a small boy waves farewell.[39] Such a depiction, completely devoid of critical reflection, is not surprising when one considers the images in *Bummi in Afrika* (Bummi in Africa), already a hit in 1969, whose hero goes to Africa to find the "African girl Sally."[40] An elephant is chosen to assist him. Geographical conditions are emphasized in passages such as the following: "The sun burns hot in Africa. Much hotter than in Berlin . . ."[41] The patterns of ignorance and unfamiliarity with the neighboring continent that we saw reflected in the Sumalgy poll were therefore not just a problem for Black children and adolescents. Interestingly, Anke Poenicke makes a similar argument in her study of the image of Africa in contemporary West German media and schoolbooks.[42]

Figures for identification beyond racist stereotypes and clichés about oppressed people who benefit from socialist aid could have been especially important for Black children's self-image. Ideologically informed expressions of solidarity in the GDR are fully evident in *Sally Bleistift in Amerika* (Sally Bleistift [pencil] in America) by Auguste Lazar, a very popular GDR youth book that is representative of many others.[43] Its problematic message of international understanding and shared class struggle is based on an image of the world that can almost be labeled a manifestation of "positive racism," if I may be permitted such an oxymoron. On the one hand, a detailed and only slightly ideological critique of the system, including some remarks about Russian pogroms—otherwise not deemed suitable for discussion in GDR circles—is presented. The main character is an amiable, feisty, and wise old lady who fled the pogroms of Russia and is now actively involved in the struggles of Chicago's working class. By portraying her as assertive, affectionate, and resolute, the text offers an image of Jewish resistance in contrast to the prevalent GDR discourse on the Jewish victim. On the other hand, the text draws on openly racist stereotypes of Native Americans and Blacks, who have become minorities in the idealized society of the city's working-class neighborhoods. Whereas the white characters have proper names like Billy, Mrs. Smith, or granddaughter Betty, the representatives of difference have names representing specific features. The only Black man in the story is friendly, strong, clever, and revolutionary, but his name is "N****rjim." Two foundlings are called "Redjackett" and "Negerbaby" (Negro baby), "Negerjunge" (Negro boy), or "*Negerlein*" (little Negro). Almost a whole chapter is devoted to the search for a name for "Negerbaby"; eventually the baby is given the name of a white man opposed to slavery—John Brown. The story includes obvious references to socialist ideology in its efforts to unite all proletarians. It differentiates only along lines of skin color, or, as the literature of the 1970s and 1980s demonstrates, along lines of racial category.

Surely the most positive example of internationalist youth book culture is Ludwig Renn's revolutionary story *Camilo* (1970).[44] It tells the story of a little boy who grows up amid his parents' involvement in a resistance movement and tries to find his own identity. The book's introductory scene presents an image deliberately opposed to contemporary racist stereotypes. When the boy asks his grandfather why the Yankee lady drops her money into his hand without touching him, the grandfather replies: "After they touch a Black human being, they immediately wash their hands. I don't think you are all that dark. You just have black frizzy hair and dark eyes." The following sentences make it clear that the blond Yankees think they are something special but that having black skin does not make one uglier: "Does this mean the Yankee lady thought she was prettier? Her pale face, painted lips, and her washed-out blue eyes, are they supposed to be more beautiful?"[45] Other positive drawings of the island's inhabitants, lacking additional racist labels, also illustrate the book's nuances.

Was Pittiplatsch[46] Black? Comics in the GDR

Whereas the GDR designated West German comics as prohibited material, the GDR's own comic books—such as *Atze* and the "Digedags," the little white goblins who remain white European boys (first published in 1955)—were upgraded into politically motivated series very early on. As the only GDR magazine to survive the unification process and still be read throughout Germany, *Mosaik* can justly claim its status as the longest-lasting German comic book.[47] In various series (the America, Orient, and Far East Series) and faraway countries, *Mosaik*'s heroes engage in difficult struggles against injustice, violence, and misery, critically address the evil in the world, and accomplish feats that influence world history (such as the liberation of slaves in the southern United States). These stories often entail a hyper-identification with the stylized minorities in question.[48] The GDR comic books construct a utopia based on a belief in human goodness, the hope for its realization, and love for humanity, whereas fear, deception, hate, and despair characterize the image of a society that is easily unmasked as the so-called dystopia of capitalism. Good and evil, between the superior (in this case, socialist) culture of the West and the inferior culture of the "others" (exotic, submissive, suffering, passive, resigned), are presented as a simple hierarchical opposition between moral socialism and the immoral world of capitalism. Black and white characters, set side-by-side in contrasting contexts, convey a double-edged message. There is the "self," surmounting all obstacles, and there is the "other," more or less succumbing to fate. Within this binary logic, the characters manifest a collective repertoire of differentiation according to racial and national categories. Strategies of ethnicization and devaluation are combined with strategies of affiliation. The "others" thus appear as a difference that can be readily consumed, such that the heroes' inner life appears as hybrid. In this fashion, a medium very popular among young people provides a sense of global heroic adventure within the context of socialist togetherness, international friendship, and multicultural solidarity. Yet the images are steeped in racial stereotypes. Expressions such as "Redskin" and "N****r Sam" and references to the apparently incoherent speech of Blacks and slaves are used pervasively. The images sometimes avoid such stereotypes, however, as when Blacks and whites are shown living together in peace in the romantic idyll of nineteenth-century Louisiana.

Socialization in the Schools

Schools in the GDR, primary mediators of education and socialization, supported identification with the GDR's own national culture. Introductions to national history and literature offered students patterns of interpretation that were meant to help them see themselves as members of the national and political body. Historical traditions from other cultures were only rarely addressed. (The situation in West Germany was much the same in this regard.) Access to these alternative traditions was therefore not generally available to young Black Germans in the GDR. Paragraph five of the Education Law of 1965 outlines the following task for schools: "to raise and educate young people such that their solid knowledge and capabilities enable them to think creatively and to act independently, that their Marxist-Leninist world view permeates their personal convictions and behavior, that they feel, think, and act as patriots of their socialist fatherland and as proletarian internationalists." The SED program of 1976 formulated the following educational objectives for schools:

1. the development of ideological and political attitudes toward citizenship;
2. the teaching of skills and knowledge that are useful in later professional life;
3. the development of social skills.[49]

These objectives of course included a GDR national identity with appropriate national sentiments. With that ever-present objective but without any positive role models, and because they did not identify with a society that regarded "whiteness" as normal, Black German adolescents lacked the feeling of being part of this GDR. The schools were, therefore, a site where a specific form of discrimination against ethnic minorities was actively produced and practiced.

Conclusion

Debates about morals and guilt regarding Germany's twentieth-century past raise many new questions about the possibility of a common identity in unified Germany. Research in this field uses various modes of historical interpretation as it searches for answers. The modes of inquiry we choose to pursue influence our behavior in the present, just as present-day experience and needs influence our views of history. Racism has clearly intensified since reunification. There are many helpful strategies for analyzing the ways in which both postwar German states dealt with "others" after the end of the Nazi dictatorship. But an analysis that focuses solely on racist violence in the new *Bundesländer* (federal states) with facile reference to the political legacy of a socialist dictatorship is inadequate to explain the sociopolitical structures of the 1990s and beyond. Instead, future scholarship must look more closely, not only at the differences between East and West German policies regarding foreigners and migration but also at a shared legacy of colonial and Nazi vintage.[50] Contemporary Germany cannot be understood with an eye narrowly focused on the present, but only with a broader optic that considers new approaches to its many beginnings.

Translated by Peggy Piesche, Leslie A. Adelson, and Sara Lennox

NOTES

An earlier version of this essay appeared as Peggy Piesche, "Black and German? East German Adolescents before 1989: A Retrospective View of a 'Non-Existent Issue' in the GDR," in *The Cultural After-Life of East Germany: New Transnational Perspectives*, ed. Leslie A. Adelson (Washington, DC: AICGS, 2002), 37–59. It is reprinted here in revised and abridged form by permission of the American Institute for Contemporary German Studies.

Despite intensive efforts by the author, the legal successors of the former Kinderbuchverlag der DDR and the Militärverlag der DDR could not be found. Although some rights of the Kinderbuchverlag have been transferred to various publishing houses in the Federal Republic of Germany, holders of the rights to many of the sources used in this paper could not be identified. Any possible claims should be directed to Peggy Piesche.

1. Since the German Democratic Republic in fact completed its life cycle when it legally ended on October 3, 1990, the descriptor "former" is both historically inaccurate and belittling, vilifying, and completely unnecessary.
2. See Andreas Wimmer, "Der Appell an die Nation: Kritische Bemerkungen zu vier Erklärungen von Xenophobie und Rassismus, " in *Das Fremde in der Gesellschaft: Migration, Ethnizität und Staat*, ed. Hans-Rudolf Wicker, Jean-Luc Alber, Claudio Bolzman, Rosita Fibbi, Kurt Imhof, and Andreas Wimmer (Zurich: Seismo, 1996), 173–98.
3. This unfortunately is also true for West Germany. However, since most of the (current) debates on race and racism in Germany focus on the particular inheritance of the GDR to explain contemporary problems mostly in the East German provinces, this absence in the post-unification conceptualization of the GDR is greatly significant.
4. The acronym PEGIDA stands for Patriotische Europäer gegen die Islamisierung

des Abendlandes (Patriotic Europeans against the Islamization of the Occident). It is a German right-wing movement founded in Dresden in October 2014 that actively promotes anti-Islamization politics.

5. Alternative für Deutschland (Alternative for Germany) is a Eurosceptic and right-wing populist political party in Germany founded in 2013.
6. Lutz Rathenow, "Die DDR höret nimmer auf: Die verdrängte Wirklichkeit und nicht nur ein Buch," review of *Geschichte der Opposition in der DDR: 1949–1989,* by Ehrhart Neubert (Berlin: Links, 1997), 1998, http://www.oeko-net.de/kommune/kommune8-98/krathe8.htm. Unless otherwise indicated, all English translations of quotations are provided by Peggy Piesche in consultation with Leslie A. Adelson.
7. See Christian Th. Müller and Patrice G. Poutrus, eds., *Ankunft—Alltag—Ausreise: Migration und interkulturelle Begegnungen in der DDR-Gesellschaft* (Cologne: Böhlau, 2005).
8. Rathenow.
9. See also Patrice Poutrus, review of *Fragmented Fatherland: Immigration and Cold War Conflicts in the Federal Republic of Germany, 1945–1980,* by Alexander Clarkson, *German Studies Review* 38, no. 1 (February 2015): 224–26.
10. Jan C. Behrends and Patrice G. Poutrus, "Xenophobia in the Former GDR: Explorations and Explanations from a Historical Perspective," in *Nationalisms across the Globe: An Overview of Nationalisms in State-Endowed and Stateless Nations,* ed. Wojciech Burszta, Tomasz Dominik Kamusella, and Sebastian Wojciechowski (Poznan: School of Humanities and Journalism, 2005), 155–70.
11. For a bibliography on this topic, see Peggy Piesche, "Identität und Wahrnehmung in literarischen Texten Schwarzer deutscher Autorinnen der 90er Jahre," in *Auf-Brüche: Kulturelle Produktionen von Migrantinnen, Schwarzen und jüdischen Frauen in Deutschland,* ed. Cathy S. Gelbin, Kader Konuk, and Peggy Piesche (Königstein: Ulrike Helmer, 1999), 195–205. See also Tina Campt, Pascal Grosse, and Yara-Colette Lemke-Muniz de Faria, "Blacks, Germans, and the Politics of Imperial Imagination, 1920–60," in *The Imperialist Imagination: German Colonialism and Its Legacy,* ed. Sara Friedrichsmeyer, Sara Lennox, and Susanne Zantop (Ann Arbor: University of Michigan Press, 1998), 205–29.
12. One exception is Ulrich van der Heyden, *Die Afrikawissenschaften in der DDR: Eine akademische Disziplin zwischen Exotik und Exempel* (Hamburg: LIT, 2000). Van der Heyden's interesting account of African studies in the GDR relates his research on minorities to research on the GDR itself.
13. See Irene Runge, *Ausland DDR: Fremdenhass* (Berlin: Dietz, 1990); the reference to a "complex reality" appears on p. 5. On the problematic of exclusion and inclusion in the GDR, see also Margarete Mitscherlich and Irene Runge, *Der Einheitsschock: Die Deutschen suchen eine neue Identität* (Düsseldorf: ECON-Taschenbuch, 1995).
14. Sabine Kriechhammer-Yagmur and Brigitte Proß-Klapproth, eds., *West Meets East* (Frankfurt/M: IAF, 1991).
15. Bernd Bröskamp, Eva Engelhard, and Ahmed Farah, eds., *Schwarz-Weiße Zeiten: AusländerInnen in Ostdeutschland vor und nach der Wende: Erfahrungen der Vertrags-*

arbeiter aus Mosambik: Interviews—Berichte—Analysen (Bremen: Informationszentrum Afrika, 1993).

16. Patrice Poutrus, Jan C. Behrends, and Dennis Kuck, "Historische Untersuchungen der Fremdenfeindlichkeit in den neuen Bundesländern," *Das Parlament* 39 (2000): 15–21.
17. The research Patrice G. Poutrus and his colleagues did over the last years is of course important to point out (see previous references). However, it is also necessary to note that this research concentrates on a general notion of xenophobia that combines different kinds of discrimination against all those legally regarded as foreigners in the GDR (e.g., members of the Soviet army or other white immigrants from socialist countries).
18. Ann-Judith Rabenschlag has recently concluded a dissertation at the University of Södertörn, Sweden, on images of the foreigner in the GDR titled "Völkerfreundschaft nach Bedarf: Ausländische Arbeitskräfte in der Wahrnehmung von Staat und Bevölkerung der DDR." It is available on line as Stockholm Studies in History 102, Södertörn Doctoral Dissertations 100.
19. See Jeanette Sumalgy, "Afro-deutsche Jugendliche im Schulsystem der ehemaligen DDR—unter Berücksichtigung ihrer bi-nationalen Familiensituation und die Bedeutung für ihre weitere Lebensplanung," Diplomarbeit Katholische Fachhochschule Berlin, 1996. Current research shows no evidence of a statistically significant number of Black Germans in the GDR prior to 1961. Statistically significant data could be obtained only for those born prior to 1971, since members of this group completed their school-based socialization in the GDR. For the purposes of the present article on the GDR, the term "Black Germans" refers to those children born to a German mother and a father from one of the so-called *Vertragsstaaten* (contract states). These children were citizens of the GDR and therefore not foreigners in any legal sense.
20. Kathrin Schmidt, *Die Gunnar-Lennefsen-Expedition* (Cologne: Kiepenheuer & Witsch, 1998), 65–66.
21. See Kriechhammer-Yagmur and Proß-Klapproth, 48ff.
22. Both foreigners who came to study and those who came as contract workers had only limited permission to stay in the GDR.
23. See Runge, 42ff and 74ff.
24. Kriechhammer-Yagmur and Proß-Klapproth, 282–85.
25. See Poutrus, Behrends, and Kuck, 18 and passim, for more on this practice.
26. Runge, 113.
27. Poutrus, Behrends, and Kuck, 17.
28. Kriechhammer-Yagmur and Proß-Klapproth, 48.
29. See Runge, 110–18, especially 112.
30. See Kriechhammer-Yagmur and Proß-Klapproth, 288–91, on the "Verordnung zur Gewährung des ständigen Wohnsitzes für Ausländer vom 30.11.1988" (Regulation granting permanent residence to foreigners of 11.30.1988).
31. Schmidt, 67.

32. See Sumalgy, 9.
33. Schmidt, 15.
34. N. N. Tscheboksarow and I. A. Tscheboksarow, *Völker, Rassen, Kulturen* (Leipzig: Urania, 1973).
35. See Sumalgy, 24–25.
36. See the foreword to *Gedanken zur Kinderliteratur—Den Teilnehmern der Zentralen Pionierleiterkonferenz der Freien Deutschen Jugend, überreicht vom Kinderbuchverlag Berlin, dem Verlag der Pionierorganisation "Ernst Thälmann"* (Berlin: Kinderbuchverlag Berlin, March 20–21, 1975), 2.
37. Klára Fehér, *Der Garten der Indianer* (Berlin: Corvina, 1973); Edith Klatt, *Der Indianer* (Berlin: Kinderbuch Verlag der DDR, 1958); Kurt Kauter, *Flieg Kondor Tupac Amaru* (Berlin: Militärverlag der DDR VEB/Das Taschenbuch, 1982).
38. This is taken from the cover of Kauter's book.
39. Hiltrud Lind and Rudolf Schultz-Debrowski, *Kinder in Afrika* (Berlin: Kinderbuch Verlag der DDR, 1969).
40. Ursula Werner-Böhnke, *Bummi in Afrika* (Leipzig: VEB Deutscher Verlag für Musik, 1969), 3.
41. Werner-Böhnke, 14.
42. Anke Poenicke, *Afrika in den deutschen Medien und Schulbüchern* (Hannover: KAS-Publikationen, 2001), http://www.kas.de/publikationen.
43. Auguste Lazar, *Sally Bleistift in Amerika* (Berlin: Kinderbuch Verlag der DDR, 1977).
44. Ludwig Renn, *Camilo* (Berlin: Kinderbuch Verlag der DDR, 1970).
45. Renn, 7.
46. Pittiplatsch is a small black goblin beloved by children in the GDR and later in united Germany. He first appeared as a hand puppet in a 1962 GDR children's television program but has since featured in films, books, audiobooks, comics, live puppet shows, dolls, stuffed toys, board games, and sweets.
47. The extremely sparse research on GDR comics accompanies historical reprints of *Mosaik*. See Reinhard Pfeiffer, *Digedag-Universum* (Berlin: Junge Welt, 1996), and Thomas Kramer, *Das Mosaik-Fan-Buch*, vols. 1 and 2 (Berlin: Dietz, 1993 and 1994).
48. See Mitscherlich and Runge, 65.
49. See Barbara Hille and Walter Jaide, *DDR-Jugend, Politisches Bewusstsein und Lebensalltag* (Opladen: Leske und Budrich, 1990), 83 and 278.
50. As Patrice Poutrus argues in a new commentary on a discussion paper that was first published in 2000, both scholars and public debates still fail to recognize the necessity for merging these arguments. See Patrice G. Poutrus, "Das Fremde bleibt fremd! Zur Aktualität zeithistorischer Forschung: Ein Kommentar zum Thesenpapier: 'Historische Ursachen der Fremdenfeindlichkeit in den neuen Bundesländern' aus dem Jahr 2000," published in September 2015 at http://www.zeitgeschichte-online.de/sites/default/files/documents/thesenpapier.pdf.

12

Blackness and Its (Queer) Discontents

FATIMA EL-TAYEB

That conferences such as "Remapping Black Germany" and the conventions of the Black German Heritage and Research Association can take place, including artists as well as activists, blurring the line between scholars and their subjects of study, and paying tribute to the community roots of "Black Germany," certainly shows that Black German studies has moved beyond a state of mere affirmation, of having to "prove" that Black Germans exist and matter. That good news, however, leaves us with the question of where to go from here. Most answers seem to indicate that Black German studies cannot and should not be merely additive, that the geographical expansion of our definition of the African diaspora has to go along with an expanded understanding of the very nature of this diaspora. The dominant methodological framework developed to grasp the particulars of the American experience cannot necessarily be applied to other parts of the world, and, additionally, the growing knowledge of the Black condition elsewhere might in turn change our understanding of the diaspora in the Americas. Black studies scholars increasingly argue that diasporic thinking beyond the national paradigm is a necessary prerequisite for an inclusive Black subjectivity—that is, one that does not create its own internal Others.[1] I would argue that it might even require thinking beyond the Black paradigm as we understand it now. This does not put into question the validity or necessity of national Black studies or the usefulness of "Black" as a political category, but it does raise the question of whether a growing number of national Black studies will merely coexist and occasionally interact under the umbrella of the African diaspora or whether a truly transnational and interdisciplinary diaspora studies will emerge. The latter seems the more adequate response to a geopolitical climate in which trench mentalities thrive while old binaries are successfully revived in "clash of civilization" scenarios.

A departure from essentialist notions of identity and a move beyond national limits and disciplinary boundaries seems more important than ever, and coalition building between increasingly embattled groups and disciplines appears to be the logical way to get there. Fields like Black studies cannot avoid addressing these developments, not only because they are favorite targets of neocon culture warriors but also because their very existence fundamentally challenges the supposedly neutral but heavily ideological boundaries between politics and scholarship, "real life" and academia, community and intellectual.[2] But how to negotiate between a normative "unity" that does not allow for contradictions and disagreements on the one hand and anti-essentialist approaches in danger of being too inclusive, too non-prescriptive, to be effective on the other? The Black German experience might offer some surprising insights, pointing to the potential contributions of "marginal" Black communities to the emerging field of African diaspora studies. In this essay, I will sketch some potential fields of inquiry: the idea of a Black Europe; the link between African and Muslim diasporas; and, finally, the potential of a "queer" diasporic memory.

Europe, in spite or possibly because of its marginal position within Africana studies, offers an ideal terrain to explore and advance the possibilities of new conceptualizations of minority identity, inclusive of but not necessarily limited to Black communities. Viewing the Black German experience in a European context—that is, in relation to Europe's other Black communities as well as to other communities of color—thus makes a lot of sense. Europe's history in its totality, national differences admitted, does show important commonalities, rooted in the perception of Europe as a "white" continent that lives on in current debates on postnational identities.[3] Consequently, the continent's various Black populations are increasingly subjected to the same conditions and confront an ever more homogeneous image of a continent that until now has excluded its residents of color. A comparative approach to these Black populations thus seems crucial. To adequately discuss the idea of a Black Europe, however, it is necessary first to systematically explore the conditions under which not only concepts of race but also racialized minorities were created. But instead the perception of these minorities in European public discourse is traditionally determined by pseudo-biological, implicitly racialized concepts of national and, by extension, European identity that invariably position them as Other. And there is still little awareness of the actual ethnic diversity representing not only contemporary but also historical Europe, more sophisticated approaches notwithstanding; when push comes to shove, "white and Christian" seems to be the lowest common denominator to which debates on European identity are reduced.[4] To explain this persistent denial, one needs to look at its historical roots, not the least of which is the colonial legacy and its repression in national and European histories. Relations among different communities of color in continental Europe are partly shaped by the common experience of European colonization, linking populations originating in Africa, Asia, and the Middle East (and even Eastern Europe, if the continental empires of Austria, Russia, and Turkey are included).[5] Europe's communities of color frequently share a history of colonization and migration, and often the religion of Islam creates a link to a transnational community that is ethnically diverse but largely nonwhite. The latter aspect, interacting and at times overlapping with discourses around race, is rapidly gaining importance, with ambiguous consequences: while Europe's Muslim population is large and fast-growing, the implicit definition of Europe as (Judeo-)Christian erases Islam's contributions to the continent's history and culture and forecloses the possibility of a secularized Muslim European identity, instead constructing Islam as antagonistic to "European values." Thus, while their shared religious background creates common ground among minority communities, it also adds to their perception as "outsiders" within dominant discourse.

This perception is supported by studies of ethnicity in Europe that focus on migration processes rather than on the emergence of native minorities, implying an invincible divide between (white) Europeans and migrants (of color). Migrants' identities are defined along lines of ethnic classifications, and various generations of a particular ethnicity are grouped together, while similarities between populations of different backgrounds are neglected. In addition, the almost exclusive focus of European migration studies on the first generation of migrants has resulted in a lack of comprehensive studies of second- and third-generation migrants on either a national or a continental level, which both reflects and reinforces the belief that there are only migrants, no minorities.[6] The complex interactions of race, religion, migration, and colonialism constitutive of the situation of minorities of color in Europe could be explored instead through a shift from a vertical look at one ethnic group, covering various generations and their move from "home" to "host" country, toward a horizontal approach across various ethnic divides. Such an exploration could uncover identifications that are trans- rather than binational, resulting in identities that are inadequately represented by the dominant models of European migration studies.[7] So far, however, continental European developments have been largely excluded from theoretical debates within postcolonial and diaspora studies, leaving a methodological void for the analysis of colonial and postcolonial migrations both within and to Europe. A more inclusive approach could not only give new impulses to comparative studies of minorities in Europe but also forge political bonds between different groups that have confronted similar strategies of exclusion.

An exploration of the continued importance of colonialism is not just a prerequisite to understanding "racial Europeanization," to use David Theo Goldberg's term. It could also effectively challenge the marginalization of Black Europe within Africana studies, which is largely due to Europe's supposedly secondary role in the central theme of the African diaspora, the transatlantic slave trade. The focus on the latter lets diasporic populations who have entered the West through other trajectories necessarily appear as less representative of the "Black condition" in the West.[8] A "cross-ethnic" exploration of processes of racialization in Europe would thus also require rethinking our notion of Blackness: while a generalized definition of "Black" is both methodologically justified and politically necessary, diaspora discourse to a certain extent produces its own subject. This representational power needs to be examined: Who is considered a proper Black subject, and why? A shift from a national focus to a diaspora perspective means that the specific cultural, historical, and political conditions that produced dominant notions of the Black subject within Black studies need to be examined—and challenged, if necessary. For example, the focus on African populations in the Americas and on the transatlantic slave trade that brought them there necessarily left the diasporic link to the non-Western world of Islam largely unexplored and several important questions unanswered: Where are the similarities and differences in racialization processes in the Christian/Western world? How is Blackness/race negotiated in a transnational community that is largely nonwhite and non-Western? How are discourses transported, adapted, and countered between "West" and "East," and how does Africa function as a space of contact in between?

North Africa, direct neighbor to both Asia and Europe, is a promising starting point in attempting some preliminary answers. Nevertheless, it has largely been excluded from Africana studies, based on a consensus that follows a framework established by, among others, Hegel's division of Africa into three distinct parts, of which the North is supposedly the "European" one.[9] This adherence to limits produced by a racist Western discourse is a reminder that African diaspora studies are "of the West" in productive and less productive ways. The model of sub-Saharan Africa as the "real," Black Africa largely worked for an Africana studies focused on the Americas, but it is just that—a working model, not a reflection of realities. Thus it cannot be generalized; rather, the question of whether it can and should be applied to other contexts must be answered for each individual occasion. Otherwise, Africana scholarship unwittingly affirms supposedly clear racial boundaries that in fact are ideological constructs, invented to serve strategic purposes. Within this ideology, the fact that North African populations are extremely "racially" heterogeneous becomes proof that Black North Africans are not really Black, or African, rather than proof of an actual diversity that has been discursively erased by race theory. Instead, the interaction of "Africanness" and "Blackness" must be reexamined based on local dynamics rather than on preconceived universalist notions. In this case, the regional, religious, continental, and racial identifications of (North) Africans affect internal as well as external group relations in ways that cannot be approached with a methodology based on the American situation.

This becomes very obvious when one returns to Black Europe and its close links to Africa. Consider the significant number of Black Europeans of "supra-Saharan" descent and their relationship both to other Black Europeans and to Afro-Europeans of North African descent who are not Black (but are sometimes part of the same family). The 2005 "riots" in the French *banlieus* brought into focus a group that is neither ethnically nor "racially" homogeneous. Rather, the French system produced a homogenized, racialized economic underclass based on certain markers of "foreignness," including race as well as religion (something that with good cause can be considered a general European condition). Traditional diaspora discourses do not account for these complications, which does not make them unusable—but neither should they be considered ultimate definitions of the Black experience. From a "marginal" perspective, in which the American experience still appears central in many ways but not as paradigmatic, the African diaspora can be seen as the result of various globalizations—not only the enormous, violent one of the Middle Passage but also, among others, that of the rapid spread of the Muslim empire across North Africa and the Middle East into Europe and East Asia, bringing with it huge population movements. Similarly, a study of the long history of Afro-Asian interactions would situate developments within the West in a broader perspective.[10]

A Black Mediterranean focus would take into account that, at least until the rise of the Franconian and Muslim empires, the Mediterranean as a space of cultural, political, and economic exchange was much more important and meaningful for the surrounding cultures than "Europe" or "Africa." And a contemporary understanding of a Black Mediterranean brings into focus the fact that Black European communities are linked to migration in a very different way than Black American communities are. For the latter, immigration is the factor that separates them from (most) other communities of color. "Blackness" was something that immigrant groups of color had to distance themselves from to enter the American mainstream; in fact, the existence of the African American community as native underclass arguably allowed and continues to allow this assimilative "upward mobility" toward whiteness. In Europe, on the other hand, immigration often is coded Black, even though the actual number of African immigrants is minor compared to that of Asians or Americans and, above all, to internal migration from East to West.[11] Nevertheless, the "Black tide" across the Mediterranean from Africa to Europe has been a consistently popular European trope, fed by images of thousands of young West African men trying to climb the barbed wire fences separating African Morocco from the Spanish exclaves Melilla and Ceuta. Despite the enormous death toll among potential immigrants, Europe tends to see itself as victim in this process, a demographic David desperately defending itself against the Black Goliath of the global South. The high symbolic value that African migration has for Europe reflects Africa's key role in European discourses on race, enhanced by the continents' geographic proximity and the history of colonialism, and also by the ways sexuality and gender are used in racist discourses: it is relevant that the migration from Africa to Europe is largely that of young men (in the public mind, almost exclusively so), feeding long-standing tropes pathologizing Black masculinity. Since the 1980s, these tropes have fed into public images of migration in Europe that were clearly divided by gender: the young African male (often portrayed as a criminal, usually a drug dealer) stood for "illegal" migration, while labor migration (and its accompanying cultural difference) was represented by the veiled Muslim woman.[12]

In light of the continued marginalization and silencing of Black populations by mainstream European discourses, academic as well as political and popular, it is of utmost importance to note that the Black Other is a key trope in the European migration discourse—a discourse that in truth is often much more one of an internal racial policing. This role has very real consequences, among them the disproportionally high number of Black victims of institutional as well as "informal" racism—which, disturbingly, is still routinely denied in European public discourse.[13] Equally important, however, is that racial dynamics work differently in Europe than in the United States, where any migrant group's relation to whiteness depends directly on its relation to Blackness: moving from one toward the other is what assimilation means. In Europe, whiteness is exclusive: while "Blackness" is the most powerful shorthand for racial Otherness, nonwhiteness and foreignness are considered synonymous. The narrower definition of whiteness goes along with the often-noted shift from biological to cultural racisms; the latter in turn are increasingly linked to a long tradition of racing religion, which partly explains the much more central role that Muslims play in migration and "clash of civilization" discourses in Europe.[14] And while this development is certainly not restricted to Europe, it affects Europe in particular ways. Its practical meaning for the relationship between Black and Muslim populations in Europe (and for Black European Muslims) depends on many factors; clearly, however, this interaction is an aspect of African diasporic relationships that remains seriously understudied and needs to be explored in a cross-ethnic, transnational framework.

The dominant disciplinary focus on national histories facilitated the exclusion of European minority communities through the marginalization of colonial and postcolonial ties between Europe and the rest of the world and of forms of organizing and identification that are translocal, such as those represented within the African and Muslim diasporas. Diaspora studies potentially offers an alternative, more balanced approach, but it too is frequently accused of magnifying rather than overcoming the nationalist, heteronormative, and essentialist biases often characterizing nation-focused histories. This criticism leads a number of migration scholars to categorically deny the usefulness of diaspora studies for the European context: "Home is thought of not just as a territory, but as a homogeneous culture from which the diasporic community has been displaced, but which it must maintain at all cost to safeguard its identity. . . . Today's hyphenated and migratory cultures develop different structures of experience which may make the traditional understanding of diaspora as linked to roots, soil, and kinship indeed highly questionable."[15]

Is diaspora nevertheless a useful concept for approaching Black European minority communities? I would argue that it is, though only if the meaning of "diaspora" is transformed from a term of temporal and spatial displacement focused on the past to one of permanent productive dislocation focused on the future. The African diaspora in the Americas offers a different perspective on the situatedness of diaspora within the nation than the one cited by critics of diaspora studies, in which the lost "home" is a symbolic if not metaphorical term and not necessarily the one most central to creating a communal "we." This makes it possible, using Édouard Glissant's terms, to replace "root identity," centered on origins, with "relation identity," leaving behind the idea of "sacred territories" and moving toward the possibility of accepting the messiness of "situational communities."[16] Here the diaspora community is closely intertwined with the host societies' past and present but is confronted not only with the systematic destruction of collective memories predating the diaspora but also with a minority memory that is explicitly at odds with official commemorations of the past, leading to radically different perspectives on "national" history. Accordingly, Black Americans had to find ways to create, maintain, and pass on a collective memory outside of the official national discourses silencing them.[17] Such counter-memory discourses and the (re)discovery of narratives of past agency are central concerns for European minority communities. The quest, on the other hand, to erase or marginalize the presence of national racialized Others lies at the heart not only of national histories but also of the European (non-)memory of colonialism. The memory of being colonized by European powers is brought to the continent through migration by diverse populations. Their narrations of this experience, however, clash with the European memory of colonialism, expressed in an official narrative of colonial rule as largely benevolent, marginal to Europe, and, most importantly, without negative repercussions for the present.[18] The experience of being written out of or misrepresented in majority histories therefore is often more relevant to minority communities in Europe than the supposed desire to recreate an ideal home—especially when one begins to see colonialism as a (repressed) part of European national histories: think, for example, of the problems French of Algerian descent both face and pose regarding the "French" memory of the Algerian war.[19] Postcolonial populations in Europe challenge dominant histories on various levels; to give them a voice in the debate about Europe's identity and future would mean a contestation of the official narrative and acknowledgement of the subjectivity of the dominant European position.[20]

The current debate over the transnational "European memory" could offer a perfect opportunity to overcome the structural (self-)exclusion of migrants and minorities so often lamented in mainstream discourses. Despite the professed desire to "integrate" reluctant "foreigners," however, the internalist focus of national histories will instead more likely be reinscribed in twenty-first-century postnational discourses. This also means that the myriad ways in which Black minorities are part of this history will still be almost completely ignored. That exclusion is based on what Haitian anthropologist Michel-Rolph Trouillot calls "archival power"—"the power to define what is and what is not a serious object of research and, therefore, of mention."[21] By deeming irrelevant, for example, the involvement of non-Western and nonwhite populations in World War II and the war's effect on them, the idea that "world history" is *white* history is again reproduced, events of global importance are shown to take place in the West alone, and Western ignorance about the rest of the world is thus excused. Equally important, this model is necessary to the claim that "migrant cultures" and European cultures did not touch until the postwar period. Consequently, so-called second- and third-generation migrants (a category exclusively applied to Muslim Europeans and Europeans of color) are constantly confronted with discourses denying them any form of continuity beyond the absurdly permanent state of "migration," fixing their identity eternally to their (grand)parents' moment of arrival and creating a discursive limbo of hybridity within which minorities seem forever lost between "here" and "there." The (re)creation of a sense of history within the "host society" is therefore a central concern of minority activism; moreover, it can be considered indicative of the shift from migrant to minority communities.

Black Germans are a main target of the paradox of culture in dominant European discourse, which presumes the importance of certain factors in defining "integration" and belonging, such as adherence to "Western values," while denying the relevance of others, namely racialized difference.[22] In most cases having one white German parent and one Black, non-German parent, and often having grown up in largely white neighborhoods, Afro-Germans are likely the most highly assimilated German minority, according to official standards: "culture," language, education, and—last but not least—citizenship. They are, however, also the minority generally perceived as being most "un-German." Through the decades and across the East-West divide, the stubborn conviction persists that Black Germans must "really" come from either Africa or the Americas.[23] While the implicit racialization of Germanness as "white" and thus of Blacks as racial *and* national Other would be an obvious explanation for this apparent paradox, public discourse rejects this analysis as meaningless within a discursive framework shaped by an Enlightenment universalism that for centuries has managed to claim race as irrelevant while simultaneously treating it as all-important. The case of Afro-Germans, whose presence seems oxymoronic within the nation and equally dissonant within the African diaspora narrative, makes explicit the implicit stakes of diaspora nationalism and transnationalism.

A historical grounding of a contemporary community-in-the-making can be achieved in many ways. The desire to create an authentic, tangible history and identity is certainly a present reaction to Afro-Germans' double displacement; also obvious, however, is a departure from essentialist concepts of home toward an embracing of these "disidentifications."[24] This does not preclude the desire for "roots," for a sense of history on which to base positionalities in the present. This history is constructed, however, via a "queer memory" that directly relates to the central role of transnational Black feminist positions within the Afro-German community. In the mid-1980s an Afro-German movement emerged that claimed an identity as Black *and* German and as part of a larger African diaspora. The particular shape the 1980s Black movement in Germany took had been made possible by the interventions of US third world feminism in the revolutionary nationalist discourses of the 1960s and 1970s, effectively deconstructing the pure, authentic, masculine identity of the diasporic subject.[25] This discourse extended way beyond US borders, inspiring Black feminist organizations in other parts of the diaspora and especially in Germany, where the first collective expressions of a Black German consciousness took place in an explicitly feminist context.[26]

The movement attempted to create a past and memory within the nation but simultaneously beyond it. This process involved the creation of a genealogy that moves as far away from essentialist notions of "roots, soil, and kinship" as possible: while blood relations—histories created through the parents' family lines—are of varying importance to individual Black Germans, a sense of an Afro-German community and history was created (almost) exclusively through a shared experience *in* the host nation. A sense of a continuing African diaspora presence in Germany, the existence of forefathers and foremothers, is built around a group of people who rarely shared family ties or even cultures a priori but who are, if not a community of choice, at least one of chosen identification. This type of community building could be called "queer," in part because a sense of community and family beyond blood ties is most pronounced in the LGBT community,[27] but more so because this strategy denaturalizes ideas of kinship, nation, and linear genealogies in rather queer ways.[28]

Queer theory's value as a political strategy is disputed, especially among communities of color who have quite different investments in questions of identity and subjectivity than the often white and middle-class authors dominating queer theory. Nevertheless, sexual and ethnic minorities potentially share an investment in denaturalizing and complicating essentialist categories of identity. This shared concern finds its most explicit expression in queer of color critique, a school of thought (and practice) explicitly placing itself in the tradition of the women of color feminism that so decisively shaped the Afro-German community. Challenging normative assumptions in queer as well as Black studies, queer of color critique aims to "elaborate the terms of a potential liberation"[29] by grounding a queer critique of heteronormativity, including the one present in Black and diaspora theories, in an understanding of the central role of race and class in these systems.[30] I believe that queer of color critique can offer useful methodological tools for exploring Black Europe, in part because of the particular conditions of the African diaspora there sketched above, but also because European minority activists, without necessarily reflecting this theoretically, use "queer" strategies to continuously rearrange the components of the supposedly stable identities assigned to them.[31] The realization that identity is not natural but rather highly performative (both in the sense of *performance* and *performativity*) is a consequence of the daily fight for survival in a system that has no space for ethnic minorities.[32] This activism shows that the deconstruction of identities such as "Black" does not necessarily imply a retreat from politically charged notions of identity but can, on the contrary, be a strategy to create them. This supports Judith Butler's claim that "if the notion of the subject, for instance, is no longer a given, no longer presumed, that does not mean that it has no meaning for us, that it ought no longer to be uttered. On the contrary, it means only that the term is not simply a building block on which we rely, an uninterrogated premise for political argument. Rather, the term has become an object of theoretical attention, something for which we are compelled to give an account."[33] This, I think, should be our position toward the "Black subject": a constant critical inquiry aimed at the subject's de- and reconstruction, not its abolition. "Marginal" diasporic experiences might irritatingly mess with established concepts of Black identity, but I believe they do so in productive ways. There certainly are and likely always will be more questions than answers, but if it is the process of creative inquiry that constitutes an African diaspora identity, asking these questions can only be beneficial, rather than threatening to the "unity" of the Black community. Ideally, the inquiry into the limits of Blackness will help keep diaspora studies a dynamic field of exchange. To this process the Black experience in Germany could have much to contribute.

NOTES

1. See Tiffany R. Patterson and Robin D. G. Kelley, "Unfinished Migrations: Reflections on the African Diaspora and the Making of the Modern World," *African Studies Review* 43 (2000): 11–50; Brent Hayes Edwards, *The Practice of Diaspora: Literature, Translation, and the Rise of Black Internationalism* (Cambridge, MA: Harvard University Press, 2003); and Michelle Wright, *Becoming Black: Creating Identity in the African Diaspora* (Durham, NC: Duke University Press, 2004).
2. See, e.g., the largely successful attempts to dismantle affirmative action at the state level in the United States, dramatically reducing not only the numbers of Black students but also support for the curricular inclusion of positions going beyond the dominant perspective, or the continued resistance to the inclusion of minority voices in European university curricula.
3. David Theo Goldberg, "Racial Europeanization," *Ethnic and Racial Studies* 29, no. 2 (March 2006): 331–64.
4. See Mark Terkessidis, *Die Banalität des Rassismus: Migranten zweiter Generation entwickeln eine neue Perspektive* (Bielefeld: Transcript, 2004), and Hito Steyerl and Encarnación Gutiérrez Rodríguez, eds., *Spricht die Subalterne Deutsch? Migration und postkoloniale Kritik* (Münster: Unrast, 2003).
5. I am not suggesting that they can be equated with colonial overseas empires. I do believe, however, that they constituted a form of spatial and ideological governance much closer to the colonialism practiced by other European nations than to the inner-European contestation and shifting of borders taking place at the same time.
6. See Steyerl and Gutiérrez Rodríguez; Maurice Crul and Hans Vermeulen, "The Second Generation in Europe," *International Migration Review* 37, no. 4 (Winter 2003): 965–86; Mark Terkessidis, *Migranten* (Hamburg: Rotbuch, 2000); and Alec G. Hargreaves and Mark McKinney, *Post-Colonial Cultures in France* (London: Routledge, 1997).
7. Fatima El-Tayeb, "Urban Diasporas: Race, Identity, and Popular Culture in a Post-

Ethnic Europe," in *Motion in Place/Place in Motion: 21st Century Migration*, ed. Toshio Iyotani and Masako Ishii (Osaka, Japan: Japan Center for Area Studies, National Museum of Ethnology, 2005), 133–55.

8. Paul Gilroy, *The Black Atlantic: Modernity and Double Consciousness* (Cambridge, MA: Harvard University Press, 1993).
9. Olufemi Taiwo, "Exorcising Hegel's Ghost: Africa's Challenge to Philosophy," *African Studies Quarterly* 1, no. 4 (1998): 3–16.
10. See Vijay Prashad, *Everybody Was Kung Fu Fighting: Afro-Asian Connections and the Myth of Cultural Purity* (Boston: Beacon, 2002), and Vijay Prashad, *The Karma of Brown Folk* (Minneapolis: University of Minnesota Press, 2000).
11. For current numbers, see Migration Policy Institute, http://www.migrationinformation.org/datahub/europe.cfm.
12. In contrast to that, and despite occasional short-term (and usually prewar) attention to the oppression of Muslim women, the face of Islam in the United States is male, and linked more closely to "terrorism" than to culture or immigration. This leads to significant differences in US and European discourses of fear (which at the same time share "clash of civilization" and "war on terror" tropes), differences that point to the significant role of gender in all race discourses. While the Muslim woman remains the symbolic manifestation of Muslim migration, the angry young (violent, sexist, homophobic, anti-Semitic) Muslim man increasingly entered public discourse after 9/11.
13. The degree of this denial became obvious in the case of a middle-aged Black German man almost beaten to death by two white attackers in Potsdam. His cell phone's voice mail recorded part of the attack, documenting that, among other things, he was called a "dirty n****r." Nonetheless, Germany's then-secretary of interior Wolfgang Schäuble publicly criticized the federal attorney general for treating the case as the German equivalent of a hate crime (in itself an extremely unusual reaction). In his attempt to prove that the motives for the attack were entirely unclear, Schäuble added insult to injury by stating that "blond and blue-eyed people get attacked as well, sometimes by foreigners." While this reaction might seem extreme in its unselfconscious explicitness, it illustrates a structural European insistence on ignoring racism as an explanation for anything (within the continental limits); this is also evident in French reactions to the riots in the fall of 2005 and in the continued downplaying of violent racism in Eastern Europe. See, e.g., "'Blonde Opfer': Empörung über Schäuble," *SpiegelOnline*, April 20, 2006, http://www.spiegel.de/politik/deutschland/0,1518,412195,00.html.
14. See George L. Mosse, *Toward the Final Solution: A History of European Racism* (New York: Howard Fertig, 1978).
15. Andreas Huyssen, "Diaspora and Nation: Migration into Other Pasts," *New German Critique* 88 (Winter 2003): 151.
16. Édouard Glissant, *Poetics of Relation* (Ann Arbor: University of Michigan Press, 1997).
17. Elizabeth Alexander, "Can You Be Black and Look at This? Reading the Rodney King Video(s)," *Public Culture* 7 (Fall 1994): 77–94.

18. See, e.g., the "European Union Declaration on Colonialism" in the wake of the UN conference on racism in Durban 2001 (European Commission, Council Conclusions 2001), or the French law, passed in February 2005, requiring high school teachers to emphasize the "positive effects" of French colonialism (repealed a year later after massive protests—see Claude Liauzu, "Une loi contre l'histoire," *Le Monde diplomatique,* April 2005, 28).
19. As expressed, for example, in the lack of commemoration of the 1961 Paris massacre in which police viciously attacked Algerian residents protesting a curfew directed specifically at them, resulting in at least one hundred dead. See, e.g., "Paris Marks Algerian Protest 'Massacre,'" *BBC News,* October 17, 2001, http://news.bbc.co.uk/2/hi/world/monitoring/media_reports/1604970.stm.
20. Apart from the more obvious contestations of colonialism's effects on the colonized, this also includes episodes of intra-European policies such as the forced resettlement of several million people in southeast Europe after World War I, which was repeated on an even larger scale after the next war (Götz Aly, *Rasse und Klasse: Nachforschungen zum deutschen Wesen* [Frankfurt/M: Fischer, 2003]). These massive interventions could be seen as signs of "the persistence of administrative methods and habits acquired during contact with 'indigenous' populations, which, after having been 'projected' into colonial space during the decisive period of the formation of the republican state apparatus, were reintroduced and 'naturalized' in the metropole" (Étienne Balibar, *We, the People of Europe? Reflections on Transnational Citizenship* [Princeton, NJ: Princeton University Press, 2004], 39).
21. Michel-Rolph Trouillot, *Silencing the Past: Power and the Production of History* (Boston: Beacon, 1995), 99.
22. For an example, see the German discussions around the "naturalization test" aimed specifically at Muslims who are applying for citizenship and are suspected of not sharing "Western values" such as tolerance for homosexuality and commitment to the equality of women; acceptance of these values is supposedly "tested" in the process. While this discourse has many of the characteristics of farce—clearly many if not most Germans, certainly including the former pope, would not pass the test—the public discussions around it have quite serious consequences for Germany's largest religious minority by further stigmatizing it as antidemocratic and premodern. (For English-language sources, see "Über-Citizens: Briefing on the Recent Naturalisation Tests in Germany," Islamic Human Rights Commission, May 2006, www.ihrc.org.uk/file/060511ubercitizens.pdf; and Andreas Tzortzis, "In Europe, Quizzes Probe Values of Potential Citizens," *Christian Science Monitor,* April 10, 2006.)
23. See Jeanine Kantara, "Schwarz. Und deutsch. Kein Widerspruch? Für viele meiner weißen Mitbürger schon," *Die Zeit,* September 7, 2000; Olumide Popoola and Beldan Sezen, eds., *Talking Home: Heimat aus unserer eigenen Feder* (Amsterdam: blue moon, 1999); Cathy Gelbin, Kader Konuk, and Peggy Piesche, eds., *Auf-Brüche: Kulturelle Produktionen von Migrantinnen, Schwarzen und jüdischen Frauen in Deutschland* (Königstein: Ulrike Helmer, 1999); and Katharina Oguntoye, May

Opitz, and Dagmar Schultz, eds., *Farbe bekennen: Afro-deutsche Frauen auf den Spuren ihrer Geschichte* (Berlin: Orlanda, 1986).

24. See José Estaban Muñoz, *Disidentifications: Queers of Color and the Performance of Politics* (Minneapolis: University of Minnesota Press, 1999): "Disidentification is meant to be descriptive of the survival strategies the minority subject practices in order to negotiate a phobic majoritarian public sphere that continuously elides or punishes the existence of subjects who do not conform to the phantasm of normative citizenship" (4).
25. See Gloria T. Hull, Patricia Bell Scott, and Barbara Smith, eds., *All the Women Are White, All the Blacks Are Men, But Some of Us Are Brave: Black Women's Studies* (Old Westbury, NY: Feminist Press, 1982); Audre Lorde, *Sister Outsider* (New York: Crossing Press, 1984); and Combahee River Collective, "A Black Feminist Statement," in *Capitalist Patriarchy and the Case for Socialist Feminism*, ed. Zillah R. Eisenstein (New York: Monthly Review, 1978), 362–72.
26. Anne Adams, "The Souls of Black *Volk*," in *Not So Plain as Black and White: Afro-German Culture and History, 1890–2000*, ed. Patricia Mazón and Reinhild Steingröver (Rochester, NY: University of Rochester Press, 2005), 209–28; and Fatima El-Tayeb, "'If You Cannot Pronounce My Name, You Can Just Call Me Pride': Afro-German Activism, Gender, and Hip Hop," *Gender and History* 15, no. 3 (November 2003): 460–86.
27. All existing gay/lesbian essentialism aside, the ever-expanding letters alone are a sign of the negotiability of inclusion.
28. It could also be called "dialogic" in the Bakhtinian sense Michelle Wright employs in *Becoming Black* (cited in note 1), and one might extend Wright's argument about the importance of gender and sexuality for Black subjectivities by speculating that the central role of female activists and transnational feminism in the early years of the Black German movement is not coincidental in producing a queer memory discourse.
29. Rinaldo Walcott, "Outside in Black Studies: Reading from a Queer Place in the Diaspora," in *Black Queer Studies: A Critical Anthology*, ed. E. Patrick Johnson and Mae Henderson (Durham, NC: Duke University Press, 2005), 91.
30. See Muñoz; Roderick F. Ferguson, *Aberrations in Black: Toward a Queer of Color Critique* (Minneapolis: University of Minnesota Press, 2004); Gayatri Gopinath, *Impossible Desires: Queer Diasporas and South Asian Public Cultures* (Durham, NC: Duke University Press, 2005); and Johnson and Henderson.
31. El-Tayeb, "Urban Diasporas."
32. Within her analysis of sexual power regimes, Judith Butler differentiates between those who in discourses around gender and sexuality represent the opposite of the norm and are thus indispensable for its definition—male homosexuals, in the case of heterosexuality—and those who do not even appear within the discourse but are an invisible aberration without discursive space and thus remain without a place from whence to resist their normative exclusion. In Butler's example, it is lesbians who appear as the discursive (un)subjects of heteronormative power systems

(Judith Butler, "Imitation and Gender Insubordination," in *Inside/Out: Lesbian Theories, Gay Theories,* ed. Diana Fuss [New York: Routledge, 1991], 13–31). But with all necessary caution, one can transfer her analysis to the discourse around normative European identity. In this discourse, only the seemingly unambiguous and opposing options of white/Christian/European vs. "migrant" are presented as valid, while ambiguities and transgressions are discursively silenced. In other words, second- and third-generation migrants and minorities are invisible and mute between the antagonism of "native" norm and "foreigner" aberration. This means that the experience of those who violate the image of European ethnic uniformity has no place in the various national narratives, which thus can remain unchanged, not only allowing the continuing survival of illusionary notions of unambiguous, pure, and inalterable national identities but also preventing a constructive approach to the irreversible multi-ethnic reality of contemporary Europe. Europe likes to imagine itself untouched by "race matters," a color-blind continent in which difference is marked along lines of nationality and ethnicized Others are ascribed a permanently transitory status as migrants of the *n*th generation, turning minorities into muted "(un)subjects."

33. Judith Butler, "The End of Sexual Difference?," in *Feminist Consequences: Theory for the New Century,* ed. Elizabeth Bronfen and Misha Kavka (New York: Columbia University Press, 2001), 419.

13

Looking Backward and Forward

Twenty Years of the Black Women's Movement in Germany

KATHARINA OGUNTOYE, KATJA KINDER, MAUREEN MAISHA EGGERS, AND PEGGY PIESCHE

What we now call community was like a train that got longer and longer and faster and faster and just couldn't be steered in one single direction anymore.

The Black Women's Movement in Germany as the Complex Product of Activist Interventions Taking Place at Different Times and Places

A conversation between four activists from different waves of the movement. Katharina Oguntoye, Katja Kinder, and Maisha Eggers met in Berlin-Kreuzberg on a Monday evening in July 2012. Peggy Piesche led the discussion.

The First Groups of Black Women Activists: Of the Necessity of Uniting as Black Activists

PP: Katharina and Katja, for me you're the first generation of Black women who came together in the 1980s and in a marvelous way created structures of the movement that the middle generation, in which I'd include Maisha and myself, could grow into. When I came to ADEFRA in 1990, I was most fascinated by stories describing the earliest encounters and meetings and finally the founding of ADEFRA. They were always very diverse and took place all over at the same time. One story stood out especially, and that was of course the one about the red plush room where you all met.

KK: Yes, we met at Jasmin Eding's in Munich—in the red salon—to found the group, the initiative ADEFRA. Later in the early nineties the official association was also led mainly by women from Munich.

KO: I thought that was in Cologne. At Gloria's in Cologne? But I don't remember anymore who lived in Cologne. My memory begins in Cologne. We traveled to Cologne and from there to Utrecht.

KK: I remember that. We met Jasmin in Utrecht. Then we went with Elke Jank—Ja-El today—and some other women to Jasmin's in Munich. Then we sat together in Jasmin's apartment. It was totally moving that we seven or eight Black lesbians were gathered together in one place.

KO: We looked for a name. ADELE: Afro-German Lesbian Group was the first suggestion. But that didn't sound so great, we weren't from Swabia. That just sounded too German to us.

KK: And also sort of too funny. That ". . . dele."

KO: ADEFRA sounded a lot better. It was also about visibility, in the name too. And ADEFRA sounded like Afrekete[1] and not at all like ADELE. That's interesting, because it really made a big difference. Katja and I came from the women's movement, and it was important for us in the women's movement to be visible as lesbians. ADEFRA [Afro-DEutsche FRAuen] as Afro-German Women's Group didn't make us quite so visible at first.

KK: Although it was always quite open and well known. We were all out. That was an important step—making ourselves visible in the community.[2] Heterosexual women who were connected to ADEFRA got a lot of funny looks and comments. But nevertheless we had a strong standing in the community. And that continues to be the case.

KO: After all, we were all women, and any woman could join.

KK: Right, it was an open group for Black women.

PP: But that was a kind of invisibility. It doesn't say on the package what's inside, so to speak. So that made clear that invisibility occurs at all sorts of levels.

KO: Yes, but maybe that was okay then. That meant that the group was open. But for me it just wasn't my starting point, so to speak.

Connecting to the Resistance Strategies of Black Women Activists Who Went Before

Establishing connections with other Black women's movements with a longer history was a great help to the young movement in its earliest stages. Trips that the German women activists took together played an important role in their efforts to organize. Theater and writing workshops and exchanges with Black women activists from London and Amsterdam contributed to their ability to thematize and analyze the lives of Black women in Germany. One result was a number of literary texts representing the autonomous Black female subject. The magazine *Afrekete* is one of those texts. Because of these efforts, Black women's political activities were much more frequently documented.

PP: That brings me to the question of what these first meetings, the beginnings for you activists right from the outset, actually mean. I know the two of you are very modest when you think about your involvement. But your experiences in the movement were always very important for me, since I came later and could build on what you went through and made happen. And of course it was also very exciting. Looking back, how do you see it now?

KO: The word movement always sounds like lots and lots of people. But it wasn't like that.

KK: Well, there were a lot of us sometimes. And movement can also mean that something is in motion. And we were certainly very much in motion.

KO: Yes, later. But when we started it was mostly just you and me.

KK: Especially you! You could always be counted on. You kept calling me up and telling me where something was happening. Other women came later. Jasmin, Eva von Pirch, Ria Cheatom, Judy Gummich, and many, many others.

KO: Eva and Elke . . . But right at the beginning, I mean, who were you with in the Sub?[3] We were always the only ones there. I can still remember Yara. She was one of the first Black women that I met in the Sub. What I mean is, I knew other women in other contexts, but just not in the political movement. That's because you could be in the lesbian movement without being political. There were different contexts—for instance, I remember an older Black lesbian that I knew then. She helped to build up Ban Ying,[4] but she wasn't there in other contexts. What I want to say is that we were often isolated, though we were there, and everybody was visible only when you belonged to all these different contexts. But it was just you and me who brought it all together, who were also interested in an Afro-German women's group. And that's where you were very active.

KK: Well, I thought you were the one who was so active. Do you remember, I met you at a reading during the Lesbian Week in Berlin. You read from *Showing Our Colors.* So I screwed up all my courage and went up to you and said that I was Black and a lesbian too. For me the Black women's movement especially meant feeling like I belonged. Belonging, that was important, that meant being recognized. I often had the experience that I wasn't always read as Black. That hurt me, and Katharina really supported me. Katharina had a very infectious enthusiasm. You knew about a theater workshop in Utrecht led by Black women from Utrecht. So that's where we went. That was a totally empowering, and also painful, experience, but good.

PP: So there were events that didn't just happen in Berlin? You traveled around a lot together? Those are the stories we heard later on. You earliest activists on the road between Berlin, Utrecht, and Munich. And that was all before you put together *Showing Our Colors?*

KK: Exactly. The book was central. Black women's / lesbian history, biographies, by and for us. That's empowerment, reflecting about language, thinking carefully about an approach to biography that's authentic because it's told from a Black perspective. Then of course more and more people joined us. Via the book and via our word-of-mouth strategy, we just went up to sisters on the street.

The Encounter with Audre Lorde in the 1980s in Berlin as the Initial Spark for Organizing in a Larger Context

Encouraged by Audre Lorde, Black women activists in Germany learned to make deliberate connections with other Black women. That took place as a gradual process in various places like the women's class at the Free University of Berlin. The search for a common language for Black German women activists' shared experiences culminated in the name they gave themselves: Afro-German, and later, Black German. The book project *Showing Our Colors* was a product of these developments.

KO: I was of course an old-time activist and had been active in the women's movement for a long time. But everything really began with *Showing Our Colors.* When Audre Lorde was invited to the Free University and I was in the women's class of the student-run high school, I went to Audre's seminar to brush up my English for the high school leaving exams. Those were great days—it was fun. I knew Audre Lorde from her work and had admired her a lot before I ever met her personally. *Macht und Sinnlichkeit* had just been published.[5] In the German women's movement that text was well known and well received. Today I still think it's one of the most radical texts that exists. Then she discussed her analysis of racial power structures with us in the seminar. That's why I decided to attend the seminar and to sort of try out the university. Then Audre also met alone with us, the Black women students. That's how I got to know her personally. In her time at the Free University and in Berlin Audre had asked the white feminists where the Black people were. She'd been presented with an image of Germany in which there were no Black people. The country after the Nazis, so to speak, in which there were no Blacks.

ME: It's kind of amazing how frequently people are presented with a white image of Germany or even of Berlin. bell hooks criticizes the film *Wings of Desire* for exactly this reason.

KO: Yes, that's right, but then there was the conference in Cologne, and there we met and made contact with May Ayim, who back then still used the name May Opitz. So that's how May joined up. Then we had a bunch of meetings. Then the Orlanda Verlag said—well, it wasn't called Orlanda Verlag yet—that it wanted to do another book with Audre. But Audre answered that she didn't need a new book. Not that she wouldn't have liked to keep on publishing books, but that was just her political position: "I would find it much more exciting to do a book with the Black German women," she said. And that is how *Showing Our Colors* came about. That was pretty incredible. May and I were still pretty young. Up till then we hadn't really had anything to do with anything public. But then we were already in the middle of the process. That lasted two whole years, with weekly meetings. In the process we met lots of other women and also included them in the book.

PP: That's just the way I've always imagined the beginnings of an activist movement. Taking steps toward becoming visible, which here in Germany were connected to the book. But also getting to know each other better, Black women and lesbians. And then via the distribution of the book getting to know even more Black women and lesbians. It might be that *Showing Our Colors* offered us a way of making networking possible.

KK: It was particularly important that the book provided us with a common political language, positive and not negative. That was very empowering for me. Yes, and then even more activists joined up, and the community got bigger and bigger.

KO: What you're calling community now was more like a train that got longer and longer and faster and faster and just couldn't be steered in one single direction anymore.

KK: Yes, and the important thing was really the language. Naming ourselves, that was a huge step in the direction of politicizing ourselves more. I was still very young then and could profit from all the lectures, readings, and discussions far into the night. We developed our own voice, and that strengthened and empowered us. Then everything really got started. The ISD[6] was founded, and a lot happened all at the same time. In a movement there are always all these simultaneities that connect up to each other.

PP: That's exactly the strength of a movement.

ME: Coming up with your own name is an important moment for a movement. *Showing Our Colors* produced a common focus. It's an important resource that stretches far beyond the borders of metropolitan Berlin, Munich, or Hamburg.

Counter-Structures and Personal Networks of Black Women Activists

Black women activists entered the movement at different points in their own biographies. Building community and conceptualizing subjectivity within the movement were especially characteristic and important for the movement's first and second waves. Part of conceptualizing an activist subjectivity is developing one's own autonomous perception of oneself as a Black woman and of the conditions of one's own life in the context of racism and sexism.

KO: It was a time when a lot of people of the same age came together. A critical mass, so to speak. For instance, there was the Frankfurt/Wiesbaden group that was meeting at the same time as we did. Eleonore Wiedenroth and others who at the beginning didn't have much to do with *Showing Our Colors.*

PP: And then it all came together again. Maisha, what was it like for you when you came to the movement, to ADEFRA, in 1993?

ME: I think I mainly found out about it from movement texts. I learned about ADEFRA by reading the texts of Black women activists in Germany. Back then I bought *Showing Our Colors* in a small alternative bookstore in Kiel along with two other books with the voices of Black women activists, including the anthology *... und wenn du dazu noch schwarz bist.*[7] The lovingly reflective perception of the conditions of one's own life was new and refreshing for me—I didn't have to be a Black female subject observed and depicted by others.

KO: Yes, I still remember that one book. Not its title, but the picture on the cover. I found it quite problematic because it was a false representation of the reality of our lives. So it was very important for me that *Showing Our Colors* was clearly anchored in representations that we as activists had decided on. Black women in Germany, and not some symbol that was going to be understood as somehow "African." People were going to have to deal with our social location here when they looked at the cover of *Showing Our Colors.*

PP: And of course historicity too, Black history made visible in Germany. The cover gives expression to this history as social subjects made it, it's not a history of objects.

KO: There were four generations on the cover! People had to take that in. It was supposed to disturb people. It was important to us that we thought about all these details.

PP: How do you look back on the beginnings of ADEFRA today?

ME: I think it's really exciting to hear about the settings in which the first meetings took place. Audre's initiative, her interest in making contact and having conversations with Black women activists, are fascinating. That she had to ask, where do I find Black women activists here, how do I contact them? That's unfortunately a question that I often still hear from Black women activists who are invited to Germany by white organizations. They have to take the initiative and ask pointed questions. That just happened again with a woman professor from Chicago who gave talks at the Berlin universities. She had to set up contacts with Black women activists all by herself.

KO: Does that mean that the forums where such meetings could happen don't exist?

ME: I don't know, I think it's more the problem that ongoing coalition work isn't happening anymore. The people who invite activists from the USA do know about ADEFRA, do know our work and us personally. It seems like it's more the problem that this isn't an urgent question for white activists. Black transnational networking is something that we continue to have to initiate ourselves when other Black people are invited by white organizations.

KO: Well, it's been ten years since the end of the women's movement was proclaimed. I think it's already a gain that people are willing to use the word "feminist" again. There was an important break back then.

ME: For me it's exciting to see how important making connections was.

KO: But that's what I mean. There aren't any forums anymore. Where do you meet Black women or lesbians anymore? There used to be the Lesbian

Week, the women's class in Berlin, the Lesbian Film Week, and other forums. So we could try out ways of spending time together and getting to know each other. All those clubs don't exist anymore.

PP: Of course that was a very specific time. It was the atmosphere, the *Zeitgeist* of the eighties and nineties, in general a pretty activist and autonomous time. It's different today and maybe not tied so much to specific spaces, which are always an expression of their time. It seems to me that Maisha means something else here that isn't necessarily connected to the continued existence of these forums or spaces. I find it very important that you've pointed out how the same problems are still just as urgent for us today. Maisha, your thoughts make me ask what happened to all those enthusiastic and activist women who were so touched by Audre Lorde back then.

KO: Do you mean the Black women? Well, the movement doesn't exist anymore.

PP: I actually mean the white women. Those women still exist. As for our movement, I think it's still there. Just different and in different spaces. A lot got written down, turned into books and other projects.

KK: I think what the spaces look like is always an expression of a movement. After all, a movement consists of people. We were present in a really physical way. Visibility was important. That meant for instance that we'd go to the Sub together so that nothing would happen to any one of us. That's probably not so urgent for us anymore.

PP: The 1990s was a decade of events in cafés, in the Free School, or in autonomous women's projects. We organized readings, exhibitions, and workshops there. Today those events are probably part of university projects and take place in their spaces. Maybe that's the problem?

Forging Connections to Black People Who Strengthen Us and Our Movement

In the transition from the second to the third wave of the movement, impulses and new political orientations deriving from other movement contexts continue to be important. Movements are nourished by the concepts and theories of leading social activists who take the risk of initiating or encouraging public debate. Social engagement demands that activists are constantly prepared to overcome the artificial divisions between political and personal topics and between theoretical knowledge and political praxis.

ME: I think it's a question of a need instead and not so much of a problem. You need connections to people, that's how I see the first meetings with Audre. We had to make connections to Black people who would strengthen us personally, as individual activists and as a community. That's the way I see it today. We kept inviting people to Berlin who made connections to urgent topics of our community with their poetry, music, and texts and thus met people's needs. Resistance is communicated on a lot of different levels. We need people who make these connections possible and are willing to share their networks of resources.

KO: Yes, maybe that's a little bit the problem in Germany, that our "famous" people just aren't so political. Which is really a shame, because that means that we lose out on the kind of impulses that you're describing.

PP: But that too seems to be really an expression of our time. So often I run into events or situations at which I can only shake my head, because it seems almost like feminism never happened. So I'm not surprised that so many of the early issues are still important to us today. Has anything changed for us? Is racism the same as it was twenty-five years ago?

KK: Racism kills. That's as true today as it was twenty-five years ago. Racism is rooted deep in the self-concept of white Europe and thus also of Germany. A long tradition that you can't just wipe out. In this sense we're still combatting the same structures as back then. We made inroads and make them every day. Some days are productive in this respect, others not so much. Thinking and acting in ways critical of dominant structures, producing changes in social interactions, in social structures, and in the symbolic order are as important for us as for coming generations. I do see changes here when I think of my own family—conditions are better for our Black children. It's maybe the case that our activism changed daily life.

PP: Maybe we can see that as a learning process, that activism means something different today, that we can't anymore just compare it to our organizing work in the 1990s.

Bringing Together Black Women Activists from East and West Germany in the 1990s

The first meetings of Black women activists socialized in the East and those socialized in the West after the fall of the Wall in 1989 represented a caesura in the movement. Those encounters mostly took place in unified Berlin in the communal households of autonomous feminists. The activist, literary, and societal contributions of Black women activists from East Germany like Ina

Röder-Sissako, Peggy Piesche, and Raya Lubinetzki had an important impact on the movement as it made the transition from its second to its third wave.

KO: Peggy, what was it like for you back then to encounter the movement?

PP: Munich was the beginning and my entrypoint. In 1990 I'd been in Tübingen only four months, newly released from the old GDR, so to speak. And in the women's bookstore in Tübingen I saw the announcement for the all-German ADEFRA convention with the marvelous slogan, "Leave Your House and Dare Your Life." That applied exactly to me. Those were the days of my coming-out, which took place in a kind of remarkable way. My lesbian coming-out was relatively easy, I just realized that up to that point I hadn't had any words for it. In my white lesbian communal household everything was so "normal," I just hadn't been able to name it before. I was very strongly influenced by the male language of the GDR. Of course that was completely embarrassing. But then I just realized that that was it. The language, the spaces—women's space. That was just it. But the poster was another new challenge: Afro-German women. So another, a new coming-out awaited me. I didn't find it very easy to travel to Munich all by myself. My lesbian coming-out, which I dealt with pretty quickly in contrast to my Black coming-out, was briefly shaken up one more time in Munich. That was when Ria announced to the convention that the Black German lesbians would meet in another room. As I hesitantly peered around the corner into the room, about half the convention was in the room! That's when I met all of you. Ina, from the GDR, was there, and we could talk for the first time. That was just a wonderful experience. A comforting normalization for me. All the parts of my identity were represented and present.

KK: That was a big step for most of us. To go to that kind of meeting at all. The great thing was, it was like a sounding board, I saw many parts of myself in the other sisters. It was a confirmation. But also enormously existential. We were all very young, full of energy, it wasn't always free from conflict. Everybody showed a part of herself, an important step in telling each other about our vulnerabilities and forging bonds with each other.

PP: Yes, exactly. Somehow we all came of age in this movement.

The Influence of Real Black Women

The women activists taking part in this discussion have been active in the Black women's movement in Germany for nineteen to twenty-seven years. Looking back on our many years of involvement, we had to ask how we sustained our motivation. What inspired us to get involved? What inspires us to keep going today? The issue of examples, influences, inspiring work by Black women, their societal contributions, is central here. Encouraged by dynamic, energetic Black women, women activists have proven themselves, despite setbacks, in various areas of society.

KO: What role models did you discover for yourselves?

ME: I entered ADEFRA circles very specifically via Ina Röder-Sissako, who came from Dresden. In Kiel I'd been part of a wen-do women's self-defense workshop. It was important for me back then to learn to deal with experiences of racism and sexism in ways that strengthened and protected me. I learned about workshops being offered by and for migrant and Black women. That's how I met Ina and Modschgan Hamzei, leaders of the workshop, at a location where we could thematize these issues in a connected way. That was existential for me. I knew that I had to stick with it so that all parts of myself could emerge. Afterwards I went to my first ADEFRA meeting in November 1993, to a seminar called "Black Women and Power," right after the wen-do workshop. The meeting was in Krummendeich, near Hamburg. From then on I kept going to ADEFRA meetings, first coming all by myself from Kiel without knowing anybody else, at the beginning pretty alone. Slowly I formed friendships with sisters with whom I'm still friends today. I gradually realized how important it is to get to know Black women in protected spaces and to care for each other. Every Black woman who was interested in making connections and who had the courage to join was important for me and brought me nearer to my own issues, though sometimes in traumatic and painful ways.

KO: For me it was the Black women from the USA. Angela Davis, for example, but I found that difficult too because she was made into a popular symbol, so it seemed like it was really only all about her Afro. For me it was more a question of how I could achieve a Black identity and then be at home in it. Josephine Baker was also important for me. But here too the stereotypes disturbed me. At the beginning it was important for me that everybody admired her, that she was socially recognized. But of course that was difficult at the same time, because finally everything just culminated in the banana skirt.

PP: For me it was actually more a movement and a book. The campaign for the liberation of Angela Davis in the GDR ("Free Angela Davis") and then the first book that I read of my own free will, *Roots* by Alex Haley. That history of collective survival was so powerful for me.

ME: For me it was definitely *Showing Our Colors,* because it was about structural racism and because it made Black history really visible. It's a very accessible book. It plays a role in a lot of my publications. How important it is to make our history visible, the way we see it in *Showing Our Colors,* becomes clear when you think about how little Josephine Baker's life and her passionate engagement have been historicized. I first noticed that in connection with my own work, how little her story, her intellectual creativity, her accomplishments are related to her—to our—identity as Black female subjects. Who even knows that the notion of the "rainbow family" comes from her? Nobody's passed that on to us. That notion is very popular and everybody talks about it, but that it's Josephine Baker's contribution, that it comes from her life practice and activist commitment, nobody knows that. But everybody knows about the banana skirt, right?

KK: Yes, we just have to keep on digging up critical knowledge. It gets lost really easily. That's how I explain the times to myself when we seem to go backward. So a Black lesbian feminist from the United States is invited by white feminists, and she's systematically prevented from meeting with us.

ME: We just have to keep at it and keep making connections to critical voices. It's a great feeling to act, to live, in the knowledge that we're not alone. That's what touches and moves me.

KK: Exactly, critical knowledge is more fragile, mainstream knowledge seems to be more constant. Mainstream knowledge is what we've all learned. We have to unlearn it deliberately and systematically. We have to look very closely and adjust the focus of our parameters. The ironic thing is, critical knowledge is always also contained in mainstream knowledge, but just concealed. Recognizing that helps us to uncover empowering knowledge about Josephine Baker and pass it along instead of just swallowing degrading knowledge without raising questions about it. Role models are certainly important, but I'm very divided about them. For me it's the really existing people in my life who've been important and formative. Growing up in Berlin meant having contacts to lots of other Black children and children of color. That was important. But we were still without a language that would have allowed us to make racism perceptible, even to name it. For that the movement was enormously important. There we could learn to give expression to our experiences and not to act like nothing had ever happened.

Otherwise people make ridiculous claims like "I never experienced any racism in Germany." I also thought it was important for us to be visible in daily life, that I can open a schoolbook and see Black people and Black history. That's still a concern today. When I leaf through the schoolbooks of my nieces and nephews I see "white" in the truest sense of the world.

PP: Yes, exactly, it's important that we don't just see Black people on the streets, but also in the functions of daily life, as bus drivers or bank tellers.

Community Empowerment, Critical Knowledge Production, and a Vision of Our Own Infrastucture

After a period of great change and great transformation, the same thing has happened to the Black women's movement as to other social movements. There isn't a mass of people anymore who make a regular date to go to the demonstration every other Saturday. Now different spaces have emerged, more virtual and less material. Both emotionally and organizationally, we've made a central investment in work with Black children and young people. It's a question not just of our own structures but of establishing our own infrastructure. Many resources exist already and are at the community's disposal. There's a tradition of antiracist intervention especially in education but also in legal struggles, and many cultural events (for example, exhibitions about the Black community) have also taken place and are now part of movement history.

KK: That helps our children to orient themselves, to figure out what they want to do when they grow up, based on what seems possible to them. We're working on that all the time and we've achieved quite a bit. Our children find our history much more self-evident, it's simply there and more visible because we've talked and written about it. It's accessible. For me the movement means learning about different aspects, perspectives, and bringing them into connection, so that we can extract different things from it. The different impulses that emerge from the movement are important for us. I can draw out whatever's most fruitful for my life at the moment.

PP: So the movement is something that we can pass along?

KK: Absolutely! Maybe not so much in the form of grand examples, but more generally in daily life. When I think of my nieces and nephews, I can see that they've benefited from our movement. They have the opportunity to acquire a different consciousness. We learned to give expression to our experiences, to our struggles with racism. It's important to make our critiques and our learning experiences perceptible, thus also intelligible. Our next generations will definitely profit from that. That will make an impact, outside the community too. Empowerment is always an act of coming together, of continuing to struggle, and finally: of living our lives and continuing to dare!

PP: That connects back to the first ADEFRA convention!

KO: Yes, I'm completely thrilled about the next generations that are now growing up. They want something different, have different goals, and that is wonderful. They are definitely very critical, but in a different way than we were. I see that in my work with Joliba.[8] I've been doing that work since 1997. I see the work of the organization, initiating and carrying out projects with the goal of promoting intercultural cooperation and mutual understanding among people, as engagement for generations to come. They don't have to contend with the same topics and struggles that we confronted.

ME: It's certainly a change that communication distances are shorter. Information is disseminated more quickly via distribution lists. That calls for new skills and emphases on our part. Different networks overlap a lot more today than they used to. I think online activism is totally important. And otherwise I think that we have to continue to make an impact in our own spaces and beyond. We definitely serve as foils for younger women to react to.

PP: So what are the next steps?

KK: Our own foundation, something we've thought about for a long time. That would allow us to be a lot more independent and deal with the issues that are most important to us.

PP: Certain things can only be realized at particular times. We've thought about our own foundation for a long time. And slowly it seems like the time is ripe for it. Ideas grow and flourish and emerge at particular times. Activism has changed a lot, and the movement is taking on new forms. We can now take small steps toward realizing things that seemed utopian twenty-five years ago. So now we're at the end of our conversation and have arrived at concrete proposals. That's a very optimistic outlook.

Translated by Sara Lennox

LITERATURE

ADEFRA e.V., ed. *Generation ADEFRA: Schwarze Autonomie in Deutschland?* Berlin: Selbstverlag, 2006.

Kinder, Katja. "Das Eingehen von Bündnissen ist eine bedeutende Investition!" In *Bündnisse—Ein Weg zu erfolgreicher Geschlechterpolitik? Was ist der Streit-Wert?* Edited by Gunda Werner Institut. http://streit-wert.boellblog.org/2011/10/12/katja-kinder.

Sharp, Pearl S., and Beverly Hawkins Hill. *Black Women for Beginners.* Danbury, CT: Writers and Readers, 1993.

NOTES

"Looking Backward and Forward: Twenty Years of the Black Women's Movement in Germany" is a translation of "Rückblenden und Vorschauen: 20 Jahre Schwarze Frauenbewegung," in *"Euer Schweigen schützt Euch nicht": Audre Lorde und die Schwarze Frauenbewegung in Deutschland,* ed. Peggy Piesche (Berlin: Orlanda, 2012), 12–40. It is published here by permission of Peggy Piesche.

1. Afrekete is an important figure in Audre Lorde's *Zami.*
2. Black Germans use the English word "community" to designate the Black German community.
3. "Sub" is an abbreviation for "Subkultur" and refers to Berlin's lesbian subculture.
4. Ban Ying is a Berlin organization that combats trafficking in women.
5. Adrienne Rich and Audre Lorde, *Macht und Sinnlichkeit: Ausgewählte Texte,* ed. Dagmar Schultz, trans. Renate Stendhal (Berlin: sub rosa, 1983).
6. Initiative Schwarze Deutsche (Initiative of Black Germans).
7. Gisela Fremgen, ed., . . . *und wenn du dazu noch schwarz bist: Berichte schwarzer Frauen in der Bundesrepublik* (Bremen: Edition CON, 1984).
8. Joliba is an intercultural network in Berlin promoting intercultural understanding and cooperation with a special focus on the needs of African-German families. It regularly sponsors educational and cultural events including readings, exhibitions, seminars, and activities for children, youth, and families.

Epilogue
Of Epistemologies and Positionalities

A Conversation, Berlin, October 21, 2014

PEGGY PIESCHE AND SARA LENNOX

SARA LENNOX: The project that has culminated in the present volume began in 2002 as a discussion between you, Fatima El-Tayeb, and me around a swimming pool in San Diego, California, at a reception hosted by the Alexander von Humboldt Foundation during the German Studies Association conference. There, encouraged by the excellent red wine the foundation provided, we made plans to apply for a Humboldt Foundation TransCoop grant to fund a research project on Black German studies. (Later Fatima joked that this gave the German term *Schnapsidee* ["schnapps idea," meaning a crazy idea] a whole new meaning!) We then sought a senior Black German collaborator for our team and asked Randolph Ochsmann, professor of psychology at the University of Mainz and to our knowledge the only Black German in Germany at that point with a professorial appointment in the humanities or social sciences, to join us as our German-based faculty partner. We were also thrilled that, thanks to your and Fatima's superb grant-writing skills, we received a concurrent grant from the Volkswagen Foundation that funded several conferences and a research center to which we gave the acronym BEST, for Black European studies. Because we have worked together so productively since then, I am very happy that the last piece of this project can take the form of a conversation between us about Black German studies.

Peggy, because you are widely regarded as a leading scholar of Black German studies in Germany and as a leading Black German activist, I'd like to begin by asking you to talk about the accomplishments of Black German scholars since 1986, when *Farbe bekennen* appeared.

PEGGY PIESCHE: In my early writing about Afro-German literature I maintained that Black German scholars were producing a counter-narrative, and that is how other Black German scholars understood their work too. That is comprehensible in the context of those early times, but, as more theorizing of the Black experience and of collective identities has taken place, I feel more and more uneasy about using the term "counter-." There are two aspects to my discomfort. On the one hand, I think it is energy-draining, agency-draining, to conceive of our work as a reaction to something else that went before. But even more importantly, the notion of a counter-narrative is premised upon a response to exactly those epistemologies that we are trying to draw into question. (The metaphor of "remapping" may in fact also invoke frames of knowledge that derive from the Enlightenment, including, for example, its categories of race.) Thus, instead of talking about counter-narratives, we now speak of alternative knowledge production. The current works of Black German scholars attest to that.

SL: Could you talk more about the epistemological implications of doing Black German studies?

PP: I'd like to maintain that over the past three decades, beginning with Black women's efforts to discover their life histories and understand themselves within a historical context and followed by more and more theoretical work, artistic work, and poetry, Black German studies has been responsible for an epistemological turn. We can speak of an epistemological turn because that work uncovered an archive of knowledge that made it possible to situate the Black German experience within a larger transnational perspective and history. The epistemological turn has been especially important for the next generation of young Black students at all levels, who can now find themselves at least in fragments, in pieces, in the curriculum and can ask questions that enable them to learn something about themselves. Such an epistemological turn makes it legitimate to research the history of Black people in Germany and in Europe, to research the history of racism, in images and in media, for instance, and not just as a research question but also as such questions may be focused and visualized by Black artists. Perhaps one could argue that such an epistemological turn would no longer be necessary when the majority, or the academy, has accepted something, when it has been acknowledged within the canon, but that is not my concern. I'm much more concerned about making it possible for young Black students to make use of hitherto unavailable materials and sources, to recognize themselves in and work with instructors like themselves at the level of the creation and transfer of knowledge, to understand themselves as active producers of knowledge. We've seen how important that was for feminist studies and queer studies, and it's also the case for Black German studies. However, the hegemonic academy still doesn't acknowledge how important that is. So there are people who claim the research field of Black German studies without pursuing it from a Black perspective. Something similar happens in other fields too, but it's clear what the limitations are.

SL: So could you expand on that point? You've talked about new contents and new voices that communicate those contents; now could you talk more about how the way in which those contents are treated is shaped by what feminists and others call "positionality," the social and historical location of the researcher? As a Black German, how do you undertake Black German studies differently than a white person (a white American, say, like myself) would?

PP: A Black German can't think of Black German studies as a commodity that is fashionable right now and then move on to another field when this one seems less chic. Rather, by definition Black people work on this field and research it and develop topics about it because it is a collective life reality. That was the case in the past and is in the present. It's research that is very much oriented towards the future, towards how to change life. It's completely different for white people if it's all kind of arbitrary, if Black German studies is something you do or else you do something else. That is also the case in other fields where affected people undertake scholarship that is relevant to their own lives. So we know, for instance, that men can research women's studies, but we also know that it is particularly a field for women because their life realities are touched and interwoven.

SL: Maybe you'd want to talk about whiteness, how Black German studies draws whiteness into question, and how that is something for which Black German studies necessarily and inevitably advocates.

PP: Well, Black German studies' critique of whiteness is resistance. White people's inability to concede the relevance of their own whiteness derives from their failure to recognize their own positioning and implication in power. A Black perspective focuses on that, points that out, elaborates on it, tries to make it obvious to white people because that again has been a life reality for Black people over the centuries. As long as we don't acknowledge the relevance of whiteness for scholarly production, as long as we don't understand that all fields in the hegemonic academy are white fields (as long as, for instance, we don't speak of white German studies), we won't be able to grasp that whiteness influences not only what your own perspective is but what kind of research you produce. That's not a kind of research that includes me and my life reality, my history, my collective.

SL: How would addressing other questions from the perspective of Black German studies change what German studies undertakes? For instance, German history, World War II, the Holocaust, what would be different?

PP: A lot, because it would not only include marginalized perspectives, not just adding, for instance, how colonial troops were involved in World War I, a question of commemoration, acknowledging their contribution. To do it from a Black German studies perspective, from a perspective that understands whiteness, we would have to approach questions of systemic power, showing, for instance, that World War II can only be understood in connection with colonialism, not just that a particular group feels itself to be underrepresented. That's a structural change, in a field where change comes in waves, people deal with a particular topic for a while and then other approaches come along that don't address it at all. That's impossible from a Black perspective, which involves a consideration of power structures that can be ignored from a white perspective.

SL: You've said that thinking about Black German studies as niche scholarship doesn't address such systemic dimensions.

PP: Exactly. Viewing Black German studies as a niche, as one subfield among many others, doesn't acknowledge how whiteness structures the entire field, it doesn't respect the Black German scholars who are undertaking research in the field, and it doesn't deepen the conversation. As well, and this is something I find increasingly more important, it basically throws the field open to everybody, obviously you don't have to know much to pursue it, and you can see that happening now. So people who have made a name in a field where they really know something, where they are involved and have a theoretical foundation, take up Black German studies as a commodity, as something cool and fashionable that they can just take up without considering the hegemonic framework of which they're part, without considering that there are criteria vis-à-vis which they have to qualify themselves, without knowing the sources and the theory, without understanding that Black German studies is a collective project. We've already seen all that happen in the field of critical whiteness studies.

SL: You've answered these questions from your positionality as a Black German. But now I'd like to ask another very important question: can others who occupy another positionality—let's say, scholars who do know the field well—pursue Black German studies, and, if so, what would be necessary for them to do so?

PP: Yes, that is certainly the case for other Black people, because they also can draw upon what Audre Lorde termed "our shared differences and our collective experiences." Black positionality is not primarily bound to nationality, it is a shared historical experience that includes the experience of slavery. But it should also be emphasized that young Black scholars can also very swiftly be forced into scholarly niches where they don't acquire the necessary skill sets or gain access to the necessary resources. The important thing is that these questions are addressed from a Black perspective.

SL: Do you think it is possible for white scholars attempting to undertake Black German studies to avoid a hegemonic positionality and locate themselves somewhere else?

PP: I think that it's exactly this strategy of avoidance that has brought us to the point where we are now. What do you change when you avoid something? Do you change the system when you partially avoid the exercise of power—if that's even possible? I would say you don't; on the contrary, you're prolonging it instead. And that, I think, is the problem of many so-called alliances, especially with white feminists' rejection of power, who say (a) that just doesn't apply to me and I'm a better person because of it, and (b) that qualifies me to form an alliance with the so-called Other. And then she's completely astonished and upset when the Other doesn't see it that way. We are implicated in hegemony, and that means it can't be avoided.

SL: So is it possible to step outside of hegemony?

PP: No, that's the other thing, that is exactly what people want to do, but how can they step outside of hegemony, and what kind of a goal is that anyway? It makes me more and more angry; that's a very entitled approach. People say, "Yes, that just doesn't apply to me anymore. So I don't have to take responsibility for anything anymore, also no responsibility for changing anything." On the contrary, it's an entitlement to claim—space, energy, in the strictest sense of the term, oxygen, to occupy the struggle of other people because you've declared that you've stepped outside of entitled power structures. Who anywhere can declare that she's stepped outside? That's a deeply white attitude that we've had to deal with forever, and it robs us of our energy. A genuine alliance would look like this for me, that white people reveal, make transparent, the ways that their political, activist, academic perspectives are implicated in power, label them, and set about changing them, since for centuries they've contributed to making whiteness what it is today. That's very well documented, among other things in the suffrage movement. For people to maintain that they can just write themselves out of whiteness is an affront to all marginalized communities who have been fighting it for centuries. Queer studies is a good example of this, hegemonic whiteness in combination with gender politics.

SL: But the question is still open. Can white people do Black German studies? And how could they do it, if it's even possible?

PP: In my view, no. But they're doing it anyway.

SL: Is it possible for them to do it responsibly?

PP: Responsibility starts with undertaking a critical consideration of where they are situated and of the way they consider their objects and include that as part of their analyses. Otherwise—and that's why I said no—they are just continuing to contribute to an epistemological canon that rests on our collective experiences, like enormous piles of garbage and dirt. Otherwise we just have to keep excavating, that's the way I see the work of Black activists and academics, we have to keep digging out the canon of our knowledge because every morning it's covered with garbage again.

SL: Can white scholars work together with Black scholars, and if so, how?

PP: We often have no alternatives within the academic institution, and exactly for that reason there's the question again, who sets the terms. What I described before is the going definition of alliances: the white subject defines herself and rejects particular kinds of complicity in power by declaring that she's rejected them, we aren't part of patriarchy, we don't want equal rights in the existing system, etc., and of course we take the same line as you do. Which is of course nonsense. Those are the claims that have been made for centuries, and that's the going understanding of alliances, which of course aren't alliances at all but mean that Black women have to give up their struggle and their interests because that's what's necessary for the alliance to function. It might be possible to develop another understanding of alliances, to say that white women should do their work in their own house, and that would mean that they would finally look at their complicity in whiteness. They did that for gender without thematizing whiteness and think they're finished. That doesn't qualify them for alliances in the sense that we are part of one and the same group or we have one and the same goals, because that just isn't the case. I think that that other kind of alliance would be a good one in the sense that white women would clean up their own place. That would help us a lot with alliances. They don't need Black women for that, there are lots of theoretical and methodological resources they can draw on.

SL: Well, you and I worked together on a project in Amherst called "Remapping Black Germany," more or less led by me and by Tobias Nagl [a white German]. Was that a mistake?

PP: I can't judge that, but the question is, who was it for? On that basis we can decide whether it was a mistake or not. It definitely wasn't a fundamental contribution to Black research perspectives. But it could be significant within a white field, showing what's important when we consider this theme, and why we're even doing it, and to what degree hegemonic power structures can be discerned here. But certainly not to explain their history to Black people.

SL: Does it make sense to try to make Black German perspectives and knowledges more widely known, to other Black people and to white people as well, and could that change anything?

PP: This sounds like the noble progressive white person trying to lend a voice to poor oppressed Black people.

SL: No, not necessarily. It's my perspective that the world that is founded on white hegemonic positions is, finally, not a world that I want to live in either. So in that respect I think I am doing something for myself.

PP: Yes, exactly, we would have gone a long way if this were generally the motivation. I always say, only when racism is a problem and a topic even when no Black people are in the room, then you all would be starting to do structural work, not just because Black people are there. Who either again have to take over that work themselves or white people can feel that they're now really affected [*betroffen*]. But as long as it's only these few people who feel they're affected it has no relevance for hegemonic perspectives. But given your assertion that you want to do something for yourself, for a better world in which you want to live, it would first be necessary for you to win over your white colleagues to change things in areas where they have power. So that's the question again, for whom is it useful.

SL: It's always been my idea that it has to become clear to white people that there are other perspectives, other voices, in the world besides theirs. And that's the reason I'm involved with Black German studies.

PP: So the addressees are your own people. Yes, I see it that way too.

SL: The danger of cooptation is very great. But I think it just isn't okay when, for instance, people in German studies continue to believe that nothing else exists but their own perspective on the world.

PP: Exactly.

SL: That certainly doesn't mean that I can assume a Black perspective, and I think there's always the danger, I'm aware of that, that without wanting to or knowing I'm doing it I could fall back into a white perspective. Actually it's highly likely that I'll fall back into a white perspective.

PP: Fall back means that you could escape it, and that just isn't possible. A critical white perspective would also be good.

SL: So we seem to be back to positionality again. You're of course right that I can't escape the time and place that produced me, but I hope, certainly with much help from my patient Black friends and colleagues, that I've succeeded at least to some degree in assuming a critical white perspective as I've pursued scholarship in Black German studies. I also wouldn't dare to maintain that this volume succeeds in drawing dominant epistemologies into question, but I hope that in various ways it is critical of hegemonic perspectives, including those of whiteness, and in that regard contributes to changing them.

PP: That's exactly the perspective that is most likely to destroy hegemony. Change is an ongoing process, but so is knowledge production, and that's exactly why we need these discussions and the challenge to position ourselves within them.

NOTES ON CONTRIBUTORS

ROBERT BERNASCONI is Edwin Erle Sparks Professor of Philosophy and African American Studies at Penn State University. He is the author of two books on Heidegger and one on Sartre. In addition to being a founding coeditor of the journal *Critical Philosophy of Race,* he has edited a number of collections of both primary and secondary sources on the history of the concepts of race and racism. He has written extensively on the complicity of canonical philosophers such as Locke, Kant, Hegel, Nietzsche, and Heidegger with extreme and novel forms of racism.

TINA CAMPT is Ann Whitney Olin Professor of Africana and Women's, Gender, and Sexuality Studies, director of the Barnard Center for Research on Women, and chair of the Africana Studies Department at Barnard College, Columbia University. She is the author of *Other Germans: Black Germans and the Politics of Race, Gender, and Memory in the Third Reich* (2004) and *Image Matters: Archive, Photography, and the African Diaspora in Europe* (2012). Her third book, *Listening to Images* (forthcoming 2017), theorizes the everyday practices of refusal and fugitivity in a genre of Black vernacular photographs she calls "quiet photography."

MARIA I. DIEDRICH is professor emerita of American studies at the Universität Münster; author of *Cornelia James Cannon and the Future American Race, Love across Color Lines: Ottilie Assing and Frederick Douglass, Aufschrei der Frauen—Diskurs der Männer: Der frühviktorianische Industrieroman,* and *Kommunismus im afroamerikanischen Roman;* and editor or coeditor of *From Black to Schwarz: Cultural Crossovers between African America and Germany, Monuments of the Black Atlantic: Slavery and Memory,* and *Crossing Boundaries: African American Inner City and European Migrant Youth,* among other volumes.

MAUREEN MAISHA EGGERS is a professor for childhood and difference (diversity studies) at the University for Applied Sciences in Magdeburg-Stendal. She is currently a visiting professor at the Centre for Transdisciplinary Gender Studies and the Institute of Education, Humboldt University, Berlin. She is coeditor of *Mythen, Masken und Subjekte: Kritische Weißseinsforschung in Deutschland* (2005). Her research interests include diversity, inequality, and plurality in textbooks and didactical materials; childhood studies; gender in transcultural education; critical whiteness; critical race theory; and Black women's activism. She has been an activist with ADEFRA since 1993 and a member of its board since 2005.

FATIMA EL-TAYEB is professor of literature and ethnic studies and director of the Critical Gender Studies Program at the University of California, San Diego. She is the author of two books, *European Others: Queering Ethnicity in Postnational Europe* (2011, translated as *Anders europäisch* [2015]) and *Schwarze Deutsche: Rasse und nationale Identität, 1890–1933* (2001), as well as numerous articles on the interactions of race, gender, sexuality, and nation. Her research interests include African and comparative diaspora studies, queer theory, transnational feminism, European migrant and minority cultures, Muslim communities in the West, queer of color critique, and visual cultural studies. She also wrote the film script for the movie *Alles wird gut* (1997).

HEIDE FEHRENBACH is Board of Trustees Professor in the History Department at Northern Illinois University. Her publications include the award-winning *Cinema in Democratizing Germany* (1995), *Race after Hitler: Black Occupation Children in Postwar Germany and America* (2005), and *After the Nazi Racial State: Difference and Democracy in Germany and Europe* (2009), and two edited volumes, *Transactions, Transgressions, Transformations: American Culture in Western Europe and Japan* (2000) and *Humanitarian Photography: A History* (2015). She is currently at work on a book on the visual culture of humanitarianism.

DIRK GÖTTSCHE is professor of German at the University of Nottingham. His publications include *Die Produktivität der Sprachkrise in der modernen Prosa* (1987), *Zeit im Roman: Literarische Zeitreflexion und die Geschichte des Zeitromans im späten 18. und im 19. Jahrhundert* (2001), *Zeitreflexion und Zeitkritik im Werk Wilhelm Raabes* (2000), *Kleine Prosa in Moderne und Gegenwart*

(2006), and *Remembering Africa: The Rediscovery of Colonialism in Contemporary German Literature* (2013). He is a Member of Academia Europaea and honorary president of the International Raabe Society. His research areas include German literature of the long nineteenth century and realism; Austrian modernism; modernist short prose; time, history, and memory in German literature; and postcolonial and cross-cultural literary studies.

FELICITAS RÜTTEN JAIMA is an associate scholar with the research project The Civil Rights Struggle, African American GIs, and Germany, a collaboration of the German Historical Institute in Washington, DC, the University of Heidelberg Center for American Studies, and Vassar College. Her dissertation, "Adopting Diaspora: African American Military Women in Cold War West Germany" (New York University), based on interviews with former servicewomen and military spouses, uncovers the forgotten experiences of Black American military wives and enlisted women abroad. It provides new insight into US military race and gender relations and suggests a new framework for understanding Black German identity formation and visions of diaspora.

KATJA KINDER, a founding member of ADEFRA, is an educator, an empowerment trainer, and a conflict mediator in Berlin. Her work involves counseling a wide range of organizations with regard to creating a space for critical consciousness of diversity, race, and gender in these organizations. She also teaches German as a second language as well as gender and diversity studies in Berlin and Stendal.

NICOLA LAURÉ AL-SAMARAI is an independent cultural studies scholar and historian, author of *Die Macht der Darstellung: Gender, sozialer Status, historiographische Re-Präsentation* and *Creating Spaces: Non-formal Art/s Education and Vocational Training for Artists in Africa between Cultural Policies and Cultural Funding*, a collaborator on the exhibition *Homestory Deutschland: Schwarze Biografien in Geschichte und Gegenwart*, and coeditor of *re/visionen: Postkoloniale Perspektiven von People of Color auf Rassismus, Kulturpolitik und Widerstand in Deutschland*.

SARA LENNOX is professor emerita of German studies at the University of Massachusetts Amherst, author of *Cemetery of the Murdered Daughters: Feminism, History, and Ingeborg Bachmann*, and coeditor of *Feminist Movements* *in a Globalizing World* and *The Imperialist Imagination: German Colonialism and Its Legacy.* She has published essays on twentieth-century literature, theory, feminism, postcolonialism, globalization, and transnationalism. In 2007–2008 she was president of the German Studies Association. With Fatima El-Tayeb, Randolph Ochsmann, and Peggy Piesche she coordinated an Alexander von Humboldt Foundation–funded project on Black German studies and a Volkswagen Foundation–funded project on Black European studies (BEST).

TOBIAS NAGL is associate professor of film studies at the University of Western Ontario and teaches at the interdisciplinary Centre for the Study of Theory and Criticism. He is the author of *Die unheimliche Maschine: Rasse und Repräsentation im Weimarer Kino* (2009), which won the international Willy Haas Award, and coeditor (with Janelle Blankenship) of *European Visions: Small Cinemas in Transition* (2015). He has published extensively on German film history, film theory, race and postcolonialism, Afro-German history, R. W. Fassbinder, Michael Haneke, and the Holocaust in film and memory culture.

KATHARINA OGUNTOYE is a German-Nigerian historian and author who helped to bring the Afro-German movement into being, both as a coeditor of *Farbe bekennen: Afro-deutsche Frauen auf den Spuren ihrer Geschichte* (1986) and as a founding member of the Initiative Schwarze Menschen in Deutschland and ADEFRA. Since 1996 she has directed Joliba, an intercultural network in Germany (www.joliba.de). Her book *Eine afro-deutsche Geschichte: Zur Lebenssituation von Afrikanern und Afro-Deutschen in Deutschland von 1884 bis 1950* appeared in 1997.

PEGGY PIESCHE is a literary and cultural studies scholar of Black European studies in the Academy for Advanced African Studies at the University of Bayreuth. Her book publications include *AufBrüche: Kulturelle Produktionen von Migrantinnen, Schwarzen und jüdischen Frauen in Deutschland* (1999), *May Ayim Award: Erster internationaler schwarzer deutscher Literaturpreis 2004* (2004), *Mythen, Masken und Subjekte: Kritische Weißseinsforschung in Deutschland* (2005/2009), and *"Euer Schweigen schützt euch nicht": Audre Lorde und die Schwarze Frauenbewegung in Deutschland* (2012). She is working on a book tentatively titled "Concepts of Future in MediaSpaces" that explores how diaspora is negotiated through notions of race and digitalized collective identities. She is also an activist member of ADEFRA and the Black community in Germany.

CHRISTIAN ROGOWSKI is G. Armour Craig Professor in Language and Literature in the Department of German at Amherst College. His publications comprise two books on Austrian author Robert Musil, a CD-ROM on teaching German studies, and numerous essays on German-language literature, drama, opera, film, and intellectual history. His current research focuses on the cinema and popular culture of the Weimar Republic, especially in terms of the politics of "race" (the legacy of German colonialism, the impact of African-American culture, the German-Jewish dynamic, etc.). He is the editor of *The Many Faces of Weimar Cinema: Rediscovering Germany's Filmic Legacy* (2010).

INDEX